D1294153

Eddie Foy

Eddie Foy, with his trademark smile.

EDDIE FOY

A Biography of the Early Popular Stage Comedian

by ARMOND FIELDS

DISCARDED

McFarland & Company, Inc., Publishers

Jefferson, North Carolina, and London

Library of Congress Cataloguing-in-Publication Data

Fields, Armond, 1930–
Eddie Foy : a biography of the early popular stage comedian /
by Armond Fields.
p. cm.
Includes bibliographical references and index.
ISBN 0-7864-0702-6
(illustrated case binding : 50# alkaline paper) ∞
1. Foy, Eddie, 1856–1928.
2. Comedians — United States — Biography.
I. Title.
PN2287.F65F54   1999   792.7'028'092 — dc21 [B]
99-39086 CIP

British Library Cataloguing-in-Publication data are available

Manufactured in the United States of America

*McFarland & Company, Inc., Publishers
Box 611, Jefferson, North Carolina 28640
www.mcfarlandpub.com*

Contents

Acknowledgments

Eddie Foy's descendants were proud of his accomplishments and contributions to American popular theater. In his memory, they preserved artifacts of his life and career, an historical record that made Eddie come alive.

Specific thanks go to Eddie Foy III, Madeline Foy O'Donnell, and Frank and Suzanne Foy for their friendship and for sharing their colorful grandfather with me. Special thanks goes to Irving Foy, a spry, dapper 90-year-old gentleman, the last living member of the Seven Little Foys. I dedicate this book to him.

I feel honored to have received a grant from Mike Strunsky, trustee of the Ira and Lenore Gershwin Philanthropic Fund, to complete this book. My gratitude to this unique organization which strives to preserve and promote America's rich arts and entertainment history.

In assembling this book, I received invaluable assistance from many people and organizations. They include:

John Ahouse, and the University of Southern California Special Collections Library

Miles Kreuger, Institute of the American Musical
Maryann Chach, Shubert Archive
Annette Fern, Harvard Theater Collection
Geraldine Duclow, Theater Collection, The Free Library of Philadelphia
Marty Jacobs, the Museum of the City of New York

and:

Mormon Library, Salt Lake City
University of Wisconsin — Wisconsin Center for Film and Theater Research
New York Public Library for the Performing Arts
New York Vital Statistics Department
Chicago Historical Society
Library of Congress
National Portrait Gallery, Smithsonian Institution
University of Wyoming — American Heritage Center
University of Texas — Harry Ransom Humanities Research Center
Princeton University Libraries — Department of Rare Books and Special Collections

Denver Public Library — Western History
   Department
Colorado Historical Society
Leadville Public Library
Dodge City Historical Society
Butte Public Library
San Francisco Historical Society
Tombstone Courthouse State Historical Park
University of Iowa — Keith/Albee Collection
New Rochelle Public Library
Academy of Motion Picture Arts and Sciences

   I am grateful for the additional contributions of Betsy Baytos (her knowledge of
dance), Carole Carder, Amy Henderson,
Nancy Ehlers, Don Mickey Designs, Eva
Miglioli (photographic restoration), Ned
Comstock, and L. Marc Fields. All photographs, except where noted, came from the
Foy family.
   John Farrell, an esteemed editor, aided
in bringing Eddie's fascinating and colorful
career to life. My sincere thanks to him.
   Loving gratitude to my wife, Sara, who
has lived through years of my obsession
with theater history and personalities, and
who has continually supported me in my
endeavors.

                              Armond Fields

Introduction

Colonial America was a puritanical nation. Public amusements were criticized, and acting was considered sinful. The stalwarts of the Continental Congress passed a law decreeing the closure of all places of public entertainment. In spite of this august restriction, the ban lasted less than ten years. The government was unable to implement the law; the public refused to obey it.

Theatergoing was not new in the early United States. The country's social elite had cherished and supported drama since their emigration from Europe, installing "culture" in their new land. With the growth of urbanization in the early 1800s, however, theatergoing became a major leisure-time activity for the common people, replacing the rustic, rural amusements they had left behind. Urban immigrants sought comedy to escape the frustrations and anxieties of modern city life.

A well-respected actor, Thomas Wignell, presented "The Contract" in New York City in 1787, portraying a new stage character, Jonathan, a rural, Yankee servant. Jonathan shuffled around the stage, whittled a stick, and offered homespun parables of "good-old" common sense, all performed with humor. Wignall's characterization became an immediate hit. On the theater program, Wignall was labeled a comedian, probably the first in the country to attain such recognition. A story suggests that even George Washington, who some claimed never smiled in his life, laughed at Wignall's jokes; quite an achievement, if true.

The first American comedies written specifically for the stage formulated characters like the devoted servant; the shrewd, Yankee farmer; the villain — his slick, thin mustache not sprouted until showboat days; the comic relief; and the naive young girl, all of whom have survived in popular theater productions.

Comedians had to be a tough and nervy lot. Performing on stage was a decided challenge. It was frequently a confrontation between actor and audience to determine who would control the encounter. Audiences talked and moved freely about the theater during performances. The social elite gossiped and displayed their latest finery. In the pit and gallery, audiences stomped their feet in time with the music, sang along, recited

1

speeches with actors, yelled out punch lines to favorite (or tired) jokes, and needled performers with insults.

Audiences noisily voiced their feelings and opinions about what they saw and heard. When they liked a performance, they demanded encores, be it a Shakespeare soliloquy or a popular song, temporarily stopping the show. Audiences shouted out their musical preferences to the orchestra, and because the orchestra was in the line of fire — directly between the audience and the stage — they had no choice but to comply. When audiences disliked an act, they hissed, shouted derogatory remarks, and threw an arsenal of objects onto the stage. Such spirited criticism often ruined performing careers.

With the "common folk" as audience, even Shakespeare had to be presented as broad comedy that included ad-libs with topical references, exaggerated sentiment, flamboyant gestures, and flag-waving patriotism. Comedians had to be prepared to reconfigure a show as the situation demanded, so a good performer had to have a substantial repertoire at hand or be highly creative. A comedian's ability to adapt gracefully to the immediate situation was recognized and appreciated by audiences. Many comedic reputations were built upon such improvisational skills.

The stage was a battlefield. Most comedians never really succeeded because they didn't realize the power that theater audiences exercised.

After the Civil War, American popular theater and its comedy presentations assumed a number of specific forms: circuses (clowns); medicine shows (rural fools and "plants"); minstrels (blackface endmen); boat shows and melodrama (comic relief roles); and concert hall variety (skits, monologues, and two-acts). Expanding frontiers, new settlements, railroad development, and industrialization gave entertainment-starved people in even the remotest places the opportunity to enjoy amusement, in whatever form. Thanks to medicine and wagon shows, circuses, roving variety companies, and entertainers who dared literally to risk their lives in uncharted performing territory, these new forms flourished.

Early circuses usually consisted of horse acts, a menagerie of animals, and lion-tamers performing in round tents, which provided shelter from the weather and allowed only paying customers to see the show. The success of the circus was due to its ability to take man's mundane if brutal battles with nature and the frontier and present them as a noble and colorful struggle, testifying to the power of the new nation and its people.

Circuses featured clowns, not only to provide general amusement between acts, but also as specific comedians. These clowns were featured performers — "talkers" — telling jokes, singing comic songs, and acting out physical gags. They were America's first stand-up comedians. As the circus grew to become a three-ring extravaganza, however, clowns were relegated to anonymous group frolics.

Medicine and wagon shows usually consisted of a trio of performers — the "Professor," or learned pitchman; his fool assistant, or straightman; and a "plant" in the audience, used to spur product sales. The pitchman was the comedian, with monologues and "home-spun" stories his presentation. Sales and profitability were directly related to his ability to capture, hold, and entertain the audience.

The minstrel show was an authentic American entertainment invention. It was a combination of African tribal customs brought to the U.S. by slaves, traditional church hymns they converted into "Negro" spirituals, and joyous song and dance. Borrowing these elements, and gentrifying them, white men — in burnt-cork blackface — made the minstrel show America's most popular amusement for fifty years.

Using what they claimed were genuine dialects, minstrel comedians helped compose a show filled with song, dance, and humor, supposedly portraying authentic Blacks in a

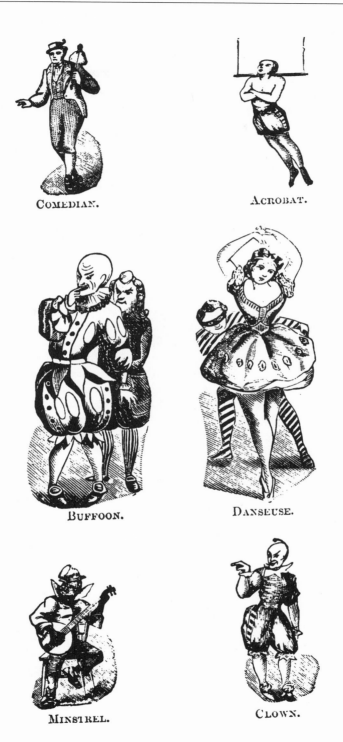

COMEDIAN.

ACROBAT.

BUFFOON.

DANSEUSE.

MINSTREL.

CLOWN.

These wood engravings of various popular performers in costume were published in the 1870s. The comedian appears in characteristic Irish workingman's garb.

benign, amusing format. In reality, the minstrel show perpetuated negative stereotypes that we still confront today. Thomas D. Rice was credited with creating a song and dance routine, "Jump Jim Crow," that gained him and his successors fame but also became a slang expression that for a century identified malignant racial segregation.

By the 1850s, the essence of minstrel comedy was performed by two endmen, "Mr. Tambo" and "Mr. Bones," sitting on either side of a line of performers on stage. Tambo and Bones always wore blackface. The interlocutor, or master of ceremonies, white and dressed in a tuxedo-like costume, was the straight man. Jokes were either one-liners (In what ship have the greatest number of men been wrecked? Courtship!) or short dialogues, usually dealing with current events, popular fads, and women, all subjects easily identifiable to audiences.

Simplistic though it might have been, this minstrel comedic form was the foundation for variety, vaudeville, revue, and musical comedy. In addition, minstrelsy integrated comedy as a prominent part of popular theater programs and elevated comedians to the rank of important performers.

Reaching their peak of acceptance during the 1870s and 1880s, melodramas were long skits or plays that centered on the conflict between common people — usually represented by a flaxen-haired, idealized heroine — and the forces of immorality — usually represented by a thin-mustached villain. Melodramas were replete with unrealistic characters and fantasy plots, a format ready-made for the comedian. He played a starring role and was integrated into the plot, offering amusement in contrast to the serious dilemmas faced by hero and heroine. The comedian never got the girl, but he always got the laughs. It was from this melodrama format that stereotypical roles like the drunk, the eccentric, and the sharp-tongued wiseguy became stock comic characters.

Like sixteenth-century Italian *commedia dell'arte*, Dan Rice (1840s–1850s) made audiences laugh by making fun of cultivated and pretentious people. He was considered America's first clown. Rice had worked his way up the performance ladder as a racehorse jockey, cardsharp, circus performer, and lion tamer, discovering in the process that, no matter the type of show, audiences wanted to laugh. Dressing in outlandish costumes and makeup, Rice told jokes, parodied songs, and ridiculed popular topics, later adding eccentric dance to his successful routines. During the middle 1800s, he had obtained as close to a national following as one could then achieve.

Following the tradition of Pierrot, the French clown, George L. Fox (1860s–1870s) excelled in pantomime and was an accomplished "mugger." His exaggerated facial expressions portraying innocence and ignorant simplicity burlesqued everything from Shakespeare to Humpty-Dumpty. Fox so epitomized the art of pantomime that, after his death, it was seldom seen in the U.S. until revived, on film, by Charlie Chaplin and the Keystone Kops some fifty years later.

Another contributor to American comedic history was Francis S. Chanfrau (1850s–1860s), who played a character from the slums of New York. Called "Mose, the Bow'ry B'hoy," Chanfrau was a rough, boisterous comic whose skits and plays revealed the gritty texture of New York City life, ridiculing both its rich and poor inhabitants. Audiences found him appealing, and he attracted people from all social classes. Most important, his performance first cultivated street-life as a fertile field for comedy and its rich variety of ethnic types as humorous examples of the "common" people. Harrigan & Hart farces popularized this comedic form, and Weber & Fields encouraged audiences to laugh cathartically at themselves and one another.

By the 1870s, variety entertainment had established itself, and comedy was a necessary ingredient in its successful expansion. The popular stage would soon lose its stigma of immorality. With America's industrialization and increasing urbanization, popular theater was widely accepted as leisure for the common people. Theaters devoted exclusively to popular performance were opened in cities and towns across the country. Railroads made it easy for traveling companies to play in a different location each week. Frequently changing audiences allowed companies to carry minimal props and comedians to repeat and refine their "business." As this new American enterprise grew, the number of aspiring actors and actresses multiplied, and the number of comedians increased commensurately. During the '70s, theater managers advertised as much for performers as they did for audiences.

The minstrels had made Blacks an object of humor. Variety, particularly in New York, made ethnics an object of humor that became a trademark of late nineteenth-century comedy. The comedian who could make audiences laugh at themselves and one another helped defuse real-life problems of assimilation and identity. That many of the comedians who advanced these stereotypes were themselves members of the group they parodied only helped to secure audience acceptance of their humor. They developed stock characterizations: Dutch (German) comedians wore chin whiskers, derby hats, checked pants, and sported large (padded) stomachs; Jews were hooknosed, stooped, shuffled, and rubbed their hands together; Irishmen wore side whiskers, plug hats, danced jigs, and drank liquor; Blacks shuffled, wore old clothing, and spoke in malapropisms. All wore exaggerated costumes, almost clownlike, to provide easy identification of their characters for unsophisticated audiences. All spoke in the jargon of their ethnic characters, again amplifying verbal and intellectual stereotypes.

The Irish two-act was an example of ethnic comedy found on the variety stage. Typically, it consisted of a straight man and

Wood engraving of an Irish comic, circa 1875. At the time, most comedians on the popular stage were Irish. Rather than attempting to escape the stereotype, they used it to advantage, enabling the audience to recognize and identify the character portrayed and, thereby, the kind of entertainment offered.

a comic; one tall, the other short; one smart, the other dumb. They dressed in stereotypical costumes, performed comic dialogues, sang, and clog-danced. Though beginning in friendly conversation, most of the routines ended in fighting. The act centered on drinking, invariably graduating into belligerence and physical combat. The skits usually identified the performers as irresponsible manual laborers, happy in spite of their hard life, a stereotypical perspective of Irish immigrants living in the Bowery. Most of the popular New York theater comedians who later became successful had an Irish act or character in their repertoire.

Ethnic two-acts became the heart of vaudeville comedy, the replacement for variety in the 1890s. Thanks to the contributions of theater managers like Tony Pastor — owner, operator, touring performer, and publicist of his own theater in the Bowery — vaudeville acquired structure, form, and standardized performance formats. It developed a class-rating among performers and initiated advertising and promotional techniques. This urban sophistication was projected to the provinces by the ever-advancing railroads, able now to reach even the smallest towns. Vaudeville theaters were always located in the center of the city and always reasonably priced, making them accessible to everyone. Theater behavior, however, had changed little from earlier times; the comedian still had to "capture" the audience to satisfy them.

Vaudeville quickly became more business than art, spawning the development of theater chains, booking agents, and a class of owner-operators who, by the early 1900s, gained control of the industry. The successful comedian's venues became more limited, but his salary and popularity increased. Again, a comedian's accommodation to changes in audience tastes proved the difference between success and failure. The most enduring comedians were those who could play many different roles in many different shows across the country.

American comedians have demonstrated their ingenuity in meeting the needs and desires of diverse and demanding audiences. Their evolution from colonial times to the present has followed a swift and relentless course, slicing through our shifting culture and challenging established norms. At the same time, like a social salve, comedians have forged new communal relationships, new bonds, and new habits that permit us to laugh at ourselves, our roots, and our universal sense of self-righteousness.

Comedy relaxes us. It stretches our viewpoint, loosens our inhibitions. At once beautiful, coarse, satiric, forceful, multi-colored, venturesome, primitive, happy, and sophisticated, comedy plays a significant role in the drama of our lives. It is deeply ingrained in our American heritage.

Comedians, purveyors of the laugh, bring emotional release and a measure of serenity to the public. They remind us that laughing is healthy and laughter a unifying element in an otherwise ferocious society. They argue against our feelings of self-consciousness and disillusionment. By revealing our society as amusing, they give us hope. Comedians are profoundly American characters, soothing our psyches and lubricating raw sensibilities with the healing balm of levity. Today, as we seek to identify heroic icons in our society — sports figures, movie stars, corporate executives, or White House occupants — we ought not overlook the comedian as a hero of our times.

Familiarizing ourselves with the lives of these rare individuals can provide some insight into what ingredients make a comic and what makes us laugh. Like all of us, comedians have their own full share of tears, conflict, hard labor, and painful moments. Yet they choose a profession whose purpose is to make us laugh. Pleasing the audience becomes their "bottom line." Comedy, the most demanding and unforgiving of any kind of performance, is uniquely perishable. What comedians do next must always be better than what they have done before. Conceivably, if we learn more about their lives, we can smile more about our own.

Eddie Foy was a consummate comedian, making the American public laugh for more than half a century. During the years from the Civil War to the Roaring Twenties, few performers brought laughter to audiences the way that Eddie Foy did. A versatile performer, he spanned the development of popular theater from its poverty-inspired Irish two-acts to its lavish musical comedies. Sensitive to changes in audience tastes, he tailored his comedy to offend no one and entertain everyone. He created a unique persona on stage — a clown for all seasons — one that made him a perennial star. He was innovative and daring, unafraid to push comedic performance beyond its traditional formats. He cared about and helped his fellow performers. But Eddie was tough on himself, strongly motivated, and committed to always doing his best in front of an audience. That Eddie Foy survived and prospered, as he journeyed from the streets of the Bowery to Broadway's most glamorous theaters, makes his life all the more instructive and compelling.

This biography has a two-fold purpose: to tell the colorful story of a revered comedian and to understand the nature and popularity of comedy in our society.

Though it will follow the development of the comedic art form over half a century, the book is not intended as a definitive history of nineteenth- and early twentieth-century American comedy. Instead, it will trace Eddie Foy's life and career, as popular theater entertainment became one of America's primary leisure-time pursuits. Foy is one of the finest examples of how early comedians evolved, revealing the trials and tribulations they endured, the successes they embraced, and the contributions they made while inspiring the public to laughter.

Some people argue that the comedy performed by Foy has vanished. They also contend that, if it were resurrected, it would be found naive, simple, and out-of-touch with contemporary culture. They have already forgotten the comedy of Milton Berle, Sid Caesar, and Red Skelton.

But it is exactly such perceptions that make comedy viable. Comedy constantly changes but never disappears; it is always everywhere around us. Comedy can be observed in all aspects of our life. The gifted comedian not only observes this antidote to life's tragedies; he points it out to us. We, as the audience, need to recognize it and integrate it, in that idiosyncratic way that creates laughter. That collaboration is the essence of comedy.

Chapter 1

KID: *Say, Dad, what kind of things are ancestors?*
DAD: *Well, son, that means your relations that have
gone before you. I'm one, and your granddad is
another.*
KID: *Then why do people go around bragging about
them so much?*

During the summer of 1860, England's Prince of Wales set sail for a royal visit to the United States. He was to be honored by New York City's elite with a lavish parade and banquet. On the afternoon of his arrival, the prince was greeted by government dignitaries, led by Mayor Fernando Wood, and prominent financial tycoons, headed by John Jacob Astor III and Hamilton Fish.

It was reported that 300,000 people lined Broadway from Battery Park to the Fifth Avenue Hotel, anxious to get a glimpse of the young, slender, handsome heir to the British throne and welcome him to America. But as his ornate, open carriage, drawn by six magnificently liveried horses, clattered through the Bowery's Irish neighborhoods, the prince was greeted with more jeers than cheers.

Many of the Irish sidewalk observers had not long before emigrated to America because of their native country's devastating potato famine. Near starvation, uprooted from their farms and villages by the English, their only hope for survival seemed to be the promise of America. More than half a million had come to New York between 1845 and 1860, most of them to live in the fetid ghettos of the Bowery. These people had not forgotten England's role in provoking the famine and mass migration, nor her later "apology" and offers of rehabilitation that never quite seemed to arrive.

In contrast to the elegant apartments and mansions on upper Broadway and Fifth Avenue, clapboard houses on the lower East Side, in an area called Greenwich Village, were in obvious deterioration. The streets and sidewalks were always dirty, littered with the detritus of daily life. Houses sheltered two or three families, the more unlucky living in cellars with no ventilation, sharing their rooms with a variety of vermin. The streets were lined with grocery stores, pawn shops, and second-hand stores that featured perpetual going-out-of-business sales. Next to these enterprises were the small entrepreneurs selling their expertise — a tailor, a carpenter, a dressmaker — out of the front rooms of their houses.

Gangs of hoodlums, many comprising pre-teens and teens, roamed the neighborhoods seeking money and diversion at the expense of residents who dared to be seen on the sidewalks, especially after dark. Complementing these gangs were thieves and prostitutes who used street-corner barrooms as bases of operation.

Entertainment was available at the myriad grog-shops, "concert halls" and dancehouses found in nearly every neighborhood. Vagrant children wandered everywhere, begging for a few pennies and searching the gutters for scraps of food. In the evenings, sidewalks were filled with vendors, adults and children alike, selling everything from hot butter-slathered corn to stolen goods. Fortunate children, some of them as young as six, were lucky enough to get legitimate jobs as newsboys, an occupation much preferred to collecting rags or stealing.

In each neighborhood, there was a Catholic church and a political headquarters, the former to succor those in poverty, the latter to make sure they voted for the preferred candidate. Like their congregations, the churches were also poor, except when local politicians — who happened to own the bars and brothels — made donations to assuage their guilt.

Few families were lucky enough to rent an entire house and support their children adequately. Such a family, however, were the Richard Fitzgeralds.

In the spring of 1855, the family — Richard, a tailor; Ellen, his wife, who was

pregnant; six-year-old daughter Catherine; and Richard's mother, fifty-two-year-old Catherine — had landed at Castle Garden, New York's immigration facility. They had come from Dublin, Ireland, escaping the aftermath of the potato famine like many thousands of their countrymen. Actually, the Fitzgeralds had been somewhat shielded from the effects of the famine, since they lived in the city and Richard's occupation was not directly tied to agriculture. But as the country sank ever deeper into social chaos and even skilled people found it impossible to feed a family, the Fitzgeralds left Ireland to seek sustenance in America. It took them over a month to reach New York, having had to negotiate a circuitous route through England to find room on a ship. So many people were leaving Ireland, there were not enough vessels available to transport them.

Thanks to help from relatives already living in the Bowery, the Fitzgeralds had somewhere to live, at Eighteen Trinity Place, within a few blocks of the docks where they had landed from Castle Garden. The neighborhood was a teeming Irish enclave.[1]

Working out of his front room, Richard was able to establish his tailoring business quickly. Few Irish immigrants had tailoring skills. Ellen could do little but take in washing, since she was in the last months of pregnancy.

A second daughter, Mary, arrived in May 1855, born at home. Richard's increasing income and the need for more living space pushed the Fitzgeralds to move to a two-story clapboard house at Twenty-three Eighth Avenue, just north of Abingdon Square, in East Greenwich Village, a decided improvement in living conditions. Within two months, Ellen was pregnant again.

Possibly because of the Fitzgeralds' now strained finances, another family moved into the second floor. Others would later move into the cellar. Ellen took in washing to supplement Richard's earnings; seven-year old Catherine cared for baby Mary.

Edwin Fitzgerald was born on March 9,

1856, at home. According to family recollections, the Fitzgeralds were loving and nurturing parents, as well as devout Catholics. Richard strove to maintain his tailoring business and Ellen continued taking in wash. Besides going to school, Catherine looked after Mary and Edwin when her mother was working. But Ellen's fourth pregnancy and the birth of baby Ellen in 1858, put additional pressures on Richard at a time when New York was enduring an unprecedented wave of crime and disorder, which greatly diminished his clientele.

Because Mayor Wood was able to control neither the police force nor the criminal elements roving the streets and attacking citizens, particularly in the Bowery, the governor of New York State established a Board of Commissions to oversee the police. The mayor, however, refused to relinquish control of the police. Battle was joined, and the army was dispatched to arrest the mayor. Two months of street fighting culminated in a confrontation between organized gangs and metropolitan police, aided by the army.

When the Prince of Wales came to New York City in 1860, it is likely the Fitzgeralds were among the thousands of Irish on hand to deride him. Richard undoubtedly belonged to one of the many patriotic organizations that existed in the Bowery, groups that played an influential role in the lives of recent immigrants. These organizations, consisting entirely of men, also served as a focus for friendships and venues for various entertainments. It was at this time that Richard began to show signs of a mental disorder.

Since the Republican Party victory and Abraham Lincoln's election in 1860, a number of Southern states had seceded from the Union; civil war seemed imminent. The Democratic Party in the Bowery expressed its opposition to war and recommended that New York secede from the Union, declaring itself a "free city." This proposal was positively received among Democratic politicians, and a secret group was formed to pursue the possibility. The actual outbreak of war, however, created such patriotic fervor in the city that most Democrats were swept along in the prevailing tide of excitement. Not surprisingly, local patriotic organizations began recruiting members to join the Union Army.

The Fitzgerald household was cast into turmoil when Richard announced he intended to join the army, leaving his wife and four children with no means to support themselves. As a Yankee soldier, Richard would earn only $13 a month, a meager sum. To support the family, Ellen would have to become a washerwoman full-time; Catherine would have to leave school to work; and Edwin, not yet six, would have to find a job, making it impossible for him to attend school.

All parks in the city had been turned into barracks for soldiers preparing to leave for Washington. Abingdon Park, a block away from the Fitzgerald house, was no different. In early 1862, the regiment for which Richard volunteered marched away to the accompanying cheers of friends and neighbors. Ellen Fitzgerald, however, was wondering how the family would survive while her husband was gone.

That Richard was ever permitted to enlist in the army attested to its urgency in accepting volunteers. He was clearly suffering from some sort of mental condition; however, it was ignored, if not totally overlooked. Yet two months in the army proved enough for authorities to recognize the obvious, and Richard was hastily discharged. While the family were elated to have him home, they quickly became aware of his increasingly aberrant behavior. He was unable to work. Nor could he manage even the simplest tasks. Though not violent, he was becoming more disoriented every day.

Finally, after months of anxiety and distress among family members, Richard was taken to Blackwell's Island, New York City's insane asylum. Two months later, in September 1862, Richard Fitzgerald died, his death attributed to paresis, a disease of the brain caused by syphilis.[2] Paresis affects the central nervous system, inducing mental and emotional instability, as well as paralytic seizures. The disease is slow to develop, usually taking four to five years before death occurs. It would appear that Richard was infected sometime after Edwin's birth.

After Richard's confinement on Blackwell's Island, the family never saw him again. He was buried in a government cemetery, no family members in attendance. In later years, Edwin vaguely remembered Richard as "a rather good-looking man and a kindly father."

Because they had little money, the family had to move to smaller quarters, at Thirty-nine Eighth Avenue, an apartment building just up the street. Besides Catherine, seven-year-old Mary was now working. Edwin became a bootblack, one of the few jobs available to a six-year-old.

At first, he was allowed to work only in his own neighborhood and during daylight hours. Gradually, he was permitted to expand his territory to include other sections of the Bowery. One day, observing a competing bootblack, Edwin too began dancing on the street to attract clientele. And when he saw other bootblacks dancing for customers, he deftly copied their steps, quickly increasing his own repertoire.

The Fitzgeralds were in mourning again when the youngest child, Ellen, only four years old, died of anemia in April 1863.[3] It seems likely that she had contracted her father's disease, since he acquired it before she was conceived. Just after Ellen's death, the family faced another physical crisis, this one spreading across all Manhattan, especially threatening to those living in poverty.

The U.S. Congress had just passed the Enrollment and Conscription Act. Passage of the bill was viewed by New York City Democrats as a Republican ploy to reduce their political power in places like the Bowery. In retaliation, the Democrats used one of the law's provisions — exemption of any man from active military service if he paid

three hundred dollars — to spread discontent among the impoverished. Democrats firmly believed the law discriminated against their constituency; more men would be drafted from Democratic districts because the poor couldn't afford the cost of an exemption. The law particularly affected the Irish living in the Bowery.

On July 4, 1863, Governor Seymour addressed a meeting of Democrats and suggested that implementation of the law might precipitate civil disorder. Actual draft selection began July 11; 1,200 names were chosen. Subdued yet restive crowds surrounded the draft offices on Third Avenue and Forty-sixth Street.

On July 13, before the draft offices opened, in what appeared to be an orchestrated event, bands of men and women assembled and moved up Sixth Avenue, persuading workers in businesses along the street to join them as they marched toward Central Park. Now a large crowd, they proceeded to the draft offices on Third Avenue. Police stationed at the offices were unprepared for such a throng. The office building was attacked and overrun; the interior destroyed and set afire, as were adjoining buildings. A group of soldiers attempted to stop the mob but found themselves overwhelmed; rioters beat the soldiers with their own weapons.

Reports to police from various parts of the city suggested that the crowds were being directed by unknown leaders and that their objectives were more than merely stopping the draft. All other draft offices were closed, but the rioting continued. Police telegraph wires were cut, and omnibus tracks torn up. Rioting continued throughout the day and into the evening, with many buildings burned and streets barricaded. One such building, housing an arms manufacturer, was attacked and set afire. The rioters seized guns and ammunition.

When crowds headed down Broadway to attack the police center, Commissioner Acton directed a contingent to stop them, ordering "make no arrests." A battle ensued, lasting an hour. The dead, dying, and injured littered Broadway.

The next day, New York City was in a state of siege. No stores were open. No trains or coaches were in operation. Flames were seen all over the city, and smoke hung over devastated neighborhoods. Crowding onto the few available ferries, thousands of people attempted to flee the city.

From Twenty-first Street to Thirty-second, a running battle took place along Second Avenue. Police and troops with rifles and cannon faced crowds of men and women armed with stones and brickbats. The bands of protesters were quickly dispersed but moved to other neighborhoods to continue their disturbance. On Eighth and Ninth Avenues, near the Fitzgerald house, rioters took downed telegraph poles, carts, and wagons and lashed them together to form barricades. What had begun as a dispute about the Conscription Act now turned into mob violence venting white, largely Irish frustrations against Blacks living in the area. Blacks were held as scapegoats, viewed as responsible for the war and hence the draft. Many were killed, and their property destroyed.

In Abingdon Square, a block from the Fitzgeralds', a Black was hanged. Edwin, along with other neighborhood children, ran to see what had happened. With a child's fascination, he watched in horror as the hanged man dangled, witnessed his body cut down, left lying in the street. Frightened and sickened by the event, Edwin ran home. As Foy reflected later in life, the episode had a profound effect on his feelings regarding prejudice based on race and ethnicity.

After four days of riots, thirteen regiments from the Army of the Potomac subdued the crowds and placed the city under military control. One thousand, two hundred people had been killed; millions of dollars of property destroyed. The Fitzgerald neighborhood was littered with debris for weeks.

The combined impact of riots and the inability of the Fitzgeralds to find sufficient

Edwin Fitzgerald, age 8, dressed in his Sunday best. He had already experienced the realities of street life in New York's Bowery and Chicago's Irish ghetto.

work persuaded Ellen to move her family out of the Bowery. A relative in Chicago suggested they would do better there and wired railway tickets for them.

It was a great adventure to travel to Chicago. For eight-year-old Edwin, his face pressed against the window to capture every passing scene, it would be the first of hundreds of railroad journeys across the country during his life. The trip took over three days, the Erie Railroad route passing through Albany, Buffalo, Cleveland, Fort Wayne, and along the southern edge of Lake Michigan into Chicago. Traveling across rolling hills and farmland, rattling over trestle bridges, and rumbling noisily through villages and towns was an exciting experience for Edwin, the kind of adventure that often creates a later longing to be "on the road."

Just before the end of the Civil War, Chicago was a boom town of more than 200,000 people. The city was about to complete construction of the Union Stock Yards, which would make it the leading cattle center in the country. It had already become the leading grain market. Chicago was the hub of ten major railroads, with nearly 100 trains arriving in and leaving the city daily. Because its manufacturing industries were growing rapidly, the city was attracting immigrants from Germany and Poland, as well as from the impoverished districts of Eastern cities. The increase in Chicago's population also brought overcrowding, inadequate shelters, and concomitant problems with sewage, garbage, and sanitation.

The Fitzgeralds' living quarters were located in the First Ward, just south of the Chicago River, in an Irish immigrant neighborhood. Employment was immediately available for Ellen, Catherine, and Mary; but Edwin could only find work as a bootblack again, earning a few cents each day.

Working full-time on the streets of downtown Chicago meant Edwin had no opportunity for schooling. In his autobiography, Foy recalled having attended night school for a few months when he was twelve years of age. It proved an abbreviated experience because his teacher once saw him polishing shoes. Painfully embarrassed about his work, Foy never returned to her classroom.

Having learned from his Bowery experiences, Edwin was able to utilize his dancing to attract customers. It appears he spent the next few years contributing whatever he could to the family income. At twelve, he decided to sell newspapers. It was a riskier enterprise, but one with the chance to earn more money. Newspapers cost three cents each and were sold for five cents. On a good day, Edwin would make a dollar; on bad days, he was lucky to break even.

Selling newspapers gave Edwin the opportunity to stay overnight at a nearby Newsboys Home, especially when no one was at the Fitzgeralds' to prepare meals. For twenty-five cents, a boy could secure a bed and two meals a day. The Home also had an assembly room, where the boys put on shows to amuse themselves. Here, Edwin got his first opportunity to perform before an audience. Persuaded by friends, a resolute Edwin mounted the stage, turned his coat inside out to achieve a comic effect, and presented a variety of acrobatic dances, perfected by his years of street performance. Foy later reported that his dancing "made quite a hit."

Edwin could not afford to see any shows in theaters, even the cheapest ones, so he stood in alleyways watching and listening to performers through windows or open stage doors. Minstrel shows were very popular at the time and Edwin was fascinated with their singing and comedic turns. One of the minstrel performers he enjoyed most was Billy Emerson, a blackface dancer, singer, and comedian.

Having made his first professional appearance with Joe Sweeney's Minstrels about 1850, Emerson had been performing for close to two decades. He played the music halls for many years but achieved minstrel stardom after the Civil War, performing at Pastor's Theater in New York. Joining Allen and Manning's Minstrels, he played extended runs in Chicago because of their great popularity there. Emerson wrote some famous minstrel songs — "Love Among the Roses," "Mary Kelly's Beau," and "The Big Sunflower" — but gained his fame because of his versatility, dancing grace, and comedic timing. He was to be remembered as one of minstrelsy's best end men. Thirteen years later, Foy would be hired as a performer with Emerson's Minstrels.

Edwin was fifteen when he became an involuntary participant in Chicago's Great Fire. On Sunday, October 8, 1871, at about 9:00 P.M., a fire brigade was called to answer an alarm in a poor Irish section on the southwest side of the city. The brigade had been there just the day before to put out a fire that had consumed five square blocks. Because fires were common in a city built of wood, few paid attention to the blaze.

This fire, however, was fed by gale-force winds and quickly spread out of control, far beyond the capabilities of the fire department. Sweeping northwest, toward the downtown section, it engulfed another poor Irish neighborhood, Conley's Patch, just south and east of the Chicago River, where the Fitzgeralds had their cottage. (The shanty houses of many Irish immigrants were called "cottages" by local authorities, their attempt to dignify — and overlook — the squalor of the area.) At the Fitzgerald home were Ellen; Catherine, a single parent with an eighteen month old child; Mary; and Edwin. They had gone to sleep, undeterred by the alarms early in the evening. At midnight, however, they were awakened and looked out their windows to see flames just a few blocks away, rapidly heading toward them. Already, their street was choked with wagons moving north, people carrying all the household goods they could. Everyone was close to panic.

The fire soon became a firestorm that roared through flimsy structures in minutes. Just beyond the Irish section lay the municipal gas works. When the fire overwhelmed the gas works, explosions of volatile chemicals added to the conflagration, extinguished all the street lights, and plunged the city into darkness, but for the eerie glow of flames.

Ellen instructed Edwin to take Catherine's baby to friends living some blocks east, to return home next morning if their house had not been burnt. At that moment, the Fitzgeralds believed they were safe and the fire would soon be put out. Once Edwin was on the street though, swept up in a multitude of other escapees, the burden of responsibility and fear combined to all but overwhelm him. The fire was moving faster than anyone had calculated. Looking back, he could see his house already burning, the flames apparently surrounding him. Since everything was constructed of wood, even the streets and sidewalks, the entire city seemed to feed the fire.

When Edwin reached the friends' home, he found them gathering their own household goods, ready to leave. They paid no attention to his pleas for help. On his own now, he ran eastward, toward one of the bridges that crossed the Chicago River to the north. There, he encountered crowds of people surging to cross the bridge, believing it to be the only escape available from the voracious flames. Panic had jammed the bridge with wagons, bellowing animals, struggling, screaming, and desperate people. Instead of trying to fight his way across the bridge while cradling the baby, Edwin headed toward the lake.

Dashing through downtown streets, he witnessed hundreds of people crazed by the encroaching conflagration. Some carried whatever goods they could, on wagons if they were lucky. Looters smashed windows and doors of stores to seize whatever they could. Others wandered dazedly, unaware of the tumult around them. The scene was pandemonium. All of life had suddenly gone dreadfully awry.

Running east, past Michigan Avenue, Edwin was almost to the lakefront. Just south of the mouth of the Chicago River, there was a stretch of sand. Already, some people stood in the water, as if to stake a claim on the quickly decreasing haven. It was here that Edwin, clutching the baby, watched the fire reach so near that it singed hair and eyebrows, then miraculously pass, jumping the river to devastate the north side of the city.

By early the next morning, only smoke and ruined buildings remained. Those who had escaped to the sand and water were now able to rest. Many, like Edwin, slept where they lay. Foy later recalled that he and the baby were befriended by the people there, some sharing food with them.

The afternoon following the firestorm, Edwin, among many others, walked back into the smoldering downtown area, already occupied by police and army troops attempting to maintain order and help those in need. Edwin wanted to see if his house had been destroyed and discover the fate of his mother and sisters. But the neighborhood was so ruined, with fire pockets yet remaining, that he couldn't reach his street directly. Traveling south on Michigan Avenue and turning west on Congress Street, the southern border of the fire, Edwin finally reached the Fitzgeralds' street. Their house, like all the others in this Irish shantytown, was completely destroyed. There was no sign of his family. A rain welcome to firefighters only contributed to his discomfort and that of the baby, both of them hungry and cold. After wandering for hours, Edwin stopped at a church, one of many that were serving as centers for fire victims. There, at last, he and the baby were fed and found safe haven.

The great fire had burned over 2,100 acres, destroyed over 17,000 buildings. More than 100,000 people lost their homes; 21,000 of them, with the Fitzgeralds, had lived on the Near South Side of the city. Most of the people killed came from sections of the South Side where Irish cottages were located. No sooner had the fire been extinguished than people rushed to find its cause. Someone had to be blamed.

Both the cause and the culprits were embodied in Irish immigrants, the O'Learys. Typical of local Irish, Mr. O'Leary was a day laborer; Mrs. O'Leary sold milk from her cows. It was one of Mrs. O'Leary's cows that, allegedly, started the fire by knocking over a barn lantern. In the press and among people who had lost businesses, the O'Learys and "their kind" aroused strong anti-Irish sentiment.[4] The press presented the unfortunate couple as examples of the immoral Irish immigrant character. During the period after the fire, as the city was being mobilized to rebuild, anti-Irish emotions ran high. The Fitzgeralds could find no work. In order to survive, they had to stand in line for hours at soup kitchens.

The people at the church helped Edwin to find his mother and sisters at a school just outside the fire area, where they had taken refuge. Edwin learned that little of the family's goods had been saved, and none of his own belongings. But to the Fitzgeralds, there was nothing more important than the entire family's being alive and healthy. Foy remembered their reunion vividly: "We kissed each other all around and all wept in chorus, myself as freely as anybody."

A month later, the Fitzgeralds were on their way back to the Bowery, in hopes that their old neighborhood would offer them the shelter and work they required. Thanks to railroad tycoon, James Fisk, Jr., anyone wanting to go to New York to escape the ravages of the Chicago fire could obtain free passage. The Fitzgeralds were among the lucky recipients of Fisk's generosity. Old friends found them a temporary house on Cherry Street and helped them get settled. Unfortunately, the Fitzgeralds arrived on Cherry Street about the time construction of the Brooklyn Bridge began, only a few blocks way.

The Fitzgeralds found the Bowery in the early days of 1872 no better than in 1864. Jobs of any kind were hard to obtain, and the Bowery environment had deteriorated even further. Inspired by the industrial revolution and the pervasive concept of "progress," New York was transforming itself. Business was moving uptown in giant strides. Department stores, mansions, hotels, and theaters were being built along Fifth Avenue and Broadway. Elevated trains made it easy to travel from Battery Park at the lower tip of Manhattan to the countryside above 103rd Street, if one was willing to tolerate the smoke and soot. Even an underground railway was planned.

But as new development moved north of the Bowery, the area's increasing disrepair aggravated its already deteriorated state. Along with squalid tenements, vendor-crowded streets, and cheap entertainments, the Bowery had now become a center of vice, crime, and political intrigue. The Fitzgeralds found themselves strangers in these surroundings. In contrast, letters from Chicago described a city quickly on the rebound, with jobs for all. Maybe it would be better to return to Chicago. But how?

Foy wrote in his autobiography that he and his mother went to Jim Fisk's office to request return passes to Chicago. They were directed to pick up their passes the following Monday. But that very weekend, Fisk was shot and killed by an irate former business associate. Would the passes be available for the Fitzgeralds? When Edwin and his mother returned to Fisk's offices Monday morning, they had grave doubts about obtaining the promised passes. Long and anxious minutes passed while a clerk determined whether their passes were indeed available. At last, the clerk returned with passes in hand. The late tycoon had apparently approved them just before he was shot.

The return to Chicago was fortuitous. Ellen was hired as a companion, protector, and nurse for Mrs. Abraham Lincoln, under constant care due to her mental breakdown. Ellen would accompany Mrs. Lincoln on trips, as well as serve long hours at her home in Chicago. Thanks to Ellen, the last years of Mrs. Lincoln's life were preserved. In his book "Mrs. Abraham Lincoln," Dr. W. A. Evans quoted continually from Ellen's writings.[5] From 1872 to 1875, no information was available about Mrs. Lincoln except that provided by Ellen. After Mrs. Lincoln was placed in a sanitarium, Ellen had no trouble obtaining future nursing appointments, assuring her of a reasonable income until her retirement.

For his part, Edwin had no desire to return to bootblacking; nor did he want to work at any kind of manual labor. At sixteen, he believed it was time for him to attempt a career in show business, at least according to his limited perception of what show business was. He considered himself a good acrobatic dancer and recalled with pleasure the applause he had received while performing for his fellow newsboys. A friend, Jack Finnegan, who also considered himself a good dancer, agreed to team with Edwin. The pair planned to take advantage of the recent popularity of Irish two-acts. For long hours and many days they practiced, using the sand on the shores of Lake Michigan to cushion their falls. When the boys believed

Ellen Fitzgerald, Edwin's mother, a formidable woman who, as a single parent, managed to work and raise three children with loving care. She later went on to become Mrs. Abraham Lincoln's nurse.

themselves ready to perform in front of a paying audience, Finnegan suggested their names were too Irish. He was going to change his name to Edwards. What name would Edwin like to use? Edwin Fitzgerald chose Edwin Foy. Years later, Foy said he took the name from the Foy Sisters, a variety team whose Irish dance routines he had enjoyed.

For two young, unknown, and untried performers, securing a stage engagement was not easy. The only venues where they could persuade the management to hire them were beer halls, wine rooms, and honky-tonks. At such places, owners were willing to try any act, as long as it might please customers and keep them drinking. So Edwards and Foy played wherever they could, often for only a few cents a night, just to perform. They even traveled as far as Joliet and Elgin, sometimes based on nothing more than a rumor that an engagement was possible.

Even though their stage names did not identify them as Irish, their act was made up of Irish jigs and clog dances, interspersed with acrobatics and Irish songs. Their costumes consisted of plug hats, pasted-on side whiskers, and green-striped knee trousers. To their beer hall audiences, it didn't matter what the team called itself, as long as they were entertaining.

Edwards and Foy patterned themselves after the Irish two-acts of the day.[6] These skits typically consisted of robust, topical, belligerent dialogue presented in a jaunty, argumentative manner. Totally devoid of romantic themes and rhymes, the songs depicted carefree wanderers, somewhat irresponsible but likable. Often a vigorous dance evolved into a burlesqued sparring match. Their skits and routines usually conveyed, in comedic form, the less attractive aspects of immigrant ghetto life. Yet, what better people to present these harsh realities than those who had been raised among them? Typical joke topics included drunks and wives:

1ST DRUNK:	Shay, quit following me.
2ND DRUNK:	I can't. I'm going the shame plashe you are.
1ST DRUNK:	Where?
2ND DRUNK:	I dunno, thash why I'm following you.
1ST MAN:	And you divorced your wife because you found her company wearing?
2ND MAN:	Yes, I found her company wearing my pajamas.

The barrooms where Edwards and Foy performed were usually two-story frame buildings. The main floor consisted largely of a long bar; the center of the room was filled with tables and chairs, all facing a stage raised a few feet above the floor, which was usually covered with sawdust. Lit with gas lamps,

the stage had what passed for a curtain and a backdrop covered with advertising. (Variety acts came to be known as olios because such backdrops often displayed ads for oleomargarine.) Music was usually supplied by a pianist. The second floor boasted wine rooms, where bargirls persuaded their customers to buy more alcohol. The wine rooms were small, separate cubicles where patrons could drink, hug the girls, and watch the show in privacy. Shows ran late, to the early morning hours or as long as there were men drinking at the bar. Some establishments had gaming rooms. Payoffs to local police made illegal gambling a profitable enterprise. For ten turns a day, Edwards and Foy were paid fifty cents each. When the audience cheered, they might earn a few dollars. When the audience jeered, booed, and hooted, the boys received nothing.

After some months of beer hall engagements, the team obtained a week's work at the Cosmopolitan, a well-known "concert hall" in downtown Chicago. Their pay was to be a dollar for each night they performed. On the first night, they began their act well; but the acrobatic pratfalls misfired. The audience shouted "put them out" and "get somebody that can stand up." Backstage, the boys were berated by the manager, who accused them of being fakers. Edwards became so enraged, he slugged the manager. When Edwards refused to perform for the man, Edwin finished the week's work alone. It was the end of the team, and young Edwin Foy was out of work. He saw his stage career rapidly evaporating.

Determined not to fail, he convinced an old friend and fellow performer, Ben Collins, to form a new Irish two-act. Collins was a poor acrobat but talented at writing skits and songs. Thanks to Collins, Edwin had new material, providing the opportunity to expand his acting, singing, and comedic skills. Collins wrote parodies of current songs that seemed to please audiences. The jokes they told were, for the most part, taken from the minstrel patter of end men:

1ST MAN: Did you put the cat out?
2ND MAN: I didn't know it was on fire.

1ST MAN: I would like to know how long
            cows should be milked.
2ND MAN: The same as short cows.

But even with this new material, or perhaps because of it, local beer hall engagements were the only performance venues available to them.

After working sporadically for months, Collins and Foy found employment with a small circus that had just opened and was seeking talent of any sort. Circuses of this kind usually pitched their tents in a vacant lot.[7] They were ten-cent, one-ring operations with a side show. Out front with the ringmaster/pitchman — usually the owner — were a snake charmer and a tattooed lady. Among the side-show performers were a fat woman, a "living skeleton," a sword-swallower, and a performer who supposedly walked barefoot on razor-sharp blades. Music for the show was supplied by a trumpeter and a drummer. Tent performers included an acrobat, juggler, tightrope walker, and animal acts — usually dogs and horses, since they were easy to transport. Everyone had more than one job; side-show people served as helpers during the show, while others cavorted as clowns. All the performers helped tear down and set up the show each time they moved.

Concession sales were more profitable than entrance fees, so these items were continually hawked. The ringmaster tried to rush through the show as quickly as possible, so they could present a number of shows each day. As fast as customers emptied the tent, ticker sellers brought in the audience for the next performance. As acrobats, clowns, and program sellers, Collins and Foy earned three dollars a week.

After playing various neighborhoods in Chicago for a number of weeks, the circus went on tour through villages and towns in northern Illinois and southern Wisconsin. Usually, these performances were one-night

Edwin was sixteen years old when he began his performing career in Chicago's beer halls. He had to apply makeup to appear older and learn the vernacular of beer-hall patter. It was at this time he changed his name to Edwin Foy, because he considered "Fitzgerald" too Irish.

stands, a jump of fifteen to twenty miles during the week, longer on Sundays and Mondays. Circus routine was the same every day; it had to be. Travel occurred at night, all but the drivers asleep in the wagons. Early mornings meant preparations for entering the new town. Everyone was up, in costume, to make the grand entrance parade. Led by the trumpeter and drummer, followed by the main wagon, with the ringmaster/owner, clowns, and other wagons featuring the side-show freaks, the circus rolled into the center of town, stopped to announce a "presentation of grandiose proportions," and then moved on to a vacant lot to erect tents and concessions. All ran smoothly, except when it rained. Then dirt roads turned to hub-deep mud, and the covered wagons leaked. Under such conditions, it was perilous to perform "great feats of daring."

Collins and Foy traveled with the circus for more than two months. Near the end of the summer season, it became apparent the show was in financial trouble. The performers had not yet been paid for their previous week's work. The season closed abruptly in Galena, Illinois, the owner absconding with the past week's receipts. The company was nearly 150 miles from Chicago, a long way by wagon. But a ticket-seller and friend suggested to the boys they all team up, buy a horse and wagon, and continue the show themselves.

He proposed they travel to those villages where no other touring company would stop. They would perform their version of a minstrel show. This suggestion appealed to Edwin. Here was a unique opportunity to perform in blackface, be an end man, tell jokes, and emulate the famed Billy Emerson. Yet the boys had only the most rudimentary costumes available to them; along with burnt-cork faces, they wore black gloves and torn farm clothes to perform.

Traveling across northern Illinois, working their way slowly in the direction of Chicago, the one-wagon minstrel show played wherever a schoolhouse or tavern was available. The former ticket-seller acted as interlocutor; Collins was Mr. Bones, and Foy was Mr. Tambo. In the first part of their show, jokes consisted of the standard minstrel fare.

TAMBO: What's the hardest thing to beat?
BONES: A hard-boiled egg.

TAMBO: What islands are good to eat?
BONES: The Sandwich Islands.

INTERLOCUTOR: Why do ladies hate parrots?
TAMBO or BONES: Because they want to do all
                 the talking themselves.

According to Foy, even though the jokes were old, they were able to amuse their farm and village audiences.

In the second part of the show, Collins and Foy performed acrobatic stunts and sang, either together or singly, since it helped lengthen the performance. After the show, the floor was cleared; and the locals staged a square dance, with the boys calling the figures.

It took them almost three months to return to Chicago. While the boys earned very little money, their performance experiences proved invaluable. They were beginning to feel like stage veterans, able and ready to accept any engagement.

Edwin Foy was almost twenty-one now. While his family supposed he would get over his infatuation with the stage, Edwin firmly believed he could become a successful performer. Even with only a brief and mixed view of show business, he felt there was opportunity for a versatile actor who was ambitious enough to work hard and willing to take risks.

Chapter 2

STRANGER: *Nice little town you have here. What is the population of the place?*
LOCAL: *Do you intend to live here?*
STRANGER: *Indeed I do.*
LOCAL: *Well, then, the population is two.*

In 1876, the McVickers was the finest of Chicago theaters for "serious" plays. It was on this stage that performers like Edwin Booth, Dion Boucicault, Joseph Jefferson, Ellen Terry, and Sir Henry Irving performed the leading dramas of the day.

A traveling company headed by one of these illustrious actors consisted of few people, only those in the leading roles. To carry an entire company on tour proved financially prohibitive for producers and theater managers. They could not afford to cover salaries and expenses for an entire company with the receipts available from performances booked. Thus, each theater was required to supply local talent to play supplemental roles, as well as "supers" (superluminaries or extras). To obtain speaking roles, local performers had to have had some stage experience; for "super"

roles, anyone who could hold a spear and follow orders was eligible.

When Edwin and Ben Collins returned to Chicago after their long and arduous tour through Northern Illinois, they were ready to accept any kind of stage job that paid a salary and was performed indoors. The renowned actor Edwin Booth had just arrived in Chicago, and a theater call for "supers" was announced. Edwin and Ben quickly applied. Since they were able to demonstrate some experience as performers, both were hired, at fifty cents a night.

One way in which young actors learned the intricacies of stage performance was to study the stars. Now, Edwin not only had an opportunity to observe one of the greatest in action, he was also able to perform with him, playing on the same stage as the celebrated

Edwin Booth in a number of Shakespearean productions.

Edwin's first experience as a "super" was in Booth's rendition of *Hamlet*. He played a castle page. In later years, Foy talked about his initial observations of Booth, as he followed the most minute movement of the actor's performances. He recalled especially Booth's ability to precisely match action and dialogue, with no superfluous ranting or emoting. He was particularly impressed with the expressiveness of Booth's hands, a trait Edwin attempted to incorporate into his own acting.

Like many young performers of the day, Edwin hoped to one day perform tragedy; appearing at the McVickers only increased his desire to play Shakespeare. He read all of the Shakespearean plays he could obtain. At home, he recited lines from various plays in an attempt to emulate Booth, to the evident annoyance of his family.

Edwin and Ben played "super" roles for almost a year, performing in a wide variety of shows, from Shakespeare's *Hamlet*, *Julius Caesar* and *Macbeth* to French tragedies like *Richelieu* and *Virginius*. Another learning experience for Edwin came when Joseph Jefferson appeared in his famous title role of *Rip Van Winkle*. Unlike the aloof and demanding Booth, Jefferson was a relaxed and genial performer who took time to assist other actors in learning their roles. Liking what he observed, Edwin embraced Jefferson's respect for fellow performers, no matter their roles. There was no question it made for a more cooperative and productive environment, both backstage and on the boards.

Edwin played soldiers, peasants, brigands, and spear-carriers while at the McVickers. All the roles required his wearing elaborate costumes supplied by the company; they also gave him his first lessons on how to apply makeup professionally. He further learned about self-discipline on stage; serious drama allowed for no humor, no matter how funny an occurrence or a mistake made on stage might be.

Occasionally, the McVickers closed between shows or during holidays — respectable patrons of legitimate plays rarely went to the theater during Lent, Easter week, or the Christmas holiday season. During these times, Edwin and Ben performed at concert halls and variety theaters in the Chicago area. Their repertoire consisted primarily of songs, dances, and jokes derived from minstrel material, although presented in an Irish two-act format. In some of his routines, Edwin parodied both Booth and Jefferson, though it is doubtful his audiences knew whom he was satirizing.

Home life during this period seems to have been stable. Ellen worked as a nurse; Catherine was married and beginning her own family; Mary was engaged to be married. Ellen, however, uncomfortable with her son's choice of profession, was unable to fully accept Edwin's acting career. He made little money and contributed nothing to the household. He worked late hours, ate poorly, slept until noon, and, worst of all, associated with questionable people. Acting was not a respectable profession, she believed; she often attempted to persuade her son to find a better job. Edwin, however, put off his mother by waxing eloquent about the potential salaries he could earn "when I make it on stage."

Edwin and Ben Collins separated amicably at the end of their run at the McVickers. Collins had become enamored with minstrelsy; Edwin wanted to continue playing variety shows, as he was becoming ever more confident performing comedy. He had realized he had an unusual facility to remember jokes and improvise humor. Such spontaneity pleased audiences, and they laughed all the more if they believed a comedian had just "made up" the joke.

From the time he was a teenager, Edwin typically talked out of the side of his mouth. When he exaggerated this habit, audiences tended to laugh as much at his delivery as at the joke itself. During one performance, when he inadvertently sprayed the air with spittle while telling a joke, the audience erupted with laughter. These facial and "wet mouth" expressions quickly became integral to his act, among Foy's most identifiable and amusing professional mannerisms.

Still not confident enough to perform on his own, Edwin teamed with another friend named Fry to continue playing in local variety houses. Fry was the more experienced performer, although, according to Foy, "not remarkable." They teamed well, however, and were found acceptable to theater managers. The Irish two-act, absent the usual fisticuffs and physical business, remained the routine. That won them a week's work at a local theater, but it didn't offer enough versatility to stay at the same venue any longer. It usually took a good deal of time to find their next engagement; more often than not, that meant weeks without work. When they managed to find work, the salaries at these theaters netted them twenty-five dollars a week, $12.50 each. Variety performers were required to supply their own costumes, makeup, and the musical scores they wanted the orchestra to play.

Frustrated by his inability to improve his situation, Edwin persuaded Ben Collins to return. Their new act got them bookings at some variety theaters in Illinois and Iowa. Since there were no booking agents at the time, and only well-paid performers could afford managers who obtained bookings for them, all arrangements had to be made by the performers themselves. Signed contracts were rarely used; engagements were based on a verbal agreement between theater manager and actor. If an arrangement were made long-distance, a teletype message was the only "contract" that persuaded an actor to travel to another city. Travel expenses, plus room and board, were normally paid by the performer. Working these small-time variety houses earned little money, barely enough to pay for the trip itself. For Foy and Collins, however, the tour seemed to offer exposure outside of Chicago and an opportunity to sign up with other theater managers. But it didn't work out that way.

During the middle of July, firemen and brakemen on the Baltimore and Ohio Railroad went on strike due to a reduction in wages. The strike quickly grew violent, strikers attacking a train, security guards firing on the strikers. The strike spread westward and, within a few days, affected all trains west of Chicago. Federal troops were ordered to guard trains and train stations. Pitched battles between strikers and troops occurred in Baltimore and Pittsburgh; but apart from work stoppages, no serious trouble happened in other cities. Nonetheless, it took almost a month for train service to be restored.

When the strike began, Foy and Collins were playing at the Tivoli Theater in Burlington, Iowa. Along with other performers on the road in Illinois and Iowa, they were stranded, with no money and no transportation home. Luckily, at the same time the strike occurred, most rural counties were holding their annual summer fairs, which usually included various kinds of entertainment. The *New York Clipper* reported that many stranded performers moved from fair to fair to earn enough money to return home.[1]

Foy and Collins returned to Chicago in September; it took them almost six weeks to complete the return trip from Burlington. The tour, however, seemed to produce sufficient evidence of their abilities to win them an engagement at the Coliseum Theater, a variety house in downtown Chicago. They were advertised as Irish song and dance performers.

No reports exist of their engagement at the Coliseum, but they played that theater until November and then moved to Hamlin's Academy of Music, performing on and off through the holiday season. Because they were appearing at the same theater for a number of consecutive weeks, the team constantly had to develop new routines and skits. Days were spent creating and practicing new material to keep their act "fresh." The talented Collins wrote song parodies and topical skits. Edwin created acrobatic dances. In addition to their Irish two-act, they performed in blackface. Since their material was often borrowed from veteran comedians, the jokes improved. At the time, jokes about horse racing and people of dubious intelligence were popular:

> Horses are superior to human beings. You put ten horses in a race and fifty thousand people will come to see them run. Put ten people in a race and not one horse will show up.

FOY: To bad about the disappearance of Mr. Jones. He was a profound thinker.

COLLINS: Yes, he was. Always, no matter where he was. Last time I saw him he was swimming, and he suddenly called out, "I'm thinking."

FOY: You fool, Mr. Jones spoke with a lisp.

That Foy and Collins played at the two Chicago theaters for more than four months suggests improvement in their performance skills and increasing audience acceptance. If a theater manager did not believe an act was successful with his audience, a booking would last no more than a week. Theater managers referred acts to one another; so a good showing in one house could improve chances for additional bookings. Managers were keenly attuned to audience comments and reactions regarding specific acts and routines. In addition, reviews in newspapers were influential, particularly if the performers were new. These long runs even helped convince Edwin's mother that her son might have an acting career, especially since he had now begun contributing to the household expenses.

In January 1878, having obtained a job with a minstrel company at the Garden Theater in Chicago, Ben Collins again decided to go on his own. In spite of the abrupt separation, Edwin and Ben remained close friends. But now, nearing twenty-two, Edwin had no choice but to continue his career alone, at least for the time being.

Convincing Hamlin that his new solo act would be entertaining, he was able to remain at the Academy of Music. Edwin soon added to his acrobatic dancing, a form that some people started calling "eccentric." Forgoing Irish costumes and accent, he created an easygoing, almost relaxed song-and-dance delivery, interspersed with one-liner jokes. His timing was excellent, never failing to capture audience attention in anticipation of the punch line or pratfall. Facial exaggerations had become an integral part of his act.

In the little town of Fort Wayne, Indiana, a growing railroad hub, 125 miles east of Chicago, two variety theaters opened almost simultaneously, creating a unique competition for customers. The Atlantic Garden, claiming to be the town's first theater, boasted in the press about "the full tide of their success," concluding by warning professional people that the Atlantic Garden should not be "mistaken for the Arcade concert-saloon." The Arcade Concert Hall (its proper name) responded with their own announcement:

> To the profession — when you write to Ft. Wayne, Ind., for dates, be sure to direct your letters to the Arcade Concert Hall, the only first-class place of amusement in the city. Don't mistake it for a place around the corner on a dark street and known as the Atlantic Garden.[2]

Both venues ran ads in the *New York Clipper* seeking male and female talent. When Edwin saw these announcements, bolstered by a reference from Mr. Hamlin, he quickly contacted the Atlantic Garden and was booked for two weeks. Two other performing teams saw the ads and also obtained engagements to play the Atlantic Garden in March 1878 — Hall & Thompson, a song-and-dance duo, and the Howland Sisters, a versatile dance duo playing in Ohio and seeking bookings to work their way west. As Foy later described it, the confluence of these performers was soon to "turn my fortunes."

Hall & Thompson had been performing together for a number of years, playing Midwestern theaters, and had achieved a good reputation as an accomplished song-and-dance act. Just after opening at the Atlantic Garden on the same bill as Edwin, the team had an irreconcilable argument; and Hall left town. Having seen Edwin's act, Jim Thompson, a handsome young man in his twenties with an excellent tenor voice, suggested they unite. Edwin accepted:

> I accepted his proposition eagerly, and thus began a partnership which was always congenial, which lasted more than six years.[3]

The Howland Sisters — nineteen-year-old Rose and Maud, twenty-one — had been performing together almost four years, accompanied by their mother, a former dancer, who acted as both chaperone and manager. The Atlantic Garden engagement fit their touring plans perfectly.

Rose and Edwin were immediately drawn to one another and spent a good deal of time together. Apparently, Edwin's good looks and friendly manner proved attractive to Rose. Rose's mother, however, was glad when they left Fort Wayne, since she was not pleased by Rose's attention to Edwin. When they separated, Edwin promised to see Rose soon if he could manage it. They would meet again five months later.

The new team of Foy & Thompson or Thompson & Foy (they agreed to alternate billing in successive engagements) had to work quickly to put together a number of different routines. Because each had specific talents, they decided to solo showcase them, with the other partner as support. Although they did perform in blackface, their initial two-act was devoid of any other ethnic identification. Returning to Chicago, they diligently rehearsed before taking the stage again at Hamlin's Academy of Music. Local newspapers reported they performed "to the audience's enjoyment."

While the pair were playing at the Academy of Music, Val Love, a St. Louis and Kansas City theater owner and promoter, came to Chicago looking for acts to sign. Seeing Foy & Thompson perform, he offered them a contract to play in both of his theaters, at forty dollars a week. Each! Euphoric at the opportunity, they caught the next train to St. Louis.

When Foy & Thompson arrived, they soon realized why it had been so easy to obtain the engagement. Most theaters were closing for the summer and most audiences were not interested in attending the theater during the "hot months." Manager Love, however, was determined to stay open and hoped to attract audiences by lowering prices.

The new team used their two weeks in St. Louis to practice and perfect their routines. Sensitive to audience reactions, they dropped items that gained little positive response and built on those the patrons found enjoyable. When they traveled to Kansas City, Love's Theater was the only variety house open, a fact that contributed to a number of SRO evenings.

Love produced a minstrel show for Kansas City audiences. Foy & Thompson, in blackface, acted as end men, danced with the ensemble, and sang in the chorus. In small minstrel companies such as this, it was common for performers to play double or triple roles. The second part of the program was a typical "olio," consisting of a number of variety acts. A short melodrama, called the afterpiece, concluded the program. All performers played in the afterpiece, usually a farce or satire of a current play.

Since Edwin and Jim spent their days practicing and their evenings performing in the long program, the two-week run was exhausting. Their enthusiasm paid off, however, when Manager Love asked if they would be interested in playing an engagement in Dodge City:

"Where's Dodge City?" the boys asked.

"Just a leisurely day's train ride west from Kansas City," he replied, with an all-knowing smile.

Jim Thompson was Edwin's partner for six years, which included their adventurous tours of the Western frontier. Jim had an excellent tenor voice and became Edwin's accomplished straight man in their two-act sketches.

Until the late 1870s, the U.S. was not a beef-eating country. Previously, pork had been its primary meat, exploited during and after the Civil War by the livestock industry's infatuation with Army contracts. But during the '70s, railroad magnates realized that freight tonnage was more profitable than passenger traffic. Exploring ways to capitalize on the benefits of hauling freight, they developed a program to transport beef. If beef could be delivered to Midwestern and Eastern markets in an unspoiled condition, huge profits could be realized. Railroad owners built the first refrigerated cars, which, although primitive, served the purpose.

In turn, the livestock industry saw a great opportunity and quickly increased the size of herds. Cattlemen in Texas viewed the new technology as a chance to make millions of dollars by driving cattle north to railhead

stations. Between them, these economic sectors quickly changed the face of Kansas, because it was through Kansas that the cattle had to move.[4]

Dodge City had been incorporated less than three years prior to Foy & Thompson's arrival. Even before formal elections were held, temporary officials were chosen and ordinances were passed, one of which stipulated that it was unlawful to carry weapons north of the Santa Fe railroad tracks. The tracks ran directly through the center of town. North of the tracks was considered the "better" part of Dodge; south of the tracks one could "do what they want." When elections took place, the first mayor and council members were owners of bars and saloons.

In 1864, the federal government had built a fort at the confluence of the Arkansas River and Mulberry Creek. Named Fort Dodge, for General Granville M. Dodge, the garrison was strategically located at the juncture of the east-west Santa Fe Trail and the north-south trail to Texas.

During 1871, Dodge City's first permanent houses were built, about five miles west of the military reservation, specifically so that liquor could be sold to soldiers. A number of saloons and a trading post opened soon after. Next year, the railroad reached Dodge City, increasing business activity considerably. A townsite was surveyed. By the fall of 1872, townspeople cheered the arrival of the first passenger train. Along with more legitimately enterprising entrepreneurs came a coterie of professional gamblers and prostitutes.

The closest lawmen were stationed ninety miles away. Dodge City quickly became a brawling town, filled with cowboys, soldiers, buffalo hunters, and a variety of unsavory characters. The town's respectable businessmen — largely saloonkeepers and gamblers — joined forces to hire a marshall to protect their interests. For the next few years, a succession of lawmen came and went, none of them able to handle his responsibilities for long.

In 1874, Dodge City was still a buffalo hunter's town, a center receiving hides and bones for shipment east. Buffalo hunters had first come to Dodge to profit from the continuous mass slaughter of the animals roaming the nearby plains. Immense herds had already been decimated, and prices for hides were dropping. But bones remained a viable business; they could be found in massive piles along the railroad tracks, monuments to a fast-dying trade. With the buffalo's decline, Dodge City too seemed destined soon to disappear.

In 1875, however, the first large herd of cattle entered Dodge; and it was not prepared for the invasion. For months, the town was turned into a maze of barbed-wire enclosures. Overnight, Dodge City was converted from a buffalo town to a cattle town. As fast as the cattle entered, so did cowboys, whether seeking work or eager to spend their accumulated earnings. Simultaneously, hotels, saloons, and stores were built; gambling houses and brothels opened for business.

Less than two years after its incorporation, Dodge City boasted a thousand inhabitants. On Front Street, paralleling the tracks and separating the north and south parts of town, were most of the town's businesses. On the north side were the hotels and "respectable" saloons, like the Long Branch (named by the owner after his home town, Long Branch, New Jersey). On the south side were rowdy saloons, brothels, and gambling houses, just beyond the marshall's jurisdiction, unless he was investigating a shooting. The street itself was trodden dirt, dusty when dry, a quagmire of mud after a Kansas thunderstorm. Hitching posts were located in front of each store, with horse troughs conveniently nearby. At intervals along the street, large whiskey barrels filled with water provided the town's only fire protection. In front of the saloons were porches, usually covered with a wooden awning. Locals often sat on the porch to avoid the hot sun or sleep-off a binge. During daylight hours, the street filled with townsfolk going about their chores,

shoulder to shoulder with cowboys, saloon girls, and gambling house habitués. At night, only those seeking amusement roamed Front Street. By 1877, a number of dance and concert halls had opened to provide additional outlets of amusement.

Due to the continuous delivery of cattle herds from Texas, summer months offered the best business opportunities. From 300 to 400 cowboys would arrive in town each week. They would usually bring five months wages with them, about $150 to $200 each. Altogether, cowboys poured forty to fifty thousand dollars a week into local businesses. Often, a cowboy's earnings would be spent before his return home. "No point in leaving with money in my pocket" was the rule.

The summer of 1878 found Dodge City at its height. It had become the center for the cattle trade, with buyers, shippers, cattle owners, and cowboys all clogging the streets. Bat Masterson, a young gunfighter with a good reputation for being calm, levelheaded, and honest, had been made sheriff. When, shortly thereafter, Wyatt Earp came to town, he was appointed deputy marshall. They teamed with a tall, wiry, tubercular dentist, gambler, and shootist, John H. (Doc) Holliday. Together, this fearsome trio maintained order in the rowdy town. Despite the emphasis on curbing unofficial violence, saloons, gambling, and prostitution were encouraged as a normal, highly profitable, part of life in Dodge.

Springer's Concert Hall was one of the combination saloon/brothel/ theaters, located on the south (the rough) side of Front Street, full of the usual merriment and misbehavior. It was a long, narrow, two-story wooden structure, built hurriedly to accommodate the rapidly growing business opportunities. On its main floor, a long bar ran the length of one wall; round tables and chairs were crowded closely together. Girls circulated at the bar, picking up cowboys, escorting them to the tables where drinks could be ordered and other business transacted. Small shacks behind the main building served as furtive havens of privacy. The theater was on the second floor. A raised stage, lit by gas lamps, filled one end of the room. The floor was similarly packed with tables and chairs. To enjoy the entertainment, a cowboy had to find a place for his drink and his hat. In front of the stage, a small space was reserved for a three-piece orchestra — usually a piano, fiddle, and banjo — to accompany the acts. A typical show started at 8:00 P.M. and continued till the early hours of the morning. After midnight, performances often turned risqué. Performers usually played both before and after midnight, altering their routines for the later audience.

Actors enjoyed a certain respect from cowboys, who perceived entertainers to be, like themselves, wanderers, misfits, and outcasts. Those performers who could relate to the needs of the cowboys were best received. In addition to earning a larger than normal salary in Dodge City, a good performance meant a shower of coins on stage at the end of an act. Female performers were equally respected. An unwritten law dictated that they be treated with deference, unless they decided to pursue further commercial ventures.

Humor on the frontier was usually based on joking about or parodying aspects of life perceived as unpleasant by the audience. Its sole purpose was to take the psychic sting out of the loneliness, isolation, hardships, and fragility of life on the frontier. Laughter was essential to maintain a modicum of mental and emotional balance. Audiences often participated in the performance by singing, responding to jokes, commenting on skits and monologues, and emphatically interrupting whenever a performance was not to their liking. If an act was found enjoyable, encores of precisely the same material were repeatedly demanded.

Off-stage, the cowboys' rough and tumble humor took the form of pranks. These usually took place in the streets, with newcomers as the butt of the joke. While such pranks were meant to be funny, they could readily frighten the unwitting victims, sometimes escalating into deadly episodes.

The train that took Foy & Thompson from Kansas City to Dodge City made scheduled stops at Topeka and Wichita, as well as at periodic points along the way to obtain water for the engine. Normally, the trip took little more than eight hours, unless unpredictable events — bad weather, Indians, cattle crossing the tracks — interrupted the schedule. Once beyond Kansas City, the boys saw only endless miles of wasteland, long, flat stretches of rolling hills, dotted occasionally with scrub brush and stunted trees, near parched creek beds, a vista evidently unpopulated by "civilized" humanity. Marauding Indian bands were still a potential danger, and passengers had been forewarned. Nearly every man carried a gun.

Edwin and Jim watched in awe as a torrential Kansas wind- and rainstorm suddenly enveloped them, then almost as quickly passed. When the train stopped at water-filling stations, passengers could leave their cars to walk around. A loud "toot" signaled everyone's return to the coaches, to resume their journey.

About twenty miles outside Dodge City, the Arkansas River, slow-moving but wide and deep enough to flow year round, ran parallel to the tracks. Five miles east of the town lay Fort Dodge, one of the links in the Army's formidable chain of defenses protecting settlers on the Great Plains. As the train approached their destination, Edwin and Jim were astonished to find huge piles of buffalo bones near the tracks. Jim responded with alarm, "My God, Ed, they're killing people out here faster than they can bury 'em."

When the train pulled into the depot, the entire town seemed eager to greet the performers. Waiting at the station were city and county officials, merchants, homesteaders, gamblers, and bargirls; a banner hung over the station welcoming "America's best song and dance team." Promoter Val Love had unabashedly bragged about Foy & Thompson's celebrated exploits, giving townspeople the impression that the team enjoyed a sizable reputation.

Meeting them as they disembarked was Ben Springer, owner of the concert hall where they were to perform that evening. Springer introduced them to the "town fathers," including a striking, full-mustachioed man wearing well-tailored clothes and sporting two large pistols, one on each hip. "This is our sheriff, Mr. Masterson. Bat, we call him. He'll watch over you while you're in Dodge," Springer assured them. They were also introduced to Mayor Kelly; Judge Marshall; the Earp brothers; Luke Short, a gambler; Bob Wright, a leading merchant; and the local press. This group would become the team's most supportive audience.

A report in the *Ford County Globe* indicated the boys made a hit on opening night, applause and showers of coins affirming the audience's appreciation:

> Foy & Thompson are simply immense and well worth going to see. A large crowd was present to witness the opening.[5]

This was the best review they had ever received; it laid the groundwork for a successful run, much better than they had ever hoped. An episode the following day cemented Edwin's rapport with his cowboy audience all the more.

Edwin stood out from the crowd by wearing clothes that bespoke a prosperous performer in cities like Chicago or St. Louis. In Dodge, however, such fancy garb identified a despised "city slicker." On opening night, along with their usual comedy, Edwin inserted a few jokes parodying cowboys. Had the cowboys not greatly enjoyed the show, Edwin and Jim would not long have survived in Dodge. But because they were well received, only a friendly prank was planned, to "haze the dude with the Fifth Avenue swaggering strut." Robert Wright, a town merchant and town historian, recorded:

> This led to their capturing Foy by roping, fixing him up in a picturesque way,

ducking him in a friendly way in a horse trough, riding him around on horseback, and taking other playful familiarities with him, just to show their friendship.[6]

Though thoroughly frightened, Edwin pretended that the cowboys' actions did not faze him. The prank soon ended with laughter and drinks. Foy remembered that, after the episode, "Thompson and I got more applause than ever." Wright wrote that even though Foy continued to satirize the cowboys, "nothing he could say or do offended them; on the contrary, they made a little god of him."

Foy & Thompson sang Irish drinking and workingmen's songs. Their dancing was a mixture of clog and cakewalk routines interspersed with acrobatics, which made a big impression on audiences. When they deliberately made acrobatic errors, stumbling and falling over one another, the audience roared its approval. Their jokes were simple but effective:

FOY:	Go out an play on the railroad tracks.
THOMPSON:	I can't. Think of all the trains that pass.
FOY:	Well, here's a timetable.
FOY:	Is Alice a good girl?
THOMPSON:	She's so perfect, even practice couldn't make her.

A song and dance routine that Foy & Thompson performed became a familiar and often encored part of their act. Called "Kalamazoo in Michigan," it had been written a few years earlier by Ben Collins. Exaggerating his facial expressions and posturing in humorous poses while pronouncing "Kalamazoo," Foy elicited tremendous laughter. His audience demanded repeated encores. Like many odd names, "Kalamazoo" was considered funny whenever it was mentioned, no matter the context.

A month after Foy & Thompson's arrival

Rose Howland became Edwin's wife while they performed in Leadville, Colorado. A versatile dancer and singer, Rose appeared with Foy and Thompson and often played roles in stock company productions.

in Dodge City, the town's first true theater was opened. Called the Theater Comique (pronounced com-ee-cue by cowboys), it quickly became the center of entertainment. The team moved over to the new venue thanks to Ben Springer, who also happened to be part-owner of the theater. The *Ford County Globe* of July 16 reported:

> Never in the history of Dodge City has she been able to show such an array of talent as may be found at the Comique. Monday night for the first time was this favorite place of resort regularly opened, and to the largest audience that ever any one entertainment could boast of in this city. Foy & Thompson, who are filling a summer's engagement, of whom it is well said, they stand among the first artists on the American stage. In their acrobatic clogs and celebrated jigs, they are simply immense. The Comique promises fresh stars and new attractions, and in doing

so, cannot fail to retain its place in the affections of pleasure seekers.

A note printed just below this review reminded the reader of Dodge City's more mundane distractions:

> Street fights for the past week were too numerous to mention.

The Theater Comique was, indeed, a great improvement over Springer's Concert Hall. Performers enjoyed dressing rooms and running water. The latest backstage equipment and curtains were employed. Seats in the auditorium were affixed to the floor. Still, audiences were comprised primarily of men, cigar smoke hung heavy in the air, drinking was permitted, in fact encouraged, and audience behavior continued to be unruly.

Even at long distance, Val Love controlled bookings in Dodge City, first signing performers to play his Kansas City theater, then persuading them to jump to Dodge. Some, like Foy & Thompson, agreed because of the higher salaries, though they had little notion of the working conditions. One such act Love signed to play at the Comique was the Howland Sisters. When she agreed to go there, Rose was unaware that Edwin was already in Dodge City. He heard she was coming, and, to her surprise (and mother Howland's chagrin), Edwin met Rose at the depot. Her arrival in Dodge marked the beginning of an extended courtship.

Until the arrival of Rose Howland, Edwin had been enjoying the company of the concert hall's working women. Many women in Dodge were familiar with this handsome young man of enviable talent, and he was considered a desirable object of affection. It appears he freely returned their admiration and attentions. Indeed, one such episode nearly caused him to be shot.

A fellow actor named Chapin believed that Edwin was attempting to steal his girl. While Edwin was resting in his room — he and Thompson lived in a side-street shack near the theater—Chapin shot at him through a window. Thoroughly unfamiliar with sidearms, he missed; but Edwin was shaken by the incident. Chapin wasn't arrested because, it was claimed, he couldn't handle a gun well enough to do serious harm. The local newspaper often reported that gunshots and flying bullets had interrupted performers on the Theater Comique stage.

Many years later, when Foy was playing in Fort Worth, he was met backstage by four elegantly dressed dowagers, who were anxious to meet their "favorite entertainer." One of the women asked coyly, "Don't you recognize me?" Foy admitted he did not. "Oh, shame on you," she chided. "We had some great times together back in Dodge."

Rose now occupied much of Edwin's time. Mother Howland was increasingly concerned about the relationship, not only because she doubted Edwin's sincerity, but also because it could jeopardize her daughter's career. Nevertheless, Rose and Edwin were seen as "a pair" during their Dodge City sojourn.

Foy & Thompson seemed to improve their local standing every week. When they originated a blackface routine, copying elements of the minstrel format, it was a revelation to most of the audience, since they had never seen such an act. When they were feted by the townsfolk, the press reported:

> Foy & Thompson were happy on Friday night when they gazed on the crowded house which had turned out to give them, "the pets of Dodge City," a benefit.[7]

Each week, local papers noted and appreciated their performances. "Foy and Thompson outdid anything we have seen in the Ethiopian line." A few weeks later, the *Globe* talked about "that unequaled and splendidly matched team of Foy & Thompson."

During this period of successful and profitable shows, the team became friendly with the town's two lawmen, Masterson and Earp. In a town like Dodge, it was advantageous to have the law on your side; the lawmen's continuing presence at the theater often proved a calming influence.

In the middle of September, an entourage headed by President Rutherford B. Hayes and General William T. Sherman stopped in Dodge City for a day while visiting the West. All the town's leading citizens came to the station to greet them, including Foy & Thompson. In his book on Bat Masterson, Robert DeArment related that:

> The president emerged from his private railroad car long enough to hear a speech of welcome by Mayor Kelly and to wrinkle his nose at the aroma that wafted from the cattle pens. Then he retired, leaving Uncle Billy Sherman to commune with the citizenry.[8]

As Foy opined in his autobiography, "I don't think he very strongly approved of Dodge."

With their run in Dodge City nearing an end, the boys discussed their next possible engagements. Val Love had suggested a visit to Leadville, Colorado, another boom town, this one "full of silver."

Edwin was intrigued by the adventure. Jim felt they should return to the Midwest, to take immediate advantage of their recent success.

Were there even any theaters in Leadville? Love assured them there were two, in every way equal to the Comique.

How did one get to Leadville? Train to Canon City, Love replied; then stagecoach for a mere 100 miles.

Could Love secure bookings for the Howland Sisters, too? Of course. He was pleased to oblige.

On September 17, 1878, the *Ford County Globe* announced that:

> Foy & Thompson have gone to Leadville to fulfill an engagement at the Comique Theater in that city. They are good artists and will be appreciated wherever they go.

Accompanying them on the train were the Howland Sisters and their mother, all of them eager "to see and taste the excitement of a bonanza mining camp." Dodge City's civic and business leaders saw them all to the train. Foy and Thompson had in hand an invitation to return next summer.

Chapter 3

THOMPSON: *You have a pug nose. Do pug noses run in your family?*

FOY: *Only in cold weather.*

In the summer of 1878, Leadville, Colorado, burst into existence, the latest focus of the West's fast-buck mining fever. Within a period of ten months, the town had grown from a few log cabins to a bustling, roaring, crowded metropolis of 4,000 inhabitants.[1]

The site had previously been settled by a few prospectors looking for gold and not having much luck. Then it was discovered that the black sand and rock they had been throwing away as useless contained silver and lead. By the fall of 1877, there were over 300 people seeking their fortunes; and the rush was on. Since lead was still the metal of primary interest, a meeting of citizens selected the name "Leadville." The town's first post office was soon opened.

When Edwin, Jim, and the Howland Sisters arrived in Leadville, the town had

already grown to more than 6,000 people. Half of its inhabitants dug for buried treasure; the other half labored to construct stores and houses as rapidly as they could obtain lumber and nails from Denver. Observers were awestruck to find frenzied enterprise on this once all-but-deserted plateau, stark and demanding at an elevation well over 10,000 feet, scraped to barren rock by the vicissitudes of long and severe winters.

Newcomers would be quick to notice that the town had just built its first foundry, grain store, hardware store, and hotel, had recently welcomed its first doctor, lawyer, and churchman. Leadville's first public speech had lately been given by Susan B. Anthony. A new storekeeper in town, H.A.W. Tabor, grubstaked two prospectors in May 1878; two months later, they struck

Main Street, Leadville, Colorado, at the time Foy and Thompson were headliners at the Theater Comique, its sign partially visible on the left side of the street. (Denver Public Library — Western History Department)

a rich silver vein. Called the Little Pittsburgh, it was soon yielding eight thousand dollars a week. In a year, Tabor would become a millionaire. News of the strike precipitated a wild scramble to Leadville. An average of 100 newcomers daily entered the now-thriving town.

At first, people built shacks wherever they wished; however, by the fall of 1878, streets were being laid out and building plans drawn up. Not surprisingly, people had difficulty finding a place to sleep. Those who could afford a blanket and some space to lay it paid a dollar a night for the privilege. Building lots that six months earlier had sold for twenty-five dollars now cost buyers more than a thousand.

Freight arrived via railroad, to a site about twenty miles from Leadville. The cargo was then carried by six- and eight-team wagons over very rugged countryside. These wagons carried building materials primarily; but as many as were being used, they were unable to keep up with demand.

Chestnut Street served as Leadville's main thoroughfare, paralleling a ravine between two hills. All of the town's structures — stores, houses, and shanties — were built along this street, which stretched for about a mile. So many eager people filled Chestnut Street each day that many of them were forced to desert the sidewalks for the middle of the street, causing a hopeless tangle of wagons, horses, and pedestrians struggling to advance in all directions.

Among the commercial enterprises being erected were dance halls, gambling rooms, and theaters. Dance halls were nothing more than saloon extensions, seating space giving way to dancing when desired. Some saloons had their own gambling rooms; but most gambling establishments were self-contained operations, sharing their space with the ever-present brothels.

In early 1878, the first playhouse to open in Leadville was the Theater Comique, owned and operated by Captain Frank Stanselle. He had purchased a bowling alley and converted it into his version of a theater. The Comique did good business at first; but

Stanselle, having little knowledge about booking acts, could not attract enough performers to remain in business. In June, the Coliseum Novelty Theater opened, featuring a variety company brought in from Denver. The enterprising owners of the Coliseum had set aside $8,000 to pay for importing talent.

A few days later, a new Theater Comique was opened by Tom Kemp, a mine owner and entertainment promoter. The outside of Kemp's theater resembled any other storefront along Chestnut Street; but the inside revealed a well-equipped, modern playhouse. The building was a hundred feet deep and sixty-six feet wide; at the time, it was the largest building in Leadville. It offered center seating for 500 and, on either side, in elegantly fitted boxes, accommodations for 400 more. At the front of the building was a parlor, along with rooms for employees. To the left, a door opened onto an attached saloon and card-room. In the basement, at the back of the building, under the stage, were the dressing rooms. The stage itself was outfitted with all the latest equipment. A large, red, velvet curtain, with the letters T. C. emblazoned in gold, hung from the gilded proscenium. Rarely were customers charged admission, but they were expected to patronize the saloon and card rooms. Intervals between acts were long enough to satisfy patrons' gambling urges. Shows started at the Comique about nine in the evening and ran until four in the morning.

A third theater soon opened, the Athenaeum. Specializing in more risqué shows, the Athenaeum quickly drew customers away from its more respectable competitors.

A typical program at the Theater Comique began with the introduction of performers, each of whom gave a brief example of his or her act. Next, the olio portion of the program featured a trapeze performer, a female singing duo accompanying themselves on a guitar, a young man who sang and played the violin, a clog dancer, and a comedy skit, ending with a sparring exhibition,

usually employing local amateurs eager to earn a few dollars. The second part of the program was typically a minstrel show, with the entire company taking part. Occasionally, a touring company would appear, offering such melodramas as "The Black Crook" or "Uncle Tom's Cabin." Other performers then playing at the theater would also take roles in the melodrama. Some performers stayed in Leadville for extended runs, in part because of the excellent wages, in part because during the winter months, there was no available transportation out of town.

Foy and Thompson's trip from Dodge City to Leadville lasted two long days. The first and fastest leg of the journey was by train, from Dodge City to Canon City, Colorado, the end of the railroad line west. From that point on, the approach to Leadville had to be made by stagecoach. While the distance was only 120 miles, the terrain was rugged and almost entirely uphill, the trip normally taking more than eight hours. The initial part of the trail followed the banks of the Arkansas River on gradually sloping yet relatively flat ground. The last thirty-five miles were all steeply uphill. Ascending three thousand feet in a series of startling and treacherous switchbacks, the winding trail scarcely managed to etch itself into the mountain sides. Perennial snow covered the surrounding peaks, and even lower elevations were already blanketed by the first snows of the season. On "flat" levels, stagecoach horses were changed every twelve to fifteen miles; on steep uphill climbs, horses had to be changed every six miles. Passengers were usually offered food and drink at each of these stages.

Edwin, Jim, and the Howland Sisters reached Leadville in the middle of September. It was already cold, with snow on the ground. Upon arriving in town, their first act was to buy winter clothes. They then sought out a place to stay, no easy task, considering the town's lack of accommodations. Luckily, they were able to bunk backstage at the Comique until they could find more permanent quarters.

Within hours, they were introduced to Leadville's tumult, turmoil, and enterprise. The town was in the midst of a typhoid fever epidemic, probably caused by its all but total lack of sanitation. Most miners and transients lived in tents and shacks. Chestnut Street melted to mud during the day but froze hard enough by evening to support wagons.

The town evidenced two remarkable characteristics. Not only did it flaunt a high degree of lawlessness, a constant, pervasive turbulence, exemplified by whiskey-engendered fights, holdups, wagon thefts, and house burglaries; it also sported a thriving red-light district, the most notable establishment being Winny Purdy's, financed by a Leadville bank. The police force was both too small to deal with the situation and too dishonest to care. Not until the following year did town merchants form their own private force, on duty from sunset to sunrise.

Edwin, Jim, and the Howland Sisters first performed at the Theater Comique in minstrel shows. Edwin and another actor, Dick Robinson, played the end men; Jim, the interlocutor. The sisters did some dances. Reports had it that their performances "were exceptionally well done." Of necessity, it didn't take them long to learn about the town where they were committed to play the entire winter.

Yet, performing through the winter proved more rewarding than they initially expected. The combination of continued silver discoveries and increasing numbers of miners fueled Leadville's growth. Commerce thrived at fever pitch, and performers reaped the benefits. Edwin and Jim were each earning twenty-five dollars a week, plus a probably equal amount in coinage thrown on stage after each performance. Everyone lived in an extravagant fashion. As Foy admitted, "The deuce of it was that I caught the fever and lived extravagantly too."

Rose and Edwin were clearly in love. Instead of attempting to keep the two apart, Mother Howland now encouraged a marriage, realizing their relationship gave all

appearance of being permanent. The wedding was planned for the following April, shortly before their run in Leadville would end, with Foy and Thompson planning to return to Dodge City for a summer engagement. Maud Howland and her mother were booked for a theater in Denver.

In early 1879, a theater reporter's monthly dispatch to the *New York Dramatic News,* aptly summarized Leadville's increasing vitality.

> Leadville is now a full-fledged city of the second class, thanks to the rapidity of the increasing population. From 100 to 150 arrive daily; every stage, freight wagon and express being crowded, and thirty or forty come in on foot, whose sole possessions embrace a blanket and brilliant hopes.[2]

Meanwhile, entrepreneur Thomas Kemp became so preoccupied with overseeing his lucrative mines that he had to give up personal supervision of the Theater Comique. He leased the theater to William Nuttall, a former variety hall owner from Deadwood, who was given the right to expand the Comique if he wished. Nuttall immediately enlarged the stage and added lodging facilities, no doubt to take advantage of premium prices for housing. He also added rooms at the rear of the stage to house performers; Edwin, Jim, and the Howlands were beneficiaries of these renovations. Nuttall invested a great deal of his own money in the theater and, in addition, paid Kemp $1,750 a month for rent. Unfortunately, his investment was wiped out by a local bank failure, the result of mismanagement.

The Coliseum barely remained in business, thanks to some performers who, having finished their engagement at the Comique, moved over to play some additional time. The Athenaeum had already closed, soon to be replaced by the Opera House, a grand name for a beer hall, specializing in melodrama. When Nuttall could no longer pay his rent, Kemp took over active operation again, renaming his theater the Grand Central.

During their first extended engagement in Leadville, Foy and Thompson mostly performed their two-act, comprised of acrobatic dancing, singing, and comedy. Occasionally, they did skits, making fun of "refined society." When a touring company came to town, the boys played leading roles in shows like "Around the World in Eighty Days" or "Mazeppa," the plots and dialogue simplified enough for actors to learn quickly and audiences to understand. Edwin was fast becoming a versatile performer. His repertoire extended from playing Rudolphe in "The Black Crook" to a blackface minstrel end man. His increasing ability to capture an audience by his easy-going, unobtrusive, egalitarian demeanor, both on and off the stage, was proving an important ingredient for success.

On April 17, 1879, Edwin Fitzgerald and Rose Howland were married. Pastor Thomas A. Uzzell of the Methodist Evangelical Church — there was as yet no Catholic church in Leadville — conducted the ceremony, Mrs. Uzzell and Jim Thompson serving as witnesses. The *New York Dramatic News*, duly publicizing a note sent from their Western correspondent, reported somewhat romantically:

> Rose Howland was married last week to Edward Fitzgerald (Foy). Their love sprang from playing respectively Amina and Rudolphe in The Black Crook.[3]

Marriage necessitated new living quarters. The newlyweds moved into a hotel until their planned departure for the return engagement in Dodge City. A traveling company playing "Around the World in Eighty Days" occupied their time and generated sufficient income to pay for their upcoming travel expenses.

Edwin, Rose, and Jim left Leadville the same way they had departed Dodge City the previous fall, with congratulations from local leaders and cheers from the townspeople.

The *Leadville Chronicle*, the town's fledgling newspaper, declared:

> …they were great favorites and met with prosperity.[4]

As with their successful run in Dodge City, the three were asked to return to Leadville the following fall. They readily accepted the engagement, knowing it promised good wages and a long engagement throughout the winter.

High-altitude trails were still thawing in May, making them hazardous. During their stagecoach ride to Canon City, as the vehicle was rounding a curve, its right wheels struck soft ground that gave way and caused the stage to topple. The reins broke, and the stage tumbled down a slope, to be stopped finally by a tree stump. Everyone in the coach seemed to have escaped injury, except Edwin, who knew he had been hurt but remained unaware to what extent. The passengers had to wait for an emergency stage to finish their journey to Canon City. When Edwin was at last examined by a doctor, he was found to have sustained a fractured collarbone and arm.

Edwin was forced to remain in bed for two weeks. Since the trio needed money, Jim and Rose played in the town's variety theater. Within three weeks of his injury, Edwin was back on stage, singing and dancing, but without assaying acrobatics. They performed in Canon City a few more weeks, argued with the manager about obtaining their wages, and, finally paid, left on the train for Dodge City as quickly as they could. A month prior to their return, the *Ford County Globe* had proudly announced that "the illustrious team of Foy and Thompson" were coming back to play the Theater Comique.

Upon their arrival, the Foys and Jim Thompson found Dodge City had matured. Cowboys still delivered thousands of cattle and continued to dominate saloons, gambling houses, and theaters; but the town's rowdiness had noticeably subsided. Population had increased, primary contributors to the boom being merchants and skilled people, from doctors and clergymen to barbers and blacksmiths, all settling down and starting businesses. Dodge City now had a number of permanent buildings — a post office, city hall, and auditorium. Some fine hotels and restaurants graced Front Street, adjacent to the saloons. A number of churches had already been built, and church socials were a weekly event. Temperance groups had descended on Dodge City and begun waging continuos battle against the town's "drinking ruffians," a conflict that often included street fights. (A year later, Kansas passed a "dry" law, which strongly contributed to Dodge City's rapid decline.)

The Social Union Club had already staged a Fireman's Ball to raise funds for better firefighting equipment. A masquerade ball had just been given, and plans for the town's first Fourth of July celebration were being formulated. Bat Masterson and his deputies had quieted Dodge considerably. In fact, Masterson and his men were at that moment scouring the countryside for a band of robbers, confident that their absence would not cause an intolerable outbreak of crime. There were now three theaters in Dodge City; yet the Comique remained the most elegant.

Springer was still owner and manager of the Comique. The theater was now attracting a better clientele; its performances were shorter, and its acts cleaner. Women and children attended matinees. To open the Comique's summer season, Springer built a show around Foy and Thompson's return to Dodge. The local newspaper trumpeted their presence:

> Foy and Thompson, who made such a decided hit in Dodge last summer, have arrived, having been engaged for another term by Mr. Springer, of the Comique, which has its grand opening on Saturday evening. Foy and Thompson will attract a large house.[5]

For their summer performance, the team played their familiar Irish two-act routines to continued success. Their jokes had become more subtle and sophisticated, to meet the needs of a more worldly audience.

THOMPSON: How old are you?
FOY: I'm sixteen.
THOMPSON: How do you know?
FOY: My mother told me.
THOMPSON: What did she say?
FOY: Well, the last time I was home, I jumped on my mother's knee and said, "Daddy, how old am I?"
THOMPSON: You jumped on your mother's knee and said, "Daddy how old am I?"
FOY: Yeah.
THOMPSON: You call your mother "Daddy"?
FOY: Sure.
THOMPSON: Well, what do you call your father?
FOY: Oh, we don't call him; he's got an alarm clock.

Edwin also added a number of solo routines to his act. He now included satires and impersonations of local characters, some in pantomime, in bizarre costumes and makeup, apparently the first time he performed in this manner. Rose sang and danced, sometimes alone, sometimes with another actress. All three played together in closing skits, usually with topical plots.

The *Ford County Globe* again registered their summer successes.

> Foy and Thompson are general favorites.
> Foy and Thompson, old standbys, are as popular as ever.
> Foy and Thompson are well liked, and nightly draw fine houses.

By the end of the summer, the boys were perceived to be stage veterans, performing their routines so flawlessly and spontaneously that the diligently rehearsed act appeared to be improvised, which delighted audiences.

Not only did Edwin win approval while on stage, he also won the town's affection for some off-stage activities.

When some local Indians saw Edwin practice juggling with Indian clubs — they laughed at the label — they asked him to perform at their camp. He gladly did so, a gesture that only increased his popularity with them. When the town requested its citizens to clear away rubbish around their houses to prevent sickness during the "hot and sultry days of summer," Edwin made announcements from the stage in support of this activity.

At the end of September, after a rousing celebration, which elicited both cheers and tears from Dodge City's townfolk, Edwin, Rose, and Jim boarded the train for their return to Leadville. Unlike increasingly civilized Dodge, Leadville was reported to be even more riotous than it had been the previous summer.

A reporter for the *New York Dramatic News*, touring theaters in the West, submitted his analysis of Leadville's milieu during the summer of 1879. It was an astute observation of the town and its ebullience:

> The rapid growth of this city argues a possibility of truth existing in the Arabian Nights. One passes a vacant lot in the morning, the ground is covered with stumps and bushes; pass that way at night — Presto, change! — behold a frame house in process of completion, and household goods ready to move in. Lumber is getting cheaper and log cabins are giving way to frame houses. The three principal streets, Chestnut, State and Harrison Avenue, are nearly all frames, but balance of city is still in its primitive rusticity. Old miners and frontiersmen pronounce this the biggest "hurrah" camp that ever existed. On Chestnut Street, between the hours of 2 and 9 P.M., it is almost impossible to make one's way through the dense crowd, and on Saturday evenings, when the miners come down from the hills, it is in some portions impossible.[6]

Leadville's newcomers were also changing. Along with the usual slang and frontier pronunciations, arrivals from a more refined society added to the polyglot, making it difficult for people readily to understand one another. Since dress did not make the man in Leadville, "boiled shirts" were replaced by blue flannels, high boots, and large hats, essential preparation for a person to plunge into the toil and tumult of the community.

Not surprisingly, some were unable to deal with the turmoil, became dispirited, and returned to Denver, the closest "civilized" city. But their places were quickly filled by the daily influx of newcomers.

Performers, particularly, found the climate unhealthy. At more than 10,000 feet, the thin air made even ordinary exertion exhausting. It harshly affected the nasal membranes, causing colds, sore throats, bronchitis, and pneumonia. The local newspaper reported that only half the town spoke with its natural voice. A certain sameness of vocal tone prevailed, a hoarseness commonly called a "gin voice"; the longer a person stayed in Leadville, the more permanent it became. Years later, it was suggested that Edwin's characteristically coarse voice might have been caused by his early Leadville experience. To sing and dance successfully under these conditions was a challenge to even the bravest and most skillful of performers.

There were now two variety theaters and one small concert hall in Leadville, the latter euphemistically called an Opera House by its owner. The Theater Comique, again run by William Nuttall, remained the best and most ornate house in town. But getting performers to visit Leadville was still proving difficult. So difficult, in fact, that Nuttall had performers play at his theater, then rushed them to the Opera House to play again the same evening. Interestingly, the Comique had full houses; yet the Opera House was lucky to net fifty dollars a night.

Show business during the fall of 1879 was erratic, making it difficult for theater managers to pay performers' salaries. Even Nuttall was having problems, and a rumor suggested that Thomas Kemp was going to assume operation of the theater yet again. Some enterprising entrepreneurs opened a large tent show, but it lasted only two weeks. The Coliseum closed, then reopened as the Athenaeum. The number of dance halls was declining; gambling saloons were closing, in both cases because weekday pedestrian traffic had dwindled. Miners were now working even farther out of town, and felons dominated the streets by night.

Edwin, Jim, and Rose began their run at the Comique in support of Howard & Sullivan's touring company playing the "Naiad Queen." In the company were Harry Montague, an accomplished actor trying hard to become a theater manager, and the Duncan Sisters, one of whom was married to Montague. On the same bill was a former cowboy and Army scout trying for a theatrical career, W.F. "Buffalo Bill" Cody, featured in a melodrama. During this particular engagement, the entire company gave a benefit for lady members of the stranded St. Louis-based "H.M.S. Pinafore" Company, for the purpose of helping them get home.

Another actor who played in Leadville during the winter of 1879 was Charles Vivian, said to be the founder of the Elks fraternal organization. Vivian, an Englishman, was a singing actor who came to America to pursue his career. While in New York, he formed an actors' club, called the Jolly Cocks, whose purpose was to assist destitute performers. Shortly after, they changed their name to the Elks. Branches were established in other cities, and a great fraternal order was founded. When Vivian's company was stranded in Denver, Leadville's seeming prosperity attracted them to the town. Edwin befriended Vivian and his wife, assisting them in finding a place to stay.

Initially, Vivian attempted to present Dicken's "Oliver Twist" to miners; but they didn't understand it. He then went into the local variety theaters, singing Irish songs, and did well. In fact, he quickly became a local favorite. Unfortunately, Vivian contracted pneumonia and died in the spring of 1880,

with Edwin serving as one of the pallbearers.

After Vivian died, he was provided an elaborate funeral by the townspeople. Foy and Thompson, along with other performers, gave a benefit for his wife, so she could return East. Vivian's body remained in a Leadville cemetery for a number of years, his grave marked only by a wood plank on which his name had been scrawled. Later, the Elks disinterred their founder and brought his remains to Boston, where he was reburied under an elegantly engraved monument.

Leadville continued a lawless town. Holdups were routine; thefts and burglaries common. Prudent people did not walk the streets at night, unless escorted by the merchants' private force. When a local judge delayed the trial of a claim jumper and another of a murderer, some town vigilantes broke into the jail and hanged the two accused on Chestnut Street. Edwin was on stage at the Theater Comique when a man burst into the theater to tell of the vigilante actions. Everyone, including the performers, ran into the street to view the hangings. Foy mentioned the episode in his autobiography:

> There was no ceremony, no last words, no delay. Nooses had been made in pieces of heavy, new rope, and ends were thrown over a low beam, men seized them and hauled away, and the doomed victims were drawn, struggling and kicking, off the floor.[7]

After thus dispatching the desperadoes, audiences returned to the theater to enjoy the remainder of the show.

During the winter, theaters were changing ownership and names almost continuously. The Comique, Leadville's leading theater, declined because of Nuttall's financial liabilities. The Athenaeum was sold, refurbished by its new owners, and became the most handsome theater in town, drawing all the traffic. Under new management, the Coliseum offered good variety; but its richly decorated wine rooms were the primary attraction. Just down the street, Colorado's biggest and richest mine owner, W.A. Tabor, was building what was soon to become the most magnificent opera house in the West.

These constant theater changes forced Edwin, Rose, and Jim to move to any theater willing to pay them. While they had little trouble acquiring engagements, the prevalent unpredictability made them uneasy about the benefits of an extended stay in Leadville. During this period, their Irish two-act was their basic routine, always able to generate good audience response. Rose played solo, singing and dancing.

As the snow melted in the spring of 1880, Leadville began to assume the shape of a recognizable town. Chestnut Street was now almost a mile long, lined with stores, saloons, hotels, and theaters, some of them two and three stories in height. The railroad now reached only twenty miles away, and six-horse stages arrived daily with passengers. Telephones connected businesses in town with the mines. A race course was being built.

But turmoil in theater management and operation continued. The Opera House was now being used as the district court. Foy and Thompson were playing at the Athenaeum, the most popular house in town. The magnificent Tabor Opera House was yet to open.

With the reopening of the Grand Central, Foy and Thompson renewed their relationship with Kemp and played at his theater until they left Leadville. By the time they were ready to depart, Leadville was patronizing five theaters, with Tabor Opera House productions demonstrating that the town would support legitimate theater if presented in elegant surroundings. Touring companies and individual actors were being booked into Leadville, happy to add the town to their list of viable venues. Five daily newspapers promoted each theater's productions, and low admission prices made full houses routine.

When Harry Montague and the Duncan Sisters left Leadville, they traveled to Denver, just as the new Palace variety theater was about to open. Montague persuaded its owner he'd make an excellent manager and was hired to take over operation of the house. His first ad in the *New York Clipper* boasted:

> Backed by Money, Brains, Life and Energy
> Always offering the most powerful attractions; unquestionably the greatest resort in Denver for pleasurable pastime.
> Everything presented is Fresh, Animated, Sparkling and Mirthful.
> First Class Artists Needed.[8]

Montague bragged that, between Denver, Cheyenne, and Leadville, performers playing the Palace could fill six months with profitable bookings. One of his first attempts at signing acts was a telegram to Edwin and Jim to play the Palace for an indefinite period of time. As they were anxious to leave Leadville, the team readily agreed to Montague's offer, twenty-five dollars a week each, not as much as they were earning in Leadville but at a venue considerably more comfortable and secure.

When Colorado had become a state in 1876, Denver had been selected the state capital.[9] A sleepy town until the railroad arrived in 1870, Denver had quickly prospered. The silver mining boom of the late 1870s contributed sizable prosperity to the growing city, now numbering more than 30,000 citizens. Enterprising city fathers wanted Denver to possess the most modern conveniences; and they soon brought electric lighting, telephones, and elevators to its inhabitants. Denver boasted a number of theaters, featuring variety prominently, but also presenting Shakespeare and Gilbert & Sullivan operettas. Theatergoing was a popular pastime for both men and women.

The Palace Theater was located on the second floor of a brick building, twenty-five feet wide and a hundred feet deep. On the first floor was a bar and gambling room. Upstairs, the stage was wide and well-equipped with audience seats fixed to the floor. Though individual dressing rooms were available, performers still had to use a common water trough to wash.

Ten curtained boxes, five on each side, flanked the stage. In these boxes, furnished with tables and chairs, drinks were served to patrons. The main program usually started about midnight and lasted till dawn. Before the show began, a "lunch" was served, usually a meal of roast beef, pork, chicken, sandwiches, and salads. Although large program cards were prominently displayed on either side of the proscenium, Montague usually came on stage and, like a circus barker, introduced each act with elegant flourishes and soaring elocutions.

At the Palace, Foy and Thompson performed their familiar routines on a variety bill. The only indication that they were developing new skits was a single mention in the *Denver Daily News*:

> The entertainment closes with a very spicy and pleasing afterpiece in which Mr. Edwin Foy personates a supposed French darkey in tip-top style.[10]

If a touring company performing a melodrama was booked, the team would participate, taking on various roles. Montague wanted to build a resident stock company that could accommodate any and all potential programs, and the talents of Foy and Thompson lent themselves well to his plans. For an occasional change, the team would play Cheyenne for a week. Montague was true to his promise. Under his aegis, Edwin, Jim, and Rose were continually booked for almost a year, the entire time they made their base in Denver.

While in Denver, Jim Thompson married an actress, Millie Thomas; and the quartet often played together in skits. The Foys and Thompsons found living in Denver quite comfortable. For Edwin and Rose, it was their most relaxing and enjoyable situation since having met in Fort Wayne.

Montague was doing a good job promoting and filling the Palace; but when he discovered that the Bella Union Theater in San Francisco was seeking a new manager, he applied for the job, citing his Denver successes. Since competition among San Francisco's variety theaters was fierce, and Montague had a good reputation, he was hired to take over at the beginning of 1881. His company threw him a benefit, thanks for their pleasant run at the Palace. Before leaving, Montague turned to Edwin and Jim and said, "I won't forget you boys. You did me fine." Within a month of his taking over management of the Bella Union, the *New York Clipper* reported "SRO audiences."

In the summer of 1881, Edwin and Jim received a letter from Montague. The manager inquired whether they would be interested in coming to San Francisco, not to play at his theater, but at the Adelphi, where a friend of his needed a number of versatile performers to be part of a stock company. Seeing this as an opportunity to play better houses at higher salaries, the team agreed to a "Frisco" engagement. Rose and Millie were promised roles, as well.

In his autobiography, Foy related that they first traveled to Tombstone, Arizona, then a fledgling, wide-open, silver mining town, to play four weeks at the Bird Cage Varieties, before moving on to San Francisco. There is, however, no evidence available in any of the Tombstone newspapers — and there were five in operation at the time — that Foy and Thompson ever played the town. Foy's claim that he played at the Bird Cage is additionally suspect, because the theater did not open until December, 1881, when Foy and Thompson were already playing in San Francisco. Photos claiming to be of Foy, on display at various locations in Tombstone, are misidentified. (The actual identity of the actor appearing in the photos is unknown.) Had Foy visited Tombstone during the summer of 1882, when the team was again on the road, he would have found most of the town destroyed by fire.

The trip from Denver to San Francisco

took more than two days. The train went as far as Oakland, where passengers caught a ferry to one of the busiest ports in the nation, "Frisco" being the country's principal harbor on the West Coast. The city's social order had matured considerably during the previous decade. Lawless vagabonds had been replaced by businessmen in the city, cattlemen, farmers, and vintners in the surrounding valleys.[11]

The city's theater district was in transition, as well. Depression in the 1870s closed many houses, particularly those of questionable reputation. San Francisco's major theaters included the Baldwin, the California, the Standard (called Emerson's Standard when it housed Billy Emerson's Minstrels), the Bush Street Theater, the Adelphi, and Tivoli Gardens, the latter two primarily variety houses. It had become common practice to import plays and companies, brought out in special trains, directly from New York. Often, traveling companies used local talent for support. When performers had a week off from their own shows, they would assist in another. Performing at San Francisco theaters was customarily quite fluid, allowing an actor the opportunity for continuous engagements, without fear of breaking contracts or offending theater managers.

The Adelphi played both variety and traveling company melodramas. Foy and Thompson's first appearance at the Adelphi was in a five-act drama, "Under the Gaslight." Rose and Millie also had small roles in the play. It was followed by "Seven Beauties, or It's Naughty But It's Nice," featuring all four in prominent roles. In early November, for the first time, Foy and Thompson were given starring roles in a variety show. The *Chronicle* ads announced:

> First appearance of Foy and Thompson, greatest of all song-and-dance artists; also Rose Howland, Millie Thomas, etc.[12]

The show ran for three weeks to "full houses." Edwin and Jim added a blackface

Edwin was a 25-year-old stage veteran when he and Thompson played in San Francisco. Edwin's versatile acting allowed him to play variety, melodrama, and minstrel roles. His brief engagement with Emerson's Minstrels launched his career as a comedian.

routine; and Edwin did a solo eccentric dance, satirizing a pigeon-toed ballet dancer.

A drama, "Rich, or the Ocean Waif," followed for a week, the four playing various roles. At the end of the month, the Adelphi was dark; so Foy and Thompson played at the Fountain Theater, as part of a combination of "specialty artists." The Adelphi finished the year with a melodrama, "Halloween," which featured Rose and Millie. In a departure from the regular program, Foy and Thompson did a skit between acts.

Although Foy later wrote about playing with the famous actor, Dion Boucicault, while in San Francisco, there are no newspaper or theater records to support his statement.

Edwin's and Jim's performances were gaining the attention of theater managers and local critics, who saw in them an innovative, professional team who pleased audiences and could play many roles. At New Year's, the Adelphi management and company presented Foy and Thompson with a set of silver goblets, the first time they had been so honored. In particular, Edwin's stage antics were frequently reported by the *Chronicle*:

> Eddie Foy's characterization of Corrigan, the pettifogger, was well drawn.[13]

Corrigan, a local lawyer, had been jailed for embezzlement. This was the first time that any press report referred to Edwin Foy as "Eddie."

Around the corner, appearing at the Standard Theater, Billy Emerson's Minstrels were playing to SRO houses. A decade earlier, when Edwin had been living in Chicago, he had become entranced by Emerson's minstrel performances and dreamed he might someday play alongside the blackface master. When Emerson asked Edwin and Jim to join his show, the boys were dazed, but only as long as it took them to accept the engagement, at forty dollars a week each.

Minstrelsy was not new to San Francisco audiences, although Billy Emerson would turn it into his own personal art form in the 1880s. Back in 1850, Tom Maguire had built the Jenny Lind Theater, primarily featuring touring minstrel companies of the day. It was Maguire who first persuaded Emerson to come to San Francisco, made him a partner, and called the company Emerson's California Minstrels. During the '70s and '80s, Emerson toured the country with great success but always returned to the city that originally honored him. His reputation as an end man, dancer, and singer — "who will ever forget his beautiful, natural, rich, pathetic,

tenor voice" — earned him the honorific "the best minstrel that ever lived." Rarely discussed but universally acknowledged was his ability to organize and profitably operate a company made up of specialty artists.

At the time Foy and Thompson joined Emerson, the company included some of the stellar minstrel performers of the day, Charlie Reed, Burt Haverly, Pete Mack, and Gus Bruno. A versatile group of actors, they could take the roll of end men, sing, dance, and play musical instruments. Reed wrote sketches and played the lead in many of them. Haverly choreographed dance routines. Bruno was an accomplished dialect artist.

A typical Emerson show consisted of two parts: part one, the traditional blackface minstrel portion, usually concluding with a march, ironically called "The Berkeley College Boys"; part two, the olio, featuring individual performers doing their specialties. The show ended with an afterpiece, a skit in which all the performers played, in blackface and bizarre costumes. Foy and Thompson were slated to lead off part two with a comic sketch. Although they always appeared in blackface, their sketches covered a variety of subjects. The first sketch, "Mischief," concerned two salespeople in a clothing store who attempted to fit their rich patrons with ill-fitting clothing. Jokes ran from the simple minstrel question and answer:

FOY: What do you say to a little kiss?
THOMPSON: I've never spoken to one.

to typical dialect:

FOY: Here am a telegram from de boss
                in Africa. He say he is sending us
                some lions' tails.
THOMPSON: Lions' tails? What are you talking
                about?
FOY: Well, read it yo'self. It say plain:
                Just captured two lions. Sendin'
                details by mail.

Rose now had to perform on her own. While Edwin and Jim played with Emerson, she obtained an extended engagement at Woodward's Gardens, billed as a "lyric and terpsichorean artist, a lady whose marvelous voice and exquisite dancing are the theme of universal admiration." Playing with her was a young singer, Lola Sefton, with whom the Foys became friends. Harry Montague had introduced them as kindred spirits, since Sefton lived in Chicago and had played some of the same Western theaters. Edwin would not soon forget pretty Lola.

For one of the few times early in his career, Edwin had the opportunity to expand and enhance his acting abilities. Emerson allowed his company considerable flexibility to initiate new skits and routines, believing it would add fresh material to his shows. It was common for an Emerson minstrel production to replace its sketches each week. Audiences grew to expect these changes and returned frequently to see the new work, thus contributing to consistently full houses.

Having been performing now for more then ten years in a variety of roles and environments, Edwin was learning well what made audiences laugh. He was also gaining sensitivity to the changes taking place in variety entertainment and what seemed to "play best" in different locations. There was no question in his mind that popular theater was fast becoming an urban experience, one with increasing sophistication. Edwin paid special attention to the cheap-seat, gallery customers, since they were not only the most difficult to capture, but also, once won over, an actor's most loyal supporters. Gallery patrons strongly identified with Edwin's low-key, easy-going, seemingly improvisational acting manner; they wholeheartedly responded to his satirizations of current mores and privileged society. When he donned exaggerated costumes and makeup, they laughed all the more. His slippery, side-of-the-mouth delivery and husky, cracked-voice singing seemed to recommend him as a performer for the common man.

Billy Emerson was one of America's most popular minstrel actors. A talented performer and shrewd businessman, Emerson had a long and successful career in the profession. He introduced "Big Sunflower," one of the most famous of minstrel songs.

Edwin's droll impersonations were particularly well received. That these lampoons were now almost entirely of celebrated legitimate actors indicated Edwin's understanding that urban theater audiences were the only ones to have seen such actors perform. In Shakespearean costume, he parodied his mentor Edwin Booth playing Macbeth. For example, he'd swing a sword menacingly over his head, only to crack himself in the skull, the sword flying offstage. Staggering onto the boards, sword embedded in his body, would be an impaled, astonished "stagehand."

To burlesque Joseph Jefferson's signature role as Rip Van Winkle — a performance that Jefferson had been offering almost as long as Van Winkle had slept — Foy awakened as would a drunk arising from a stupor. Attempting to stand up, he tripped repeatedly over his body-long beard. Throwing the beard over his shoulder, he'd exit the stage.

Though familiar with the actor's every move and word, delighted audiences repeatedly demanded encores of these skits. No matter the redundancy, audiences wanted to laugh; and what made them laugh they wanted to see repeatedly.

Edwin's off-stage activities also enhanced audience affection for him. During his teenage years, Edwin had become interested in boxing and billiards, two sports easily accessible to him. While in San Francisco, he spent many daytime hours pursuing these hobbies. A boxing club was located near the Adelphi Theater, and Edwin was a frequent visitor, later suggesting that he had occasionally sparred a few rounds with local professionals. Now able to play frequently, Edwin improved his billiards game, which soon turned into an avid avocation. His interest in sports in which average citizens participated, conveniently mentioned in the newspapers, further advanced his standing as a popular favorite.

Within a few weeks of joining Emerson's Minstrels, Foy and Thompson were being advertised as "the monarchs of comedy in song and dance." Rose was building her reputation, as well, headlining the Woodward Gardens variety entertainment as "the most accomplished lady song and dance artist on the American stage." Acclaim for their performances had become so great that Edwin and Jim began to believe they could be their own producers and managers. This newfound ambition apparently coincided with colleague Gus Bruno's similar aspirations. Or so it seemed.

Bruno proposed to the boys that they go on tour with their own company. Along with his own wife, Edwin's, and Jim's, they could offer a small but versatile and well balanced company. Pooling their money, they purchased costumes and scenery and engaged an advance agent. The *Chronicle* reported on their enterprise:

> Gus Bruno has determined to enter the managerial field, and has organized a company in Frisco, Cal., consisting of Foy and Thompson, Rose Howland, Millie Thomas, and Mrs. Gus Bruno for a trip through Nevada and Montana. Eddie McArdle goes as advance agent.[14]

What Bruno neglected to share with his colleagues was an urgent motivation for his desire to leave town — his pending incarceration on a charge of child molestation. If he could exit the state quickly, he'd be able to escape a court date. Agent McArdle, aware of possible booking problems with the new company, dropped out.

During the middle of May, Gus Bruno's Comedy Company journeyed to its first stop, Virginia City, Nevada, conveniently located just across the state line. It was reported they were going on to Denver, then to Butte, Montana, the copper boom town that supposedly already supported three theaters.

Two weeks later, the *Dramatic News* reported:

> Gus Bruno's Comedy Co. collapsed within a week after taking the road, en route to Denver.[15]

Whether they played to poor houses, or whether Bruno believed his escape secure, he and his wife quit the company and proceeded on their own to Salt Lake City. In his autobiography, Foy stated that the company played in a number of Central California towns, closing weeks later in Sacramento. Evidence from local newspapers, however, indicates that such engagements never occurred. Apparently, when they left Virginia City, Foy and Thompson headed straight for Butte. Foy mentioned that a telegram from a Butte theater manager, which they received in Sacramento, offered them an engagement. More likely, the team saw an ad then running in the *New York Clipper* indicating that Butte's Theater Comique sought artists. In any case, the team wired interest; they were quickly engaged. Luckily, the manager sent them railroad tickets for the trip.

Copper mining was already taking place near Butte in 1873, but it wasn't until 1876 that William J. Parks found a copper vein so pure it could be "shipped to hell and back for smelting and still make a profit."[16] The Anaconda, the richest copper mine in the world, and the Colorado and Montana Smelting Company provided the impetus that transformed Butte into the West's latest boom town. Along with the rapid growth of the town came the effects of refining its copper locally. The cheapest method was heap roasting, burning alternative layers of logs and ore. It gave off a suffocating smoke, filled with sulfur and arsenic fumes, lethal to grass, flowers, and trees. It was reported that cattle eating grass on adjacent land literally plated their teeth with copper. On windless days, the smoke was so heavy in town that lamps had to be burned. These practices continued unchecked until 1885, when Butte's women's organizations protested and a clean-up program was initiated.

Like Leadville, Butte was rapidly expanding, streets being laid out, buildings erected, housing difficult to obtain. Streets were muddy, sidewalks single planks laid end-to-end, at least in front of the stores. As with other boom towns, sudden prosperity brought its ample share of gamblers, prostitutes, and toughs. Citizen vigilante committees tried to maintain order, but disturbances continued. Along with new hotels, the town's first theater was opened.

The first place for entertainment was Renshaw Hall, located above a drug store. All local dances were held there; when a theater company came to town, the Renshaw was where they played. A so-called theater was then opened a few blocks away and became the center for touring companies for a number of years. In 1880, a man named Maguire opened Butte's first "real" theater, called the Theater Comique (it seems *every* town had a Theater Comique) where high-class companies were to play. For opening night, Maguire hired a company of players from New York to perform "Adrienne Le Course," the programs printed on white satin paper, the names of the performers etched in gold. The new theater attracted Butte's social elite; however, a few months later, misfortune struck Maguire when his theater burned to the ground.

Its replacement was another house called the Theater Comique, but this new venue featured popular acts and attracted a broader audience. Except for brief trips to Cheyenne and Denver, it was the house that Foy and Thompson would play for more than six months. The new theater was a three-story brick building about forty feet wide and 150 feet deep. It had three entrance doors. Just above the middle door was a small balcony where musical groups entertained patrons prior to the show. Inside, the walls were covered in red velvet; the carpets were red plush; gas chandeliers supplied illumination. An ornate central staircase led to comfortable balcony boxes. Smoking and drinking were allowed. Before the evening came to an end, the theater was filled with smoke. At intermission, the doors would be opened to clear the air. During winter, however, audiences (and performers) had no choice but to accept the smoky atmosphere.

The Foys and Thompsons found rooms in a home on West Park Street, near the theater. It was probably one of the more comfortable places they stayed during their extended Western tour. Better wages obviously helped, as each member of the team was earning fifty dollars a week, plus the usual gratuities obtained from appreciative audiences.

The team's versatility again proved advantageous. When variety companies played the Comique, Foy and Thompson performed comedy routines, acrobatics, and Irish song and dance. When melodrama companies appeared, they played roles in the show or entertained during intermissions. It seems they achieved their increasingly predictable recognition as the local paper frequently reported to the effect that:

...Foy and Thompson gave an excellent entertainment to the usual packed houses.[17]

But more than four years touring the Western frontier had taken a toll on the Foy/Thompson relationship. While they enjoyed many successes, earned considerable money, and built a sizable reputation playing boom towns, Edwin longed for critical acclaim of the sort that he at least recognized could only be achieved by performing in Eastern theaters. Edwin wanted to "go East"; Jim seemed content with the results and potential of continued playing in the West. Another factor entered into Edwin's aspirations: Rose was pregnant.

The team began exploring East Coast opportunities, writing letters to theater managers, seeking an engagement. They found many variety jobs available, but not at the salaries they had been enjoying. Even their vaunted versatility was less attractive in the East, since Eastern traveling companies had set acts and a hierarchy of performers that dictated the company's structure and operation. Moreover, attempting to find work during the winter proved even more difficult.

When they finally received an offer from Carncross' Minstrels in Philadelphia, they accepted the engagement with little hesitation. It would occupy them to the end of the 82–83 season (May) and give them an opportunity to establish some Eastern credentials, no small benefit, since Edwin had never played east of Fort Wayne in his career.

They all left Butte in early January 1883, first traveling to Chicago, where Edwin visited his mother and sisters. Rose decided to stay in Chicago with mother-in-law Ellen, since she was having problems with the pregnancy. Edwin and Jim were to open with Carncross the end of January.

Wherever the team had played in the West, they always left with invitations to return. Their reputations as versatile, talented comedians and sketch artists had been well established, with substantial incomes reflecting positive audience approval. During the previous four years, the boys had experienced tough towns and riotous audiences, shoot-outs and hangings, axle-deep mud, bitter cold, and primitive theaters. Not only had they been able to survive these conditions, they had been able to overcome them and convert such hardships into stage success. If an actor could endure and master such challenges, they reasoned, he could play anywhere, excel under any circumstances.

Seemingly tested and self-confident, Edwin and Jim made their way to Philadelphia, eager to undertake whatever new adventures lay in store.

Chapter 4

MISSIONARY (SLOCUM): *And you don't know anything about religion?*

CANNIBAL (FOY): *Well, we got a little taste of it when the last missionary was here.*

John Carncross was called the Father of Modern Minstrelsy.

Born in 1834, in Philadelphia, of Quaker parents, he was educated as a civil engineer. It was his voice, however, that led him to the stage and would make him one of early popular theater's greatest ballad singers.

While in his teens, Carncross and a few comrades sang for their girl friends, accompanying themselves on banjo and guitar. They called themselves the "Serenaders" and performed so well that neighborhood residents listened to and applauded their efforts. They suggested Carncross become a professional singer. At the time, minstrelsy was rapidly growing in popularity in Philadelphia under theater manager Sam Sanford. When Sanford heard young Carncross sing, he was signed for an engagement at the Eleventh Street Opera House. There, Carncross performed with E. F. Dixey and Sam Sharpley, and they soon became local favorites.

In 1860, Carncross teamed with Sharpley to perform in minstrel shows at the Continental Theater. When Sharpley retired two years later, Carncross and Dixey formed a minstrel company, performing to great local success throughout the next decade.

During the Civil War, Carncross and Dixey entertained Union soldiers, not only to boost their spirits, but also to encourage their loyalty to the cause of the North. In traditional blackface, they reminded audiences that war was taking place to rescue the Negro from slavery. They brought Southern plantation traditions to the stage, and Negro songs were sung. These shows were staged

John Carncross, owner and manager of Carn-cross' Minstrels, at Philadelphia's Eleventh Street Theater. Carncross presented minstrelsy, farce comedy, and travesty, to the delight of the city's better-class patrons for more than 34 years. (Harry Ranson Humanities Research Center — University of Texas)

but a few miles from the front lines. Laughing at the antics, jokes, and burlesques presented, soldiers particularly found the performances an escape from the horrors of war. And when Carncross' beautiful tenor voice floated over the auditorium singing "When This Civil War Is Over," "Mother Kissed Me in My Dreams," and concluding with "Columbia, the Gem of the Ocean," the house would rise as one in tears, applauding and cheering.

Dixey retired in 1878, and Carncross took over as owner and manager of the company. He gave up stage work but continued to write the majority of burlesques and newspaper advertisements. He endeavored to bring the highest level of entertainment to patrons, offering clean and wholesome shows for the entire family. His audiences usually consisted of the city's elite, from both social

and political circles. Even deeply religious people, not usually theatergoers, went to see Carncross shows.

An astute observer of talent, he signed up-and-coming actors and helped to launch their careers. Such celebrated entertainers as Chauncey Olcott, Francis Wilson, Weber & Fields, Lew Dockstater, Willis P. Sweatnam, Frank Dumont, and Eddie Foy all received a timely boost from Carncross. In the 1880s and '90s, Carncross's shows combined traditional minstrel turns with sharp social and political satires, poking fun at presidents, local politicians, businesses, and the social elite. Though his audiences were made up of the very people he parodied, they willingly came to laugh at themselves. These sketches played to continuously full houses.

In the early 1880s, Carncross turned his writing over to Frank Dumont and E. N. Slocum, two talented burlesque authors and performers; and the shows grew in popularity. In 1895, when Carncross believed the minstrel business was declining, he retired, having accumulated a comfortable fortune. After his retirement, Carncross severed all relations with minstrelsy, refusing even to discuss it, past, present, or future. He died of heart disease in 1911, age seventy-seven. At his death, he had remained a household word in Philadelphia's entertainment circles for more than fifty years.

The Carncross Minstrels played their entire time at the Eleventh Street Opera House. The theater had originally been a Reformed Presbyterian Church. Converted into a theater, it operated under various managers until Carncross and Dixey took it over. An imposing structure, it featured a building-high, central arch lined with electric lights over the entrance, side doors, and projecting cornices. At night, the entire edifice studded with lights, the theater looked especially impressive.

The interior boasted framed, vertical wall panels of sumptuous cloth in the orchestra and horseshoe-shaped balcony levels. A central dome chandelier and clusters of wall-mounted globes furnished illumination. The stage was large, with a proscenium width of forty feet and height to match. The distance from the footlights to the back wall measured forty-five feet. Backstage, the side walls were sixty-five feet apart. Yet there were only 528 seats in the theater, quite cozy for a playhouse of the time.

Philadelphia had a long history of enjoying minstrelsy, wholeheartedly supported by audiences from the 1840s through the early 1900s. Besides the Carncross group, a number of other minstrel companies made their permanent homes in the city. Each season, traveling minstrel companies always visited Philadelphia, because they knew the theater patrons there would bring in profits. Several factors may have contributed to this popularity and longevity.

Philadelphia was a Quaker city, known for its ethnic and religious tolerance. Since colonial times, the city had attracted immigrants from many different European countries, as well as blacks, because of the Quaker belief in racial equality. During the 1860s, Philadelphia was the center of the antislavery movement. A very prosperous city, near the burgeoning coal industry, it was also an important manufacturing center for clothing, iron, machinery, and textiles. Blacks were an important part of the Philadelphia community.

Of all the various forms of entertainment available in the city, minstrelsy seems to have been the most widely and readily accepted. Patrons ranged from blacks to religious hardliners, who would otherwise shun all theater as sinful. Early in their Philadelphia performance history, minstrel companies demonstrated a desire to appeal to broad audiences, including women and children. It became common for minstrel companies to advertise their programs as suitable "for the family." Some minstrel theaters were even labeled "family resorts." During holidays such as Easter and Christmas, special programs, exclusively for children, were performed.

During the 1880s, minstrel companies began to de-emphasize traditional blackface formats, adding musical numbers and skits that were more popular and topical. They offered social travesty to their middle-class audiences in the same way that Harrigan & Hart and Weber & Fields offered entertainment to the Bowery's immigrant populations. While minstrel performers still appeared in blackface, they did not mimic the prevailing Negro stereotype. Rather, they performed "white" material in blackface, probably to justify the presence of these acts within a minstrel program.

Carncross' shows excelled in this more enlightened form of minstrelsy, incorporating elements of variety and farce-comedy. Carncross modified the usual, rigid minstrel format, adding opportunities for popular songs to be rendered and new sketches introduced. Often, these sketches centered on contentious local issues, performers assuming the identities of well-known actual people, while wearing bizarre makeup and costumes. Of course, playing to a more sophisticated audience contributed to the success of these innovations.

In addition, Carncross brought together into his stock company a group of talented and professional performers. The frequent introduction of new sketches and roles demonstrated their creativity and versatility. When Foy and Thompson joined the company in January 1883, they must have been impressed with their colleagues' artistry.

Often called one of the most intellectual actors in minstrelsy, Frank Dumont was not only the author of innumerable songs, sketches, and plays, but also an excellent character actor. Dumont wrote most of the skits, frequently played the lead, and, in addition, functioned as Carncross' stage manager.

E. N. Slocum was considered one of the best interlocutors in minstrelsy. After operating his own company for many years, he joined Carncross to escape the burdens of managerial responsibilities. The oldest company member, he starred in "old codger" and "presidential" roles.

Having made his stage debut just a few years earlier, Chauncey Olcott was a handsome, young Irish singer and comedian. Olcott had previously appeared with Emerson's Minstrels, where he got to know Foy and Thompson. When Slocum joined Carncross, he brought Olcott along. Olcott's later career included playing opposite Lillian Russell in "Pepita," and he appeared in a number of romantic musical plays from 1892 until 1913. Songs he introduced included "Mother Macree," "Macushla," and "When Irish Eyes Are Smiling." Olcott was especially pleased to work with Foy and Thompson again.

Later in his career, Lew Dockstater received the highest salary given to any blackface performer. Already a minstrel veteran when he joined Carncross, Dockstater was an excellent actor of travesty and farce-comedy, particularly topical satire. After leaving Carncross, he produced and acted in refined minstrelsy — a mixture of minstrel and vaudeville entertainment — and performed on the vaudeville circuit until his death in 1924.

Also in the company was Fred Dart, a diminutive song-and-dance man who was building a reputation as a first-rate drag artist. Nearly every Carncross skit featured a flighty, zany female character — and Dart played the role. He was later considered one of the best and most versatile "wenches" in minstrelsy.

Upon joining the company, one of the first things Foy and Thompson had to learn was the professional slang employed by the actors and, for that matter, managers, property men, agents, and stage hands.[1] Performing in the Midwest and West for six years had not prepared them for this occupational language, so common among theater people in the more sophisticated East.

First of all, the boys were taught that they were "professionals" or "in the profession." Their assignments were "parts," costumes were "wardrobes," specified as either ancient or modern. Parts played in "ancient" costumes were "dress-pieces"; those in modern costumes "clean-shirt" plays.

They learned that "cues" were the last few words of the speech preceding the one to be spoken. A long part was called a "soaker"; a lively one a "hummer." A part that allowed one to emote was "fat"; one that assisted another was a "feeder"; one considered too short was a "bum." When an actor had to supply his own language to a role, it was called a "fake part." If he forgot his lines, he was "fishing for lines" or "shaky in his lines." Unspecified action or improvisation was called, simply, "business."

Edwin and Jim learned that their hotel was a "haskery," their room a "den," their trunk a "bumper," their hat a "cady," and their shirt a "smish." Pants were "kicks," shoes "skates," and a diamond pin a "spark." Their colleagues never hesitated to correct mistakes; to communicate correctly, it was vital to be familiar with the jargon.

When "the ghost walked," it meant salaries were forthcoming. A company that closed or was closing was "busted," "stranded," or "gone up the flume." Then, an out-of-work performer had to "hoof it," "walk on his uppers," or "kick up dust on the road."

People unaffiliated with the stage were "outsiders." Those who wished to associate with actors were called "gills," "chappies," "lunkheads," or stigmatized with an even more derogatory term, "jays." When an audience liked a performance, they were "hit hard" or "laid out cold." But when a show didn't do well, it was "rocky," "tough," or "thorny." An unsuccessful show was a "dead rabbit." When an actor was doing well, he was "velvety" or "coming smooth"; when he failed, he'd been "thrown over." In a matter of days, Edwin and Jim were required not only to learn both their lines, but also to understand what was being said to them if they hoped to survive with the company. It was a rigorous initiation into the elite levels of the acting profession.

Two new skits were being rehearsed for introduction in the coming week's program. Every morning, rehearsals for the new pieces took place at the theater. Each afternoon, current material was revised and reviewed in preparation for the evening performance. The boys quickly discovered that working in a Carncross show was demanding and strenuous. At the same time, it was exciting, because the company was so committed to entertaining audiences.

A Carncross program began with the traditional minstrel overture, in which all performers marched on stage and took their designated positions, which signified their acting roles. The interlocutor, either Slocum or Dumont, introduced the actors and initiated a few one-liner jokes:

END: If your sister fell in a well, why couldn't you rescue her?
INTERLOCUTOR: I don't know. If my sister fell in a well, why couldn't I rescue her?
END: Because you could not be her brother and a-ssist her too.

Following a brief interplay along these lines, Dockstater and Olcott rendered songs, such as "The Kerry Dance" and "Elevated Railroad," after which the entire chorus sang more characteristic "plantation" tunes. Tambo and Bones then verbally sparred with the interlocutor through a series of continuous jests; the usual topics included marriage, animals, work, and money. The grand finale of part one of the program was a skit, such as "Dime Museum Curiosities," in which the entire cast impersonated dime museum freaks.

Part Two was made up entirely of olios — short skits, songs, and dances — performed by each of the actors. A quartet sang a sea chantey. A comedy skit about mistaken identity was presented. Dockstater or Olcott sang a number of popular songs, asking the audience to "sing along." Foy and Thompson did an Irish clog dance. Another company member played a harp solo.

Then, a final sketch was performed, usually the feature of the program. This finale

presented either a travesty of a current melodrama or an original story, written by Frank Dumont, filled with topical social and political satire. The entire company participated, with all the primary actors having speaking roles. Dumont wrote skits with a Dickensian flair. His characters were given names that identified their roles and personalities: Amos Leech, a doctor; Catherine Snakeroot, a nurse; On-a-Fry, a restaurant keeper.

Foy and Thompson made their first appearance in bit roles, in a skit entitled "Lower the Ante," a burlesque of *Iolanthe*, the Gilbert & Sullivan opera. They also sang in a chorus of "city councilmen," who proposed all sorts of strange laws "for the good of the city."

For the entire spring season, at least one new skit was introduced every week. Foy and Thompson played in these presentations, but in secondary roles, as they were gradually being integrated into the company. In "Our City Society," they played comic tea drinkers; in "Hazel Korke" (a burlesque of the melodrama "Hazel Kirke"), Edwin and Jim were animal mascots.

After years as featured performers, Edwin and Jim were relegated to bit parts. After having been recognized and feted as stars, they were now practically unnoticed on stage. It undoubtedly deflated their egos. It also demonstrated to them how little they really knew about acting, particularly as members of a company. Performing in the East was significantly more professionally exacting than their frontier experiences had been. When the boys visited other Philadelphia theaters, they soon learned how sophisticated the Carncross productions really were.

It appears that Jim was particularly affected by the demotion of his stage status. By the close of the spring season, he talked about returning to the West. It was probably the primary contributing factor that precipitated his separation with Edwin, after their six-year partnership.

For his part, Edwin seemed to recognize

what he needed to learn from his colleagues and was eager to take advantage of the opportunity. There is no doubt that his Carncross experience contributed significantly to Edwin's development and maturity as a comedian and served as a foundation for his future stage persona.

In March, when a fellow actor suffered a paralytic stroke, Edwin got an opportunity to perform a more important role. It was in a skit, "Barn Door Jig," that demanded an extended dancing routine. With little preparation, Edwin stepped into the role. Audience response was so positive that he continued to play the part as long as the skit was presented. It was this effort that convinced Carncross that Edwin was a developing talent, and he asked him to return to the company for the '83-'84 season. Edwin accepted the invitation, at an increased salary of forty dollars a week.

At the close of their season in Philadelphia, Carncross' Minstrels took a five-week tour of Washington, D.C., Baltimore, and small Pennsylvania towns. They closed their season May 26, in Wilmington, Delaware; it was tagged as another in a long succession of profitable seasons for Carncross.

Edwin returned to Rose, at their home in Chicago. She was now six months pregnant and, unfortunately, feeling quite ill. Bedridden frequently the past few months, she had been cared for by Ellen. The new Carncross season was to open the end of August, which meant rehearsals would begin early in the month. Edwin, however, chose to remain with Rose until she gave birth, wiring Carncross he would be unable to join the company. Although Jim had already indicated his intent to return West, he volunteered to take Edwin's role temporarily.

The Carncross season opened August 30, to the usual SRO house. Back were most of the same performers from the previous year — Slocum, Dumont, Dockstader, Dart — plus two new members, James Quinn and Fred Hart, both already well-known in minstrelsy. A baseball burlesque, "Athletics vs.

Philadelphia" was featured and reported to be:

> ...one of the funniest absurdities seen in this cozy place of amusement for many a day.[2]

Meanwhile, Rose weakened as she approached childbirth. On September 25, unable to survive the ordeal, both she and the child died. A week later, the *New York Clipper* stated in its obituary column:

> Rose Howland, one of the Howland Sisters, died while giving birth to a son, Sept. 25, at the home of her mother-in-law. She was the wife of Ed Foy, of Foy and Thompson, and was well-known in the variety profession throughout the country. Her infant was buried with her.[3]

Edwin was deeply distressed by the loss of his wife and child. In his autobiography, he remembered:

> Now and then in life, there is a sorrow so keen that the pain of it never quite departs. My grief at the loss of my youthful sweetheart was one of these. Life seemed to stop short for a while and almost lose its reason for continuance.[4]

Foy later claimed that he immediately returned to Carncross but, because he wasn't performing well, retired from the company. He reported having then played at variety houses and dime museums for a while, until regaining his zest for performing.

In reality, Edwin returned to Carncross two months later, in early November, to perform for another year and a half and ultimately star.

When Edwin rejoined the company, Jim departed. There were tears when they finally separated. "I hope you may succeed, Eddie," Jim said. "I believe you got it in you to do it." Over the following forty-odd years, they saw one another only occasionally; Thompson died a few years before Foy.

Edwin's first roles were in a burlesque of "Peck's Bad Boy" and "Misfit Servants," still bit parts. At the end of November, however, called upon to replace an ailing Fred Dart, Edwin won a starring opportunity. Dart had been playing the leading "female" in "Young Mrs. Winthrop." It would be Edwin's first female impersonation.[5]

Men had been impersonating women on stage for centuries. It wasn't until the mid-nineteenth century, however, that the word "drag" was coined, to describe the petticoats worn by men playing female roles. The word quickly became identified with the roles themselves.

Audiences knew such a characterization was meant to be comedic. Any man who wore women's clothes was automatically a comedian; the sketches were always burlesques and parodies. The drag actor entered the stage with a broad grin, sported a wig and exaggerated makeup, and wore a bizarre assortment of clothes parodying high fashion. His voice, however, remained natural, to "prove" to the audience the act itself was a joke.

The female impersonator had available to him a unique vehicle with which to satirize society, from its elites to its domestic servants, to expose political intrigue, and to discuss the "girlish" secrets of marriage. The primary cause for laughter was the clownish anachronism of a man in women's clothes. It gave comedic sanction to otherwise taboo subject matter.

For the accomplished clown, however, drag acts were but one example of a wide comic vocabulary. To such talents, the laughter they elicited did not rely solely on female costumes and makeup. Quality drag acts essentially featured comedians at work. Speed of delivery, improvisation, a range of inflections, and the ability to capture an audience with a glance or gesture, remained the primary ingredients for comedy. All truly good comedians of the time included a drag characterization in their repertory.

Edwin seemed a natural for the drag

When Edwin walked the streets of Philadelphia looking like a prosperous businessman, no one would recognize him. Audiences knew only his stage persona, always in costume and zany makeup, often in drag. Edwin seemed to value the anonymity.

role. *The Philadelphia Ledger,* reporting on his performance, stated:

> Foy was greeted with approbation by an appreciative audience.[6]

Two weeks later, Edwin's name appeared in Carncross's newspaper advertisements for the first time. He played a starring role in a sketch entitled "Medical Mistakes," in which he portrayed an eccentric doctor who sought to operate on everybody in sight.

The famous actor, Sir Henry Irving, had just opened an engagement at Philadelphia's Chestnut Street Theater, appearing in Hamlet. His performance prompted the Carncross company to prepare a burlesque on the Shakespearean play. As Edwin was chosen to parody the famous actor in this burlesque, he went to observe Irving perform a number of times. A week later, "'enry Herving 'amlet" was featured on the Carncross bill, with Edwin impersonating Sir Henry, to the audiences' delight:

> Edwin Foy's imitation of Irving is attracting favorable attention. 'enry Herving 'amlet kept the audience in a broad grin until the curtain fell.[7]

Within a few weeks, Edwin had graduated from supporting roles to featured player in the Carncross company.

Each holiday season, Carncross presented a special program for children. This year, the program featured the presentation of "Mother Goose and the Golden Egg." During the play, performers mingled with the audience and Mother Goose, played by Edwin, brought children on stage to receive toys and candy. The show played three weeks, to SRO audiences. Local newspapers noted the popularity of Carncross's Christmas program.

The January 1884 bills offered revivals of two previously popular skits, "The Dime Museum" and "The Bigger Student":

> The first parody entitled "The Dime Museum" disclosed to view a number of curiosities so fearfully and wonderfully made up, and so comic in their actions and speeches, that long after "the trained giraffe" had disappeared the audience wore a broad grin.[8]

Edwin was the trained giraffe, who experienced great difficulty holding his head up while constantly bumping into obstacles.

> The performance closed with the presentation of a burlesque operetta, "The Bigger Student," in which beggar students, tramps, and other "distinguished and influential citizens" display their ability to do and say a number of most absurd things, all of which were received with loud guffaws.[9]

In this sketch, with much of the business left to the imaginative, improvisational skills

of the actor, Edwin played a tramp, in grotesque costume, his pant legs so long, he continually fell over them.

Spring programs featured a series of topical social and political satires, "Running for Mayor," "Our Police Plug Club," and "The Broad Street Station," in which Edward Foy — as he was now being identified in newspaper advertisements — played an Italian stationmaster. In "Stranglers of Our City," Edwin played Darkness — Black and Gloomy, a would-be anarchist out to assassinate President Chester Alan Arthur. Foy's large, black mustache was so bushy it caught in his mouth whenever he spoke his lines.

When the Barnum and Forepaugh Circus came to Philadelphia, the company produced a skit, "Barnum's Four Paws," parodying circus performers and animals alike. Featured were the two "original and only white elephants"; Edwin was one of the elephants. The show was so well received, it continued to the end of the season, though it was reported that Barnum was not pleased.

During April, Haverly's Minstrel Company played a week in Philadelphia, on a tour of Eastern cities. Haverly visited Carncross, not only to see what his friendly competitor was presenting, but also to seek out performers for a summer engagement in London, England. He had already signed Billy Emerson and Charlie Reed. When Edwin was asked to join the company, he readily signed, seeing an opportunity both to perform with a number of esteemed colleagues and to earn additional salary.

The Haverly Minstrel Company, sixty-eight in all, planned to leave New York on May 17, to open at the Drury Lane Theater in London on May 31, for a three-month engagement. A delay in departure forced the company to play a week at the Brooklyn Theater, likely for financial reasons. Then, Billy Emerson declared he would play only two weeks in London because of other commitments. Edwin, too, would have to leave the company in early August, because rehearsals for Carncross' new season were scheduled to begin at that time. The tour appeared to be in trouble, but its London opening was considered successful.

Haverly's Minstrels opened May 31, at Drury Lane Theater, to a crowded house, and are reported to have scored "quite a success."[10]

When Emerson departed the company, however, the show soon floundered. After only a month in London, Haverly's started a tour "through provincial cities of England, playing week stands." Although he found his first trip overseas quite interesting, Edwin was glad he would be soon returning to Philadelphia and Carncross for another season.

On the evening of August 24, 1884, Carncross's '84-'85 season opened. The featured cast included Slocum, Dumont, Quinn, Dart, Olcott, Dockstater, and Foy. To help initiate the season, the bill also included the team of Hawkins and Collins. Ben Collins was Edwin's old partner, from their early beer hall and traveling circus days. It was a welcome reunion, one that rekindled a warm friendship that lasted until Collins' untimely death only a few years later.

The *Philadelphia Ledger* heralded the return of Carncross' Minstrels:

Welcome news to the many patrons of this popular family resort was the announcement of the opening last night of its 22nd season. All of the old favorites were there, as well as a number of new faces, whose sweet songs and genuine humor will soon place them in the front rank with those artists whom John L. Carncross has for so many successful seasons welcomed "to the boards" at this cozy and attractive spot.[11]

On the opening, the *New York Clipper* reported:

Talbert, Foy, Olcott and Dart brought down the house with "The Society Swells."[12]

A burlesque on local banking followed, "The Third Street Brokers," or "How the Money Goes." Edwin played Garibaldi McFord, an Italian-Irish policeman. Two weeks later, the company presented "The Coachman's Bride," in which Edwin, in drag, played Rosie Nolan, an Irish belle, "one of the hits of the season."

A short skit, "Railroad Train in Motion," in which the chorus simulated the speeding up and slowing down of a train (as in the opening number of "The Music Man," almost seventy-five years later) was reported to be "among the most sidesplitting of the many oddities which have been produced at this place."

Sketches were changed frequently, almost weekly, and Edwin was now playing featured roles in nearly all of them. In a burlesque on swimming in the Atlantic, Edwin played a Negro female, Exquisite Ebony. In a skit called "Electric Shocks, or a Scientific Satire," a mad scientist invented an electrical machine that hatched and grew chickens at astonishing rates. Edwin played a giant chicken that jumped off the stage and ran clucking through the theater, bombarding the audience with artificial eggs.

A revival of the "Dime Museum" sketch featured a living head, a man/octopus, a three-legged man, Aztec midgets, and the celebrated frog boy. It was presented to satirize a struggle among local dime museums, which had been outbidding one another for freak acts.

"Kris Kringle's Visit" was the annual Carncross holiday program, a child's fantasy presentation that closed, as usual, with the distribution of toys and candy. Also featured on the bill were Lew Dockstater as "The Human Sandwich" and Dart and Foy in "Colored Flirtations," both of them playing Negro females.

A new skit, "The White House Dinners," or "Washington High Life," opened the new year, 1885. The program was described as "a host of nihilists, cranks, and dynamiters filling up the total of what is alleged to illustrate high life society in Washington." Edwin played in drag again, a spy, Dr. Mary Walker.

The press reported the skit to be "the most talked-about hit of the season."

Spring shows featured new burlesques, often parodies on local events. A scandal in a Philadelphia college inspired "The Quack College," in which a medical school was exposed as graduating unqualified doctors. "Our Roller Skating Rink," or the "Hall of the Dull Thud" parodied the latest fad among the city's elite. Just before Easter, the company presented "The Office Seekers," a burlesque on the selection of Presidential candidates, with E. N. Slocum playing President Cleveland and Edwin as Secretary Lamont, who experienced considerable trouble correctly communicating messages to and from the President.

While Philadelphia shows played to excellent houses during the spring of 1885, theater managers noticed that the minstrels were not attracting the large audiences they had in the past. In his small theater, which normally played to standing-room-only, Carncross saw his attendance declining, although his bills had steadily moved from traditional minstrelsy to social travesty. Company members noticed the decline as well, and they began to explore other bookings for the next season. Lew Dockstater was the first to declare he would not return to the Carncross organization. Chauncey Olcott indicated his intent, as well. Edwin wasn't sure yet what he wanted to do, torn between playing starring roles in familiar surroundings or taking his chances with unfamiliar touring companies. Finally, when Carncross announced the current season would close the end of April, and the minstrels would not go on tour the summer, Edwin decided to leave the company.

The Carncross company's closing show was a parody on Italian opera, "The Dime Opera, or a Ten-Cent Patti." Edwin played an Italian conductor whose instructions to orchestra members were delivered with side-of-the-mouth spray, in an unintelligible Italian dialect. The *New York Clipper* reported on the finale:

J. L. Carncross quits a good winner this year.[13]

Yet, in the same issue of the *Clipper*, an editorial noted that variety was replacing minstrelsy at an "alarming rate" in the country's popular theaters.

Edwin now began seeking a new job in earnest. The past two years had proved a fulfilling and maturing experience, in which he had progressed from a naive bit player to a featured performer in a stock company of acknowledged professionals. Edwin had enjoyed the opportunity to demonstrate his versatility as an actor and comedian, not only meeting the challenge of continuously new roles, but also developing his own unique style. Less cocky than when he first joined Carncross, he was now more confident and assured in his work. Edwin was certain his talents and abilities would win him a booking. It was simply a matter of finding an organization that could best utilize his kind of performance.

In early April, a farce-comedy company, Barry and Fay, had played a week in Philadelphia. They were now on their way West, having been engaged for the entire summer. Barry and Fay had seen Edwin perform and were interested in his joining their company. With Carncross' agreement, they contacted Edwin, offered him a good salary and featured billing. If he accepted their offer, Edwin was to join them in Milwaukee on May 18. Promising to be on hand when they opened there, he wired his acceptance.

Edwin never played in minstrels again, but the acting techniques he learned while with Carncross remained an integral part of his stage performance throughout his career. He never performed with a stock company again, but he learned the ingredients necessary to make a congenial, cooperative, and productive company. That he was now able to make orchestra patrons laugh as heartily as those in the gallery attested to his increasing professionalism as a comedian, one with appeal for all theatergoers.

Chapter 5

Some titled folks,
Some equivokes,
Some risky jokes,
A strange or lawless passion;

Some fond regrets,
Some cigarettes,
Some — well "coquettes,"
May make the play the fashion.

Making a resplendent entrance dressed as a foppish courtier, an actor sang and danced this pseudo-Shakespearean prologue to introduce Barry & Fay's new farce-comedy, "Irish Aristocracy."

Already famous for their entertaining melodramas, Barry & Fay had recently changed their familiar presentations to cater to increasing audience interest in farce-comedy. The new venture had been quite a departure from their earlier days as Shakespearean performers. Yet they were not afraid to modify their presentations in response to the prevailing interests among theater patrons.

Barry & Fay had made their reputation and fortune by presenting melodrama — America's morality play — primarily in small Midwestern and Western towns, to audiences who enthusiastically embraced this type of attraction.

Melodrama had become the most popular dramatic play during the middle nineteenth century.[1] Its classic plot portrayed a wholesome family situation, which usually featured a pretty daughter (the heroine) courted by an honest and moral young man (the hero). Danger ensued when an external force threatened this stable family life, usually in the guise of a villain whose goal it was to steal the girl's affection by discrediting the young man and menacing the family. After a plethora of perils were overcome, the story ended with dramatic flourish, the villain vanquished and the virtuous characters returned to their previously harmonious life. The play's characters were starkly good or evil; there was no ambiguity. The hero and heroine battled and bested the villain. Virtue defeated evil.

The quintessence of melodrama was restoration of the moral order. The play's action hurled audiences through a tortuous course of risk and uncertainty, toward a dramatic conclusion that, at the ultimate instant, snatched them from the jaws of danger and restored their peace of mind.

Melodrama presented a microcosm of the social and moral dilemma faced by the American public. This widely felt predicament stemmed from the destabilizing effects of a rapidly growing industrial economy, an impact that threatened the older, simpler structures of a society dominated by white, Protestant, propertied men who had, heretofore, wielded largely uncontested power. In its idealized form, melodrama captured the imagination and sympathy of audiences by returning them to life as it had been, or should have been. It portrayed the eternal human confrontation with morality, abbreviated for the stage.

But once the public became accustomed to the industrial revolution and began to realize its capitalistic opportunities, melodrama soon declined. Ironically, or perhaps predictably, it gave way to its antithesis, a new dramatic form called farce-comedy.

Farce-comedy presented a full-length musical play, within the framework of a plot that included the topical ingredients of a variety show. Instead of stylized subject matter and predictable characterizations, farce-comedy attracted audiences by means of dialogue in the vernacular, with songs and dances loosely integrated into the plot.

More importantly, farce-comedy featured wit and humor, particularly that which tended to poke fun at the very stereotypes melodrama embraced. Serious conflicts became funny mishaps. Social mores were teased; the social order satirized. In that sense, farce-comedy resembled the sketches put on by Carncross.

Farce-comedy was designed to give audiences a good time by offering familiar characters and situations in comedic form. Further, it included key figures that melodrama conveniently overlooked — the poor, people of color, independent women, and immigrants. It also taught audiences to laugh with them, not at them.

Mounting and touring farce-comedy companies was cheap; settings, properties, and costumes were minimal. Plots were flexible enough to interpolate local issues and recognizable characters. Plays gave ample opportunity for performers to exploit their talents and offered them improvisational latitude. Thus, it was not surprising that many of America's most respected comedians graduated from this stage form. Indeed, some historians have considered farce-comedy to be the root of modern musical theater.

Edwin began his engagement with Barry & Fay in the "Irish Aristocracy," playing an Irish laborer. Dressed in workman's costume, he entered the stage carrying a ladder, paint can, and brush. After some brief funny-business attempting to put up the ladder, he began painting a wall with great speed and vigor, albeit sloppily. When asked, "Why are you in such a hurry, Murphy?" Edwin replied, "Sure I want to get through before me paint runs out." After a few weeks of bit parts, Edwin earned separate billing for a number of novelty and "ridiculous" dances.

After leaving Milwaukee, the Barry & Fay company traveled to St. Paul and Minneapolis, then made a long jump to Denver. There they played at the elegant Tabor Opera House. The same ore-rich entrepreneur who had built the opera house in Leadville spent more than half million dollars in 1881 to erect the West's most ornate and modern theater. For a touring company to play Tabor's was as impressive as playing at the great Eastern opera houses. But a prestigious claim had its drawbacks when the house wasn't filled.

Even for the most renowned companies, Tabor's, with more than 1,500 seats, was difficult to fill for an entire week. Barry & Fay realized that, with only one production, they could not successfully entertain a city that had such a large theater. They decided to add two plays, "All Crazy" and "Dynamite," both of which they had presented a few years earlier. It also benefited them in preparation for an extended engagement in San Francisco at the Bush Street Theater, the city's best variety house.

During the company's three-week stay in 'Frisco, the three pieces were alternated every few days. The success of each of these presentations persuaded patrons to return a number of times, motivating the *San Francisco Chronicle* to report:

> Barry & Fay's Company have achieved a distinct success.[2]

For Edwin, however, performing in San Francisco was not all work-related. Across the street from the Bush Street Theater stood the Olympic Club, an organization devoted to training boxers in the latest pugilistic techniques. The oldest athletic club in the U.S., it had been formed by the city's business and professional men to promote boxing as a "scientific" sport. Hired for their mental, as well as physical, abilities, club instructors were the best available. Emphasis was on training and conditioning.

Boxing had been one of Edwin's interests since his teen-age years. The proximity of the Olympic Club gave him the opportunity to watch fighters in training, even to box a few rounds himself, an exercise that quickly gained him respect from club members. On one of his visits to the club, Edwin met a twenty-year-old Wells Fargo bank teller who was training to become a club instructor. Almost immediately, Edwin and Jim Corbett became friends.

Corbett was a handsome, well-formed man, six feet one-half inch in height and weighing a muscular 187 pounds. While a strong puncher, his hands were delicate, making it problematic that they could endure sustained punishment. (Bare knuckle fights often lasted fifty or sixty rounds.) To offset this potential liability, Corbett learned to box with intelligence, a style designed to wear down opponents to the point where they could be more easily knocked out. Corbett was said to have invented shadow-boxing, as well as the feint, bob, and weave, a technique that required excellent legwork and superb conditioning.

Though he had been raised in a poor Irish family, Corbett liked to associate with the club's business people and eat at the best restaurants. From this, he gained the nickname "Gentleman Jim," a sobriquet that identified him throughout his future boxing and stage careers. Though Corbett had not yet decided to turn professional, he did confide to Edwin his desire for a stage career at some later date. Edwin promised to help him if at all possible.

During that same San Francisco visit, Edwin formed another friendship, this one with William "Billy" Jerome, a fellow actor playing with a variety company touring the West. Jerome was considered an anachronism in the profession; he had been raised in a well-to-do family and had attended college to study law. Nevertheless, Jerome's ambition called for show business, particularly writing songs. In fact, he had just sold his first song, "There's a Woman at the Bottom of It All," for five dollars. Because he was required to pay for its orchestration, the song was never published.

Realizing that song-writing would not generate a reasonable salary, Jerome joined a variety company as a song-and-dance man. He had started his career at the London Theater in New York's Bowery, playing twelve weeks there for a total salary of seventy-five dollars.

During their time in 'Frisco, Jim, Billy, and Edwin were frequently seen together, often accompanied by striking young women, usually fellow performers. Edwin's most frequent companion was pretty Lola Sefton, whom he had met the last time he played San Francisco, four years previously. Lola, too, was on tour, playing a brief run in the city.

In a matter of days, their relationship blossomed. Since both still made their home in Chicago when not on the road, Edwin and Lola agreed to share an apartment there. So began an intimacy that was to continue for nine years.

From San Francisco, the Barry & Fay company headed back East, playing in Salt Lake City, Denver, Cheyenne, and Leadville. The Salt Lake Theater had originally been the home for the Deseret Dramatic Association, a Mormon group; with the arrival of the railroad, the theater became an important stop for touring companies. Since it was still owned by the Mormon Church, visiting companies were screened to ensure no questionable material would be presented. Nonetheless, city folk dressed up when attending the theater; women wore their best dresses and plush capes, a local style. The Mormon elite enjoyed specially assigned boxes and were the sole possessors of opera glasses, not only to better view the stage, but also to observe who happened to be attending the theater that evening.

Mormon parents were discouraged from bringing babies to the theater; when that didn't work, management put up signs informing patrons that "babes in arms" were ten dollars extra. In response to this admonition, parents brought their small children in carriages.

While the Salt Lake Theater was popular, it continually suffered from financial problems. The theater's economic viability was remarkably enhanced when its only competition, the privately-owned Walker Opera House, mysteriously burned to the ground.

Barry & Fay's "Irish Aristocracy" closed "a successful engagement," with Edwin's expanded role as the Irish laborer gaining attention from an audience intimately familiar with the material presented. "The specialties of Edward Foy were the special features

of the performance," reported the *Clipper's* Western correspondent.

Barry & Fay's engagement in Leadville proved a disorienting experience for Edwin. It had been only three years since he had last performed there, but he could barely recognize the town. Now a built-up city with paved streets and sidewalks, Leadville boasted a main street lined with two- and three- story brick buildings. Top theatrical productions were staged at the decorous Tabor Opera House, a high-altitude complement to Tabor's in Denver. Theaters that Edwin had played in no longer existed. The house where he lived had been replaced by a dry goods store. Moreover, remembering his early married life with Rose in Leadville surely moved him.

At the end of July, the tour came to an abrupt end in Denver when Barry became so ill he had to be hospitalized. Company members were abandoned without engagements for the remainder of the summer and with no prospects for the fall season. As a kindly (and rare) gesture to the company, Barry & Fay paid travel expenses for all to return home.

A little over two months later, Edwin was playing with Kelly & Mason's "The Tigers" Company in Buffalo, New York. How he obtained this engagement and what transpired between Denver and Buffalo remains unknown. Yet in this farce-comedy, Edwin played a leading role as Buffington Quick, an English detective. "The Tigers" was a three-act play, with a cursory plot interspersed with variety-style olios. Kelly and Mason played the leads as "tigers" looking for rich young women to marry and willing to commit crimes to gain their objectives. Business included a visit to the zoo, a restaurant lunch that turned into a riotous food fight, and an escape to a jungle. The dialogue consisted of characteristic husband/wife and he/she jokes:

HUSBAND: My wife hasn't spoken a cross word to me in two weeks.

FRIEND: When is she coming back?

SHE: When you asked me to become your wife you deliberately deceived me.

HE: In what way?

SHE: You told me you were well-off.

HE: Well, I might have said it; but I didn't know how well off I was at the time.

The company's (and Edwin's) engagement in Philadelphia was well received. The *New York Clipper* declared:

> Kelly and Mason's "The Tigers" made its first appearance here Sept. 21. The piece achieved a hit and the house was large. Lena Merville, Edwin Foy, Harry Kelly, and Kelly and Mason shared honors.[3]

Touring from Philadelphia to Boston took the Kelly & Mason ensemble three months, with intermediate stops as far west as Denver. During this time, the company played more than 100 performances in twenty-one cities and journeyed over 4,000 miles. They did quite well in smaller towns but only fair in larger cities. Critics in Cincinnati appreciated the company's cleverness but believed "the play fails to pick it up." In Chicago, it was reported "The Tigers" "played to a very slim business." By the time the company reached Boston at the end of December, much of the plot had been changed; apparently not for the better. *The Boston Globe* predicted the show's likely demise:

> Kelly and Mason pleased few audiences with the piece, which is now simply an elongated knockabout Irish and German variety sketch.[4]

The company closed down a week later, the *Globe* bluntly reporting "the combination went to pieces." Kelly and Mason officially announced their season ended, "The Tigers" shelved until further notice. At the same time, they signed a contract with Carrie Swain and her "Jack-in-the-Box" company to appear the following week in Philadelphia. To complement their new engagement, the only actor they chose to take with them was Edwin Foy.

"Somersaults made her a hit," said an old theater manager of Carrie Swain, already a veteran of variety and minstrel shows from the '70s. While playing in minstrels during the early days of her career, she excelled in dancing and imitations of Negro eccentricities. Although she was blonde, with a good figure and decidedly feminine features, Swain dressed as a boy and did somersaults as a feature of her act. Labeled a "rough soubrette" because of her strong voice, she was one of the first song "belters" to appear on the variety stage.

After separating from her husband, Swain formed her own company, one of the first women on stage to do so. They performed a combination of farce-comedy and variety, which always included a somersault routine by the star. In 1882, in "Cad, the Tomboy," Swain and her company attained featured status on the touring circuit. There was no question in any actor's mind that Carrie Swain ruled her company.

When Edwin joined the Swain company, it was in some financial and artistic trouble. Philadelphia critics questioned whether the show would continue beyond its run in that city. Kelly, Mason, and Foy were hired to improve the faltering play, its plot so confused that audiences couldn't decide whether it was a melodrama or a farce-comedy.

The hero, his father a rich landowner, was heir to a fortune. When young, the hero had left home to join a variety company on tour. (Farce-comedies always seemed to include actors or touring companies in their plots.) One night, the show was enveloped in flames. In the ensuing panic, the hero rescued a boy, Jack-in-the-Box, who became devoted to him. When the hero was accused of killing a wealthy citizen, Jack proved his mentor's innocence and found the guilty man. Happiness and prosperity were restored.

Swain played Jack and, with her songs, dances, and somersaults, was "well received."

In 1886, Carrie Swain was one of the most popular women on the variety stage. Her farce comedies filled theaters and her trademark somersaults never failed to attract cheers and whistles from the men. One of the first women to do so, she managed her own company, with mastery. (Harry Ransom Humanities Research Center — University of Texas)

The play itself, however, was considered "barely good." At this point, Swain was very close to closing the show, to replace it with her already proven "Cad, the Tomboy."

The show went through considerable revisions while playing in Philadelphia. Initially, the *Clipper* reported the play to be a "patchwork of old ideas, and baldness of plot." Three weeks later, the same reporter declared "the revision of the play judicious and a decided improvement on the old version." "Jack-in-the-Box" was now a decided farce-comedy, with considerable infusions of comic material.

Edwin played a dialect role, Professor O'Sullivan, an ex-showman, which also gave him an opportunity to present some impersonations. Along with the play's favorable report, Edwin was identified as "making an unmistakable hit." Thus encouraged, Swain

made a bold and brave decision. She moved the company to New York, to appear at the Union Square Theater. For Edwin, it would be his first New York performance.

"Jack-in-the-Box" survived New York for three weeks, to "fairly successful business." "As bright as ever," Swain carried the show. Edwin, identified in the review as Mr. Fry, was singled out for his burlesque ballet dance, which gained him a number of encores.

The first part of the road tour, from March to May, included cities in New England, where the company was greeted with generally good houses, thus encouraging Swain that her show might have some longevity. With the advent of the summer season in the East, she decided to jump the company to San Francisco for an extended run.

The Swain company opened at the Bush Street Theater, presenting her familiar standby, "Cad, the Tomboy." Audiences were so large that the company moved to the more spacious Alcazar Theater to continue their run. In the middle of June, sustaining attendance, "The Ragamuffin" replaced "Cad." The *Chronicle* declared:

> Carrie Swain is doing nicely in the title role. The reception accorded Miss Swain and the new play was most cordial. She has been quite successful here.[5]

But while Swain was apparently "a source of profit for the management," Edwin was refused a salary increase, although he argued that his contributions had helped save the show and extend its life. Angry at Swain's refusal, Edwin left her and briefly joined the Alcazar Theater stock company to appear in "A Desperate Game," an emotional drama. Two weeks later, he joined Kate Castleton's "Crazy Patch" company for a three-week run at the Alcazar. Old friend Charlie Reed was Castleton's leading man, playing the role of Felix McGlue, an Irish policeman. Reed made stage history by his entrance on roller

The Alcazar was San Francisco's most elegant theater for two decades. By the time Edwin played there, however, other theaters had been opened; the Alcazar was relegated to farce comedy and burlesque programs.

skates. Since roller skating was the latest craze at the time, he scored a big hit.

Edwin played the role of William Smith, a deranged man who imagined himself to be John L. Sullivan, the world champion boxer. To better perform his role, Edwin visited the Olympic Club and sought the aid of his friend Jim Corbett. That Edwin was encored repeatedly for his impersonation suggests that he collected and interpolated some decidedly funny material about boxing.

For his work in San Francisco, Edwin received recognition by being asked to participate in a benefit for David Belasco, a West Coast producer and director who had moved to Broadway and seemed to be on his way to an outstanding managerial career. Included in the benefit program were McKee Rankin, Maurice Barrymore, and other legitimate theater actors. Only Edwin and Carrie Swain represented popular theater. Edwin did some imitations of prominent actors, among them Sir Henry Irving. He recalled in his autobiography, "It made me rather proud to be called upon to do a single act along with such distinguished company."

Castleton continued on tour, but Edwin chose not to remain with the company, opting instead to return to New York to join Mr. and Mrs. George Knight's company in "Over the Garden Wall." Kate Castleton, however, would not forget Edwin's performing talents and audience appeal.

The Knight organization was a well-known and respected farce-comedy group. Mr. Knight wrote all of their material; Mrs. Knight was an excellent singer and comedienne. They had been performing "Over the Garden Wall" for three successful years, each season brightening the script with new songs, comic sketches, and new actors. Edwin was hired because of his comic ability and versatility, since he would not only play a role in the piece, but entertain between acts, as well.

The Knights opened their season in Paterson, New Jersey, August 27, to try out their renewed version of "Over the Garden Wall." Three days later, they were in Boston, preceded by extensive playbilling throughout the city. The *Clipper* reported business at the Globe Theater to be "very good" and mentioned that the specialties of the St. Felix Sisters and Ed Foy "were received with approbation."

After a few weeks touring through New England to finalize and polish the play, the company opened at the Windsor Theater in New York to "very good attendance." Edwin played Julius Snitz, Jr., nephew to George Knight's leading role. At the beginning of the second act, he did some burlesque imitations and dances; near the end of the third act, he performed some eccentric character songs and a "pas-seul" ballet number. According to the *New York Post,* he was "much applauded in his amusing burlesque."

Following a successful week in Baltimore, the Knights traveled south, to play in medium-sized and small towns in Georgia, Alabama, and Tennessee. The Knights had already established a good reputation in the South, but it was Edwin's first experience there. He quickly discovered Southern audiences were different: they applauded politely, rarely asked for encores, and enjoyed speeches by performers at the conclusion of the play. Admission prices for "better" shows were also lower, ranging from twenty-five cents for the gallery to one dollar for the parquet. Nor were specific performers singled out for their specialties. Returning to Midwestern theater audiences brightened the company's disposition and enthusiasm, and they played to full houses in St. Louis, Cincinnati, and Chicago.

Foy later wrote that, while in Cincinnati, he and Lola Sefton had been married. Yet an examination of records for all cities in which he played from 1886 to 1893 shows no recorded marriage. At the time he claimed the marriage took place, Sefton was performing with a small variety company in Iowa. Since Foy and Sefton were already living together, this may have been an attempt to legitimize (or cover up) their real relationship. One wonders about his memory and motivations, since Foy wrote his memoirs in 1927, having already admitted in a 1916 court case that he had never married Sefton.

The Knights returned to the New York area for the holiday season, playing a total of six weeks in Brooklyn, Harlem, and New York to "fairly good houses." The now tired "Over the Garden Wall" was replaced by George Knight's version of Bronson Howard's "Baron Rudolph," presented for the first time at the Fourteenth Street Theater. It was during rehearsals for "Baron Rudolph" that George Knight first revealed some episodes of irrational behavior on stage.

In February 1887, the Knight company went on tour again. But "Baron Rudolph" was replaced by "Over the Garden Wall" because Knight seemed unable to finish the new play. Boston attracted "a good sized audience," as did other small towns in upstate New York. Detroit's "business was good," but a comment in the Detroit newspaper implied that Knight was ill. The suggestion was affirmed when the *New York Clipper* announced that "Ed Foy and W. H. Sloan are said to have secured 'Over the Garden Wall' for next season." The announcement was apparently premature because, in a Chicago newspaper release, George Knight angrily declared he would continue to play the piece.

No mention of Edwin managing the play occurred again, but it was obvious among company members that Knight and Foy were not getting along. Nor was Knight friendly to the company in general, as his health was rapidly deteriorating. It was only Mrs. Knight's kindness that kept the company together. Edwin began seeking another engagement; since the company was planning to play in San Francisco in another month, he made his inquiries among managers there.

By the time the Knight contingent reached San Francisco, Edwin had made up his mind to leave as soon as he could. By chance, Lola was playing an extended run in a variety company at the Vienna Garden Theater, so she and Edwin spent some time together. Jim Corbett often joined them for dinner and a tour 'on the town.' When Billy Emerson arrived for a visit, the four of them were seen together. Among other reasons for good cheer, they were celebrating Corbett's decision to become a professional boxer. After handily knocking out the Olympic Club champion, Corbett boasted he was going to take the world championship from John L. Sullivan in the near future.

In spite of its apparent internal problems, "Over the Garden Wall" was well received at the Bush Street Theater, playing "to immense houses." *The San Francisco Chronicle,* already a Foy supporter, reported that the Knight cast included Edwin Foy, "a favorite of the boys, who made a great hit." Those comments only served to increase the tension between Knight and Foy. It exploded when Edwin abruptly left the company at the end of May. Knight then claimed that his company had been detained in San Francisco because of Foy's departure, and he threatened a lawsuit for lost revenue. A month later, Knight took out a lawsuit against his entire company, claiming that their contracts required them to dress well on and off the stage and conduct themselves like ladies and gentlemen. A short time later, Mrs. Knight placed her husband in a sanitarium where he remained until his death.

Edwin was quickly hired by the Alcazar Theater management to appear in their stock company. "Harbor Lights," a melodrama about the Boston Tea Party, played for three weeks, with Edwin in a supporting role. When Gus Williams, the German dialect comic, opened at the Alcazar in "Oh, What a Night," Edwin was one of the featured performers. The *Chronicle* reported Edwin to be "very clever."

The next week, Williams put on "One of the Finest," a farce-comedy about New York City life. While the *Chronicle* theater critic panned the piece as "sorry stuff," Williams "kept the audience in a continuous laugh." As Mort Devine, the masher, Foy:

Another manager of and actor in her own company, Kate Castleton gave Edwin his first opportunity in a starring role. Unfortunately, Castleton's colorful personal life always seemed to intrude on the professional, just when she was on the threshold of a successful stage career.

...plays an indescribable comedy part with an appearance of genuineness that is remarkably clever. He does not overdo the thing.[6]

"Capt. Mishler" followed "One of the Finest" and, even though the piece was no better, Williams and Foy "pleased the public to a large extent." During Williams's last week at the Alcazar, he presented "Kepler's Fortune," another German dialect farce-comedy. A teenager, Maude Adams, played the ingenue, with Edwin as her sweetheart. Williams wanted Foy to remain with the company, but he refused. At the same time, Frank Daniels was forming a company to do burlesque and asked Edwin to join him. Again, he turned down the offer.

Kate Castleton had not forgotten Edwin. When he let her know of his availability, she wired him a proposal to join the "Crazy Patch" company for the season, at seventy-five dollars a week, the most he had ever earned. Edwin was on the next train to Duluth, Minnesota, where Castleton's season would open.

Kate Castleton was described as having "the pearliest teeth, roguish eyes, buoyant bashfulness and wicked kicks," and to be an exponent of "naughty satire." Originally a music hall singer in England, Castleton began her U.S. career as a comedienne in E. E. Rice's 1882 "Surprise Party." She then obtained a leading role in "Pop," with headliner John A. Mackey. Castleton formed the "Crazy Patch" company in 1885 and had already toured successfully with it. She would have become a commanding actress but for her tempestuous marital problems.

Early in her career, Castleton had married Little Joe Elliott, a master forger, who had already spent various periods of time in jail. Elliott had formed a partnership with Adam Worth, called the Napoleon of Crime by the Pinkerton forces; together they negotiated a number of high-profile capers. When Elliott met Castleton, he pursued her intensely. After a few years of marriage, however, he left her for Worth and England. In early 1887, he returned, and they reunited. Because Elliott was jealous of her success and many male admirers, they quarreled, and she left him. Castleton claimed she "could suffer Elliott's abusive behavior no longer." At the time Edwin joined the company, divorce proceedings were in progress, threatening to derail the "Crazy Patch" tour.

Edwin was signed to reprise the role he had played before, William Smith, the lunatic pugilist. His increasingly exaggerated clowning, makeup, and costumes were gaining him a reputation as an "eccentric farceur." Castleton wanted to take advantage of this following, particularly in the cities they were planning to visit.

The "Crazy Patch" company played in thirty-one cities and towns in three months, beginning in the Midwest, traveling through the major Eastern cities, crossing into

Canada, then back into the Midwest again, this time playing one-night stands in small towns. Overall, the tour was quite successful. In Philadelphia, the *Ledger* not only complimented the company, but also singled out Edwin for his comic business:

> The Kate Castleton Company, in "Crazy Patch," opened to a good house and did very well for the week. They are always popular here. The howling lunatic (Foy) considerably brightened the presentation.[7]

When the company played in Pittsburgh, one of Edwin's routines was noted by the *New York Clipper:*

> Eddie Foy and Harry Battenberg indulged in a nose-pulling contest last week. They came out with honors even.[8]

It was one of those improvisational moments of stage business that initiated the episode. Positive audience reaction turned it into a skit in which fake noses were used and, with each pull, grew longer. By the time the company played in Memphis, Tennessee, during the Christmas holidays, audiences called for the skit to be presented and demanded encores.

Castleton's recent successes, however, were marred by an article in the *Clipper* commenting on her divorce proceedings against Elliott. The action was not only distracting her, but the company as well, because of its possible negative influence on continuing their tour. The court case was delayed; all relaxed for the moment.

During the early part of 1888, the company visited a few Southern cities and returned to playing one-night stands in Indiana and Illinois, on their way to Chicago. Castleton received continuous praise for her work — "Kate Castleton sang and danced to full houses" — as did the company.

In Chicago, at the Haymarket Theater, "Crazy Patch" played to "full houses" the entire week. "Kate Castleton was the star," announced the *Chicago Tribune,* "and Edwin

Foy delighted the audience." Edwin's gallery supporters cheered him constantly and begged for encores so often he had to come on stage to thank them and point out that "the show must go on."

Down the street from the Haymarket Theater was the imposing Chicago Opera House, recently leased by impresario David Henderson to introduce his fairy-tale extravaganzas, complete with casts of hundreds and lavish sets and costumes, "all imported from Europe," he claimed. The *New York Clipper* had just announced:

> The summer attraction of the Chicago Opera House will be a new burlesque, "The Crystal Slipper," which Manager Henderson assures the *Clipper* will be the most elaborate spectacle Chicago has ever seen. There will be nearly 150 people on the stage, about twenty of whom are already under contract.[9]

However, until he saw Edwin in "Crazy Patch," Henderson had not yet signed anyone for the leading comic role. When Henderson asked for an interview, Edwin was reluctant. He knew Henderson had a reputation as a "hard manager" who paid low wages. At almost the same moment, Kate Castleton's divorce case was nearing resolution. She had charged Elliott with cruelty and drinking; he claimed she had liaisons with other men. There was no doubt the company's tour was going to be affected.

Edwin accepted the engagement with Henderson, at a salary of sixty-five dollars a week, less than what he had been earning with Castleton. He had to report for rehearsals early in May because Henderson planned to open the show in June. Since all Henderson shows originated in Chicago and played long runs there, Edwin envisioned long periods at home, very different from his years of almost continuous touring.

But the "Crazy Patch" tour was not yet ended. After leaving Chicago, the company headed West, to play in small towns like Lincoln and Hastings, Nebraska, Pueblo and Leadville, Colorado. The trip seemed doomed, however, when Castleton announced the company would close its season April 14, in Kansas City. While in Pueblo, a snowstorm marooned them for almost a week. A railroad engineer's strike prevented them from making all of their planned stops in Kansas. Some company members left early for newly acquired engagements.

Since they were both playing in Denver at the same time, Edwin and Lola were able to spend a week together. When he told her of his new employment with Henderson in Chicago, she was pleased enough to suggest cutting back on her own career to be with him.

The "Crazy Patch" company ended their tour in Kansas City to "one of the largest houses of the season." On the final night, all the leading actors were asked by the audience to give speeches. When Edwin was called upon, he received a standing ovation.

Somewhat embarrassed by the reception, he thanked them for "giving me the opportunity to entertain you."

During the past three years, Edwin's career had encompassed a wide expanse of both experiential and geographical territory. He had performed for five different farce-comedy companies, with short runs in various stock companies, playing almost continuously. He had played in more than one hundred different cities, from Boston to San Francisco, Duluth to New Orleans. He had appeared in many roles, particularly as an eccentric comedian. Taking advantage of these opportunities, he had learned and developed new material that quickly contributed to his growing reputation as one of variety's premier clowns.

Performing in Henderson's extravaganzas would now offer new horizons and open a new era in Edwin's flourishing career.

Chapter 6

It was five minutes to nine in the morning when Edwin passed through the side gate of the stage entrance to the Chicago Opera House. Just inside the gate, he stopped, motionless and undecided, before entering the building. Glancing to the right and left, seemingly overwhelmed with the size and opulence of the majestic theater, he marshaled his courage and entered the stage door. Immediately, he was confronted by an old doorman.

"And what might you be wanting?"

"I'm Edwin Foy," he replied. Then added hesitantly, "the actor."

He wondered whether his name would actually appear on the actors' list. The doorman shuffled through the papers on his desk, seeking the *bona fides.*

"O.K., Mr. Foy, go right in. Down the corridor and to the left. You'll find the stage at the end of the hall. Good day to ye," he said cheerfully, giving Edwin a casual wave of acceptance.

Inside the auditorium, Edwin was met by a cacophony of sights and sounds. In various clusters, more than two hundred people were present, talking, dancing, and playing music. He saw three distinct groups on the stage: to the left, workers were assembling scenery; on the right, actors were blocking out their stage positions; at the rear of the vast stage, members of the ballet troupe were taking their morning exercises.

Among the seats of the auditorium, other groups were also busy. Surrounded by seamstresses, the stage manager examined

One of America's first great impresarios, David Henderson was credited with establishing Chicago as a major theater center, second only to New York. His employment of hundreds of performers, with lavish costumes and opulent sets for his extravaganzas, was unprecedented and attracted SRO houses across the country. (Harvard Theater Collection)

Impresario David Henderson was a man of many talents, outsized and splendiferous and effusive. Born in Edinburgh, Scotland, in 1853, he began his career as a newspaperman with the *Edinburgh Courant*. He came to America in 1872, at the age of eighteen, and worked for various newspapers, from New York to San Francisco, finally settling in Chicago. Henderson soon became interested in the theatrical business. Within a few years, he was managing a number of theaters and touring companies. With some other investors, he built the Chicago Opera House, the largest and most opulent in the city. In 1887, Henderson launched the first of a series of fairytale musical extravaganzas. Their success was immediate and overwhelming.

The men Henderson gathered for the creation of these elaborate productions all came from countries outside the U.S. Heading the group was Richard Barker, who had produced all the Gilbert and Sullivan operas at the Savoy Theater in London. Henderson recruited an Englishman, Fred Dangerfield, and a German, William Voegtlin, as scenic designers and artists. George Bowles, a Canadian, was Henderson's business manager. Master of the *corps de ballet* was Filiberto Jesus Maria Marchetti, a fiery Italian, whom Henderson obtained from Cairo, Egypt, at whose opera house Marchetti had staged "interpretive" oriental dances that proved the rage of Europe. Captain Alfred Thompson, a friend, investor, and writer, had proposed to Henderson a summer season of fantastical extravaganzas, because the immense Chicago Opera House couldn't make a profit by depending solely on its regular theatrical season. Thompson wrote Henderson's first production, "Aladdin, Jr.," in 1887. The piece played 392 performances, a record for any show ever presented in Chicago, and garnered a sizable profit for Henderson.

costumes. Orchestra members discussed musical cues. With large sheets of paper laid out on a table before them, impresario David Henderson and his colleagues seemed to be arguing about stage lighting, judging from their vigorous gestures and pointed gesticulations.

At first, Edwin wasn't sure what to do. Best to report directly to Henderson, he finally decided, let the man know of his arrival and readiness for work. Henderson briefly acknowledged him, introduced Edwin to the play's author, musical conductor, and choreographer, then directed him to join the assembled actors doing blocking exercises.

"You can pick up your script from the stage manager," he told Edwin. "Try to have it all memorized by the end of the week." Henderson's reputation was "all business." Indeed, his demeanor supported the contention.

David Henderson was a man of contradictions, making it problematic for theater colleagues and performers to respect and cooperate with him. To assert he was a dictator would not be far wrong, according to many who worked with him during his Chicago Opera House years. Henderson was imaginative and stubborn, courtly and arrogant, a dashing and flamboyant adventurer, a tremendous money-maker who despised money, generous yet tyrannical, suspicious yet an ostentatious braggart. He presented family entertainment, yet disliked children. Showman that he was, never hesitant to promote an offering, he was adamantly opposed to salacious entertainment. Henderson's splendid and immense productions were perceived by audiences as being well worth the price of a ticket. His expenditures on shows were so great yet were made so casually, hardly anyone comprehended or appreciated their magnificence.

Henderson was also a stage innovator. To improve stage lighting, he used electricity instead of gas — at a time when very few theaters were wired for electricity — enrapturing audiences with the effects achieved. He was the first to use the self-focusing arc lamp and strip lights to kill shadows. His vision created a blending of scenery and costumes; and he sent the plans to Europe to be manufactured, resulting in a stunningly total visual harmony on stage. He devised the display style of theatrical advertising, turning what had been mere statements of fact into ornamental eye-catchers, complete with zigzags, curlicues, and elaborated wording like "Matinee Today" and "Bring the Children." Henderson watched weather conditions carefully; when he observed clouds and the possibility of rain — which could portend reduced receipts — he would offer free drinks at the theater that evening to maintain the box office.

A Henderson extravaganza cost over $25,000 to produce, a colossal sum at the time. Leasing the Chicago Opera House cost him $35,000 a year. For each production, he employed from 150 to 200 performers, as well as dozens of stage hands. Yet his productions were so successful, they consistently cleared more than $200,000 each year. These successes only exacerbated his spendthrift

and arrogant behavior. According to Eastern critics, the fact that he accomplished this success in Chicago rather than New York, made it all the more amazing.

"The Crystal Slipper" or "Prince Prettiwitz and Little Cinderella" was set to open June 1888. It consisted of a prologue and four acts. There were more than 150 cast members, of which twenty-seven were specifically identified in the program. The libretto was written by Thompson and Harry B. Smith, later to become the most prolific librettist and lyricist in American theater history.

The prologue was represented as occurring next to the catacombs of "She" (of Rider Haggard fame), where "She" is enjoying an argument with the fairy Graciosa about the best school of fiction. Graciosa introduced the story of Cinderella, singing:

One of these dear old stories I'll revive,
The folly of your selfishness I'll prove,
And Cinderella will teach the power of love.

Act One takes place in Pretzelstadt, where a fair is in progress. Enter Baron Anthracite (R.E. Graham), his two cruel and ugly daughters, Angostura (Charles Warren) and Flordefuma (Topsy Venn), and his valet Yosemite (Foy), with Cinderella (Marguerite Fish) following. The Prince, Polydore Von Prettiwitz (May Yohe), arrives, since the fair is given in honor of his coming of age. He is infatuated with Cinderella but continually interrupted by a series of songs identifying the principle cast members and their roles. Cinderella and Yosemite sing, "A Cent for This and a Cent for That." The first act concludes with a maypole dance, performed by two prima ballerinas, Clara Qualitz and Madeline Morando, as well as a *corps de ballet.*

Act Two takes place in the Baron's kitchen, where the sisters' tyranny is demonstrated. Cinderella is consoled by her only friends, Yosemite and Thomas Cat (Eddie Rategan). The Baron intercedes upon an argument between Yosemite and the cat — a comic boxing bout — and engages Yosemite in an eccentric baseball game. Graciosa appears and declares Cinderella shall go to the ball. The fairy godmother furnishes a coach and six, a ballroom dress, and jewelry for Cinderella to make her debut in society. First, however, Cinderella is given a glimpse of fairyland, presented in a ballet of nursery rhymes, in which all the favorite children's characters perform.

Act Three, Scene One, starts in the palace yard, where all the prominent personages are welcomed by the Prince as they arrive. The Baron and his daughters arrive with Yosemite, closely followed by the Duchess of Cantelope, who is really Cinderella. Cinderella and Yosemite sing, "When the Wheel Goes Round."

Scene Two includes a ballet representing a combined banquet and ball. The dancers impersonate all the features of an elaborate menu. At the conclusion of the third act, the drop curtain represents Cinderella clothed in rags, rapidly descending the palace steps at the stroke of twelve.

Act Four, Scene One, opens back in the Baron's kitchen, where the Prince's ambassadors invite Cinderella to the palace to try on the crystal slipper. Scene Two features a march of beauties of all nations, a musical and visual spectacle of enormous proportions and impact. The slipper can be worn only by Cinderella, who weds the Prince. A final transformation scene represents the Temple of Time, with Graciosa bringing wedding gifts and a huge clock marking a cycle of hours, each hour embodied by the *corps de ballet*.

The *New York Clipper* correspondent, on hand for the opening, reported:

> The Chicago Opera House has held a great many people in the past, but the theater was never more besieged by as many persons since its existence as it was on the opening night (12) of "The Crystal Slipper." The house was packed to the doors, while outside a regular mob endeavored to enter at all hazards. From the time the curtain arose until the

end, the audience persistently applauded every scene. In the ballroom scene, however, the crowd arose, while shouts of "Bravo!" came from hundreds of throats. Repeated calls were made for Manager Henderson, but he failed to respond.[1]

Edwin sang two songs and appeared in two comic sketches, the second of which involved a dance identified as "eccentric," the first time the label had been attached to one of his particular sketches. For Edwin, this triumph capped a long and arduous road, one that had begun with his initial awkward attempts at Irish clog dancing in Chicago beer halls, only a few blocks from where the Opera House now stood.

However, what gained everyone's attention that week was a fire that almost totally destroyed the McVicker's Theater, where Edwin, as a "super," had begun his career. The fire took place early in the morning, so no one was injured. Starting in a basement saloon, the blaze quickly engulfed dressing rooms and stage paraphernalia, invading even the auditorium itself. The entire interior was destroyed and would have to be totally rebuilt. Investigation of the event suggested the building was a fire trap. According to the fire department, new ordinances had to be passed to protect future audiences. To this time, the McVicker's had been considered the most handsome and safest theater in the city. As a consequence of the fire, Henderson had the Chicago Opera House inspected, and some modifications were made. But theater fires remained a fear prevalent among all performers, heightened and intensified when one occurred so near.

"The success of 'The Crystal Slipper' continues unabated at the Chicago," declared the *Chicago Tribune*. "The house was jammed." Reaction to the entire production was so strong it seemed to overshadow individual performances; none of the leading performers received any mention during the first month of the extravaganza's run.

In contrast, Manager Henderson was

often mentioned as the premier theatrical magnate in Chicago. Thompson was reported to have signed a three-year contract to write more fairy-tale spectacles. Fred Eustis, the musical conductor and arranger, was signed for Henderson's next production. Henderson's brother, Wemyss, was sent to Europe to "secure dancers and unique specialty performers," as well as cast replacements.

A few weeks after opening, some of the actors had expressed unhappiness with Henderson's regimen and submitted their resignations. A few others claimed pre-existing fall engagements. In addition, Henderson discharged two of the leading women in the cast because of an argument. None of these changes, however, seemed to dampen audience enthusiasm for the production.

In the middle of July, Henderson introduced a "second edition" of the piece, which included new performers, songs, and skits. The show continued to do "immense business." Now, however, individual performers and specific skits were mentioned, particularly those of an English dwarf, Little Tich, whose comic impersonations and dances appeared to overshadow Edwin's individual efforts. A "third edition" was introduced in August. New scenery was added by Voegtlin, and an expanded ballet, in new costumes, performed new numbers.

"The Crystal Slipper" closed September 1 in Chicago, after an extremely successful run, ready to go on tour. Packed into a seven-car private train — four cars for the scenery, three for the performers — Henderson decided to make a long jump to Boston to take advantage of the opening of the theatrical season there. He hoped to play at the Boston Theater for six weeks, and his decision resulted in a very profitable engagement:

> The Crystal Slipper made an instantaneous hit by reason of its superlatively excellent stage mounting. Eddie Foy, Rob Graham, Tom Martin, merry Marguerite Fish and Topsy Venn all made indisputable successes. The old Boston Theater was crowded, and

Madeline Morando was a talented and attractive ballerina from Milan, Italy, employed by Henderson. She and Eddie performed in the same productions for six years. A year after Lola Sefton's death, they married.

> the big audience liked the show better than anything they've seen for many a night.[2]

This was the first time Edwin had been mentioned in a review of the show.

The six-week run in Boston was reported by the local press to have been "a heavy financial success." When a rumor appeared in the *Clipper* that "Edwin Foy has got the starring beetle in his bonnet," Henderson raised his salary to one hundred dollars a week. At the same time, Edwin was given "added opportunities for the exercise of his humorous talents." A new comic dance, this one in combination with the *corps de ballet*, pleased audiences. It also gave Edwin the opportunity to discover a young Italian beauty, Madeline Morando, one of the cast's prima ballerinas.

Madeline Morando was twenty years old, a native of Milan, Italy, born into a family of musical artists. By the time she joined Henderson, she was already a veteran ballerina, having been on tour for years, performing in Rome, Paris, Vienna, and Moscow. When Henderson hired Marchetti, the Italian ballet master persuaded Madeline and Clara Qualitz to join "The Crystal Slipper" company as featured dancers. Accompanying Madeline was her older sister, Clara, a former ballerina, now serving as her younger sister's chaperone.

An attraction arose between Edwin and Madeline, but Henderson's control over his performers and Clara's protection of Madeline inhibited the opportunity for flirtation.

"The Crystal Slipper" played to packed houses in Philadelphia and to capacity in Baltimore. While the company played in Philadelphia, many of Edwin's friends from Carncross came out to cheer him. In Washington, D.C., the show lost money because the theater was too small.

The next stop on their tour was to be New York, Henderson's first attempt to entertain the city's sophisticated theatergoers. He was apprehensive that audiences in that city might react negatively to his definition of spectacle. At the end of November, the company arrived at the Star Theater, hoping to play a month's run in one of the country's most demanding theater environments. To Henderson's relief, the critics of both the *New York Clipper* and *Dramatic Mirror* gave the production a positive, if qualified, review:

> The Crystal Slipper has drawn to the Star a series of large and pleased houses, who have viewed a spectacle of uncommon beauty, acted with considerable spirit. This endorsement of Capt. Thompson's extravaganza, however, stops with its pictorial excellences. The text is as weak as that of "Arabian Nights" and most *Clipper* readers know how weak that is. The costumes, scenes and effects are elaborate, almost to garishness; the chorus is of good size, and the ballet is better than average.[3]

The *Clipper* also singled out Edwin's work, one of the few times he had been mentioned since the show opened.

> Most of the humor is interjected by the comedians, Robert E. Graham and Edwin Foy.[4]

The combination of critical recognition and salary increase gave Edwin a satisfaction he had not felt since his performances in Dodge City and Leadville. This time, however, the pleasure he felt had more to do with his own discernment and artistic professionalism than with the inebriated uproar of unsophisticated audiences. In his autobiography, Edwin recalled his first flush of success making people laugh in New York.

> I could not but be happy in a success which was of a quality and completeness such as I hoped for and dreamed since boyhood; not only financial success, but the ecstatic laughter of grown-ups and little children.[5]

As the company made ready to return to the road on its way back to Chicago, Henderson replaced some cast members and had some of the "old" material dropped. This meant additional rehearsals to integrate new people, new songs and dances, much to the consternation of the company. Morning rehearsals to learn new material became mandatory, while matinee and evening performances continued with the current production. As the new business was learned, it was gradually incorporated into the show; not an easy task for performers, but a characteristic Henderson scheme to avoid the "downtime" of non-playing days. As part of these changes, Edwin added his impersonation of Henry Irving to the sketch with Baron Anthracite and Thomas The Cat.

"The Crystal Slipper" returned to the Chicago Opera House in early January 1889, for a three-week run — a supposed "break" for the company — before beginning a tour of Midwestern cities. The *Clipper* reported on the production's continued phenomenal success.

> The Crystal Slipper came back with all its glories and the result was a great success. Crowds packed the house every night and applauded as if they had never seen the piece before.[6]

Box office profitability had come so quickly, Henderson began planning for his next spectacle, another fairy tale extravaganza, "Bluebeard, Jr." Like "The Crystal Slipper," the production would open in June at the Chicago Opera House.

The "Crystal Slipper" spring tour included stops in Cincinnati, Kansas City, St. Louis, and Milwaukee, all of them to full houses. The Grand Opera House in Cincinnati "was not large enough to hold the people." Kansas City reported "the banner week of the season." The Grand in St. Louis drew "a full house at every performance." Edwin was mentioned as "catching round after round of applause."

After playing a week in Minneapolis, the company was in the process of moving to the St. Paul Opera House to begin rehearsals for their week's run at that theater. Two hours before the company was to arrive, however, the theater caught fire and burned to the ground. Luckily, no cast members nor stage equipment had yet reached the St. Paul Opera House.

For performers in the 1870s and 1880s, theater fires were relatively common. Most companies had experienced or knew of friends who had been involved in a theater fire. They were fully cognizant of the fire hazards they faced. The use of gas, arc lights, and highly flammable scenery and costumes created a tinderbox environment, one primed for a small spark to explode into a blazing inferno. One of the first things actors did when entering a new theater was to seek out the fire escapes. Their greatest fear was to confront a fire during a performance. Beyond his youthful experience of the Chicago fire, Edwin had seen theaters ablaze in both Leadville and San Francisco.

To close out the final weeks of the tour — and they were always the toughest weeks — the company played Detroit, Cleveland, Pittsburgh, and Washington, D.C. SROs and profitable box offices continued. The season was to end April 29; but at the last minute, Henderson informed the company he had booked them into Louisville and St. Louis, thus delaying the close of their season for another two weeks. Again, Henderson alienated many cast members by this decision. For those who had already negotiated summer engagements, it meant a possible loss of jobs. For those who remained with the Henderson contingent, it meant no time off before rehearsals began for his next show.

Edwin, however, was pleased to hear from Henderson that he was wanted for the next production, with a concomitant increase in salary to $150 a week. He was further pleased to hear that Madeline Morando was also signed for next season.

"Bluebeard, Jr." or "Fatima and the Fairy" opened June 11, 1889, to an SRO audience at the Chicago Opera House. The evening was so hot and humid, house management allowed all doors in the stuffy and sweltering theater to stand open to offer some respite. Hundreds of people stood outside the doors simply to listen and applaud the music. In the next day's edition, the *Chicago Tribune* enthusiastically exclaimed:

> Manager Henderson's latest spectacular production is all that was expected of it, and business should be in excess of The Crystal Slipper. The burlesque is enlivened by all sorts of good entertainment. The principals, Lilly Post, Kate Uart, Ada Deaves, Edwin Foy, Harry Peakes and Ignacio Martinelli made a good show by themselves. The ballet was well-drilled and effective, and the costumes are all pleasing and artistic. Its success is assured.[7]

The *Tribune* went on to report that the company contained over two hundred people, including a ballet troupe of sixty, headed by Mlle. Clara Qualitz and Mlle. Madeline Morando. Henderson stalwart, Richard Barker, again directed the production; Voegtlin and Hoyt designed and painted the scenery. Costumes were by Dazian, all manufactured in Europe. Fred Eustis composed and arranged the entire musical score; and the ballets were choreographed by Marchetti's assistant, Mamert Bibeyran, of Milan. The production consisted of a prologue, four acts, and a grand transformation scene, which served as epilogue.

B. R. Graham was Bluebeard, the villain. Kate Uart played Zara, the Genius of Truelove, and Lily Post played Selim, a Persian officer. Post and her brother officers were all women playing men's roles, a common practice for these types of productions in Europe but unique to the American stage. Edith Murilla was Fatima, Bluebeard's eighth wife. Critics considered her costume so revealing, it had to be modified almost immediately after opening night. Edwin had the role of O'Mahdi Benzini, Fatima's father. As comic lead, his role was poetically described in the program:

> His fondness for his daughter, though is trivial, Compared to his penchant for tastes convivial.

Also in the cast, in a bit part, was an actor new to the popular stage, William Collier.

The play begins with a brief prologue in the Gloomy Grotto of the King of Chestnuts, staged as a satire on the traditions of the legitimate stage, with some similarities to a typical minstrel opening. The fairy Zara orders a modern performance of Bluebeard.

The marketplace of Constantinopolis opens Act One, where a party of picnickers are entertaining Fatima. Enter Benzini, who tells his daughter he has promised her to Bluebeard, for considerable money, although she loves Selim, captain of the police.

Edwin sang, "Drop a Nickel in the Slot," proclaiming his love of money. Along with the song, he performed a short "eccentric" dance that included an across-the-stage shuffle.

Bluebeard arrives in his state barge and claims Fatima as his bride. She accepts him, but only to save her father from financial ruin.

Act Two takes place in Selim's quarters in the barracks. He is being consoled by his company for the loss of his sweetheart. Benzini enters, full of resentment because Bluebeard has not yet paid him for Fatima. Together, Benzini and Selim plan to rescue her. Benzini succumbs to his thirst and becomes drunk. His most memorable line comes when he is challenged: "You don't mean to tell me that your memory is absolutely perfect?" Benzini answers: "Well, I can honestly say that I cannot remember a single thing I have ever forgotten."

After a brief sketch playing a comic drunk, Benzini falls asleep and dreams of a grotto of fantasy, danced by a ballet costumed as birds and insects. Morando danced the role of the Firefly.

Scene One of Act Three opens in the streets of Constantinopolis, where plans to rescue Fatima are being made. Benzini appears, still angry about Bluebeard's nonpayment for Fatima, and prays for something that might place Bluebeard in his power. When Bluebeard and the bridal train appear, Benzini catches the villain kissing a village maiden. Benzini threatens to reveal the tawdry liaison, so Bluebeard pays him the money and also proclaims Benzini Pooh-Bah of Bluebeard's private household.

Scene Two takes place in Bluebeard's palace, where the wedding pageant is taking place. In the pageant, Benzini sings "When Johnny Gets His Gun" (an interpolation of "When Johnny Comes Marching Home"). The act ends with the entire ballet company dancing "The Light of Asia."

Act Four opens in a chamber of Bluebeard's palace. Benzini is seen surrounded by harem slaves. "A veritable pig in the clover," as stated in the program, Edwin sang his hit song, "He's on the Police Force Now," with pointed allusion to the various extra benefits one may enjoy while guarding a harem.

Bluebeard is angry about being superseded in his own domain. Fatima is given the keys to the house but is warned not to open a secret closet. Curiosity overcomes discretion, and Fatima opens the closet. To her horror, she finds the heads of Bluebeard's seven dead wives. Bluebeard reappears and condemns Fatima to death. While the execution is being planned, Captain Selim attacks Bluebeard's castle, captures and punishes Bluebeard, and wins the love of Fatima. An elaborate finale, the "Grand Transformation" scene, with the entire cast of 200 on stage, exhibits humanity's progress from darkness into light and beauty.

Included in the cast were sixteen children who performed in the fantasy ballet. They were added by Henderson to attract families to the production.

While the program identified him as "Edwin Foy," newspapers and critics now began referring to Foy as "Eddie," using the familiar diminutive affectionately, in recognition of his emergence as a leading comedian. While everyone called him Eddie from this point on, it would be another five years before the diminutive was used in a theater program.

The production's run in Chicago was excellent, even more profitable than "The Crystal Slipper." Each month a revised edition was presented and, according to the *Clipper*, constantly improved the show with the introduction of songs, dances, and sketches.

> Bluebeard, Jr. continues to fill the house at every performance. The performance is much more bright and spirited than it was at first, and highly entertaining specialties are introduced. There was new march music and several new ballets and some new comedy situations have been evolved.[8]

One new comedy situation was a children's feature, which included "forty or more

At 34, Eddie had become a dapper dresser, abetted by his selection as the star comedian in David Henderson's fairy-tale extravaganzas at the Chicago Opera House. Eddie's drawing power with Chicago audiences continued throughout his entire career. (Museum of the City of New York)

little ones having been trained to a ballet entitled 'The Children's Heroes.'" It also featured Eddie in a comic sketch of "The Old Woman Who Lived in a Shoe," with Eddie playing The Old Woman. The act proved so amusing, it had to be encored several times (for each show). Coincidentally, Henderson publicly announced he had signed Eddie to a five-year contract.

Now typical of Henderson's productions, changes in cast were as frequent as changes in the production itself. A number of the leading players were either dropped or had to honor other engagements for the forthcoming season. One of them, William Collier, left to be replaced by another newcomer to the stage, Lee Harrison. With all these substitutions, Eddie was fast becoming the senior member of the cast, as well as a role model.

On August 27, the 100th performance of "Bluebeard, Jr." was given. Along with flower tributes and speeches, an elaborate souvenir program, filled with photographs of the leading actors, prima ballerinas, and grand scenes, was distributed to the entire audience. While this celebration was taking place, Henderson was in Milwaukee preparing for the show's first stop on tour. The city was plastered with playbills two weeks in advance of "Bluebeard's" opening night. His efforts paid off handsomely, the *Clipper* reporting:

> Bluebeard, Jr. was presented to immense audiences at the Grand. It was voted the most beautiful spectacular production ever witnessed here. The topical songs of Eddie Foy, Arthur Dunn and Esther Williams were enthusiastically encored.[9]

Fresh from its triumph in Milwaukee, the company traveled to Cincinnati and Philadelphia, stops along the way to a run in New York. Because of the production's size, only theaters with large stages and substantial seating could accommodate the show in each city, all of which required careful booking.

Large theaters were no deterrent; splendid weeks and crowded houses continued. But when the company was ready to move into the Amphion Theater in Brooklyn, they were required to lay over a week because the show currently playing was doing so well that the theater manager had extended its stay. The action threatened to wipe out Henderson's financial reserves. He was heard to have threatened the theater manager and went to court to attempt getting the current play thrown out of the theater. Although claiming the manager's decision had cost him thousands of dollars, which it undoubtedly had, he failed in his legal struggle. Hundreds of new posters had to be printed and rebilled to reflect the changes in schedule. Since performers were not paid when they weren't working — even in the middle of a tour — they had to use their own money for room and board while they waited.

Eddie had enjoyed a comfortable summer at home in Chicago with Lola. Their off-days had been spent on picnics or visits with his mother or sisters. When he began "Bluebeard's" road tour in September, Lola obtained a job with C. W. Hassett's "Braving the World" Company for a tour of Iowa theaters. Their both going on the road again allowed Eddie the luxury of paying less attention to family and more attention to cast members, particularly Madeline Morando.

When the "Bluebeard" Company opened in Brooklyn, the cast was ecstatic about returning to work; audiences seemed to reflect their enthusiasm. The *New York Herald* stated:

> Bluebeard did the largest business of the season. The house was packed from pit to dome at every performance.[10]

Manager Henderson was particularly pleased that critics in New York liked his new production, not only because of its beauty and scenic effects, but also its performers. Eddie was singled out for his delineation of "a drunken man awakening from a stupor with all the horrors of the delirium tremens," called by the *New York Post* critic, "an exceptionally fine piece of acting."

Confident that he could increase his profit and make up the week's layoff, Henderson raised ticket prices for "Bluebeard, Jr." Again, his evaluation of the situation was astute. Advanced prices in Baltimore, Cleveland, and Washington, D.C., seemed only to make the show even more attractive. "Bluebeard had SRO," came the report from Washington, D.C. In Cleveland, the production "had large houses." When "Bluebeard" opened at the Tremont Theater in Boston for a four-week holiday run, the *Globe* remarked about Henderson's advertising acumen:

> The piece has been picturesquely billed and very decently advertised. These are cardinal essentials in the monetary success of a theatrical performance, and for that reason,

we apprehend a good measure of success from this booking.[11]

The *Globe* was correct in its assessment. Even with advanced prices, "Bluebeard" was "the rage" for its entire run, consistently "attracting the big stomachs and bald tops into the front rows of the Tremont." Henderson was so elated by the apparent success of his advanced-price decision, he hastily booked the show back into New York in the middle of January, at Niblo's Garden. Critics told Henderson he was overly optimistic to return to New York only a month after he had played in the city and, with regard to his advanced-price philosophy, he "was daft."

Again, they were mistaken. "Bluebeard" played to full houses every performance. In addition, Eddie and Madeline were highlighted in the review.

> Eddie Foy caught the house in fine style, and was the recipient of honest encores.... Madeline Morando also requires special mention for her terpsichorean endeavors.[12]

While Eddie and Madeline were savoring the praise of their work, Lola and her fellow performers were experiencing problems in Iowa. The "Braving the World" company was attracting poor attendance and Manager Hassett was unable to pay salaries. Taking direct action, members of the company attached a lien to the box office in order to secure enough money to pay their board. When Hassett discovered what had happened, he went on stage before the performance, announced to the audience the show would not go on, and instructed them to get their money back at the box office. The company objected and got a policeman to arrest Hassett. After some delay, the show went on without him. When the company got to Des Moines, the local manager had to advance sufficient money to pay the performers' train fares. In the meantime, Hassett returned to Chicago to organize another company. The company continued on the road because they still had engagements to honor.

Even though the "Bluebeard" engagement in New York had been a profitable undertaking, Henderson ran afoul of the Gerry Society, a.k.a. the Society for the Prevention of Cruelty to Children. Led by evangelical socialite Elbridge T. Gerry, this private organization had been given the power to enforce laws concerning the appearance of children under sixteen on stage. Gerry demanded that Henderson remove the children from "Bluebeard" because they were underage and were thus being exploited, "led into sin," he claimed. Henderson was forced to drop the children from the show, which meant Eddie's "Old Woman in the Shoe" sketch had to be excised, as well. Some years later, Eddie would encounter Gerry's threats again.

Henderson vigorously appealed to the mayor to let the children appear, since they were considered by the press "one of the most attractive features for the little people and lady patrons of the show." But municipal counsel advised the mayor he had no power to grant permission, as the entertainment could not possibly be classified under the law as a concert. The *Dramatic Mirror* reported on the results of this latest confrontation between company managers and the Gerry Society:

> The S.P.C.C., therefore, wins a complete triumph in this case, as it has in many another similar one.[13]

Eddie's old friend, William "Billy" Jerome, now a recognized song writer, had written "He's on the Police Force Now," which Eddie sang so successfully in "Bluebeard." Their renewal of friendship prompted Eddie to ask Jerome to write other songs, exclusively for him. Jerome quickly came up with a parody on "Annie Rooney," which Eddie included in his act.

Jerome seemed to understand Eddie's comedic appeal so well, he could craft songs that became identified with the comedian's performances. At the time, a new song gained immediate popularity when performed by a particular entertainer. When the song in turn achieved wider success, it reflected positively on the performer. Stage stars like Marie Cahill, Annie Russell, and Fay Templeton gained a good deal of popularity by becoming identified with songs tailored to their delivery. For Eddie, it contributed to his growing reputation to have his name (and picture) appear on music sheet covers sold for home use.

The spring of 1890 tour continued through Detroit, St. Louis, and Kansas City, with a two-week return to Chicago to fill an empty slot in the Opera House's schedule. Henderson was now paying scant attention to "Bluebeard," since he had begun planning for his next summer's extravaganza. This time, however, it would surely be more difficult, because professionals like Barker and Eustis were committed to other projects. After exploring a number of different fairytale librettos, Henderson decided to revive "The Crystal Slipper," at least for the summer, hopefully replacing it in the fall with a rendition of "Babes in the Woods." In response to his announcement, critics suggested that Henderson was losing his impresario's touch, noting that extravagant shows were not normally repeated so quickly.

When Henderson announced his intentions to "Bluebeard's" cast and told them he intended to play the current attraction until the middle of May, three weeks longer than originally planned, a cast member asked, "And when do rehearsals for 'Slipper' begin?"

"The following week," Henderson responded. "We open at the Opera House June 19."

Again, it meant no vacation time between productions. Cast members already signed to continue with Henderson were unhappy with the new arrangements, and loyalty to the production deteriorated rapidly. Henderson's reaction to their reluctance was to threaten them with unemployment. Cast members not signed were glad they had made other plans.

When Eddie returned to Chicago, he found Lola at home. With no one to book their advance engagements, the company with whom she was performing had been unable to sustain their tour. After a month of playing small towns in Michigan, the company had disbanded. Lola was seriously considering retirement.

Eddie also discovered that Ben Collins, his old friend and early partner, had just died while performing in Boston. Collins' body was being returned to Chicago for burial. Eddie knew that Ben's mother, Mrs. Dorand, was poor, having lived on the money her son sent home. Within a week, Eddie organized a benefit for her.

The benefit took place at the Columbia Theater, to a crowded house of performers, friends, and Collins admirers. Along with Eddie, Henry E. Dixey, Ross and Fenton, John T. Kelly, and John D. Gilbert performed. Manager Al Hayman, of the Columbia, donated the use of his theater and assisted in collecting donations from other theater managers who had known Collins. More than one thousand dollars was collected, enough to pay for the funeral and burial. Later, Mrs. Dorand especially thanked Eddie for "the kindness extended" to her and her son.

Anxiety and anger continued to preoccupy the extravaganza troupe. To calm the company, Henderson offered them a week off with full salary, before rehearsals for the new summer show would begin. Eddie and Lola took this opportunity to vacation in Mt. Clemens, Michigan, a resort that had become very popular among theatrical people.

The revised edition of "The Crystal Slipper" opened at the Chicago Opera House on June 19, to an SRO house. The Chicago correspondent of the *New York Clipper* wrote:

> The Crystal Slipper in costumes is far more gorgeous than the old, with a new libretto that far excels the old, opened to a packed house, and has had only standing room since. Eddie Foy, Ida Mulle, Louise

Montegue, Babette Rodney, Fanny Duball, Topsy Venn, Marie Williams, John Gilbert and all the old favorites were received with applause, and the piece went with all the old time snap and vigor. Clara Qualitz and Madeline Morando led the ballet and give some clever Japanese character dances.[14]

Eddie continued his old part as Yosemite, but with some new songs and comedic sketches. He sang "I Was Dreaming, That Was All" and "Second Thoughts" and performed a comic dance with Topsy Venn. When, in the production's "second edition," a children's ballet was added, Eddie danced with them. Madeline Morando had taught the children; she had to have been impressed by the way Eddie embraced, encouraged, and assisted them in their acting needs. Like last year's children's ballet in "Bluebeard," the dance was well received by theatergoers.

As had now become common, Henderson tinkered with his cast, giving notice to those who didn't meet his expectations, telling others they would be terminated at the end of the summer. Since most performers did not have long-term contracts, they knew they were subject to quick dismissal if Henderson so desired. When the *Clipper* announced that Henderson was in New York "engaging novelties to strengthen the production when it became necessary to drop out some of the present ones," some performers decided to obtain new engagements before Henderson made any further cast changes. This served to disrupt the continuity of the production and affected performance. The *Chicago Tribune* noted the cast's discontent and questioned why Henderson, with another hit in hand, should announce changes in the cast. Backstage conflicts arose; one in particular, involving Eddie, reached the newspapers.

According to the local press, John D. Gilbert threatened to leave the company because of "punishment" he was supposedly receiving from Eddie. In one sketch, when

Lola Sefton (Conlick) was in fact Edwin's paramour for seven years, though they claimed to be husband and wife. Lola retired from acting and cared for their home in Chicago until her death in 1894, shortly after giving birth to Catherine, Edwin's first child.

Gilbert recited some funny poetry, Eddie was to strike him with an ax in his well-padded stomach. While the business was very funny and "captured the house," Gilbert complained Foy was attempting to upstage him. Eddie agreed to omit the ax-wielding portion of the sketch, but Henderson wanted it continued because of the audience's positive response. Angry, Gilbert abruptly resigned from the cast, causing the sketch to be temporarily discontinued. Eddie was perturbed because Gilbert, an excellent actor, had been forced to leave the company due to Henderson's priorities.

The ballerina team of Qualitz and Morando were now getting press reviews almost every week. To encourage the press coverage, Henderson ordered them to develop new material every few weeks, thus retaining the critics' attention. In late July, they created a new ballet that captured the eye of the *Clipper* correspondent:

Clara Qualitz and Madeline Morando appeared in a Calabrian dance, entitled "The Cicciara." It is something entirely new and has never been danced in America or in any cities outside of Calabria, except Paris and London.[15]

However, Henderson's pressure on Qualitz had apparently upset her. She handed in her resignation, effective in two weeks. Until she quit the company, no one had been aware of her dissatisfaction with Henderson, nor that she was seeking another engagement. A week after she had left "The Crystal Slipper," Qualitz was working for P.T. Barnum. This left Madeline as the sole prima ballerina in the cast, bearing the entire responsibility for the children's ballet as well.

In spite of the increasing hostility between Henderson and his cast, "The Crystal Slipper" played its 450th performance at the end of July. As if to bolster his own confidence, Henderson released a statement proclaiming the production's continued and future success:

Louise Montegue and Ida Mulle have signed contracts for the traveling season of 1890-91 and Eddie Foy extended his contract to 1893. The ballet of children and dolls has proved one of the best features of the piece. At the close of the Chicago season, the Crystal Slipper will be presented for one week at St. Louis, whence it will journey at once to San Francisco. The company will number ninety-eight persons and occupy a special train of seven cars, aside from four baggage cars.[16]

All thoughts Henderson had once entertained about producing "Babes in the Wood" had now been set aside, as "Crystal Slipper" continued a box-office winner. The production's last week in Chicago was "the largest the Crystal Slipper has ever enjoyed." In its latest edition — the one designed for the

road — new songs and dances were introduced, along with a comic sketch by Eddie and a Hungarian dance by Madeline. Eddie's sketch was a shadow pantomime and the mechanical effects were said to be outstanding.

In addition to his continuing relationship with Lola in Chicago and his interest in Madeline while they toured together, Eddie indulged in liaisons with other women of the Crystal Slipper cast. Unfortunately, one episode reached the local newspapers.

Jenny Eddy evidently had a strong fondness for Eddie. During a restaurant interlude one evening, shortly before the company was to begin their tour, she and Eddie argued. Suicidally distraught, Jenny suddenly swallowed an entire bottle of morphine. A doctor was called immediately, and Jenny was rushed to the hospital for treatment. Luckily, she recovered; however, she was unable to join the company on tour. No information is available regarding Eddie's reaction to the incident, nor that of any other party.

Packing the Grand Opera House, the show's success continued in St. Louis. It "was pronounced the most magnificent spectacular production ever seen in this city." The long jump to San Francisco gave Eddie the opportunity to catch up with Jim Corbett. Since turning professional, Corbett, with his unique style of boxing, had already won a number of heavyweight matches and was now training for another. He was now talking of seriously challenging John L. Sullivan for the heavyweight championship of the world.

The three-week engagement in San Francisco was so popular, standing-room-only patrons were turned away, even though prices had been advanced. Local newspapers reported daily on the production's "phenomenal success."

Nonetheless, backstage tensions remained high, as Henderson constantly ordered new songs and dances and demonstrated his iron control by firing two performers for "unprofessional behavior." About this time, Eddie asked Henderson for a meeting to discuss a salary increase. Henderson refused to discuss the issue with him, delaying any meeting until they returned to Chicago to play a Christmas season engagement.

On their way back East, the "Crystal Slipper" company played in Denver's Tabor Opera House "to its capacity," with a brief side trip to Leadville. The town had begun to decline as silver mines "played out." In three years, Leadville would become a ghost town. Stops also included Kansas City, St. Louis, Detroit, and Milwaukee. Even with advanced prices at these theaters, they played to packed houses.

While in Milwaukee, Eddie was reported to have come down with a severe cold and was unable to perform. Actually, he was protesting Henderson's denial to meet with him regarding a salary increase. In response, Henderson demanded that Eddie show up on stage when the company opened in Chicago for their holiday run. As reported by the *Chicago Tribune:*

> Eddie Foy made his reappearance, but is far from recovered, and will be obliged to retire again shortly.[17]

"A severe hoarseness" was declared by Henderson to have kept Eddie off the Chicago stage for a week, but it was the dispute with the manager that precipitated the action. Using his "draw" in Chicago as leverage — some gallery audiences stomped their feet in unison while yelling for Eddie's appearance — Eddie persuaded Henderson to raise his salary to $250 a week, making him the highest paid performer in the company. Miraculously, Eddie was back performing the second week of the show's run, apparently fully recovered.

At the close of "The Crystal Slipper's" engagement in Chicago, Henderson startled everyone by announcing that:

> Next summer, the management of the Chicago Opera House will produce a new extravaganza according to usual custom.[18]

Critics wondered whether Henderson, with all his successes, could afford another show. Where was he getting the money to pay for the elaborate trappings of his productions? Wasn't he aware of increasing competition from comic opera and vaudeville, which delivered full houses at much lower costs? Would any performer willingly play for a man who so easily alienated his cast?

Yet Henderson had sufficient funds from the profits of the previous two seasons and showed no reluctance to make his next production even more opulent. What other managers seemed to fear most about Henderson was that his successes had been gained by breaking all the usual rules. That he consistently charged advanced prices and advertised in unorthodox ways also bothered them. To guarantee future available venues in Pittsburgh, Boston, Philadelphia, and San Francisco, Henderson leased theaters in those cities, probably one of the first showmen to extend control in this manner. While these management decisions suggested Henderson was going to be in business a long time, and his star comedian was himself well rewarded, Eddie was not entirely satisfied with Henderson's treatment of performers. It was obvious to Eddie that, unless they felt satisfied and secure, the company would soon collapse. For many cast members without long-term contracts, Henderson's seemingly erratic activities only contributed to their apprehension.

The company returned to the road again in January 1891. Their first stop was the Duquesne, in Pittsburgh, one of Henderson's recently leased theaters. Thanks to heavy advertising, SRO signs were already out at 7:30 P.M. every evening. Clara Qualitz had just returned to the cast; apparently, circus life was not as rewarding as stage spectacle.

The "Crystal Slipper" cast then jumped to the Star Theater in Boston for a two-week engagement. It might have been a relatively pleasant run except for another fire scare, this one immediate. Early in the morning, at the Camden Hotel, where the company was staying, employees discovered a fire in the kitchen. The blaze quickly spread to the stairwell and reception area. Hotel staff alerted the guests, but easy egress was denied because of fire on the stairs. Firemen arrived in good time and were able to control the flames. Using their new scaling ladders for the first time, firemen rescued many guests, including members of the "Crystal Slipper" cast, from upper floors. Luckily, there was no loss of life.

The company began to believe their tour was jinxed. When theater people get such notions, irrational or not, their performance is often affected. It is not a feeling or behavior that audiences readily notice, but heightened sensitivity to quirky incidents is amplified among the performers themselves.

From Boston, the company traveled to Cincinnati, Pittsburgh, and Philadelphia, an unusual route; but Henderson was using his recently leased theaters to enhance and extend the tour. They arrived in Philadelphia at the beginning of Lent, a season when theater patronage was usually low. According to the *Ledger,* the "Crystal Slipper" was "one of the several attractions that suffered the most."

Meanwhile, the trials between Eddie and Henderson continued. While in Washington, D.C., a disagreement about Eddie's performing a new sketch precipitated a relapse of "throat trouble." After missing the entire week's engagement, Eddie returned to the company when the proposed sketch was dropped. Eddie's argument with management agitated the company, and other minor grievances surfaced. When they returned to Chicago, Clara Qualitz again retired from the company because of a quarrel with Henderson.

On their way from Chicago to Minneapolis by private train, a number of the cast became ill. They immediately claimed to have been poisoned. Investigation revealed that a new buffet car had been added to the train, and a coffee urn in this car had caused the trauma. The train was stopped and a doctor called to minister to those afflicted. He stayed with his patients until they reached Minneapolis, where they were transferred to a hospital. Two of the cast members were so ill, they never returned to the company. As viewed by the cast, yet another frightening twist of fate.

The cast had anticipated the end of their tour in Minneapolis and St. Paul. Henderson, however, unnerved them again by announcing an extension of their route for another two weeks, playing small town one-night stands in Wisconsin and Iowa. Representing the company, Eddie challenged the decision and made it clear to Henderson that the cast had had enough disruption. To emphasize his indignation, Eddie left the company and returned to Chicago. An irascible Henderson fined Eddie one week's salary for "being in an unfit condition" to play in Minneapolis. In addition, he stated he would prevent Eddie from playing with any other company because of his long-term contract. Joseph Doner took Eddie's place.

While the company waited on the depot platform in Superior, Wisconsin, Doner was attacked by a number of drunken gamblers, who attempted to stab him. In defense, Doner pulled out a revolver, but one of the men slashed his face and hand before they ran away. Doner was treated by a doctor and continued with the company. A week later, the gamblers were caught and brought to trial. They admitted being drunk and angry because Eddie Foy had not appeared in the show that evening.

While Eddie was known to "fly off the handle" occasionally, he rarely revealed that behavior in front of cast members or in the theater. His confrontations with Henderson, however, frequently reached shouting stage. As Henderson was a stubborn man, the two quickly reached an impasse. Eddie refused to return to the company. Henderson refused to fire him and threatened to withhold his salary for as long as Eddie was absent from the theater. Henderson's new summer extravaganza, "Sinbad," was to begin rehearsals the middle of May. Eddie waited at home for a note from Henderson. Henderson waited for Eddie to apologize and return.

Chapter 7

ALI BABA: *He's quite a prominent politician, is he not?*
CASSIM: *Oh, no, he's a statesman.*
ALI BABA: *Well, what's the difference?*
CASSIM: *A statesman is one who is a politician because*
              he has money. A politician is one who has
              money because he is in politics.

(Eddie Foy as Cassim in "Ali Baba")

Henderson's new extravaganza, "Sinbad," or "The Maid of Balsora," opened June 11, 1891. Although his name appeared in the program, Eddie was missing from the cast.

Having been persuaded by Henderson to return to Chicago, Richard Barker once more directed the entire production. Harry B. Smith wrote the libretto in his now all-too-familiar pattern. Dangerfield and Voegtlin designed and painted the scenery in the same rococo style they had employed for previous productions. Dazian continued as supervisor of costuming. Ballet master Marchetti was again on hand for choreography. Along with Marchetti, prima ballerina Clara Qualitz returned from Italy to team with Madeline Morando once more. Obviously attempting to replace Eddie, Henderson hired Louis Harrison to play the principal comic role.

Now having been given responsibility for advertising, business manager George Bowles planted articles in local newspapers with the purpose of building patrons' anticipation for the opening of Henderson's new fairy-tale extravaganza:

Those who have followed the rehearsals say that it will far outshine any of its successful predecessors, not only in brilliancy and catchiness of the libretto, but in the wealth and magnificence of the scenery and costumes, and also in the dramatic action, spectacles and ballet effects.[1]

"Sinbad's" opening was greeted by a crowded house; even SRO patrons had difficulty seeing the stage. The *New York Clipper* heartily applauded the production's mechanics:

> Manager Henderson's spectacle is, as it was promised it should be, the handsomest yet produced on the stage of the Chicago Opera House. The scenery and mechanical effects upon which the play largely depends are superb.[2]

However, the *Clipper* cautioned:

> There is only one trouble with the production. The company is weak in spots and even the talented members in it have not enough to do. These are defects which the management seems to be even more acute than the public is in discerning.[3]

Less than a week after the production's opening, Henderson contacted Eddie to discuss their differences. While neither apologized, they did agree that Eddie would return to the cast, with an increase in salary. Their mutual distaste remaining, this was strictly a business arrangement. Aware of Henderson's increasingly obsessional penchant for production and cast changes, Eddie and other company members knew that disagreeable issues would undoubtedly arise in the future.

Eddie appeared on stage for the first time at the beginning of "Sinbad's" third week, coinciding with the introduction of the show's "second edition." Immediately upon taking the stage, Eddie was given a standing ovation, and he was compelled to make a short speech before the audience allowed the show to continue. The *Chicago Tribune* gleefully acknowledged both Eddie's return and the show's improvement:

> Sinbad couldn't do better if it tried. This week, several changes will be inaugurated. The piece has been considerably altered, and the changes made are all for the better. The second edition of Sinbad was given 25, and was additionally marked by the reappearance of Eddie Foy.[4]

"Sinbad" consists of four acts and a grand finale, identified in the program as "The Morning of Life." The first act opens on the port of Balsora at daybreak. Cupid (Fanny Ward) appears, and by way of prologue, explains to the audience the secret of the plot. Ninetta (Ida Mulle), the only daughter of ruined merchant Nicolo, is betrothed to Sinbad (Louise Eissing), a factory apprentice. However, Nicolo has promised his daughter to Snarleyow (Harry Norman), captain of the smugglers, for financial considerations. A foreign nobleman, Count Spaghetti (Herbert Gresham) arrives in search of a wife and is himself raffled off, won by an old school mistress (Fanny Duball). To escape her, the Count enlists one of the smugglers. Snarleyow and his men arrive and carry off Ninetta. To protect her, Sinbad and his apprentice comrades sign on the fleeing ship as recruits.

Act Two takes place at sea, aboard the smugglers' ship. Sinbad and the apprentices lead a conspiracy to scuttle the ship. One of the apprentices is Fresco (Eddie Foy). Nicolo, also aboard, is seeking revenge on Snarleyow because he refused to pay Nicolo the price of his daughter's hand. A mutiny takes place; aided by a timely hurricane, the ship sinks. A tableau at the end of the act depicts everyone thrown into the sea as the vessel goes down.

Act Three opens on an island full of pigmy cannibals. All the characters have survived, to land on the island, under Cupid's protection. Enter Fresco, who is actually King of the Cannibals and now controls the lives of all the people from the sunken ship. Fresco appoints the Old Man of the Sea (Arthur Dunn) to guard his Valley of Diamonds. From Cupid, Sinbad learns the secret of the Valley of Diamonds. He drugs the Old Man, obtains the magic key, and rescues Ninetta. Fresco calls his cannibals together and the blood-thirsty crew all head for the valley.

Scene Two is located in a jungle, with Cupid guarding Sinbad and Ninetta as they flee the others. Scene Three displays a tableau of the Valley of Diamonds.

A ballet, "A White Carnival," concludes Act Three. Dancers represent snowbirds, snowflakes, icicles, sleigh riders, and skaters. During the finale of the ballet, Sinbad escapes on a giant roc, with the treasure of the diamond valley in hand and his pursuers baffled.

Act Four opens in Sinbad's palace. He and Ninetta are about to be married, when Snarleyow and his crew arrive and prevent the nuptials by producing the contract the smuggler had made with Nicolo for his daughter's hand. At the beginning of Scene Two, Snarleyow carries off Ninetta again, along the way eagerly seeking a justice of the peace. Sinbad comes to the rescue. A duel ensues; Sinbad defeats Snarleyow, and Cupid awards Ninetta to Sinbad.

Featuring the entire company and ballet on stage, more than 150 performers in all, the third and final scene of Act Four, called "The Morning of Life," provides a glimpse of the lovers' future happiness.

Eddie sang one song in Act One, "Mary and John." In the second act, he had the show's hit song, "He Never Came Back," after a sketch impersonating a clog-dancing statue. In the third, Eddie performed a comic duet with Fanny Duball (the old school mistress) and burlesqued caricatures of various popular forms of entertainment. As King of the Cannibals, Eddie wore a brightly colored, garish costume, replete with feathers and bells, which constantly got in the way of people trying to talk to him.

One of the production's songs, "The Bogie Man," sung by Snarleyow and his crew, not only became a popular hit but also gave birth to the expression "the Bogie Man will get you if you don't watch out," an admonition used for years thereafter by adults toward naughty children.

By the end of July, the third edition of "Sinbad" had been introduced, complete with the usual Henderson-demanded changes — new sketches and songs, an entirely new ballet ensemble. Yet, the show's success continued:

Ida Mulle starred in a number of Henderson productions. Her association with Eddie likely contributed to divorce proceedings initiated by her husband. Mulle continued to play leading roles in comic opera and musical comedy until 1900, when she retired.

By retaining all the good things and discarding the old or easily worn out for new, Sinbad has become the most attractive of all the Chicago Opera House extravaganzas.[5]

Coincident with Henderson's replacement of a number of cast members, the *Clipper* published an announcement, attributed to Eddie, regarding his future plans:

Edwin Foy, the comedian of Sinbad, has written a play called "Comrades." Mr. Foy has also purchased a play by John Gilbert, the burlesque comedian, entitled "In Your Mind." When Mr. Foy's contract with Mr. Henderson expires, he will go forth as a "star."[6]

To what extent the information was genuine (or merely a reminder of Eddie's tenuous relationship with Henderson) was never determined. The shows mentioned in the article were never again cited.

The 100th presentation of "Sinbad" took place August 26. Exactly one half of all the performances had displayed SRO signs. Business manager Bowles reported that "Sinbad" was exceeding the financial average of "The Crystal Slipper" by more than sixty dollars a night, a considerable sum. He neglected to mention, however, that ticket prices for "Sinbad" had been increased.

As the production was being prepared for its annual tour, which meant new material and a smaller cast, Henderson boasted that he never had enjoyed "such a popular extravaganza in his career." His comment was corroborated by local press reports that:

Sinbad continues to astonish even its owners with its drawing propensities.[7]

Henderson also announced that Eddie would have "entirely new material" when the company went on tour — four songs, a parody, and a burlesque. In addition, the company was reduced to 100 people, including a much smaller ballet ensemble. St. Louis was to be the first stop on the way to a gala San Francisco engagement.

A related article in the *Chicago Tribune* reported that one of Henderson's primary investors had decided to "pull out." At the time, no one speculated on what effect this might have on the impresario's future operations.

David Henderson had quickly learned that the essential ingredients for the commercial success of his extravaganzas consisted of popular stars, beautiful girls, comedy, singable songs, and elaborate dance numbers — all this two decades before Ziegfeld's first Follies. Henderson was particularly enamored of dance, a compelling attraction that never failed to excite audiences. The *corps de ballet* he employed were the most professional on the American popular stage. In addition, his inclusion of children in the dance numbers made his shows decidedly more attractive to families. His sumptuous ensembles overwhelmed audiences with their colorful dramatics that were, literally, show stoppers, or "enders," since they characteristically concluded the production with a dazzling flourish.

Henderson was also aware that comic dance was an important component, hence his extensive use of Eddie in that role, no matter their ongoing disagreements. In the three years of Eddie's tenure as resident comedian, he had matured into an able and attractive "grotesque" dancer. Even for the most knowledgeable critics, defining Eddie's dancing genres and techniques proved difficult. Unlike the documentation that librettos, music, or stage sets offered, Eddie's dance sketches were simply unique, all but impossible to categorize. The best description that critics could muster, "grotesque" dancing, delineated it as a brief, unscripted moment of muscular motion, made identifiable only by the creativity and daring of the performer. But no one discussed dancing in this manner in reviews or production synopses. It would be some years yet before "classic" dance steps and routines were preserved, discussed, and copied.

Twenty years earlier, when young Edwin

Fitzgerald had observed and copied the rudiments of dance on Bowery streets, he was most likely exposed to the Irish jig and clog dances. His early performances in local beer halls and Western frontier towns included these dances. The Irish jig utilized rapid leg and footwork, with the tapping of toes and heels. Arms were kept close to the body, and the torso was held stiffly erect. It came off as a fast, bouncing, and happy dance.

The clog was a "sounded" dance, utilizing wooden shoes to pound out the measures of the music. It too demanded erect upper-body posture but additionally required passive facial expression.

In addition to these Irish dances, Eddie also acquired acrobatic skills while playing with the circus and minstrels. Acrobatics captured audience attention and encouraged involvement. When performed in garish costumes, these demanding athletic movements usually garnered substantial applause. Unlike circus acts presented above the ground, acrobatics were on-the-ground work, a do-it-yourself act, one that included a multitude of cartwheels, somersaults, tumbling, flips, and spins, an array of efforts made all the more breathtaking when performed in a wig, skirts, and baggy pants. Such acts later came to be exclusively circus clown routines, but in the early days of variety, most popular theater dancers included them in their repertoires. Eddie had first added acrobatics to his act while playing in the West, but he transformed these skills into compelling pantomime as his routines grew ever more sophisticated.

Evidently with Carncross, Eddie learned soft shoe, also called the "song and dance" step. Even more important, however, was his education in the structure of successful dance. It had to be correctly paced, begun with an interesting entrance and ended with a rousing exit, imaginative steps in the middle, and no dead time. Each new routine in a Carncross skit demanded new dance steps, each performer solely responsible for his or her own material. This continuous challenge gave Eddie the constant opportunity to add new approaches and techniques, always experimenting to determine what gained audience attention and approval.

When Eddie played in Castleton's and Swain's musical farces — they believed comic dance to be vital — he learned about integrating song and dance into a plot, rather than performing dance as an olio solo. It was here that he added the buck and wing dance to his repertoire. The buck was a gliding step, achieved by heel and toe movements that propelled the performer across the stage in slow tempo. The wing was a horizontally executed air step. This combination very likely contributed to the evolution of Eddie's characteristic across-the-stage shuffle and his relaxed, swaggering gait.

Eddie was first hired by Henderson to be a comic dancer, a role that relied on characterization and plot to make the act. Thus, he was funny for who he was, as well as for what he did.

While he was with Henderson, Eddie's "grotesque" dancing was redefined as "eccentric." Actually, critics were labeling "eccentric" all performers who developed highly individualistic acts that created humorous effects through ludicrous posture, grotesque behavior, and unique physical mannerisms. Jo-Jo, the dog-faced boy, was an "eccentric" performer by way of his appearance, as was a comic juggler called W.C. Fields. To be labeled "eccentric," however, did not mean that a performance was undisciplined. To the contrary, to earn the sobriquet demanded hard work, calculation, experimentation, and endless practice, along with the approval of audiences.

Eddie's special way of moving, his facial expressions (enhanced by mime-like make-up), his scratchy-voiced song renditions, and his droll joke-telling technique established him as an "eccentric" comedian, all ably abetted by George Bowles's advertising and promotional tactics. Soon, because of this unique combination of humorous attributes, some perceptive critics began to call Eddie a clown — indeed, a compliment paid to his acting ability.

The first stop on "Sinbad's" tour was the Grand Opera House in St. Louis, one of Henderson's leased theaters. As reported by the *Clipper*:

> The Grand was packed long before the curtain went up to see Sinbad and the audience was not disappointed in the scenery or the burlesque.[8]

On the long train ride to San Francisco, a scuffle broke out among a few of the actors, apparently due to some last-minute changes in the script. Though duly reported when it occurred, nothing more was said of the incident; it appeared to have no negative effect on performance. The 'Frisco newspapers lauded "Sinbad" as a show of "great magnificence."

A planned two-week run in San Francisco was extended to four weeks because of the production's "immense business." The engagement in Los Angeles was abruptly canceled. Instead, Henderson decided to take the company to Portland, Oregon, and Tacoma and Seattle, Washington, where new theaters had recently been opened. "Sinbad" met with enthusiastic receptions in these cities — audiences had never witnessed a show of this magnitude — but little if any profitability. In Salt Lake City, the production "played a banner engagement," although some ballet costumes had to be modified because locals considered them too revealing.

Henderson then returned the company to Chicago for the holiday season, to play a run of four weeks, before beginning the Eastern portion of the tour. A train delay nearly ruined the opening matinee at the Chicago Opera House, but a patient audience waited for the scenery to be set up, and the show started six hours late.

The episode exemplifies Henderson's business dealings with suppliers. The trip from Denver to Chicago (1,127 miles) was contracted to take twenty-six hours. Henderson had negotiated an unprecedented arrangement with the Union Pacific Railroad: for every hour the train was late, the railroad had to forfeit $100. The original cost for transporting the company was seven hundred dollars. Because of the delay, Henderson paid only $100 for the trip.

While "Sinbad" played to SRO audiences for its entire run in Chicago, as usual, Henderson replaced some performers and ordered some new songs to be added. Another argument with prima ballerina Clara Qualitz apparently caused her to leave the company yet again. Total responsibility for the ballet again reverted to Madeline Morando.

Cincinnati and Pittsburgh were the initial Eastern stops, the latter at another of Henderson's leased theaters, the Duquesne. In both cities, the houses were crowded as extravaganza devotees anxiously awaited the arrival of Henderson's new production.

In late January 1892, the company played three weeks in Boston and realized the greatest response to any Henderson production in that city. The *Globe* reported on Henderson's success:

> Sinbad, with its wealth of magnificent spectacular staging, gorgeous costumes, catchy music, beautiful girls and mirth-provoking situations, has drawn splendid business. The production has proved to be the most telling and catchy of the season and the results, financially, will exceed any for a long time at this house.[9]

Audiences and critics were no less enthusiastic in Philadelphia:

> In the opinion of many, unquestionably a majority, Sinbad outdoes anything in the way of spectacular burlesque that has ever been seen in this city.[10]

But rumblings of discontent were recorded by the *Clipper*. In Boston, they reported that Henderson attacked the theater's orchestra leader with a cane. The man was not injured, but he refused to play for "Sinbad." Two more performers were dismissed. For two days, Eddie was unable to play in Philadelphia because of "throat trouble." The *Clipper* suggested Henderson should leave the company and return to Chicago to preserve morale.

Instead, the entire company returned to Chicago in March for a three-week run. This allowed Henderson to begin work on his new summer production, "Ali Baba," at the same time keeping a close watch on the current show. The impresario publicly proclaimed that this would be his biggest production, featuring a cast of 250 people and three ballets. Richard Barker would again direct the entire production; Harry B. Smith would write the libretto, with Voegtlin and Dazian preparing scenery and costumes, respectively. "No money for the production will be spared," Henderson declared.

When the company plunged into its Midwestern tour, they were already a tired troupe. Audience approval of their performances remained enthusiastic, but minor problems surfaced. Two stagehands were injured moving sets. Orchestra instruments and music were late arriving in Kansas City. Stage appliances broke down in St. Paul. And when Henderson told the company they had been booked for two weeks of one-night stands in Illinois and Iowa to end the season, cast members nearly revolted. Only the intervention of the starring performers prevented many of the players from deserting. They all returned to Chicago May 9. Like Eddie, those people signed for Henderson's next extravaganza immediately launched into rehearsals for "Ali Baba," supposedly to open June 2, less than four weeks away.

"Ali Baba" or "Morgiana and the Forty Thieves" did open June 2, on schedule. It was a remarkable undertaking for a cast of more than 150 people — not 250 as claimed by Henderson — to rehearse such an elaborate production in only three weeks. Henderson was no longer satisfied with public

adulation as manager and head of production; he now insisted on being identified as originator and designer of the entire spectacle.

Problems between Eddie and Henderson continued. Just prior to the opening, it was announced that Eddie would not appear. "Throat trouble" was the now familiar excuse. The article further stated that Eddie had been "granted a leave of absence." Actually, Eddie and Henderson had again argued about a salary increase; they remained deadlocked. Alfred C. Wheelan, an English comedian, was quickly hired to replace Eddie.

In its initial review, the *New York Clipper* effusively praised the mechanics of the production but gave only brief space to the libretto and performers:

> Ali Baba, the new extravaganza, was ushered into the world before a packed, enthusiastic house June 2, and bids fair to repeat and even surpass the successes of its predecessors at this house. The scenery and costumes are gorgeous, and are far ahead of anything yet attempted by Mgr. Henderson. The auditorium has been decorated in the Moorish style, relieved by figures in light blue and olive with red as a prevailing tint. The play was well presented and passed off very smoothly, considering the fact it was a new production.[11]

The *New York Dramatic News,* however, revealed the production's weaknesses:

> The book or libretto is remarkable only for dense stupidity. Messrs. Henderson, Harry B. Smith and John Gilbert are accused of perpetuating it. There is scarcely a legitimate laugh in the entire book and the players are seriously handicapped. What is needed most is an infusion of new lines, music and ginger. Eddie Foy is greatly missed in the cast. Alfred C. Wheelan, an English comedian, does not succeed in infusing much of the comedy element.[12]

The production was in trouble. To save it, immediate surgery had to be done. At the end of the first week, Henderson announced "the piece is being worked over and improved." He also announced that Eddie was returning to the cast in two weeks. Eddie had demanded (and received) another salary increase; apparently the deal had been consummated only after the production seemed in jeopardy.

The production was radically changed — shortened considerably, complete with scenes redone, new ballets arranged, and new comedy material developed, Gilbert and Eddie writing the sketches. The final transformation scene was altered to introduce a gigantic silken cocoon that, at the climax of the show, opens and releases a large butterfly that flutters in midair. The forty thieves were fitted with helmets featuring incandescent lights, a highly entertaining feature for the audience but taxing and dangerous for performers, as they all had to carry twenty-pound batteries under their costumes.

As a result of the libretto changes, "Ali Baba" now consisted of four acts. Ali Baba (Louise Eissing the hero again) is in love with Morgiana (Ida Mulle), his slave — but so are several other characters. The city of Baghdad is being overrun by the forty thieves, and the Caliph (Thomas Martin) has been elected to rid the city of these marauders. He decides to cooperate with them instead and appoints as his chief of police Arraby Gorrah (Henry Norman). To deceive the people, the Caliph offers a reward for the thieves' capture — the hand of Morgiana — knowing that the forty thieves have been safely co-opted. Through Zamora, the chief of police's daughter, Ali Baba is given this information; he begins a search for the thieves' booty. Using the celebrated password, "Open Sesame," he gains access to the riches. Cassim (Eddie Foy), Ali Baba's brother — described in the program as "a vagabond, the world owes him a living, which he collects" — is also after the booty. Abdallah (Bessie Lynch), the captain of the thieves, and his band attack Ali Baba, and an exciting combat ensues. Ali Baba succeeds in escaping with much of the riches, builds himself a magnificent palace, and enters

Baghdad politics to rid the city of the duplicitous Caliph. After Ali Baba is elected Caliph, the thieves are destroyed and "all good people have happiness meted out to them."

By the beginning of July, after all the changes had been incorporated into the production, the *Clipper* reported that "Ali Baba had scored a genuine financial and artistic success." Cast changes did not go unnoticed, however. Some friends of the actors dismissed by Henderson claimed that he was firing all those people previously hired by Thomas Prior, the former stage manager, due to an altercation between Henderson and Prior that resulted in the latter's being relieved of his responsibilities. When Eddie was queried about the cast turnover, he stated that, at the conclusion of the season (he was still under contract to Henderson) he would leave the company and star jointly with Della Fox, a musical comedy performer.

"Ali Baba's" third edition was challenged by extremely hot weather in Chicago (101 deaths from the heat in a single week) and attracted poor audiences. In response, Henderson made further changes in the cast and libretto to produce a fourth edition, which also prepared the show for its upcoming road tour.

At about this time, another quarrel involving company members, this one domestic, reached the newspapers. Ida Mulle, one of the featured players, was brought to court by her husband; he demanded a divorce, the claim being adultery. Eddie was named the corespondent. Mulle made no defense, and the divorce was granted. No further information on the issue was ever revealed, but Lola Sefton and Madeline Morando had to have been fully aware of the affair.

In his own, inimitable fashion, Henderson continued to antagonize people; this time, Chicago's fraternal order of Elks bore the force of his ire. At their annual summer fund-raising picnic, with more than 5,000 people in attendance, Henderson pulled his company out of the entertainment at the last moment, "owing to a real or fancied slight," as reported by the *Tribune* .

Yet in spite of the adverse publicity, "Ali Baba" continued to SRO houses. In fact, the show proved so profitable to Henderson, that he delayed the road tour for almost the entire fall, playing a total of 200 performances in Chicago before leaving town. In September, Henderson announced that all previous attendance and box-office records had been smashed by "Ali Baba." Though changes had been made in both the cast and in seat prices, "all had been for the better," he claimed. Henderson also revealed an agreement with the railroad for a 12,000-mile tour of "Ali Baba," which included 115 road company members in a special train of seven cars. This time, however, the railroad did not agree to his proposed fee reduction for running late.

Of interest to Eddie and all the country's Irish that September was the world's heavyweight championship boxing match between "Gentleman Jim" Corbett and John L. Sullivan. Displaying dazzling footwork and devastating punching ability, Corbett knocked out Sullivan in twenty-one rounds, in what most boxing enthusiasts considered an upset. Eddie received teletype reports in his dressing room; when the results of the bout were dispatched, he announced them to the audience. The fact that Corbett now held the championship also helped to make him an attractive performer for the variety stage. He opened a month later at the Haymarket Theater in Chicago, with thanks to Eddie for providing stage pointers to enhance the champ's display of pugilistic artistry.

The last night of "Ali Baba" at the Chicago Opera House, the production's 200th performance, was more than the ordinary SRO sellout. At the end of the evening, all the star performers gave short speeches (Henderson was absent), and the audience, standing and cheering, sang *Auld Lang Syne*. Very early next morning, the company entrained for St. Louis and points west.

In Kansas City, the theater manager

Eddie as Cassim, in Henderson's "Ali Baba," which played continuously for more than a year, and was featured at the Chicago Opera House during the World's Fair. Eddie usually designed his own costumes. (Harry Ransom Humanities Research Center — University of Texas)

spent $3,500 of his own money to enlarge the stage to accommodate the extravaganza, yet still was rewarded with a handsome profit. Denver proved equally profitable, but the proposed stop in Salt Lake City had to be canceled because the local stage was too small for all the scenery and performers. On to San Francisco, to play a four-week engagement during the Christmas holiday season. The *Chronicle* declared:

A theater photocard of Eddie distributed to Chicago Opera House patrons at "Ali Baba's" 200th performance. Eddie displays the relaxed confidence of a popular theater headliner.

Ali Baba has captured the city. SRO has been the rule at every performance.[13]

The newspaper's final report reiterated the successes of the production:

People were turned away nightly. The engagement was a big success financially. The company leaves for the East.[14]

Throughout January 1893, Henderson's "Ali Baba" troupe played Denver, St. Louis (a return engagement), Cincinnati, and Pittsburgh to "the largest business of the season." At this time, Henderson decided to perform "Ali Baba" during the entire Chicago World's Fair, from May until the fall. For a change, the company expressed satisfaction with the decision; it not only promised continuous employment throughout the summer, but also meant no travel. Yet, no sooner had they celebrated the news than they heard that Henderson's brother, Weymss, was on his way to Europe in search of "new novelties" for the company.

A planned one-week engagement at the Globe Theater in Boston was extended to three weeks. The *Clipper* reported the production's success:

Ali Baba has been drawing rattling good business. It is a revelation in stagecraft, and its record beats that of any of David Henderson's previous productions in its line.[15]

Boston had become an Eddie Foy town, and local critics discussed his hilarious antics repeatedly, his "eccentric" dancing particularly.

A return to Pittsburgh captured capacity houses. (No one questioned Henderson's booking policies anymore.) From Pittsburgh, the company jumped more than 600 miles to Minneapolis and St. Paul, usually the final stops of the season. But because the production was scheduled to run the entire summer at the World's Fair, Henderson booked additional engagements in Milwaukee, Indianapolis, Louisville, and St. Louis (a third time) before returning to Chicago. In each city, the capacity of the house was continually tested.

In a rare enlightened moment, Henderson closed the production for two weeks, giving the entire company a week's pay while resting, no doubt due to his elation with the financial results of "Ali Baba," and the opportunity to play the same show for the entire summer. The extravaganza was to re-open May 28, for a projected, continuous, eight-shows-a-week run until October.

The financial panic of 1893 occurred almost simultaneously with the reopening of "Ali Baba." While the panic nearly closed the World's Fair, shuttering a number of banks that contained the money of many exhibitors, it seemed to have little impact on the crowds of people lining up to see "Ali Baba." While the World's Fair Commission sought to attract tourists, "Ali Baba's" patrons were people already enamored of Henderson's extravaganzas. Some downtown theaters "went dark"; others played to reduced audiences. The Chicago Opera House packed the theater "beyond the standing room limit." The *Clipper* reported this deluge of support for the production:

> From the size of the crowds which have thus far marked the seventh annual engagement of Manager Henderson's American Extravaganza Co., one could well imagine a successful outcome if their reign were made perpetual. Louise Eissing, Ida Mulle, Ada Deaves, Eddie Foy and Joe Doner still remain in prime demand. Ali Baba nears its five hundredth production, when fitting memoirs are promised.[16]

With effects of the panic abated, improved weather, and a decision by the Fair Committee to remain open three nights a week until 11:00 P.M., as well as open Sundays, (a major defeat for local religious authorities), attendance at the fair rocketed to more than 100,000 a day in July. In addition, tourists were now visiting Chicago in large numbers, fueling fair attendance.

For Henderson, "Ali Baba" had become SRO heaven. In late July, the *Clipper* declared:

> Manager Henderson is profiting this summer in the same degree as in seasons gone before. Ali Baba, staged more gorgeously than ever, and handled by quite the same cast as when last seen here, continues to put the weeks behind it, with accompanying profits of monster proportion. Standing room only, and often times precious little of that, is the gratifying portion of this simon pure Chicago offering.[17]

In conjunction with "Ali Baba's" successful run, Eddie was also enjoying a more leisurely respite. Working for an extended period in Chicago reduced much of the stress of touring. Now permanently retired from the stage, Lola was again at home. Eddie often visited his mother and sisters, and he purchased a house for his mother.

Due to the fair, Chicago was at least as replete with top performers and shows as New York would have been during its regular theater season. Tony Pastor's variety troupe, Weber and Fields, Lillian Russell, Denman Thompson, and De Wolf Hopper were all playing extended runs at downtown theaters. Jim Corbett was giving boxing demonstrations on the Midway Plaisance at the Fair. Flo Zeigfeld featured his strong man, Sandow. Sinuous "Little Egypt" offered her sultry "Dance of the Seven Veils" to ogling fairgoers. The Barnum & Bailey Circus enjoyed considerable prosperity and planned to remain in Chicago until the end of the circus season.

It became common to see famous entertainers together, enjoying one another's company at restaurants, picnics, and the race track, as well as performing benefits for needy children or the disabled. Eddie was often seen with Jim Corbett, and the two of them attended the races with Lillian Russell. Eddie recalled marveling at Russell's star power and her traveling retinue of "camp followers." At least once a month, various combinations of performers appeared at local charity events and, from all reports, collected large amounts for the sponsors.

Eddie even assisted Corbett in a suit his friend took out against the *Saturday Evening Post*. The magazine had written an article about performers on the Midway at the fair, insinuating that Corbett was "in no great danger of growing wealthy on the proceeds of the Midway Plaisance venture." Corbett claimed he was embarrassed by the "slanderous" statement. He broadened the suit to include the *Chicago Herald* when they published "an oily account" of Corbett's career on the Midway. Eddie testified on behalf of Corbett, emphasizing his fledgling career as a variety artist. Like most similar lawsuits, the case was thrown out of court. However, such suits did generate a good deal of publicity for the litigants.

By late August, the "Ali Baba" cast again showed signs of unrest, likely due to Henderson's replacing a number of cast members, including Ida Mulle, who was given two-weeks notice after an "encounter" with the impresario. Tension heightened even more when Henderson told the cast they were to begin rehearsals for a new show at the same time they were performing "Ali Baba." The replacement was to be a revival of "Sinbad," to open October 12, with "Ali Baba" playing its last show October 10. As usual, Henderson claimed that "Sinbad" was "to excel in splendor its former presentations." Those cast members who balked at the onerous rehearsal schedule were summarily replaced.

"Ali Baba" had played a total of 629 performances in sixteen months, over 100 more than any of Henderson's previous productions. That it had proven itself a highly profitable enterprise was never questioned. Yet, at this point in Henderson's management of fairy-tale extravaganzas, all of his investors had sold out or retired from the show, leaving the impresario in a precarious financial situation. It seemed his decision to revive "Sinbad" had more to do with money than the show's previous success. The '93-'94 season was crystallizing into a daunting fiscal challenge for the impresario.

It didn't start well. When the fair closed, all theater companies experienced a considerable decline in attendance at downtown theaters. In addition, Henderson erred by opening "Sinbad" just four weeks before he had to vacate the Chicago Opera House for other previously contracted engagements. While preparing the show for its tour, he was even more ruthless in trimming cast and staff to conserve money. It was reported that Eddie had pointedly told Henderson this would be his last extravaganza tour. When reporters asked Eddie what his plans were, he replied, "You'll be surprised when it happens." Eddie started the tour ill, unable to perform for two weeks because of "a bad throat."

Box-office success on the road came more easily than at home. Cincinnati was the first stop, to "a standing room house." Kansas City, St. Louis, and the long jump to San Francisco followed. The production played four weeks in 'Frisco, the entire holiday season. It was labeled an enormous success:

> Sinbad has achieved a triumph beyond description. The attendance has been exceedingly large. The SRO sign is nightly displayed.[18]

Eddie played the entire San Francisco engagement and was enthusiastically received. All his old friends turned out to cheer him, forcing him to make brief speeches during each show; they begged for encores of his songs. Henderson argued that these encores delayed the presentation, but performers refused to relinquish the opportunity to reprise their acts and so disappoint their publics.

When a play booked into the Chicago Opera House for six weeks suddenly failed, Henderson was forced to return "Sinbad" to Chicago to fill the time. It was a financial disaster for him, not only because he lost money on the failed production, but also because he had to give up lucrative stops at advanced prices in four other cities. Not surprisingly, the crowds to see "Sinbad" in Chicago were not nearly as large as when it had first opened. It took almost the entire run to generate the usual full houses. The *Clipper* paid some attention to Henderson's problems:

> Business thus far has been good, but not quite up to the standards hoped for, and far short of the merits of the production.[19]

In other words, Henderson had suffered a financial shortfall. It was an ominous warning.

Eddie now had six unexpected weeks at home with Lola. Just when he and the company were preparing to leave Chicago to continue their tour, Lola informed him she was pregnant. There is no evidence to indicate how Eddie responded to the news, but no sudden marriage to Lola took place. Apparently, Eddie believed he could maintain the fiction that he and Lola had already been married for a considerable time.

Louisville, Indianapolis, and Pittsburgh were the initial stops on "Sinbad's" Eastern tour. The Pittsburgh stop coincided with very cold weather and the effects of a financial panic, and the show "nearly did well." Even a two-week engagement in Philadelphia, normally a banner city for Henderson, failed to meet his expectations. The *Ledger* reported:

> There was no rush for seats last week, which will be placed on record as one of the lightest experienced this season by this attraction.[20]

In what appeared to insiders a denial of impending financial problems, Henderson boldly proclaimed his next summer spectacle to be "Aladdin," or the "Wonderful Lamp," an "entirely new and wondrous extravaganza." He claimed he was going to spend more than ever before on the production. Yet not only were his finances now almost totally depleted, his inner circle was in turmoil as well. Henderson found Eddie intimately involved in this turbulence.

Business manager George Bowles was in Cincinnati to promote the "Sinbad" engagement. He was also talking to theater managers about fall dates for a new musical comedy, starring Eddie Foy.

A number of secret meetings had recently been held, involving Eddie, Bowles, Fred Eustis (Henderson's musical arranger), Sam Davidson (owner of the Davidson Theater in Milwaukee), John D. Gilbert, and investor Sherman Brown. They were working out the details of a production to be introduced in Milwaukee in September, then toured throughout the country. Bowles and Eustis had expressed unhappiness with Henderson and were seeking other opportunities. They were also the people who had the most knowledge of Henderson's financial difficulties.

Henderson was reportedly borrowing heavily to fund "Aladdin, Jr." When he was sued for $5,000 by a "colored" patron, for having refused the man a seat in the theater even though he had purchased a ticket, Henderson couldn't raise enough money to pay a lawyer. The suit went to court, and the local press gave it prominence. The issue reached the front pages when Henderson lost the case and was required to pay the offended patron $525. Theater people were convinced that Henderson was now close to bankruptcy, if not bankrupt already.

The company's internal torment was made public when Henderson fired Eddie while "Sinbad" was playing its final week of the season in Milwaukee. Apparently, Henderson discovered the plans for Eddie's new show and the Bowles/Eustis/Davidson involvement. The *Clipper* disclosed:

> Comedian Edwin Foy was given notice by Manager Henderson that his services with that company would terminate immediately. In the notice, Mgr. Henderson accuses Mr. Foy of violating the rules of the company and various other offenses.[21]

Eddie replied that Henderson untimely broke contracts and frequently abused cast members. What appeared more than simple coincidence was an announcement in the *Clipper*:

> Eddie Foy will star next season in a spectacular farce-comedy, entitled "Off the Earth," of which Mr. Foy and John D. Gilbert are the authors.[22]

Feigning disdain for his dilemma, Henderson started rehearsals for "Aladdin, Jr.," and defiantly declared that Hallen Mostyn, of Rice's "Venus" Company, had been signed as principal comedian. But his cash flow was so limited he was having trouble signing cast members.

George Bowles then released to the newspapers a statement that he planned to manage Eddie Foy in "Off the Earth"; in turn, Fred Eustis indicated he would be musical arranger for the show. No sooner had Henderson denounced his former colleagues than a number of crucial cast members — Louise Montague, Kate Uart, Joe Doner, and Madeline Morando — stated they had signed for principle parts in Eddie's new show.

Henderson was only three weeks away from opening "Aladdin, Jr.," and still had important holes in his cast. Luckily, a troupe was assembled in time; the new production opened on June 8, to mixed reviews. Misfortune seemed Henderson's companion when a local transportation strike occurred just days after "Aladdin, Jr.'s" opening. The *Chicago Tribune* reported that Henderson "gave some thought to closing the Chicago Opera House for a time, but determined to weather the storm." A month later, it was reported that business was still below expectations, "enough to discourage the bravest heart," said the *Clipper* correspondent.

In the meantime, planning for "Off the Earth" had begun. Eddie disclosed that his troupe had been named the American Travesty Company. A reporter asked if this was perhaps intentional mockery of Henderson's

American Extravaganza Company. Billed as an operatic travesty, "Off the Earth" was to contain two acts and five scenes. The production had been adapted from the English stage, and scenery and costumes from its English incarnation were to be used by the Foy company. When a brief description of the new show was provided, it sounded very much like a smaller version of a Henderson extravaganza, with emphasis on beautiful girls, stunning scenery, and splendid costumes.

"Aladdin, Jr." ran through July and August but "continued a losing venture for Mgr. Henderson." Theater people attempted to analyze why a production by a celebrated showman such as Henderson had declined so rapidly in popularity. Some cited the effect of the transportation strike, but it had lasted only two weeks. Some suggested that the public had tired of opulent extravaganzas, but others pointed out the success of equally elaborate comic operas. Most agreed, however, that the loss of key people — performers and management alike — probably had had the most telling impact. Nor did Henderson's public pronouncements help draw patrons to his theater. David Henderson's reign as "king of the extravaganza" was at an end. He would never recover from this debacle.

"Off the Earth" was to open at the Davidson Theater in Milwaukee on September 10. Meanwhile, Lola was in the middle of a difficult pregnancy, being cared for by Eddie's mother, Ellen, and his sister, Mary. For Eddie, Lola's precarious condition only added to the stresses of the moment.

For the first time in his career, Eddie was now the leading actor in his own production, as well as manager and stage director. While he had the benefit of solid collegial support, the shows' finances were as precarious as Lola's physical condition. There would be little room for error. And new challenges were about to unfold.

Chapter 8

Isn't that a wonderful actor. He can actually make one feel hot or cold, happy or sad, at his slightest fancy.

That's nothing. We've got a janitor that does the same thing.

From the moment he lit it, at the entrance to Chicago's Columbia Theater, Eddie savored his cigar with greater enjoyment than ever before. He was about to step on stage as the bona fide star of his own show, as well as director of his own company.

Eddie was thirty-eight and a half years old, with more than twenty years' acting experience, having performed in thousands of venues, under all types of working conditions. Eddie Foy was not merely a successful survivor of the rigors of the profession. Rather, he was fast becoming one of the most unique comedic innovators on the popular stage. As a highly versatile performer, Eddie had "seen it all" and "done it all," at least everything except starring in and running his own company. And he was more than sufficiently confident in his ability to deal with these new challenges.

Photographs of Eddie in 1894 reveal a casual, poised, handsome man. He was a "dresser" off-stage — "dressing" manifested an actor's prosperity and signified legitimacy — but more conservative than flashy. He wore no jewelry. An ascot and well-tailored suit made him appear more a prosperous businessman than a popular entertainer.

Eddie's demeanor was friendly and appealing, communicating the impression that he was approachable, easy to talk to, accepting, and unpretentious, all of which attributes were in fact true. He was courteous and respectful, yet unafraid to voice his own opinions. Some called him opinionated, but when the subject at hand was performance or other aspects of life on the stage, colleagues paid close attention to his remarks. There was no question that personal charisma was one of his notable assets, and its impact was made even more attractive by his easy-going manner.

Possessed of an "Irish" temper, he could "fly off the handle" on occasion. Except when he believed a theater associate had gone beyond the bounds of propriety, such episodes were more likely to occur within the family. Offstage, Eddie could drink, swear, and entertain women as well as any actor of his day. In the theater, however, he insisted that material had to be clean, actors respectful of one another, women and children esteemed. Anyone breaking these rules would be sternly reprimanded. Nor did he easily forgive a person who abused these values.

There is no question that Eddie was a hard worker, highly committed to his profession. He could not have become a star had he not devoted his entire being to the endeavor. In the late 19th century, obstacles to success were plentiful, the odds against an aspiring performer all but overwhelming. To attain the status of an accomplished and recognized performer required study, practice, perseverance, good health, and good luck. It took a unique combination of creativity, innovation, psychology, and performance skill to gain and sustain audience approval. Eddie possessed all these qualities. And his ultimate goal was always to please the patron.

He had little formal education, having attended elementary school for no more than a few years. It was only through his theatrical apprenticeship that he came to speak articulately. He was a "fast learner," with an excellent facility to read and recall lines. Moreover, he could gracefully improvise and adjust his "business" to meet the needs of particular audiences. Most important, Eddie developed a deep and respectful understanding of theater.

Considering the disposition of his early years and the conditions under which he lived and performed, Eddie's health was remarkably good. Rarely was he ill; an actor could not afford to be ill. There were, however, occasions when feigned illness was used to prove a point with management. Such strategic withdrawals had become a familiar ploy utilized by performers in their on-going battles with management. But only stars could use the tactic effectively. Eddie enjoyed eating, drinking, and smoking; but never to excess. A strong constitution, the athleticism of his acting, and the careful attention he paid to personal health kept him trim, muscular, and in good physical condition. While in the theater, he never drank. Smoking cigars seems to have been an occasional treat rather than a habit.

Eddie had two obsessional hobbies, boxing and billiards, both of which he learned to enjoy during the early years of his career. He frequently visited boxing clubs in the various cities he toured, making friends with many professional boxers and their managers. Jim Corbett, for example, became a lifelong friend. Over the years, Eddie perfected his billiards game to the point where he entered tournaments and won awards. He often went to the race track, but rarely bet.

Eddie was not skillful, however, at handling his own finances. While never a spendthrift, he regularly seemed to be short of money. This was no doubt partly due to the costs of being a leading actor. One did have to look and act the part. In addition, performers had to pay for their own room, board, and transportation while on the road. Another cause may have been the many and varied financial responsibilities Eddie assumed, always sending money to his mother and caring for the other women in his life. Nor was he one to turn down requests for money from a needy actor or worthy charitable organization.

Eddie had been raised in a devout Catholic family. Though he respected the tenets of the religion, he was not particularly religious. Except for marriages, baptisms, and funerals, he rarely went to church.

One of Eddie's most admirable characteristics, evident early in his career, was his lack of prejudice toward others. The ease and comfort with which he made friends gave people the feeling he respected who they were and what they represented. His ability to achieve rapport with diverse people — from cowboys, miners, and Indians to the professional and social elite — seemed to dissolve any and all barriers based on race or religion.

In large measure due to his years on stage, Eddie certainly developed a strong ego. Yet it was never overblown, nor ever used to upstage a colleague. If anything, given the nature of the profession, Eddie may have been too low-key, too unpretentious, since he rarely did or said anything for the purpose of self-promotion. His career might have progressed more quickly had more self-promotion taken place. Unlike many other actors, Eddie's name rarely appeared in gossip columns, nor did he habitually publicize his professional plans or intentions. In fact, at this point in his career, nearly all press reports about Eddie had derived from other sources.

Whether because of heritage or training, Eddie was a first-rate storyteller. Nor did he hesitate to reconstruct history on occasion. Yet this did not seem an attempt to brag or make himself a hero. Rather, his "tall tales" tended to relate to actual historical events in which he claimed to have played a minor role. His alleged trip to Tombstone (for the celebrated shoot-out at the OK Corral) and to the mining towns of Central California were evidently fictitious, as was his claim that Rose Howland's death affected his career. His phantom marriage to Lola Sefton was probably prompted by a concern for her respectability. Yet, in perspective, his attempts to revise personal history were no different than those of other star performers of the era (or today). And often more artfully imaginative.

Eddie worked diligently the entire summer preparing "Off the Earth" for a September opening. In his autobiography, Eddie mentioned being delegated to travel to Europe to select scenery, costumes, and dancers for the upcoming production. He claimed that, after stops in London, Paris, Switzerland, and Italy, he hired a former colleague, prima ballerina Madeline Morando, for his new show.

In reality, Eddie never visited Europe the summer of 1894. His entire summer was spent in Chicago working on the new production. Scenery and costumes had come from the show's London run. Actors were engaged from local sources, some of them from Henderson's company, including Madeline Morando, who had played in all of Henderson's shows since 1889. Yet, in his book, Eddie makes no mention of his defection from Henderson nor his solicitation of investors for "Off the Earth."

Rehearsals for the show commenced the beginning of August. Company enthusiasm attempted to overcome what was perceived as a weak libretto. A month before opening, the company moved to the Davidson Theater, in Milwaukee, to complete rehearsals. Enterprising George Bowles gave a reception for the local press, at which he outlined the production's plot, exhibited scenery and costumes, and had performers present a few of the show's songs. It was a first for Milwaukee, and the hometown reporters were duly impressed.

"Off the Earth" was scheduled to open in Milwaukee; Manager Davidson was one of the show's primary backers, and the production would inaugurate the city's new theater season. Thanks to Bowles's extensive promotional activities, large crowds were anticipated. Yet the choice of initial venue was also influenced by current realities in Chicago. Attendance at Chicago theaters had significantly declined throughout the summer, and the press predicted little improvement in the fall. In addition, investors did not want their production to compete with or be compared to Henderson's "Aladdin, Jr."

While rehearsing in Milwaukee, Eddie returned to Chicago each weekend to visit Lola, whose condition was worsening as she approached childbirth. The prognosis was not good. He had been advised there existed a strong possibility that neither mother nor baby would survive. For Eddie, the strains and anxiety were palpable.

"Off the Earth" opened on September 10 and, in the language of critics, made a great hit. Eddie had to have been particularly pleased by their reaction to his comedic role. Further, Milwaukee papers were excited by the event itself:

> One of the most notable theatrical events in the history of our city was the initial production of "Off the Earth" at the Davidson 10, and the handsome theater was packed to the doors by a representative audience bubbling over with the most kindly feeling for the success of the piece. Eddie Foy's ability to please his audience seems unlimited.
>
> The new Davidson was crowded from pit to dome and the audience manifested its pleasure in a manner sufficiently demonstrative to satisfy the most fastidious manager.

Even the *New York Clipper* recognized the new production:

> The premiere of Off the Earth, the travesty by John D. Gilbert, in which Eddie Foy commenced his tour as a star, occurred at the Davidson Theater last evening, and proved an unqualified success.[1]

A production's first night was usually crowded with enthusiastic audiences who clamored for encores, presented a stageful of bouquets, and shouted for actors to speak. "Off the Earth" was no exception. The show received even louder acclaim because it was the first new play to be given its initial performance in a Milwaukee theater. Every song was encored, some many times. At the end of the first act, Eddie, Sherman Brown (the producer), and John Gilbert were called to the stage and asked to speak. Eddie's speech was short: "Ladies and gentlemen, this welcome is mutual." Audience response was deafening. Simultaneously, the stage was strewn with flowers thrown by the clamorous crowd. At the end of the show, leading performers were called to the stage yet again to receive the accolades of the appreciative audience.

Even though there was much praise for Eddie's work and the beauty of scenery and costumes, Gilbert's book was panned. The *Clipper* excused the libretto by suggesting that it should improve as the show progressed. The *Milwaukee Sentinel*, however, was brutal in its evaluation.

> The composer of "Off the Earth" was as well left to a kindly oblivion. He scored a lamentable failure. Not a whiff of consistency nor unity nor originality blows through the windy, noisy nightmare "Off the Earth."[2]

Eddie and company had only one week to rework the production before exposing it to a more discerning Chicago audience. Louis Harrison was hired to write new novelties; and as quickly as he submitted material, the company incorporated it into the show.

Sunday, September 16, was the traveling day to Chicago. For Eddie, it was a day filled with conflicting emotions; pleased with "Off the Earth's" first week of box office receipts, but worried about Lola's condition. Lola was in labor, tended by Ellen and Mary at home; childbirth was imminent. No sooner had Eddie arrived than Lola gave birth to a healthy baby girl, whom Eddie named Catherine, after his grandmother. Lola, however, remained very ill; in fact, close to death. For the time being, Mary, Eddie's sister, would care for Catherine.

Overcome by events, Eddie could not bring himself to take the stage in "Off the Earth" the next evening; and the production had to be postponed one week. While Eddie's financial backers were deeply concerned, they were pleased to discover that none of the patrons returned their tickets, waiting patiently to honor their favorite star and attend his new offering.

Amy Leslie, the *Chicago Tribune's* eloquent theater critic, trumpeted Eddie's return to the Chicago stage, a triumph for the comedian she now declared "a decided star":

> The house was packed with Foyites; it was money a knee deep and admiration irrational, real and sugar-coated.... Success? Well, rather! There has never been so terrifying a success as this personal hit of Eddie

Foy.... It is ours, our own and we cannot keep it dark. Eddie has come to stay; he will star and star and star as long as he lives; it is all Chicago's fault and she is dead glad of it.[3]

The *New York Clipper's* initial report of "Off the Earth" was less enthusiastic but positive, nonetheless:

> The chief event of the week was the local debut of Eddie Foy as a star and, as evidence of his personal popularity, the Columbia was packed to the walls. Louise Montague, Sadie McDonald and Kate Uart carried off most of the honors, but Mr. Foy's every appearance was a signal for boisterous enthusiasm in the upper gallery, where his friends seem to center. Last night the house was filled completely, and the three weeks' run of Off the Earth seems likely to bring big profits.[4]

"Off the Earth" is described in the program as a fantastic operatic travesty, in two acts and five scenes. Act One opens in a department store run by Stag Party (Hallen Mostyn, fired by Henderson when he failed to succeed in Eddie's former role), a confidence man who, having failed at some specific professions, is now trying them all together. His man of all needs, Cluster (Eddie Foy), not only does all the work, but also impersonates various freaks in a sideshow, an extra activity in the store. (Eddie made a unique entrance, standing on a canal boat pulled by a donkey, upon whose back was a Negro child.) Gavotte Tripplie (Laura Clements), a romantic young maiden writing a book, calls on Stag Party to be hypnotized, so she can realize her romantic ideals. She is accompanied by Charley Prince (Louise Montague), her lover. Cad Daverous (Sadie McDonald), a sumptuous exponent of physical culture admired by both Cluster and Stag Party, enters. Gavotte is hypnotized, and all the characters become idealized. Luna, Queen of the Moon (Kate Uart), suddenly appears and, falling in love with Charley Prince, transports all the characters on clouds to the moon. Cluster, however, takes his trip

upon an aerial bicycle. (During Eddie's trip to the moon, he encountered various atmospheric phenomena, to the delight of the audience.)

Act Two opens upon the Fairy Forest of the Phosphorescent Fungi. Luna tells her handmaids of her adventures on Earth, as all the characters arrive. Cluster burlesques with the fairies, and he and Stag Party duel for the hand of Cad Daverous. The final scene takes place in Luna's palace, where a magnificent celebration takes place to honor the nuptials of Luna and Charley Prince. Under cover of buffoonery, Cluster steals Luna's magic diadem, deposes the queen, restores Charley Prince to Gavotte, and anoints himself Man in the Moon.

In Act One, Scene One, Eddie sang four songs: "Back Among the Old Jokes"; "Combination Freak," while impersonating sideshow freaks; "Tuscalina Brown"; and, in combination with the company, "Away We Go," on their way to the moon. In Act Two, Scene One, Eddie rendered the show's hit song, "Still His Whiskers Grew," as he impersonated various well-known people; sang a duet with Stag Party, "Don't Drink, My Boy, Tonight"; and another with Cad, "The Chinese Dolly." For all these songs, Eddie constantly modified his costume to identify with the song's characters.

In Act Two, Scene Two, Eddie harmonized in a quartet, "When the Moon Is Turned on Full," while dancing with the fairies. In this scene, Cluster has a nightmare in which he confronts various animals — all of them played by George Ali, one of popular theater's most accomplished animal impersonators — and mirrors each of their behaviors. The final scene showcases the *corps de ballet*, led by Madeline Morando, in which she performs a variation solo.

Each night, during "Off the Earth's" first week in Chicago, Eddie was called to the stage prior to the curtain's being raised. He sang a song and thanked his friends for their "magnificent reception." "After all," he deadpanned, "I'm just a combination freak." The

A drawing of Eddie, appearing in "Off the Earth," published in the *New York American* in 1895. The show was Eddie's first as a star and manager of his own company. While the show was fairly successful, the experience persuaded Eddie he could not perform and manage at the same time.

audience cheered wildly before the show had even begun.

"Off the Earth" was undoubtedly a *tour de force* for Eddie, for he was on stage nearly the entire length of the production. He sang eight songs and performed seven comedy sketches. Still, the *Chicago Tribune* reported, there was "not too much of Foy."

Unfortunately, the initial financial success of "Off the Earth" was short-lived. Harrison's story revisions were not well received, and critics continued to deride Gilbert's libretto. Backers of the show were reticent to invest additional money to pay for proposed changes. George Bowles had problems booking the show in other cities. Moreover, as predicted by critics before the start of the season, Chicago's theater attendance generally remained weak. While Eddie was lauded for his own work, "Off the Earth" generated no profit.

Meanwhile, Lola was failing. Eddie asked his sister Mary to care for and raise Catherine, as he planned to be on the road for a considerable time. Mary would serve as substitute mother to Catherine more than eight years.

"Off the Earth," now struggling to survive, went on tour in mid-October, its first stop the Albion Theater, Pittsburgh. Eddie was singled out for a fine performance, but attendance was "less than half a house." By the time the company reached Philadelphia, the libretto had been rewritten again by Harrison. This time, critics received it more favorably; patrons crowded the Walnut Street Theater, prompting the run to be extended an additional week. One of Eddie's most enthusiastic supporters, John Carncross, turned out a number of times, just to cheer on his former employee.

Now more confident and encouraged, "Off the Earth's" company played almost the entire month of November in Boston. The *Globe* declared:

> At the Park Theater, "Off the Earth" was seen for the first time in this city and drew a fine house. It is a play of sterling merit, and was well acted by a sterling company. Eddie Foy as Cluster made a hit, and his able support adds much to the success of the play.[5]

At the same time that the production earned its first profits, the *Clipper* announced that backers Sherman Brown and Gerard Coventry had sold their interests in "Off the Earth" to Manager Davidson. Since Brown and Coventry were the show's primary backers, Eddie was very concerned.

After an exceptionally successful engagement in Boston, scheduling problems forced the show to return to Chicago, with intermediate short stops in Syracuse, Buffalo, and Detroit, along with a number of off-days.

"Off the Earth" was rapidly running out of money. Ironically, on its return to Chicago, the production was booked into Henderson's Chicago Opera House because the impresario needed money to continue "Aladdin, Jr." Returning was also essential for Eddie; Lola was dying.

During its second presentation in Chicago, "Off the Earth" did better, sustaining good crowds for its entire three-week run. Most of the production's new features were well received, including some new songs and sketches that Eddie performed.

On the evening of December 16, while Eddie was on stage, Lola died. Grief-stricken though he was, her death had been expected; Eddie continued playing the entire engagement. Lola's death was not revealed to the public, nor was her funeral two days later. A simple death certificate declared that Lola Conlick, age unknown, had died of pneumonia. No relatives were listed.

Looking back on the event years later, Eddie wrote:

> The comedian is never allowed to sorrow long. The funeral baked meats are not cold before he must be back with painted face, grimacing under the spotlight, and woe be unto him if he fails to make the patrons laugh![6]

After undergoing further script, song, and dance changes, "Off the Earth" was on the road again a week later, for another Eastern tour. Even though the production had played Philadelphia two months earlier, the show was well received. The *Clipper* reported that "good business" resulted, mainly due to "several new features added since Off the Earth's appearance here earlier in the season."

The show played for a week in Brooklyn and another in Harlem, though not consecutively, due to booking difficulties. At considerable cost, the company traveled to Baltimore and back between these engagements. Still, both the Brooklyn and Harlem engagements were good, "packing the house." Reviews of the new version suggested that the company worked hard and Eddie sang several new songs, while a synopsis revealed considerable plot changes since the show's introduction four months previously.

The revised libretto opens in a big department store, one in which everything can be bought, from a diamond to a ton of coal. The oft-bankrupt proprietor, Stag Party, is now a successful entrepreneur. Cluster is his number-one employee and salesman. When the heroine, Gavotte Tripplie, loses the family jewels, Party hypnotizes her, and she locates them. Luna, Queen of the Moon, transports everybody to her home to show her friends how humans behave. Cluster is sentenced to 100 years imprisonment for killing the Sacred White Buffalo. He escapes by stealing the Queen's diadem, proclaims himself Man in the Moon, and returns everyone else back to Earth.

Eddie now had only four songs and four comedy sketches to perform. Key members of the cast remained the same; animal impersonator George Ali and prima ballerina Madeline Morando received special attention.

From Harlem, the company had four days off because of a long jump back to Milwaukee, Manager Davidson's theater. Davidson reported profitable box office receipts, although "Off the Earth" had played in the city only four months earlier. For the next six weeks, through the early part of 1895, engagements in St. Paul, Kansas City, St. Louis, and Cincinnati proved successful, playing variously to "immense houses" and "good profits." An innovation in scheduling, opening a week's run on Sunday, instead of the usual Monday night, resulted in the biggest weekly box-office receipts ever at Cincinnati's Walnut Street Theater. Bowles and Foy agreed to continue Sunday openings wherever possible, even though Sunday was also a day to travel to the next engagement. Unfortunately, the decision never took effect because Bowles was unable to book week-long runs for the remainder of the season. From the middle of March to early May, only

one- and two-night stands were available; and those in Illinois, Michigan, and Ohio's smaller towns. Aware that playing one-night stands in small towns at the end of a long season invariably precipitated stress, Eddie worried about company morale.

A female performer accused Joe Doner of assault and calling her "vile names." She obtained a warrant for his arrest. In Mansfield, Ohio, Eddie and George Bowles were arrested for giving a theatrical performance without a license and were taken to the city jail. When they appeared in court the next day (forced to cancel their scheduled engagement), Eddie protested to the mayor, whom he defied to arrest him. The mayor ordered Eddie locked up for a day and fined him fifty dollars, subjecting the company to another day's delay before traveling to the next engagement.

Chagrined, Eddie took it out on Bowles, upbraiding him for his inability to obtain good bookings. Some scenery and costumes were temporarily lost between Cedar Rapids, Iowa, and Grand Rapids, Michigan.

In the middle of April, Thomas Prior, lately the stage manager of Henderson's company and one of his principal collaborators, joined forces with Eddie as investor in the production. Prematurely, Prior announced that he:

> has decided to present a new extravaganza at the Schiller Theater (Chicago) this summer. It is called Little Robinson Crusoe, the libretto of which is by Harry B. Smith. Eddie Foy has been secured as the leading comedian, and Marie Dressler will have a leading part.[7]

Bowles was irate. Where did he fit in? Why hadn't he and Davidson been informed of Prior's plans? Swiftly, Eddie assured Bowles that he would retain his full rights and responsibilities, as would key performers, if they so desired. Eddie hoped that Prior's involvement would mean a financial transfusion for his ailing American Travesty Company. Whatever had been negotiated, the entire company was glad when the season's last presentation of "Off the Earth" took place in Evansville, Indiana, on May 2.

All things considered, "Off the Earth" had enjoyed a fair season. Even with its scheduling problems and erratic cash flow, the show played the entire year, to good reviews and responsive audiences. Unfortunately, the production made no profits for its investors.

Eddie's first season as star and company manager had proven both promising and enlightening. As a first-time star, he gained considerable notice and augmented his following. Moreover, he continued to develop his signature roles and improve his comedy turns.

As company manager, Eddie was good with fellow actors, creating a professional rapport that made performing fun, but he demonstrated limited ability in dealing with the administrative aspects of the operation. Nor did he display much knowledge of, or interest in, the production's constant financial adversities. He likely was aware that the show's accessories cost a great deal to manufacture and maintain, at the same time that its operation was underfunded. Investors showed only a fickle commitment to the production. When they believed profit might not be generated, they pulled out early in the season. Scheduling was a constant worry; much money was lost by inefficient routing and downtime. Because of insufficient financial resources, minor money matters became major problems.

When Eddie and his partners planned the next production, he readily agreed to concentrate his efforts on performance. Thomas Prior would handle stage management, and George Bowles would handle all scheduling and advertising. Yet adequate financing of the new production remained problematic.

It was now more than eight months since Lola's death, and Catherine was nearly one year old. During the summer, Eddie was at home and, along with his daughter, enjoyed some semblance of domestic life. His interest

in Madeline Morando (and hers in him) reignited. She had decided to join his new company the previous summer, giving up a secure position with Henderson. Further, she agreed to continue in Eddie's new show, fully aware of the risks involved. They were seen together often, off stage as well as on. "A love affair in progress," George Bowles observed. At this time, however, they did not consider marriage a prudent choice, since the new show could fail, and both might be unemployed.

After a number of temporary delays, "Little Robinson Crusoe" opened at the Schiller Theater, June 15. Yet, the production's debut with Chicago audiences was immediately inconvenienced:

> After some vexatious delays in getting the curtain up for "Little Robinson Crusoe," the introductory bow was made 15. A large crowd gathered Wednesday evening, which had been announced as opening night, and were disappointed to find a notice to the effect that the opening had been postponed.[8]

And, when critics finally reviewed the new effort, they issued ominous warnings:

> It is agreed that the piece possesses the elements of success, the chief criticism on it being the placid way in which material to make it bright has been borrowed from previous successes. The piece is certain to get a fair share of the summer business, but it will be necessary to keep Eddie Foy more under subjection before the production fulfills all of its possibilities.[9]

All those responsible for "Little Robinson Crusoe's" development wanted to capitalize on Eddie's reputation with Chicago audiences by featuring him for almost the entire length of the performance. Unfortunately, there was not enough original material to support him, nor were co-stars Marie Dressler and Sadie McDonald satisfied with secondary billing.

Thanks to Bowles' extensive advertising, the production attracted good crowds. On hot and humid nights, Bowles offered free iced tea to patrons at intermission, an innovation quickly adopted by competitors. But the show continued to receive more than its share of complaints, as reported by the *Clipper* correspondent:

> With the only new thing in town, things have been coming easy for the Schiller since Little Robinson Crusoe opened. There has been plenty of criticism for the production, much more than there would have been had it come here from New York, instead of having its initial production in this city. The chief complaint is that the music and many of the situations have a decidedly familiar air.[10]

Now, with the stage situations more evenly balanced among the performers, critics noted:

> Opinion is fairly divided as to who is the star, Eddie Foy or Marie Dressler.[11]

Marie Dressler was twenty-six years old, pug-nosed, hefty — even by prevailing fashion standards — and a "shouter," already a veteran of variety and comic opera. She admitted to having been born ugly and choosing comedy to take advantage of it. Dressler was also among a younger generation of aspiring actresses who sought equal billing and salaries with actors. In the view of various theater managers, this ambition made her difficult to get along with. She had not yet reached star status (that would come in another year); but she demanded — and obtained — more lines and stage time in "Little Robinson Crusoe." Eddie didn't seem to mind. Still, Dressler continued her demands.

"Little Robinson Crusoe" was billed as an operatic burlesque, in three acts. The prolific Harry B. Smith wrote the libretto, and the music was composed by W. H. Bachelor. Both were ex-Henderson people.

The story opens on what the program describes as "the anti-fat Summer Hotel." Robinson Crusoe (Adele Farrington), a captain of marines, is in love with Polly Perkins (Sadie McDonald), who in turn is loved by Ben Bolt (Bobette Rodney), captain of the press-gang. Hockstein (George A. Beane), a philanthropist, and one who has had Polly in pawn for money borrowed, seeks revenge upon Crusoe, who has turned his marines loose to loot Hockstein's pawnshop. Hockstein persuades the press-gang to abduct the hero. The entire company go aboard ship, suffer shipwreck, and are lost upon a desert island. Dare Devil Willie (Eddie Foy) is an amateur pirate, the skipper of a canal boat, who makes the acquaintance of a deaf-and-dumb saltwater fairy. Ophelia Crusoe (Marie Dressler) is the operator of the hotel and joins Willie in opening a saloon on the island. Although the island was uninhabited before the shipwreck, the newcomers start a theater and race track for the benefit and pleasure of the survivors. Hockstein and Bolt are defeated by Robinson Crusoe, and he sails back to civilization with Polly. Willie and Ophelia stay on the island to run their business and make money.

Eddie sang four songs and performed as a swashbuckling pirate (with rubber sword and oversized boots), a myopic skiff skipper, and a race track tout. He also presented a pantomime with the deaf-and-dumb saltwater fairy, a burlesque of mistaken communication. The dancing chorus of racehorse jockeys was led by Madeline Morando.

Writers called in to refurbish the libretto worked hard to improve the show. By its third week, critics acknowledged "Crusoe might hold its own with other attractions." By the fourth week, the production was seen as "settling down to business"; Eddie was viewed as improving, as well:

> Eddie Foy is doing better work than he has done before, and seems disposed to drop a few of the clownish ways that have characterized his recent performance.

By late July, "Crusoe's" second edition was introduced and improved business even more. The *Clipper* suggested:

The second edition of Little Robinson Crusoe is taking very well with audiences, and the Schiller is well-filled at each performance.[12]

Dressler and Eddie were featured in new sketches and reported to be "working well together." One particular sketch performed by Eddie, "The New Woman," in which he burlesqued an upper-class woman shopping in a department store, was well received. However, the new sketches seemed to have little relation to the libretto, resembling variety-style olios, rather than being integrated into the plot. Nevertheless, audiences enjoyed them; the show was beginning to generate a profit.

Early in August, Gustave Frohman, the oldest of three brothers who made names for themselves in the theatrical management business, took over the Schiller Theater lease from Thomas Prior. The other principals in the management of "Little Robinson Crusoe" had been unaware that Prior had accumulated debts of more than $15,000 during the preparation of the production and was about to file for bankruptcy. Had he filed, the show would have closed. Frohman generously assumed the accrued debt, thus allowing "Crusoe" to go on tour.

Upon leaving the "Crusoe" company, Prior joined the "Little Christopher" company and promptly hired away Sadie McDonald. "Crusoe" management attempted to prevent McDonald from leaving by filing an injunction against her, but she barricaded her apartment door, departed through a rear exit, and left on a train for New York to join her new employer.

The "Crusoe" company was in turmoil. A replacement for McDonald had to be quickly signed, and new material devised for the replacement's sketches and songs. Preparations were being made for the road tour, but Frohman had to be consulted on all expenditures. Dressler informed the management she was looking for another engagement. Eddie was rightly concerned that the production was in jeopardy.

Frohman caused additional problems by hiring stage hands from another theater to assist backstage, much to the displeasure of "Crusoe's" staff. It seemed almost a miracle that "Little Robinson Crusoe" survived to leave for St. Louis, the first stop of its tour, still intact.

The first few stops on the road attracted good audiences and profits. In St. Louis, "the show caught on well with the crowd, encores were frequent, and Mr. Foy received an ovation." In Pittsburgh, "Eddie Foy, in Little Robinson Crusoe, did excellently." Yet events in Cincinnati again raised doubts about the viability of the show. Frohman announced that Thomas Prior had been rehired — he had left the "Little Christopher" company after two weeks — and would take over stage management again. To no avail, Eddie argued against rehiring Prior.

The following week, after an engagement of "good audiences" in Louisville, scheduling problems surfaced anew. For the next fortnight, the company played ten one-night stands, even in large cities like Cleveland and Toledo, and suffered a number of off-days.

By the end of October, "Little Robinson Crusoe" was near closure. Prior was again fired. Salaries were two weeks behind, and the company refused to perform until they received some pay. Marie Dressler abruptly left the company for another engagement.

Apparently, her departure was hastened by an on-stage episode between her and Eddie. Performing a sketch, in which she played the hotel manager and he a pirate, Dressler moved downstage to recite her lines, playing solely to the audience. In response to this upstaging, Eddie immediately improvised, inserting new lines into the dialogue and temporarily confusing Dressler:

"Send the chambermaid quickly."

Dressler was surprised, but she kept her composure, answering, "Why, what's the matter? Is anything wrong?"

Foy replied, "I want some towels."

"Aren't there any in your room?" inquired

Dressler, not sure where Eddie was taking the dialogue.

He quickly responded. "Yes, one. But I dropped it, and it broke."

While the audience laughed heartily at the joke, Eddie escorted Dressler to the door of the hotel, closed it behind her, and strolled offstage.

Dressler and Foy played together some years later, albeit reluctantly. Off the stage, they seemed to share a formal, if distant, respect. On stage, they played their comedy sketches with gusto. In her autobiography, Dressler referred to Eddie as "the prop comedian," because he seemed to be constantly hunting "funny accessories for business." She blamed Eddie for her aversion to their use, although, examining her performances, it becomes clear that she herself consistently used them to further her own comedy.

Fortunately for the production, a theater investor, Arthur Stine, purchased the show and assumed its debt from Frohman. "Crusoe" was soon revived. George Bowles took over temporarily from Prior. Eddie revised the entire third act.

"Little Robinson Crusoe" played in St. Paul and Minneapolis to full houses, but reporters noted the company's continuing financial turbulence. As they were preparing to leave Minneapolis, police attached box-office receipts and scenery for debts due from the production's previous owners. Stine, Bowles, and Eddie went to court and succeeded in averting the attachment, then hustled the company onto the train for their next engagement, in Keokuk, Iowa. They were scheduled to play a few more one-night stands before arriving in St. Louis.

Rumors about "Crusoe" were reported daily, most predicting its demise due to insolvency. It was reported that a St. Paul investor would purchase the play; Henderson would take over management; scenery and costumes had been appropriated. Box-office receipts in St. Louis seemed to have been affected by these rumors:

Eddie Foy is a favorite here, but his return date of "Little Robinson Crusoe" has failed to draw the patronage it deserves.[13]

At the conclusion of its St. Louis engagement, the Kansas City date was canceled and the company disbanded. Still optimistic about the show, Eddie returned to Chicago with ideas to form a new company. He immediately rehired performers from the disbanded troupe, wrote new material, and secured an engagement at a local theater.

As preparation for the new production took place, Eddie and Madeline decided to marry. Evidently, love had triumphed over concerns about job security.

They were married on December 16, 1895, in a Chicago Catholic church. A brief ceremony was attended by Eddie's family and theater colleagues. Since Madeline did not appear on stage for the next seventeen years, she likely decided to retire at once. For the foreseeable future, she planned to travel with Eddie while he was on tour. Catherine remained in Chicago under Mary's care.

With great effort, Eddie procured sufficient funds to reconstruct "Little Robinson Crusoe." He secured the former production's scenery and costumes and persuaded a few of the leads to join his new company. The remainder were recruited from local sources, including a number of variety acts appearing in vaudeville houses. Little of the libretto was retained from the original show. Ironically, Eddie booked the revised "Crusoe" into the Chicago Opera House, to open December 22, hopefully for a two-week run. The production's first week was inauspicious, however. According to the *Clipper's* analysis:

Even the moderate prices at the Chicago failed to make "Little Robinson Crusoe" go; the attendance last week was small.[14]

By the end of the second week, Eddie had no choice but to close the show. "Crusoe" was unable to attract sufficient audience even to pay salaries. The *Chicago Tribune* announced the cessation:

The Little Robinson Crusoe Company is disbanded, their two week engagement at the Chicago being probably the last time that the piece will be seen.[15]

With the show's closure, Eddie was unemployed. For more than a month, he was unable to book any vaudeville engagements, the quickest way to return to the stage. His financial situation had not yet become desperate, but Eddie was anxious about maintaining his recently acquired star status while negotiating future engagements. He was aware that the life of an unemployed actor, no matter how celebrated or even adored, was at best uncertain.

Thanks to Jim Corbett, Eddie met with William A. Brady, Corbett's agent. In recent years, Brady had become a highly successful agent-producer, and he was proving to be an influential theater impresario.

William A. Brady came from humble beginnings in San Francisco's Irish neighborhood. An aspiring actor, Brady quickly realized his dramatic deficiencies and, in 1888, turned to producing plays. His initial attempts failed when he was accused of pirating works for presentation. Just as the boxer was turning professional, Brady discovered Corbett and became his manager. After Corbett defeated John L. Sullivan for the world's heavyweight championship, Brady featured Corbett in a number of vaudeville and farce-comedy productions. While these were rather amateurish shows, they proved highly profitable for Brady.

At the time Eddie and Brady met, the producer was negotiating leases for a number of theaters, including one in New York. He was looking for shows to fill engagements at these theaters. In addition to Corbett, Brady managed Maurice Barrymore, two touring melodramas, two farce-comedies, and a new play about Bowery life. Brady wanted Eddie to star in one of his farce-comedies, "The Strange Adventures of Miss Brown."

While Eddie believed the vehicle to be inadequate for him, he signed a contract

A formal portrait of Madeline Foy just after she and Eddie married. Madeline retired from the stage and, a year later, gave birth to their first child, Bryan.

because he needed employment and the salary of $400 a week. Immediately, Brady announced the signing of "the great Eddie Foy," and booked "Miss Brown" for an opening at Hooley's Theater in Chicago, March 11, 1896.

From its beginning, the production was poorly managed. The company had only two weeks of rehearsals before opening. Scenery and costumes were borrowed from Brady's other shows and made to fit. Supporting performers were obtained from local sources, none of them ever before having played in a first-class show. Dance routines and music were hastily incorporated into the sketchy plot, appearing more like olio interpolations than integrated scenes.

At the time this picture was taken, "Gentleman Jim" Corbett had just defeated John L. Sullivan for the heavyweight championship of the world. Corbett's popularity persuaded promoter William A. Brady to tour him on the variety stage, performing boxing exhibitions. It signaled the beginning of Corbett's long career in vaudeville. (Museum of the City of New York)

"Miss Brown's" story tells of a well-known socialite who is kidnapped, while her place in society is taken by a janitor (Eddie Foy), who spends most of the show impersonating Miss Brown. Little information about the production's libretto is now available; Eddie was reported to have used previous material for his signature sketches; his performance in drag, however, was seen as "an emphatic hit."

Eddie was correct regarding his assessment of "Miss Brown." The *Chicago Tribune's* review indicated the production was in some distress:

> A big crowd was on hand to see the first performance of "The Strange Adventures of Miss Brown." The play did not produce a favorable impression on the audience, and it is doubtful if it will draw another audience as large as on opening night.[16]

Almost immediately, Brady and Foy inserted new material into the production. Still, Chicago critics remained skeptical, noting that there were a variety of opinions about "Miss Brown," all of them negative. Rather than attempt to deal with what seemed to be a losing battle, Brady decided to put the show on the road.

For the next two weeks, Brady had "Miss Brown" playing one-night stands in Iowa and Illinois, close enough to Chicago that, if the show failed, costs for returning the company would be small. Surprisingly, audiences in these towns enjoyed "Miss Brown" and filled the theater. Brady was so pleased with the results that he booked "Miss Brown" for a run in San Francisco. The *Clipper* published Brady's press release:

> Wm. A. Brady's Company, headed by Eddie Foy, in "The Strange Adventures of Miss Brown," opened its touring season in Streator, Ill. Mr. Foy is said to have made a big hit in the role of Miss Brown. The tour extends to California, including two weeks at the Baldwin Theater, San Francisco. Mgr. Brady has arranged to have Mr. Foy continue under his management. Next season, he will have a new farce-comedy.[17]

From Illinois, the company played in St. Louis, Omaha, and Kansas City, to "good business." After a week in Denver, they visited Colorado Springs, Pueblo, and Leadville. Eddie received a returning hero's welcome at the Tabor Opera House in Leadville, but he could see the town had lost its frontier enthusiasm and was now in rapid decline.

Initially, San Francisco's response to Eddie and "Miss Brown" was excellent:

> At the Baldwin Theater, "The Strange Adventures of Miss Brown" was presented last evening for the first time here, and Eddie Foy received an ovation from his many admirers. The success of the play seems assured for the two weeks of the engagement.[18]

Unlike the positive reactions the show had received in small towns, however, San Francisco's more sophisticated patrons found the production "only fair." Baldwin attendance declined during the show's second week. A week in Los Angeles attracted only "light audiences." A long jump to the Pacific Northwest ensued, for engagements in Portland, Oregon, and Tacoma and Seattle, Washington. Receipts and reviews alike were disappointing, with only fair business. Brady knew the production was doomed. He decided to close its tour and return the company to Chicago.

Nostalgically, for Eddie, "Miss Brown's" last performance took place in Butte, Montana. He had last played Butte thirteen years previously, performing variety sketches with Jim Thompson and Rose Howland. Aware of his attachment to the city, the audience cheered him almost continuously throughout his performance, demanding encores of not only songs, but also comedy sketches.

In fact, "Miss Brown" had done amazingly well for a weak show that appeared to have no life. Brady later admitted to its haphazard creation, crediting Eddie for keeping the show alive for its ninety-one performances.

In June 1896, Eddie was again unemployed, with no prospects for the fall season. And Madeline was pregnant. He had learned two significant lessons: running one's own company was a constant struggle, and the relative security of performing in inferior shows challenged an actor's commitment, both to the profession and to his audience.

Beset by doubts and anxieties, Eddie had been sorely tempted to tell the audience in Butte his favorite gag about unemployed actors. It had an increasingly poignant immediacy, now that the joke was on him:

"I'll have you know I come from a long line of actors."

"Yeah? Outside what casting office?"

Chapter 9

I'm in lower three. Is my berth ready?
No sir. I thought you politicians made up your own
bunk.

"Hotel Topsy Turvy"
(Washington, D.C., engagement)

Do you know how to make a baby buggy?
Yeah, put him in bed with the dog.

"Hotel Topsy Turvy"
(Davenport, Iowa, engagement)

ACTOR: *I come from one of the oldest families in*
New York.

DIRECTOR: *I want a man to act, not for breeding pur-*
poses.

"Hotel Topsy Turvy"
(Los Angeles engagement)

An actor does not know what it feels like to be out of work until it actually happens. For more than fifteen years, Eddie had enjoyed regular employment. Now, for the third time in a year, he was unemployed, with no engagements or prospects in sight.

Madeline was five months pregnant. She and Eddie were living on the last of his earnings from "Miss Brown," and that income was threatened by a judgment in favor of William Brady to repay a loan. Brady had advanced Eddie "living expenses" prior to the opening of "Miss Brown," because he had been paid no salary the previous seven weeks. What did Eddie do about this predicament?

First of all, he contacted friends, fellow actors, and stage managers, seeking leads on specific company openings. He wired theater managers around the country, asking about possible roles in upcoming productions. He talked to writers of librettos and music who might be composing new shows or renewing old ones. He avidly scanned weekly editions of *The New York Clipper* and *The Dramatic Mirror* seeking announcements of new productions or ads looking for touring company acts. He frequented bars and saloons where fellow performers shared the latest gossip.

When it was disclosed that Eddie was considering an engagement in vaudeville with two professional billiardists (he would sing and dance between billiard exhibitions), observers noted he was having considerable difficulty finding a job. Though comedians of his rank were hard to come by, Eddie was unable to attract offers of employment.

Eddie's star status had been undermined by his recent history of show failures. Though critics acknowledged that, in his case, the star was often better than the production, even carried the production, a premature closing or losing season usually reflected negatively on the *actor*. In contrast, when a show was highly successful or profitable, managers and producers received the accolades.

In addition, Eddie had so successfully perfected his unique persona as an eccentric comedian that managers were hesitant to hire him for traditional comic roles. Most writers of musicals were unable to prepare librettos for Eddie's style of comedy, and they still considered comedy to be secondary to music and dance. Besides, Eddie wrote a good deal of his own material; writers were reluctant to share their authority.

Fortunately, the role and style of stage comedy were about to change. In September 1896, Weber & Fields, already successful managers and performers of travesty and satire, would open their own theater on Broadway, legitimizing zany comedy as a production's *raison d'être*. Their artistry would open the creative door to comic invention, promoting a marriage of comedy with song and dance, a union unexplored to this point. In coming years, Eddie's career would benefit from this expansion of comedic style.

For the moment, however, Eddie's biggest barrier to employment was his salary. He was certainly one of the highest-paid comedians of the time, earning no less than four hundred dollars a week, more than $16,000 a year for a theater season. (In current dollars, he would have commanded more than $150,000 a year.) Most productions could not afford that level of salary for a comedian. Even the most generous stage productions of the day, those of comic opera, had little room for a comedian of Eddie's stature, particularly one who might outshine a show's high-priced prima donna.

Nor did Eddie wish to succumb to vaudeville. Stage stars had not yet come to perceive a stint in vaudeville as an enhancement to their careers. Eddie had achieved stardom in musical comedy and was determined to continue in that genre. He decided to hold out a bit longer.

Fortuitously, a month later, Manager Davidson contacted Eddie and offered to help underwrite a revival of "Off the Earth." Eddie was ecstatic, not only because it meant employment in his chosen realm, but also because he believed the show had a good deal of potential, management mishandling having been responsible for its premature closure.

Davidson, John W. Dunne, and James E. Sullivan were all both investors and active participants in the new production. Davidson supplied his theater and promotional savvy for "Off the Earth's" opening; Dunne produced the show; Sullivan not only directed, but also played the role of Stag Party. The remainder of the company, however, consisted of unknown and, in some cases, untried performers. Scenery and effects were available from the former production. Sullivan and Eddie attempted to freshen up the libretto with new business. John Gilbert continued to get credit for the libretto, but he likely would not have recognized it.

"Off the Earth" opened at Milwaukee's Davidson Theater September 28, 1896. Those connected with the production hoped the show would survive. Critics noted the play had done "fair business" with "poor support from the company," but apologized by suggesting that audience familiarity with the show might have contributed to poor attendance. When the production played in Minneapolis and St. Paul, the *Clipper* reported "good business," since "Eddie Foy is always popular here."

For the next six weeks, "Off the Earth" played one-night stands through small towns in Wisconsin and Illinois, to some profit. Near disasters threatened the company a number of times, but they survived, and the tour continued. In Madison, Wisconsin, in the middle of the first act, a severe wind storm shook the theater and blew off the roof. The audience bolted for the exits; luckily, no one was injured. In Danville, Illinois, the sheriff seized the evening's box-office receipts to make sure that all expenses would be paid before the company departed.

Brief runs in Indianapolis and Cincinnati not only helped sharpen company performance, but also gained enough funds to pay salaries in a timely manner. When "Off the Earth" visited Chicago at the end of November, playing the Haymarket Theater, the *Chicago Tribune* reported that:

> Eddie Foy, in "Off the Earth," was applauded by one of the largest audiences ever seen at this theater.[1]

The Chicago engagement afforded Eddie an opportunity to spend time with Madeline, who was very close to giving birth. Ten days later, while performing in Lincoln, Nebraska, Eddie received a telegram announcing that "his wife presented him with a son, December 8." They named him Bryan (after William Jennings Bryan) Lincoln (after Abraham Lincoln) Fitzgerald. It was reported that Eddie played an "excellent performance" that evening.

St. Louis audiences gave the company big houses and self-confidence as they headed South. For many of the performers, this was unknown territory. During January 1897,

"Off the Earth" played in twenty cities and towns through Tennessee, Arkansas, and Texas. For the most part, the show was well received. In February, it was presented in seventeen cities and towns, the largest being New Orleans, Louisiana, the smallest, Macon, Georgia. There were a few stops where business was only fair; yet in the main, it was reported they "did good business." Most Southern audiences had never before seen Eddie, and they were quite amused by his comedy style, particularly his eccentric costumes and dancing.

When the company reached the rarefied atmosphere of a high-class theater in Washington, D.C., everyone was pleased they had mastered the Southern tour and continued to receive weekly salaries. In Washington, Eddie and Sullivan were persuaded to offer additional performances at matinees and at midnight, a novel bit of scheduling. Within six days, the company presented fifteen performances, which included daily matinees and three midnight shows. Box-office receipts were good; but Eddie swore never to work that schedule again, because of its effect on the company. Both John Dunne, the producer, and Mary Marble, a leading lady, left the company because of unhappiness about the scheduling. Although Eddie and the company were lauded for their merry-making, the loss of Dunne (also an investor) and Marble nearly closed the show. A stop in Cincinnati had "big houses," but "Off the Earth" closed a week later in Marion, Indiana, a somewhat cheerless ending to a tough but otherwise satisfying six-month tour, since the results had proven to far exceed what anyone had hoped when the production opened. Anxious to see his five-month-old son for the first time, Eddie returned to Chicago. He also had to begin seeking his next engagement.

During the summer of '97, Eddie was occupied with a number of theatrical activities. He participated in charity benefits, performing old minstrel skits. When Billy Emerson was in town, the vaudeville theater at which he was appearing suddenly closed, stranding the performers. Emerson was broke; Eddie gave him a place to stay and helped him return to San Francisco. Of course, Eddie continued his own search for a fall engagement, but he seemed unable to find the proper showcase for his talents.

In early August, Eddie was approached by the firm of Klaw and Erlanger, at the time an emerging power in the newly-formed Theatrical Trust. They offered him the leading comic role in their touring production of "In Gay New York," a musical review that had already experienced a successful year's run. The show's original star, Walter Jones, had departed the company for another engagement. Although the salary was good, Eddie was reluctant to sign, because Klaw and Erlanger were rapidly earning a deserved reputation for being unsympathetic to actors. Nonetheless, since the new theater season was about to begin, and he had no other prospects, Eddie agreed to perform for them.

The Theatrical Trust, more commonly known as the Syndicate, was soon to become the most powerful, influential, and feared organization in the theatrical business. In an era of free-wheeling, monopolistic practices, its objective was to gain complete control over theaters and performers throughout the country. For more than a decade, with Klaw and Erlanger as exemplars of predatory greed, the Syndicate accomplished their goal of almost total domination.

Mark Klaw, a man of hawk-like features and piercing eyes, had studied law. His introduction to the theater occurred when he litigated pirated productions of "Hazel Kirke" on behalf of Gustave and Daniel Frohman. The ever-keen Abe Erlanger soon noted Klaw's success.

Abraham Lincoln Erlanger started his career by selling opera glasses in a Cleveland theater. When financier Mark Hanna bought the theater, he hired Erlanger as treasurer. Hanna's obsessive, suspicious nature regarding commercial transactions seemed to feed Erlanger's own business instincts. In time,

Erlanger came to be regarded as a cold, hard, relentless, and often less-than-scrupulous negotiator.

Klaw and Erlanger formed a partnership, moved their offices to New York, and immediately purchased the Taylor Theatrical Exchange, a previously relaxed and rather disorganized booking agency. To expand their business, they produced a number of modest shows, using actors and theaters under their control. They also built two theaters in New Orleans, which gained them effective control of bookings in most other Southern theaters.

About this time, theater manager Al Hayman teamed with Charles Frohman, who had just opened his own booking bureau. In 1895, Klaw, Erlanger, Hayman, and Frohman met with theater owners Nixon and Zimmerman of Philadelphia and Rich and Harris of Boston to form the Theatrical Trust. Its operating head was Abe Erlanger. By February 1896, they announced control of thirty-seven theaters and hundreds of actors. Any productions or actors who wished to be booked into their theaters would have to join the Syndicate. Initially, few heeded their threat.

By 1897, however, the Syndicate had gained control of theaters in the Midwest and West, in cities from Chicago to San Francisco, and routes through Pennsylvania and Ohio. Companies who wished to travel west had no choice but to stop at these theaters, since long jumps to Western theaters were generally unaffordable. The essential idea of the Syndicate's system was to force theater managers to accept the plays the Syndicate offered, with performers they booked, receiving, in turn, an unbroken schedule of shows for the entire theater season. By doing so, the Syndicate argued, theater owners would get better terms and actors would be guaranteed constant work. When independent theater owners and producers balked, threatening to take their plays to second- and third-class houses, the Syndicate called their bluff, betting that managers of lesser houses

Marc Klaw and Abraham Erlanger, the powers behind the Theatrical Syndicate. Erlanger dealt mercilessly with anyone who refused to abide by the Syndicate's terms. Because Eddie supported the White Rats actors' union, he was unemployed for almost a year.

would be loath to raise prices for the shows and displease their regular clientele with attractions that didn't fulfill patrons' expectations.

As for actors, obtaining a promise for an entire season's booking was still too new a notion to judge its success. To this point, few top performers had signed with the Syndicate; new productions had not yet encountered booking problems in major theaters. Still, stories of abuses toward actors, particularly on the part of Erlanger, had begun to circulate. He was already urging his partners to agree to a scheme to charge actors a fee for guaranteeing their seasons.

"In Gay New York" was a review in three acts, created by three stage veterans: Hugh Morton, book; Gustave Kerker, music; and George W. Lederer, director. A typical review (later redesignated "revue") included pretty girls, lavish settings, individual performances by headliners, and ensemble skits. It closely resembled variety, with its olio turns, but offered a loosely unified theme and a story with a beginning and an end, all the while competing with comic opera in its absurdity. One of the chief advantages of a review was the flexibility it offered managers to change acts and actors without disrupting the show. It also had the advantage of persuading audiences to return often to the theater, because the production regularly featured new performers and new business, a very profitable enterprise for the Syndicate.

The "Gay New York" company was composed of thirty-five performers, but only two, Eddie and Lee Harrison, were well-known. With the exception of the two stars, each performer had to perform multiple roles. For example, a young actress, Gertrude Zella, played Sally Tompkins in Act One, Sally Brown in Act Two, and Lurline, The Water Queen, in Act Three, adding bits to her original costume in each act to identify her new role. Eddie portrayed Edgardo Macbeth Boothand Barrett Todd, a stranded actor.

The story tells of a group of actors stranded in Maine, who are mistakenly booked into New York's celebrated Casino Theater. The portrayal of small-town performers in the big city, exemplified by episodes at Grand Central Station and the Waldorf Hotel, constitutes the action of Act One. The second act is set first in the lobby of the Casino Theater, then moves to its stage, giving performers the opportunity to deliver their specialties. Act Three takes place at Coney Island, where the entire ensemble exhibits their happiness about having played "the big time."

Eddie appeared in all three acts, impersonated various well-known social and political personages (from the familiar actor Sir Henry Irving to President Grover Cleveland), and sang a number of undistinguished songs. In one skit, Eddie and the chorus performed while standing on their hands, eliciting astonished gasps from the audience when the girls flipped over in vivid display.

"In Gay New York" opened at Klaw and Erlanger's new Harlem Metropolitan Theater (142nd Street and Third Avenue) on August 28, 1897. It was the theater's official opening, and critics seemed more interested in its opulence than in the production itself:

> The theater presents a magnificent appearance, covering the greater portion of the block. It is built of Indiana limestone and terra cotta. The house proper will seat 1,600 comfortably. The interior decorations are in old gold, ivory, salmon pink and Nile green, artistically combined throughout. The house was packed from top to bottom.[2]

After only one week in New York, the company embarked on an extensive tour, combining week-long runs in Cleveland and Cincinnati with one-night stands through the states of New York, Pennsylvania, and Ohio. Overall, the production generated good business at all of these venues. It wasn't until reaching Milwaukee, however, that Eddie was individually recognized as star of the show.

In mid-October, the company played Chicago for a week's run. Eddie returned home, not having seen Madeline and Bryan since early August. During this brief visit, Madeline became pregnant again.

From Chicago, the company traveled to St. Louis for a week's engagement. "'In Gay New York' is known here as a good thing and Eddie Foy scored well," reported the local newspaper. Along the route to Denver, short stops were made at small towns in Missouri and Nebraska. Most of these venues were witnessing a high-class, New York-based show for the first time.

With the rapid opening of modern theaters in smaller towns, venues owned or leased by the Syndicate, touring companies were forced to include them in their routes. While it meant frequent stops and more performances, it also meant shorter jumps and good box office receipts, as local audiences jammed theaters to see well-known performers. These engagements gained headliners national recognition at the same time they educated small-town audiences to be more sophisticated theater patrons. Demonstrably, popular entertainment was expanding throughout the country.

Most of these engagements were one-night stands, hard on performers but profitable for managers. Some weeks, performers saw only that part of a town between the train and the theater. A typical week of one-night stands for a large, well-mounted production like "In Gay New York" had to be tightly scheduled. Usually, the company traveled on its own train, comprised of passenger cars where the company slept, ate, and rehearsed, along with box cars filled with scenery and costumes.

A press representative preceded the production by two weeks. He had two objectives: to initiate billboarding and promotion for the show, and to hire backstage staff and additional musicians for the orchestra. Press reps usually carried a show's primary advertising. They met with influential townspeople, attended local social gatherings, and bought drinks strategically to ensure strong support for the show's upcoming visit. A good press agent was almost as valuable as the production's star.

A company would arrive during the early morning hours on the day of the show. After breakfast on the train, the entire company went to the theater to rehearse, gain familiarity with the stage layout, and coordinate with stage hands. For members who had completed their tasks, lunch was served back on the train. Early afternoon was usually rest time. An early dinner was served, because everyone had to be back at the theater by 6:00 P.M. to prepare for an 8:00 P.M. curtain. Performances usually ended by 11:00 P.M., with the entire company back on the train by midnight, ready to depart for the next town. On Wednesday and Saturday, matinees were presented. Performers rested between shows, then ate a light dinner, while in costume. A full season likely lasted thirty weeks. A typical tour in the late 1890s usually meant an equal number of weekly runs and one-night stands. Sundays were the only off-days, almost always taken up with travel.

In Denver, the company played at the elegant Tabor Opera House, "the house packed at every performance." Their engagement in San Francisco was extended from two weeks to three, due to Eddie's popularity in that city. He was "often encored, and curtain calls were frequent." On the way to Los Angeles, they played one-night stands in Oakland, San Jose, Sacramento, and Stockton. From Los Angeles, the company made a long jump to El Paso, Texas, to begin a quick tour of Southern cities — San Antonio, Houston, New Orleans, Mobile, Birmingham, and Atlanta — all one-night stands. Returning through the Midwest, they played engagements in a number of Canadian cities before closing out the month of January 1898, in Philadelphia.

Over a period of six weeks, the company had played fifty performances in twenty-two locales, having traveled over 4,500 miles. A number of cast members departed because of other commitments, were fired, or simply grew tired of touring. Replacements seemed to have no negative effect on profits.

In February, "In Gay New York" returned to New York, playing Harlem and Brooklyn theaters "for two weeks of good houses." The *Clipper* noted:

> "In Gay New York" succeeded in renewing its popularity last week and will continue to boom things during the current week. Although there have been a number of changes in the cast, since it was last seen here, no complaint was heard on that score.[3]

Having performed satisfactorily for Klaw and Erlanger, Eddie was confident he would finish the season with the show. His employers, however, already had other plans. Although having done reasonably well, "In Gay New York," now completing its second year, was running out of venues. When a successful show reached this point in its existence, managers, aware that its future life would likely be short, sought to unload the production and gain whatever additional profit they could. Since the selling price was usually reasonable, there were plenty of interested parties.

While the show was playing in New York, Klaw and Erlanger sold it to Lederer and McClellan. Walter Jones, who had played in the original cast, was rehired as company manager and also assumed his original role, replacing Eddie. Eddie was summarily given notice that the New York run would be his last with the show.

The Syndicate was gaining a reputation for such actions. Unfortunately, an actor had no protection. Contracts were meaningless; litigation was expensive and often thrown out of court. Some leading actors, like Nat Goodwin, Francis Wilson, and Richard Mansfield, tried to organize opposition to the Syndicate, declaring their concerns in the harshest terms. Mansfield wrote:

> I consider the existence of the Syndicate a standing menace to art. Its existence is, in my opinion, an outrage and unbearable.[4]

In defense of performers, Francis Wilson stated:

> Dramatic art, in America, is in great danger. A number of speculators has it by the throat, and are gradually but surely squeezing it to death.[5]

When Wilson drew a cartoon that represented the Syndicate as a giant octopus, each appendage labeled with a characteristic transgression, no newspaper would publish it, fearful of losing the Syndicate's contribution to advertising revenues. The *Dramatic Mirror,* operated by a fierce opponent of the Syndicate, Mrs. Harrison Grey Fiske (the former actress Minnie Maddern), published an article condemning their practices:

> Its characteristics are greed, cunning, and inhuman selfishness. Every actor in America should at once join the Actor's Society of America.[6]

Yet all of these protests failed to convince other actors to join their organization. It was too late. The Syndicate already owned a sufficient number of theaters to control most routes. They also controlled booking for enough performers to dictate the operation of many productions. Forced to accept Syndicate dominance, a number of actors nonetheless began plotting ways to overcome their oppressors. But it would be another two years before they could openly challenge the Syndicate again.

In addition to being unemployed, Eddie was furious about having been treated so badly by Klaw and Erlanger. While there was nothing he could do about it at the time, he was determined to fight the Syndicate at such time that his involvement would assist in defending his profession. In the meantime, he returned to Chicago to seek another job.

For many years, Charles E. "Honey Boy" Evans had been a popular dancer in comedy two-acts. He and his partner, William F. Hoey, asked colleague Frank Dumont to write them a sketch, which proved to be a vaudeville success. When they persuaded writer Charles Hoyt to expand the sketch into a full-length play, "The Parlor Match" made Evans and Hoey national headliners, until their separation in 1894. Evans then bought the Park Theater in New York City, refurbished it, and renamed it the Herald Square Theater, using the venue to produce plays he authored.

Evans had just completed a new musical comedy slated for a September opening. Knowing he was available, Evans asked Eddie to take the role of leading comedian in "Hotel Topsy Turvy." Nixon and Zimmerman, Syndicate members, were planning to route the show; however, Evans assured Eddie that he controlled the production's management. The show seemed right for Eddie, and it was being opened in New York. Having been out of work four months, he accepted Evans's proposal. Rehearsals were to begin in late July.

During that summer, Eddie's attention was occupied by two events. One was joyful; the other tragic. On June 12, 1898, Charles, Eddie's second son, was born. All agreed that he looked just like Eddie.

In late August, while Eddie was rehearsing in New York, Jim Corbett was training in Asbury Park, New Jersey, preparing to fight Bob Fitzsimmons, who had won the heavyweight championship from him the previous year. From his brother, Harry, Corbett received a telegram stating that their father had shot and killed his wife and himself. Corbett was devastated. The papers reported that the senior Corbett had been in poor health for some time and had become demented. Mrs. Corbett had been shot in the head while she slept; then her husband killed himself by discharging the revolver in his mouth.

Eddie rushed to Corbett to console him. Although seeming to recover from the tragedy, Corbett never regained the championship, winning only one bout over the next five years, after which he retired from the ring.

When the cast for "Hotel Topsy Turvy" met for the first time, Eddie discovered his leading lady was again to be Marie Dressler. While they worked well together on stage, their offstage demeanor was distant. Both Evans and Eddie were quite aware of Dressler's propensity to break contracts, but she and Eddie were an excellent comedy team.

"Hotel Topsy Turvy" opened at Nixon and Zimmerman's Lafayette Theater in Washington, D.C., on September 19, 1898. The production was an Americanized version of "L'Auberge du Tohu-Bohu," a musical farce first produced in Paris, in 1897. In addition to Evans, Arthur Sturgess and Edgar Smith adapted the libretto from the French. Victor Roger and Lionel Moncton wrote the music. The production was billed as a vaudeville operetta.

The action of the play takes place at Bourg Fleury, a small village in France. Cluny's Colossal Combination, a troupe of acrobats, have pitched their tent in the town. Owing to a lack of money, they are in debt to Mme. Malicorne (Carrie Perkins), hostess of the White Horse Inn, who has refused them further credit until their bill is paid.

M. Moulinet (Ed J. Connelly) and Mme. Moulinet (Emma Brennan), residing across the street from the inn, depart on a trip because they can't tolerate the noise from the troupe, leaving their nephew Louis (Frank Doane) in charge. Paul Blanchard (Aubrey Boucicault), a friend of Louis's, arrives to visit Cecile Dremer (Mae Lowrey), with whom he has fallen in love. Paul has heard that M. Dremer (Frank Smithson) has planned to marry his daughter, Cecile, to Count Zarifouli (Alexis Law Gisiko), a nobleman, and that Dremer, the Count, and his daughter are to meet at the White Horse Inn that evening to finalize wedding plans.

Paul and Louis, touched by the distress of Mme. Flora (Marie Dressler), manager of Cluny's Colossal Combination, provide the acrobats financial aid. Flora proposes they change the sign of the inn to the house of

Moulinet and, in disguise, disgust Dremer with the Count, leaving the way open for Paul to win Cecile's hand. Lebeau (Eddie Foy), a trapeze performer, impersonates Dremer; Flora represents Cecile; and Paul and Louis play waiters at the supposed inn. Flora/Cecile disgusts the count with her vulgarity; Lebeau/Dremer does likewise. In the midst of this hubbub, the Moulinets return to find their tranquil home turned topsy-turvy.

After numerous ridiculous mistakes and misunderstandings, Mme. Malicorne arrives with gendarmes to arrest M. and Mme. Moulinet for stealing her sign. The truth unfolds; Dremer gives his daughter to Paul, while the Count falls in love with Flora.

A scene of the acrobats at supper turns into an orgy, featuring serenades with tin pans as accompanying instruments, acrobatic feats, and can-cans. By the end of the act, the stage is strewn with food, broken bread, smashed plates, seltzer water, and champagne bottles.

Dressed in white tights, with baggy shorts and floppy hat, Eddie first played an acrobatic clown. In a later foppish costume, he impersonated Dremer with an accent that fractured the English language, poured soup into his waistcoat pocket, strode atop the dinner table, swung on the chandelier, played music on plates and tumblers, and sang a few songs, all delivered with a serene yet ludicrously pained expression.

According to the *Washington Times*:

> In a curious combination of Gallic triviality, British stupidity, and American rowdyism called "Hotel Topsy Turvy," the piece itself may be dismissed curtly, without injustice. The honors, however, were won by Eddie Foy.[7]

The *New York Clipper* was even less generous to the play:

> Those who had gathered here in point of humor were doomed to disappointment. In fact, but for the vigorous and painstaking work of Marie Dressler and Eddie Foy, it is doubtful if the work would have lived throughout the first performance.[8]

Still, after introductory weeks in Washington, D.C., and Baltimore, "Hotel Topsy Turvy" played twelve weeks in New York to full houses. The New York press called the show "of slight fabric, harmless and diverting." The public responded with crowded theaters and hearty approval for the uproarious stage business.

By "Hotel Topsy Turvy's" third week, the *Clipper* reported the production "had been greatly improved." By the sixth week, they declared:

> It is constantly improving by the addition of new songs or other matter, and is likely to make a good record.[9]

Of even greater significance, New York critics "discovered" Eddie Foy. *Times* critic, Edward Dithmar, wrote in his column:

> Mr. Foy is not a newcomer, exactly. He has been on view before. He ought not to be permitted to lapse again into obscurity, for he is as funny a fellow as our stage knows.[10]

The critic from the *New York Telegraph* was even more eloquent:

> Mr. Edwin Foy's clown is the best bit of legitimate burlesque seen on Broadway in many years. Foy, though a comedian of great experience, is likened to some newly discovered genius of the footlights. Foy's inimitable clown has developed into a stage character that is quite as worthy as the "Humpty Dumpty" of the late George L. Fox, the "Fritz" of the elder J. K. Emmet, or the "Dundreary" of E. A. Southern, and it is safe to say that Mr. Foy is one of the luckiest actors with whom the gods have played kindly pranks in the past dozen years.[11]

No sooner was the production hailed as one of New York's top entertainments than an announcement by George W. Lederer unsettled the company. Lederer told the press that he had just engaged Marie Dressler for a new show, to open about Christmas. Distribution of souvenirs at "Hotel Topsy Turvy's" fiftieth performance was overshadowed by rumors of the show's impending demise.

To everyone's surprise, however, Dressler did not defect. In fact, she was reported to be working "with added vigor" when the production's second edition was initiated at the beginning of its ninth week at the Herald Square. The *Clipper* correspondent reported the show had "new impetus and showed marked improvement."

After the show's 100th performance, quite an achievement for a musical farce on Broadway, the company began preparations for an extended tour by playing two short engagements, in Buffalo and Rochester, over the Christmas holidays. While "Hotel" was in Rochester, Dressler suddenly left the company. Scrambling to find a replacement and reintegrate the show, the company had to return to New York to regroup. Belle Thorne was hired to replace Dressler, but she lacked Dressler's comic touch. Eddie expressed his displeasure with the entire episode. Coincidentally, he injured his ankle and was on crutches for a week. When the show moved to the Newark Theater for a week's engagement to begin the new year, Dressler just as surprisingly rejoined the company, and Eddie regained his health. No one seemed to know or cared to reveal the reasons behind these strange events.

At the Chestnut Street Opera House in Philadelphia, "'Hotel Topsy Turvy' delighted audiences" and filled the house the entire week. The *Ledger* declared:

> The laughter, applause and expressions of approval clearly showed the favor with which the attraction was received. As amusement is the only object strived for, Marie Dressler, Eddie Foy and the others in the cast deserve credit for their success in creating fun.[12]

Because of large audiences, the engagement was extended another week. Yet when the company returned to New York to prepare for their Western tour, Marie Dressler again retired from the company. This time, however, the managers were prepared to deal with Dressler's erratic behavior. She was quickly replaced by Amelia Summerville, an equally competent comedienne. Unfortunately, the continuous disruption affected company performance, and Cleveland's theater critic noted its decline:

> The attraction was hardly up to the high standard set, and much adverse criticism was heard. Amelia Summerville and Eddie Foy are easily the shining lights of the show; the former, on account of her statuesqueness and diaphanous drapery, made quite a hit with the male element. Eddie Foy, however, is not himself and is not equal to his former successes.[13]

Following the Cleveland engagement, "Hotel Topsy Turvy" visited Washington, D.C., where the production had opened its season seven months before. Midway through its run, it was announced the show would close its season because of "deservedly poor business." Disheartened, the company returned to New York. After eight months on the road, Eddie continued to Chicago to see Madeline and the children. He had an important question to discuss with her.

Like other headliners, Eddie firmly believed that New York had become the center for popular theater productions. It was New York where deals were made, performers hired, productions prepared and opened. Based on the Gotham critics' recent discovery of his comic talents, Eddie was convinced that living in New York would provide the best opportunities for him. When he discussed the possibility of moving with Madeline, she agreed.

But when should they move? Eddie replied it would depend on his employment for next season.

Eddie was correct in his assessment of

The Foy family, just before they moved to New York. Bryan stands next to Madeline. Charles sits on a cushion. Richard is in Madeline's lap.

New York's ascendancy as the center of popular theater activity. At the turn of the century, New York was presenting hundreds of musical comedy, comic opera, and vaudeville productions every year. Syndicate booking power was located in New York. Production money came from New York investors and banks. Most of the authors of librettos and music were centered in a small area of Manhattan, humorously labeled Tin Pan Alley. Broadway, the street that epitomized theater entertainment in New York, was now becoming a national symbol for theater glamour, prestige, and success. What played well on Broadway, it was believed, would play well throughout the country. Touring companies from Broadway were transforming naive audiences into sophisticated patrons and judges of theater arts. Increasingly, wise performers lived in New York for the vast array of job opportunities it provided.

As Eddie contemplated where and when his next engagement might occur, he was surprised to receive a telegram from impresario David Henderson. Henderson inquired about Eddie's interest in a new extravaganza currently in preparation.

During the past five years, Henderson's business had suffered. "Aladdin, Jr." had been his last fairy-tale production, a failure at the box office. He lost his lease on the Chicago Opera House. He had been reduced to managing small touring companies, with mixed results. Still, his charisma as a theater impresario remained; he had finally gathered sufficient investors to mount a production reminiscent of his previous extravaganzas. Announcing the new show, he boasted, with typical Henderson bravado, that it would cost over $50,000 and no money would be spared to make it a success. Henderson believed that Eddie's heightened popularity would help make his show a hit.

Eddie knew Henderson's character and operations all too well. Yet he believed this engagement would gain him further visibility in New York and other Eastern cities. Promised six hundred dollars a week, Eddie accepted Henderson's offer. When he joined the company to begin rehearsals, Eddie discovered they had only three weeks to opening night, usually insufficient time to prepare a large production.

"An Arabian Girl and Forty Thieves" was a revival and reworking of Henderson's "Ali Baba." The extravaganza opened at the Herald Square Theater April 29, 1899. J. Cheever Goodwin had rewritten the libretto. Julian Mitchell, fresh from successes at Weber & Fields' Music Hall, produced the play. Henderson had hired old colleague Fred Dangerfield to design the scenery; the costumes were prepared in Europe, as before, and Signor Marchetti was again in charge of the ballet. William Parry, late of the Metropolitan Opera House, was stage manager. Not surprising, then, that the *New York Clipper* critic declared the opening of the production "a Chicago Opera House night."

The extravaganza was mounted in four acts and ten scenes, the plot essentially copied from its original libretto. Ali Baba, a poor woodcutter, formerly a member of Baghdad's 400, now down on his luck, was played by Dorothy Morton. Morgiana, a slave girl in love with Ali Baba, was played by Clara Lane. Arraby Gorrah (J. K. Murray) was the nefarious chief of police. Eddie played the vagabond Cassim D'Artagnan, Ali Baba's brother. As stated in the program, "the world owes him a living, which he collects." Old friend George Ali played Ali Baba's donkey.

Taking the stage for the first time, Eddie held a lantern "to see where he came in." He performed a pantomime with the donkey, sat in a collapsing chair, and tripped down stairs. He sang only two songs, "Pictures" and "The Hoo-Doo Man," neither of them memorable hits. Yet the humor of his character, his delivery and timing, grotesque costume, and understated fun completely captured the audience. The production was lavish; the girls gorgeous; the libretto trite, and prosperity questionable. But Eddie was a hit.

New York critics were united in their assessment of the show. One called it "simply atrocious." Another wrote, "the language of the piece denotes paresis and is well calculated to produce it." More generously, another called the show, "inoffensive, and it will not harm anybody. 'The Arabian Girl' is better furnished for travel."

In contrast, reactions to Eddie's performance were excellent:

> Most of his business, including his encounters with Ali Baba's donkey, are reminiscent of the era of Grimaldi.
> Eddie Foy cannot help being amusing and he scores a big hit. His personal humor provided a goodly share of amusement that was not in his lines.[14]

"The Arabian Girl" played to full houses the first week of its engagement, but patronage gradually declined. At the beginning of the show's third week, surprising both his investors and the company, Henderson filed for bankruptcy. Of his total liabilities of $130,000, most had been incurred in Chicago, when he owned the Chicago Opera House. Naturally, he had not shared this information with his investors. Henderson's debts were principally for salaries, material, rent, and hotel bills. There were 170 creditors listed, including four banks and many private investors. His assets consisted of a paid-up life insurance policy worth $7,500. The *Clipper* announced the fourth (and final) week of "Arabian Girl," because it "lacked sufficient patronage." None of the company, including Eddie, received any salary for the abbreviated engagement. Henderson's days as a theater impresario had ignominiously ended.

At about the time "Arabian Girl" closed, Evans, Nixon and Zimmerman sold their interests in "Hotel Topsy Turvy" to Dunne and Ryley, managers of a number of second-class productions. Quickly, they offered Eddie the role he had played in the show, at the salary he was earning at the time; Eddie accepted without hesitation. Since Eddie's salary represented almost one-fourth of the entire salary allocation for the show, most

other company members were lesser-known actors. Funds for production were also limited, even though some scenery and costumes were salvaged from the previous year's show.

The second season of "Hotel Topsy Turvy" opened at Chicago's McVickers Theater August 19. The production was received with some indifference:

> "Hotel Topsy Turvy," with Eddie Foy as star, last night opened its second season. The selection was not the best that could have been made, for although Mr. Foy was as funny a clown as ever, the piece and company failed to interest the audience to any great extent.[15]

After two weeks of mediocre patronage, the show was put on tour, playing one- and two-night engagements in Illinois and Iowa. In progress were emergency repairs to the libretto and comic turns, soon rewarded by a concomitant increase in audience approval. By the time the company reached Kansas City, the *Clipper* reported "big business," Eddie's antics "heartily applauded," and Dunne and Ryley's show "a nice production." Box office successes in St. Louis and Topeka assured the managers "Hotel" had been saved from a premature death.

Two weeks in San Francisco brought out all of Eddie's local admirers and resulted in "splendid business." The company had sharpened its presentation and now settled down to a long tour, featuring one-night stands in small towns while *en route* to weekly runs in large cities. Trips south to Los Angeles and north to Seattle attracted good business. A two-day engagement in Butte, Montana, crowded the theater to honor Eddie for his longtime association with the town. As an encore, Eddie obliged his fans by performing some of the old routines he had done for them nineteen years earlier. Audiences were delighted.

An early-season snowstorm in Minneapolis and St. Paul didn't prevent patrons from filling the theater to see Eddie and "Hotel." For all these local critics, Eddie had become the show; the rest was just scenery. To support Eddie, Billy Jerome sent him new songs and new comic material designed to keep his sketches fresh. Even his own company marveled at how often Eddie incorporated new material into his business. It seemed to make no difference to anyone that his material often had little relation to the libretto.

Throughout December, the company played one-night stands in Nebraska, Arkansas, and Texas, with a full week in New Orleans to celebrate the holiday season. To take advantage of the crowded houses, Dunne and Ryley advanced prices. The theaters continued full. Only in Austin, Texas, was the audience small, because of high ticket prices.

To begin 1900, the company continued its series of one-night stands through Alabama and Georgia, playing towns where first-class performers and shows had not previously been seen. Local critics found the show offensive; nevertheless, audiences filled the theaters. In mid-January, when "Hotel" reached Cincinnati, a popular city for Eddie, the show drew "crowded houses." The *Clipper* correspondent emphasized what critics everywhere believed when he stated:

> It was generally acknowledged that Eddie Foy saved "Hotel Topsy Turvy" from dreariness and disaster.[16]

Presented with humor by the press, an incident in Cincinnati gave Eddie front-page coverage. It was reported that, while Eddie was asleep in a hotel, a former employee of "Off the Earth" stole his clothes. She claimed Eddie owed her a salary of $25.60, and she wanted payment of the debt. Eddie was forced to borrow clothes to get to the theater and vowed he would fight her claim. The outcome of this episode is unknown. Yet a discerning local wag was curious to know how the woman got into Eddie's bedroom.

The company enjoyed a two-week rest the end of January. The *Clipper* suggested they were experiencing scheduling problems. When "Hotel" renewed its tour, the show played two months of one-night stands, verifying the *Clipper's* observations. During the break, Eddie returned to Chicago to visit Madeline and the children, not having seen them since early September. One result of the visit was another pregnancy for Madeline.

While "Hotel" continued to entertain large audiences, at advanced prices and excellent box office receipts, the company (and Eddie) seemed to have lost their zest performing. Since September, "Hotel" had played 155 performances, in sixty-four cities and towns, and had crossed the full extent of the country, east and west, north and south, in seven months. The company was exhausted, and all concerned anticipated the show's closure.

In early March, "Hotel" played a week in Philadelphia with "satisfactory receipts"; critics, however, noted the company's fatigue. Finally, Dunne and Ryley announced the show would close in three weeks, at the end of March. A short trip to Bridgeport and New Haven, Connecticut, and Providence, Rhode Island, attracted good crowds. The final week returned the company to Philadelphia and, to no one's surprise, small audiences.

On April 1, Eddie was on his way back home. Eddie and Madeline planned to move to New York during the summer and hoped to be settled before their next child was born. Now more than ever, Eddie needed a job.

Chapter 10

Now hypnotism is the force by which the world is ruled,
It heals the sick and by its use the wisest men are fooled;
I've studied hypnotism and I practice it each day,
When I do things that others can't, I often hear them say:
It must have been Svengali in disguise,
With his bright hypnotic eyes, we were taken by surprise,
I do my work so well that everyone I mesmerize,
Says, it must have been Svengali in disguise.
 "It Must Have Been Svengali in Disguise,"
 sung by Eddie Foy in "The Wild Rose"

Finding Eddie lying on the grass, under a large elm tree in front of his recently rented cottage, an observer would think he was thoroughly enjoying a few, rare, quiet moments off stage. His children roamed the neighborhood, accompanied by the Foy maid, gathering newly discovered treasures to show their parents. Madeline worked in the kitchen with her older sister Clara, who had joined them when the family moved to New York. By her own admission, Clara had asserted her intent to bring order and discipline to the Foy household. It would prove an admirable pursuit, against substantial odds.

Manhattan's West Ninety-eighth Street was still remarkably rural, with only a few houses on the street. There were no sidewalks. The street was paved with packed clay, not unlike those Eddie recalled from some of the Western towns he played. Only Broadway, a block east of the Foy house, was paved. Yet, looking south, just over the trees, one could see multistory apartment buildings seeming to creep farther north every day.

The Foy cottage contained four bedrooms: one for Madeline and Eddie; another for Clara and almost six-year-old Catherine; a third for Bryan and Charles; and the fourth for the maid, who would very soon be sharing her room with the new baby. The living room was somewhat smaller than the dining room, the latter quickly becoming the center for all family activities. A barn in the backyard housed a goat and a dog and served as a sheltered playground for the children when the weather turned inclement.

Eddie and Madeline had fallen in love with their first house, even if it was only rented. A few blocks to the west, fresh waters lapped the banks of the Hudson River, active with commerce and transportation. Few vehicles drove their street. Bird songs and animal sounds abounded. Around each house in the neighborhood ran a white picket fence. After a day in the city, immersed in the cosmopolitan milieu of the theater, Eddie found his home and family an oasis, always loving, if not entirely peaceful.

Yet Eddie's frequent trips into the city these days had a specific purpose. He needed employment, and as quickly as possible. Madeline had proved an able economist, handling money matters with amazing agility. The family was living on the earnings from Eddie's long run with "Hotel Topsy Turvy," but those funds would soon be exhausted.

Eddie's inquiries now led him to a group of friends who were, at that very moment, plotting to challenge the Syndicate and another recently-hatched theater managers' organization.

An enterprising theater manager in Springfield, Massachusetts, Pat Shea, proposed the formation of a clearinghouse through which performers would be booked, for a fee. In December 1899, Shea and two other managers took their idea to E. A. Albee, partner and business manager of the Keith-Albee organization, owners and operators of more than 100 theaters throughout the U.S. Coincidentally, Albee had been investigating the potential of entering the booking business. In June 1900, Albee called together the leading vaudeville managers for a series of meetings in Boston. They included, F. F. Proctor, Hyde & Behman,

Kohl and Castle, J. D. Hopkins, Tony Pastor, Weber & Fields, and the owners of the fast-growing Orpheum company, Morris Meyerfield and Martin Beck. Together, these managers controlled over sixty of the first-class vaudeville houses in the country. The object of the meeting was the creation of an organization, to be known as the Association of Vaudeville Managers (A.V.M.). Once established, the A.V.M. would operate a centralized booking agency.

Albee persuaded the managers that a centralized agency, using Syndicate methods, was necessary for the continued growth of vaudeville. To offset the argument from performers that they would lose income under this new arrangement, the A.V.M. would guarantee forty or more weeks of annual employment. Actors would no longer need agents, nor would they be able to negotiate by forcing theater managers to bid for their services. Of course, Albee assured the managers, this was in no sense a trust or monopoly. Suspicious of Albee's intent, neither Tony Pastor nor Weber & Fields agreed to join the organization, opting to continue their independent operations.

Implications for performers were ominous. In order to get bookings, they had to join the A.V.M. In addition, they had to pay a five-percent fee for every booking they obtained. The agreement also required actors to accept any routing during the forty-plus-week season. The deal would be based on minimum railroad fares for easy jumps. Actors would have to pay out of their own pocket for unexpected, revised, or long jumps, which were a common occurrence. The contract also stated that an act could be terminated by a house manager during or before the third performance in a given week, usually a Tuesday-night show. Thus, the forty-week contract would be actually effective only once the curtain fell on the third or Tuesday performance. Potentially, this unilateral cancellation could take place each week, at each city in which the actor performed. Nor could the actor ever cancel the manager.

Performers awoke one morning in June to read in the newspapers that a new trust, the A.V.M., would now dictate what theaters they could play in, when they could play them, and at what salary. Since performers already enjoyed exorbitant salaries, the A.V.M. argued, and the supply of performers was greater than the demand, the unfit would soon be weeded out. Suddenly, actors needed protection, shelter, and a defense.

George Fuller Golden seemed an unlikely leader.[1] He was a pugilist, poet, reader of classics, an idealist, and a vaudeville artist. He had performed an interesting, if uninspiring, routine that mixed prize fighting with dancing, playing in Midwestern variety houses. He went to London in 1899 to enhance his career in English music halls but failed to gain acceptance. Stranded in London, with large debts, an ill wife, and no means to return to the U.S., Golden was befriended by a group of London music hall actors, who called themselves the Water Rats. They assumed his debts and assisted him and his wife to return to America. He arrived in New York in May 1900, precisely when the A.V.M. was announcing its intentions. Golden asked the obvious question: Why shouldn't actors in the U.S. have a collegial protective group as well?

A month later, eight men met to form what was to become the first actors' union in America. They called themselves the White Rats. At their second meeting a few days later, sixteen actors attended. By the third meeting, fifty had joined the group. When some complained that the name of the group was ill-conceived, they were educated to the fact that "rats" spelled backward was "star." The primary objectives of the White Rats of America were to protect actors from managers, preserve their salaries, and build respect for performers, in the face of powerful Syndicate forces.

Eddie attended his first White Rats meeting in July and joined immediately. He was fully cognizant of the ongoing conflict between managers and actors; his scuffles

with Henderson and his recent dismissal by Klaw and Erlanger were clear examples of managers' duplicity. Eddie quickly became an avid spokesperson and convinced many fellow actors to join the organization. When the White Rats took a public stand against the A.V.M., Eddie's name was prominent among the list of protesters. In response to this announcement, the A.V.M. threatened that no member of the White Rats would obtain a booking from them for the coming season.

At the same time this battle was unfolding, Eddie was looking for work, unsuccessfully. Even though an established star, he was forced to submit to humiliating auditions, only to be rejected with no explanation. The White Rats helped him with loans, but these were not sufficient to support his family.

In early August, the White Rats opened an office at 1418 Broadway as a clubhouse for members and a place to conduct business. At the same time, the independent management team of Buckley and Constantine interviewed Eddie for the starring role in their new musical farce, "A Night in Town." The play was mediocre, the settings of average quality, and the routes not yet established; but it was a job for Eddie, doing what he did best. Further, his partner in comedy would be Eva Tanguay, already a Broadway star, noted for her animated delivery and eccentric feathered costumes. Immediately, they began rehearsals for a September opening, on the road.

"A Night in Town" opened at the Olympic Theater in St. Louis, Missouri, September 2. There is no record of the show's plot nor its musical numbers. The production's initial review was a portent of its doubtful future:

> Manager Stuart opened his house for the coming season last week with Eddie Foy and company in "A Night in Town." The piece was poorly patronized, and got about all that was due it at that. Foy and Eva Tanguay bore the brunt of the work, and did their best, which is all that can be said of them.[2]

Short stops in Des Moines and Omaha attracted "small audiences"; however, when the company appeared at Denver's Tabor Opera House, they played to "capacity houses." Eddie had always been popular in Denver, and his appearance generated enthusiastic audiences and good box-office receipts. Had Denver patrons not responded in this manner, Buckley and Constantine were prepared to close the show.

Hearty response to Eddie in San Francisco provided additional life for "A Night in Town," but subsequent bookings were difficult to obtain. The Orpheum Circuit, a part of A.V.M., controlled most Western theaters, and they appeared to have no available time for an independent company. After a week's layoff, the company had to jump to Salt Lake City, followed by another long jump to Portland, Oregon. Although the show did well in both cities, expenses exceeded box-office receipts. Eight weeks after opening, the company concluded their tour with a one-night stand in Butte, Montana.

It took Eddie almost a week to return to New York to see his family and alert his colleagues that he was again available. It would be almost eight months, however, before he secured his next engagement.

Eddie occupied his time with frequent trips to the White Rats office, as well as to theaters with friendly managers, who allowed him to practice when the house orchestra was rehearsing. He performed in a number of White Rats-sponsored benefits throughout the fall and winter. Ironically, he received a portion of their receipts to pay his own bills. Madeline had become pregnant again, just after Eddie's return from the West, less than two months after giving birth to Richard. It was no doubt a very disconcerting time.

As the A.V.M. applied increasing pressure on actors to comply with their stipulations, conflict between the A.V.M. and the White Rats accelerated. By the beginning of 1901, a strike against the A.V.M. appeared inevitable.

Albee wanted to prevent such a con-

George Fuller Golden, President of the White Rats of America, the first actors' union. Golden was an excellent organizer but a poor strategist. Erlanger outmaneuvered him throughout their entire confrontation.

frontation, since a strike would mean sizable box-office losses for managers. He met with Golden and the White Rats board and proposed rescinding the five-percent regulation at A.V.M.'s next meeting. But no date had yet been set for the next meeting.

To show their displeasure with the delay, some members of the White Rats refused to appear for a Thursday matinee at Keith's theaters in New York, Philadelphia, Boston, and Providence. Quickly, Albee met with Golden and worked out a temporary truce, an agreement that the five-percent commission would be abolished immediately. Believing they had won an important concession from the A.V.M., the White Rats were jubilant.

The commission, however, was not abolished. Going back on its word, Keith/Albee instead approached individual members of the White Rats, those seeming to be most vulnerable, and offered them long-term contracts to book through the A.V.M. Eddie was one of the actors approached, but he refused to be compromised. The White Rats responded by staging a series of sick-outs at various Keith theaters. Managers expressed embarrassment, and theater patrons complained about last-minute changes in bills. Unfortunately, most patrons were not sympathetic to the performers' strikes, and Keith/Albee adroitly manipulated audience impatience to stir up public resentment against the White Rats.

Sick-outs continued. Finally, A.V.M. members convened and abolished the commission. Actors believed they had been victorious and returned to work. Albee, however, continued to seduce actors away from the White Rats with long-term contracts, targeting those he knew were in financial trouble. Naturally, these new contracts included a five-percent booking commission.

By June, Albee's schemes had reduced the White Rats to token opposition. They became an ineffective group due to disloyalty from within the union. It would be another seven years before actors regained any negotiating power. Nonetheless, Eddie's staunch fidelity was finally rewarded by fellow actor Francis Wilson, a long-time, outspoken opponent of the Syndicate.

Wilson was appearing in "The Strollers," a musical comedy produced by George W. Lederer. The producer was already familiar with Eddie, having been involved in a number of shows in which the comedian had starred. Wilson wanted a "different kind" of comedian to back him. Although the role was secondary, offering only a short time on stage, at a reduced salary, Eddie accepted the engagement and immediately began rehearsals. It was a welcome change, entertaining an audience instead of clashing with managers.

"The Strollers" opened at the Knickerbocker Theater in New York June 24, 1901, for an indefinite run. Lederer hoped to keep the production in New York for as long as possible to avoid booking problems with the Syndicate, an organization he thoroughly disliked. With a reasonably good libretto, adapted from the German by Harry B. Smith, and music by Ludwig Englander, the show was regarded as a "bright and merry piece designed for the hot weather." Wilson, a popular star, had the leading role, with support from an excellent company.

The plot concerns the finding of a note and a diamond necklace by two strollers, August Lump (Francis Wilson) and his wife Bertha (Irene Bentley). When they present the note in payment of a meal, the couple is arrested on suspicion. Incarcerated in a jail run by Kamfer (Eddie Foy), they lure the Prince de Bomsky (Harry Gilfoil) and his companion, a ballet dancer named Mimi (Marie George), into their cell by a ruse and escape. It later becomes evident that the prince was the original owner of the necklace and note and had offered a reward for their return. He also intended to present a paste necklace to Mimi, with whom he was in love; he had instructed a jeweler to have the imitation necklace made. After being released from jail, the Prince and Mimi encounter Lump and his wife at a mountain resort hotel, but do not recognize them. Lump has been masquerading as the Prince; however, when de Bomsky arrives, Lump is mistaken for the agent with the paste necklace. To get out of a tight spot, he turns over the real necklace to the Prince. The Prince presents the necklace to Mimi; when he later discovers it is the real one, he becomes greatly distracted. Finally, after considerable trouble attempting to explain the mix-up, the Prince is pacified and all ends satisfactorily.

Wilson's style of comedy was not too different from Eddie's. He was acrobatic; he burlesqued social conventions, and he performed them in a droll manner. However, the comedians didn't really compete because Eddie's role — a drunken jailer, a simple clown — was an excellent foil to Wilson's more sophisticated, pedagogic punning.

Though he was on stage only a short time, Eddie sang, in his gravelly voice, about a man who was too fatigued to do anything, a turn that provided ample opportunity to stagger across the stage, bump into furniture, and recite a few "drunk" jokes. For example:

LUMP: Haven't you got your key?
KAMFER: Sure, I got lotsha keys. But would
          you help me find a couple o' key
          holes.

KAMFER: (serving food to Lump and his wife)
          That's strawberry shortcake.
LUMP: Where's the strawberries?
KAMFER: That's what we're short of.

Eddie introduced a new style in hats, the kind worn by horses, and performed a pantomime about a drunk trying to slaughter imaginary foes. In the pantomime, Eddie, seated on the floor, looks blankly about until his gaze becomes preternaturally intense. Hefting a policeman's club, he strikes the empty floor repeatedly, battling imaginary snakes and vermin. Suddenly, he grows even more agitated, for this time he really sees something. He prepares to strike with his club, but arrests himself just in time to pick up an actual beer bottle and guzzle its entire contents.

Reviewing "The Strollers," the *New York Mirror News* wrote:

> The performance in every respect proved entertaining, and there is such an abundance of material, so much that is comical, that it scored an emphatic hit.[3]

The *New York Times* declared:

> "The Strollers" is an entertainment of the kind that is popular here in the summer, and as such will have its measure of success. The show is to continue at the Knickerbocker for the season, the end of which will be determined by the willingness of the public to attend an indoor performance in hot weather.[4]

Although playing a minor role, Eddie was duly recognized by critics:

It fell the lot of Eddie Foy to furnish the fun of the performance. Mr. Foy had only a small opportunity, yet his ever droll clowning made the role of a drunken jailer shine more brightly than any of the others.[5]

From the *New York World:*

> Edwin Foy was the hit of the evening. His method is easy.[6]

And from the *Green Book* came a review that reveals much about Eddie's philosophy of comedy:

> Mr. Foy is not a bit of dramatic Sevres, but the man or woman who cannot laugh at him should consult a doctor. Foy plays the role of a jailer. His broad, yet quiet humor, his assumption of the grand airs of the serious player, his willingness to earn his salary, made him a prime favorite with those who laugh because something is funny and not because it is the fashion.[7]

As an addendum to Eddie's reviews, the *Clipper* announced that, on August 16, the Foys had added a girl to their family. She was named Mary, bringing to five the number of children crowding their Ninety-eighth Street cottage.

"The Strollers" played for ten weeks at the Knickerbocker Theater, plus two additional weeks in nearby Harlem and Brooklyn. Reviews continued to be excellent, and box-office receipts profitable. By the end of September, however, Lederer had to put the company on tour and, unfortunately, subject it to Syndicate routing. To no one's surprise, the route was awkward. They traveled from New York to Baltimore and Washington, D.C., returned to Newark, and then embarked on two weeks of one-night stands through New York and Pennsylvania. Francis Wilson's appeal and positive New York reviews strongly contributed to the show's success, and profits continued.

When the company reached Philadelphia the middle of November, Lederer announced that Wilson would be withdrawn from "The

Strollers" to take the principal part in a new musical comedy. The current production would continue on the road with another prominent comedian taking Wilson's role. Eddie believed that he would be selected for the role.

At the end of the Philadelphia run, when Wilson said good-bye to the company, he and Lederer introduced John E. Henshaw as his replacement. Eddie was disappointed, but Lederer assured him that another show already being planned would return him to star status. Reactions to Eddie by Chicago audiences only confirmed Lederer's decision, even though the opening of "The Strollers" almost didn't take place.

> The opening was almost attended by ill fortune. The box containing the score and orchestra parts failed to reach Chicago in time, but the comedy went off with a rush. Eddie Foy made a distinct hit. For many years he was the fun maker of the Chicago Extravaganza Co., and an army of his old friends have turned out to give him a royal welcome back to the city. Few actors have received warmer greetings.[8]

"The Strollers" continued on tour into the spring of 1902, mostly one- and two-night stands, through Iowa, Nebraska, Missouri, and Minnesota. A number of stops had to be rescheduled because of snowstorms and cold weather. In spite of these strains on the company, they received good reviews and "did big business."

When the production jumped to Cincinnati the beginning of March, Eddie questioned Lederer's promise about a new show. "Stay with Kamfer a bit longer," Lederer encouraged. "'The Wild Rose' will begin rehearsals in Philadelphia in two weeks."

Lederer made good his word. Eddie left the company in Toledo, Ohio, his farewell punctuated by tears and cheers from company members as he boarded the train for his new engagement.

"The Wild Rose" opened at the Garrick Theater in Philadelphia, April 21. The production planned to play two weeks in that city to smooth out the rough spots before moving on to a New York opening. The *Clipper* correspondent reported:

> "The Wild Rose" received its first production last night, at the Garrick. Bright, catchy music, handsome chorus, remarkably clever principals and attractive stage pictures characterize this latest Lederer offering. The audience was large and brilliant and received the new production with enthusiasm unrestrained. The company is capital, and the efforts of its members will doubtless pull "The Wild Rose" into good shape for the New York production.[9]

On May 5, "The Wild Rose" opened at New York's Knickerbocker Theater with great fanfare. Newspapers declared they had found "considerable merit" in the production, qualities that "will presage success." The show was labeled a musical comedy. The book (libretto) was written by Harry B. Smith and George V. Hobart, with music by Ludwig Englander, adapted from a German story, "The Bohemian Girl."

Having been switched at birth with another infant, Rose Romany (Irene Bentley), in reality the daughter of Count Von Lahn (W. Wallace Bloch), is raised among the gypsies as the daughter of Mirabel (Carrie Perkins), one of the band. Mahomet (Albert Hart), the leader of the band, knows her true identity and seeks to marry her. Mirabel tries to prevent the match, as she loves Mahomet herself. The arrival of Vera Von Lahn (Marie Cahill), the actual daughter of Mirabel, along with her new husband, Victor Hugo De Brie (Junie McCree), causes further complications. These center on Paracelsus Noodle (Eddie Foy), a fake hypnotist. De Brie suggests Noodle should be hanged unless he can hypnotize a gypsy in ten minutes. Mirabel puts a sleeping potion in the food; Noodle, desperately pretending to hypnotize the gypsies, is astonished to find them all falling asleep. After presumably blowing up De Brie with a barrel of gunpowder, Noodle and Rose escape to the Cafe Militaire, Strasbourg, where Rose is adopted as the daughter of a French regiment. Mahomet, Mirabel, Vera, and De Brie (having miraculously escaped injury) follow them to Strasbourg. Mahomet exposes to the Count the truth about the exchanged children and extracts from him what is supposed to be an agreement for Mohamet to wed Rose. Noodle steals the contract; when Rose is discovered, he presents it to the Count. It turns out to be an order for the execution of the bearer, but Noodle escapes in disguise. Ultimately, Rose chooses Rudolph (David Lythgos) as her husband, and the Count consents. Everyone is contented except De Brie who, now that his elegant wife has turned out to be a gypsy, fears that Vera will not be able to support him in the style to which he is accustomed.

As Noodle, the fake hypnotist, Eddie also burlesqued as a barmaid and a melodramatic villain. As the barmaid, he dressed in Tyrolean costume, a giant bow in his hair, with two long braids down his back almost touching the floor. He sang three songs, "The Land That's Far Away," "They All Were Doing the Same," and "It Must Have Been Svengali in Disguise," the latter receiving several encores before the show could continue. All three songs had been written especially for Eddie by William Jerome.

Near the end of Act One, Eddie made his entrance by emerging from a large wooden beer mug. After whacking it with a hammer, he cried out "Hammerstein," a comic reference to the antics of impresario Oscar Hammerstein. Audiences howled with laughter for minutes before he was permitted to sing his first song. Yet Eddie's pantomime sketch with "Baby," a trained bear (George Ali), was considered the best feature of his performance.

The cast of Eddie, Marie Cahill, Irene Bentley, Marguerite Clark, Albert Hart, and Junie McCree was viewed as one of the better combinations of talent to be seen on the New York stage in years. One of the bit parts,

Eddie in 1902, just after he was signed to star in "The Wild Rose." He had reason to smile, having returned to the musical comedy stage a headliner.

Vashti, a gypsy girl, was played by a very pretty young woman named Evelyn Nesbit (later to provoke the notorious murder of her benefactor, the architect Stanford White, by Harry Thaw, her jealous, spurned husband). When Marguerite Clark left the company, Nesbit took over her role, "to good effect," reported the *Clipper*.

New York critics had seemingly rediscovered Eddie, and they again extolled his comedic virtues:

Eddie Foy is as congenially assigned as though he had gone to the playwrights and measured for the role.

Foy's rare faculty for expressive grimace, his aptitude for pantomime, his affection of stupendous gravity while telling a funny story, and his undeniably original method of rendition of a funny song stand him in good stead.

He is certainly one of the very best comedians that we know, never over-acting, never seeming to labor for effect, but doing everything easily and naturally. Foy was never funnier, and this is about the same as saying that no musical comedy ever pleased an audience more.[10]

One scene in the show featured a number of children, who sang in the chorus supporting Irene Bentley. A few days after the show's opening, agents of the Society for the Prevention of Cruelty to Children (the Gerry Society) served notice to close the show unless the children were removed from the cast. Lederer had no choice but to comply. The press noted the confrontation, and also reported that Lederer was appealing to local politicians to repeal the law regarding the use of children on stage.

A week later, Eddie interpolated a new Jerome song into his act, "A Most Unlucky Man," which included a verse concerning Lewis Nixon, the corrupt leader of Tammany Hall. Police Inspector McLaughlin and Bridge Commissioner Shea were in attendance that night and loudly disputed the apparent slur against their boss. The audience, however, loved the joke, responding with applause and requests for encores. The song remained in the show for as long as it was performed in New York.

"The Wild Rose" continued through June and July to capacity houses and excellent box office receipts. Lederer was so pleased with the results he decided to continue the production in New York to September, an unprecedented run of seventeen weeks through the summer months. In contrast to his producer's good fortune, however, Eddie's own financial situation had deteriorated so badly that, in August, he filed a petition for bankruptcy.

While Eddie was earning an excellent salary, reported to be $600 a week, debts that he had incurred with the White Rats — when he wasn't working — and advances received from Lederer before "The Wild Rose" opened took so much out of his paycheck that he could not cover personal expenses. It appeared the shortfall would continue throughout the current theater season. Eddie claimed no

assets, with liabilities of $4,600. In order to reduce expenses, the Foys moved to a house on 151st Street and Eighth Avenue, in Harlem. Bankruptcy proceedings succeeded in reducing Eddie's debt, but his personal finances remained problematic. Within a matter of months, however, his financial situation would improve dramatically.

Coincidentally, Eddie was reminded of the wide gulf between performers like himself and the economic elite who patronize theaters. "The Wild Rose" company was hired en masse by Mrs. Cornelius Vanderbilt to entertain members of New York's prestigious 400 families with a special performance at her summer estate.

The company arrived at the villa for an afternoon rehearsal and set up a temporary theater at one end of a splendid esplanade bordered by rose bowers. Commodore and Mrs. Vanderbilt were there to greet the performers. After introductions, Junie McCree, in a strong Irish accent, remarked, "They are real goods, and no pikers." Eddie reported them to be "charming people with a natural knack of making you feel at home."

The company's performance was well received, although no encores were requested, as was usual in the theaters. After the entertainment, the company were served a lavish dinner on the lawn, to the strains of a mandolin orchestra playing classical music. After the elaborate meal, Mrs. Vanderbilt graciously took her leave, admitting that her damp eyes "were tears of joy over the pleasant evening." When she noticed Eddie with tears in his own eyes, she asked, "Why this sorrow?" Eddie replied with admirable candor: "I'm crying because I'm not as rich as you. I'd like to give an entertainment having Cornelius Vanderbilt do a cake walk for me and my five kids."

"The Wild Rose" company began their tour with a two-week run at the Colonial Theater in Boston. A large advance sale suggested full houses. Even with unseasonably warm weather, the box office was excellent.

In the midst of the Boston run, Eddie

received a telegram from his sister, Mary, that his mother, Ellen, was very sick and near death. Ellen was eighty-one years old and had been in ill health for a number of years. Eddie was unable to leave because his departure would effectively close the show. Madeline and the children, however, arrived in Chicago just before Ellen died in her sleep. She was buried two days later, surrounded by family and old friends. None of the theater patrons in Boston were aware of Eddie's loss. It was only after the company left the city that local papers mentioned his mother's death.

When her will was read, Eddie discovered he had been left an estate of almost $25,000, which included the house he had purchased for his mother ten years earlier. With this money, not only would he be able to pay all his debts, the family would also be able to secure permanent housing.

"The Wild Rose" played two weeks in Philadelphia to "crowded houses." It was a good example of a show's success in New York reflecting positively on the road. The *Ledger* pointed out:

> Since its original production at the Garrick here last season, it has met with a cordial reception in New York, and comes back with this hallmark of success.[11]

A Lederer argument with the Syndicate caused some scheduling problems. After a week in Baltimore, the company returned to Brooklyn for an unplanned stop at the Montauk Theater. They then embarked on a two-week series of one-night stands in Connecticut, returning to the Amphion Theater in Brooklyn, the previously scheduled stop, prior to their Western tour.

The tour began with one-night stands in Ohio and Indiana, preceding a two-week run in Chicago the middle of November. Upon arriving in Chicago, Eddie went to visit his mother's grave, already covered with the city's first snowfall. While in Chicago, he sold his mother's home and wired the proceeds

to Madeline, to begin planning their anticipated move, preferably to the kind of rural area they so enjoyed.

Although local critics wrote some disparaging reviews, calling the production itself vulgar, stupid, and an offense to decency, Eddie was the hit of the show in Chicago, one of his premier locales. Audiences packed the theater the entire two weeks. When Eddie made his entrance (out of the beer mug), applause and cheers lasted minutes before he could recite his initial lines. Each of his songs had to be encored a number of times. At the conclusion of each show, audiences demanded that he make a speech. Usually, he just thanked the audience for their enthusiasm; but, on the final evening of the run, Eddie was eloquent:

> Ladies and gentlemen, in the name of the company, the management, the stage hands and the scenery of "The Wild Rose," I beg to thank you for the ovation which you have tendered us tonight. What can I talk about? Myself— there is little to say. Junie McCree? There is nothing to say. Miss Bentley? She has spoken and sung for herself. The chorus? You have seen all there is to be seen. Your city? How can a man talk about a great city he has lived in for years.[12]

The audience erupted in fervid applause and almost compelled Eddie to make another speech. Instead, waving to his admiring patrons, he danced off the stage.

The company arrived in New York to play at the West End Theater for the holidays, after profitable weeks in Washington, D.C., and Newark. Back home, Eddie and Madeline began their search to find a new home for the Foy family. Old friend William Jerome suggested a rural area called New Rochelle, yet warned them, it was a long ride from Manhattan.

January 1903, found "The Wild Rose" company playing one- and two-night stands in New England, an achievement, considering the severe weather that time of year. Portland, Maine, audiences didn't mind the company's playing an extra day there because frigid weather had disabled their train.

In early January, Syndicate leaders Klaw and Erlanger had just opened their new show, "Mr. Bluebeard," at the Knickerbocker Theater in New York. While it was favorably reported a spectacular extravaganza, the show ran into casting problems that forced it to be closed down temporarily. Klaw and Erlanger needed a star comedian to lead the company; otherwise, the production could be shelved indefinitely, causing a sizable loss of revenue. Eddie Foy was at the top of their wish list, but would he perform for the Syndicate?

Through Lederer, Erlanger approached Eddie to head up the "Mr. Bluebeard" cast. Erlanger offered Eddie a guaranteed contract until June, the end of the season, and an increase in weekly salary to $800. These terms were unprecedented. Apparently with little hesitation, Eddie accepted the offer to perform for the Syndicate. After battling them for two years and being blacklisted, why did Eddie agree?

Organized opposition to the Syndicate had by now all but disappeared. The White Rats had become an ineffectual organization, given almost solely to social gatherings. Most actors had deserted the White Rats when they found themselves duped by the Syndicate. Klaw and Erlanger were now the most powerful theater owner/managers and booking agents in the business. To perform at all successfully, an actor had to agree to Klaw and Erlanger-dictated terms.

At the same time, when Eddie received the contract from Erlanger, he felt vindicated. Klaw and Erlanger wanted him because he was an established star who could carry a show. In fact, they wanted Eddie so badly that they made him an extraordinary offer, even though Eddie had previously opposed them. As surely as the Syndicate could ruin an actor's career, they could support and promote a performer more vigorously than anyone else in the theatrical business. Eddie believed this engagement would help to improve his career even more. The

prospect of a stable income and new home, especially in light of Madeline's pregnancy, surely contributed to his decision.

Klaw and Erlanger were decidedly worried about this production; they had already invested many thousands of dollars to give it a successful opening. It was reported to display unrivaled scenery and costumes, boast an immense chorus and ballet, employ unique special effects and a total of four hundred people, including all those on, above, below, and backstage. The outlay for the second act alone was said to be over $38,000. To be financially successful, the show would have to play to capacity for at least four months; Klaw and Erlanger intended for it to run much longer.

The recast "Mr. Bluebeard" opened January 21, with Eddie in the lead role of Sister Anne. The show's libretto was similar to Henderson's earlier production but restored the role of Sister Anne from the original London version, presented at the Theatre Royal, Drury Lane. J. Hickory Wood and Arthur Collins were credited with the story, adapted for the American stage by John J. McNally. Music was composed by Frederick Solomon; lyrics written by J. Cheever Goodwin, and ballets choreographed by Ernest D'Auban. Ned Wayburn managed the stage direction, one of his first jobs on the way to an illustrious career. The fairy-tale plot was only hinted at in this production, which gave way in each act to elaborate choruses, ballet numbers, and spectacular stage effects.

Mr. Bluebeard (Dan McAvoy) is a cruel monster one moment, a singer of comic songs the next. Stella, Queen of the Fairies (Georgia Kelley), spends her time attempting to thwart Bluebeard's cruelties. Ima Dasher (Bonnie Maginn) seems continually to be dancing on and off the stage, while changing costumes a dozen times. Fatima (Flora Parker) is the young woman of Bluebeard's passion.

Eddie played Anne, Fatima's ugly sister. He tended children in a skit based on "The Old Woman in the Shoe," taught a baby elephant to dance, became temporarily insane, and told stories that Adam had recited to Eve. He sang two hit songs (written for him by Jerome and Schwartz): "I Am a Poor, Unhappy Maid" and a burlesque on Shakespeare, "Hamlet Was a Melancholy Dane." In the latter skit, Ophelia (Foy) dies and descends to the lower regions — flame and smoke emanate from a trap-door in the floor of the stage — whence the girl is resurrected.

Critics were ecstatic over the new production. The *Morning Telegraph* headlined:

> Mr. Bluebeard scores an emphatic hit at the Knickerbocker.[13]

"Eddie Foy scores a hit in Mr. Bluebeard," reported the *New York Post.* "Comedian the star in most spectacular pantomime ever produced here."

Allan Dale, one of New York's most eminent critics, declared:

> "Bluebeard" at the Knickerbocker last night showed the latest and the brightest, the costliest and the lightest, the gaudiest and the noisiest, all crowded together in affluent juxtaposition.[14]

Of Foy, Dale wrote:

> I take my hat off to Eddie. He was the one quiet spot in a rampageous cast, and — mark my words — Mr. Foy's value in New York will be enhanced. Mr. Foy took his place with the really clever comedians.

The *New York Herald* called "Mr. Bluebeard" a "gorgeous show," with spectators cheering every special effect.

During one ballet sequence, a dancer took flight from the stage and soared over the audience to the upper balcony, scattering carnations upon the delighted patrons below throughout her ascension. In the dance finale, more than 100 elegantly costumed ballerinas crowded the stage to perform an intricate series of choreographic maneuvers,

ultimately composing a giant fan, with twinkling, revolving stars.

The production played for seventeen weeks and closed the season the middle of May. Klaw and Erlanger immediately announced they had again signed Eddie to appear in "Mr. Bluebeard," to tour the country the following season.

While performing, Eddie encountered more than one unexpected and potentially dangerous episode. In each of these situations, he turned accident into comedy so seamlessly that audiences had no idea the untoward incidents were not in the plot. Once, in the trap-door scene, when Eddie reappeared on stage as Ophelia, the door abruptly closed on his skirt, locking him into a sitting position on stage. Continuing his lines, he attempted to wrench the garment free in a manner so hilarious that the audience believed it to be part of his act.

Another episode with the trap-door provided more ominous portent. Cavorting as Ophelia, Eddie wore a short, pleated, white skirt, a wreath of ragged cotton flowers on his red-wigged head, and two soiled, moth-eaten wings protruding from his back and extending to the floor. When he descended into the trap-door, flames burst forth from the opening. A moment later, he reappeared from the "blazing" grave wearing a fireman's hat and carrying a scroll that he unfolded for the audience to read: "No room down there."

Rising to the stage, however, Eddie was in fact aflame. His headdress had ignited and his skirt was smoldering. Since it seemed he hadn't noticed the danger, a stage assistant ran on stage and covered him with a coat to smother the flames. Never losing his presence of mind, Eddie addressed the audience directly, exclaiming, "You never can kill a bad actor." Patrons cheered as he made his exit. Yet nine months later, playing in the same show, Eddie, the company, and a crowded Chicago theater would encounter one of the most disastrous fires in theater history.

The Foys had begun their search for a home outside the city. On one such foray,

Eddie and John Gilbert drove out to look at a home in New Rochelle that the Foys were considering. They searched more than two hours for the house but were unable to find it. When they asked a farmer for directions, he chased them off his land, threatening them with a shotgun. A month later, the Foys moved into their new home. One of Eddie's most profound longings had finally been fulfilled.

The Foy summer was spent settling into a rambling, white house on wooded property at the east end of Boston Post Road in New Rochelle. The town was located seventeen miles from New York City, in southern Westchester County. New Rochelle had been incorporated only in 1899. That same year, the town acquired its first official police force. A nearby train stop offered Eddie an easy forty-five minute ride to the city. (Three years later, George M. Cohan touted New Rochelle in his musical comedy hit, "Forty-Five Minutes from Broadway.") Eddie named their new home "The Foyer."

The house was almost two miles from the business center. On several acres, the property contained a gently sloping hillside ideal for a children's playground. There were few neighbors, and the frontage road was rarely in use. Not long after moving in, the Foys acquired a cow, a horse (for the carriage), chickens, cats, dogs, and a goat. According to local observers, activity in and around the house seemed sometimes unruly. When someone asked, "Is that an orphan asylum?" the reply was, "No. That's where Eddie Foy lives." A joke among the locals suggested that, whenever police found a lost child, they immediately called to see if one of the Foy kids was missing.

Rehearsals for "Mr. Bluebeard's" second season began mid-August, for a late September opening on the road. While the libretto remained much the same, new exotic acts were now added to the spectacle. Eddie, too, added new business to his sketches.

"Mr. Bluebeard" opened in Pittsburgh,* Pennsylvania, September 28, at the spacious Alvin Theater. Enthusiastically, the *Pittsburg Dispatch* declared:

> The biggest and most magnificent spectacle ever seen in Pittsburg was presented last night at the Alvin Theater. It was Klaw and Erlanger's "Mr. Bluebeard." Stupendous is the word that best describes the production. Massive and gorgeous scenery, an immense crowd of pretty girls, magnificent costumes, colored lights, catchy music and plenty of fun were the elements that made up the entertainment. Eddie Foy, a Pittsburg favorite, was the star among the comedians. The audience could not get enough of him. Arrayed in skirts, as Sister Anne, his ludicrousness was exaggerated.[15]

In Cleveland, the show was extended a second week due to crowded houses. While Indianapolis reviewers reported the production not up to "expectations of the crowd," they praised Eddie for his work:

> Foy's fun is the same as ever — infectious — and when he bowed and smirked as Fatima's sister, Anne, and sang "Hamlet Was a Melancholy Dane," and told the stories that Adam told Eve, he scored again on the Indianapolis laugh-loving public.[16]

A week at the Century Theater in St. Louis generated "good business. The company's trip to Chicago was delayed, however, because a new theater at which they were to perform, the Iroquois, was not yet ready. While the troupe waited in St. Louis, Eddie entered a billiards tournament and won the grand prize. Local newspapers gave his victory more prominence than "Mr. Bluebeard."

The grand opening of Chicago's Iroquois Theater had been postponed a number of times because construction had been slower than anticipated, much to the embarrassment of the city fathers. Installation of lighting had proven more difficult than planned. Ropes and pulleys were found to be inadequate to

---

*The spelling "Pittsburg" rather than "Pittsburgh" is retained in quoted material to be consistent with its usage at that time.

support the asbestos curtain. Some audience seats had not yet arrived. To add to the builders' woes, a streetcar strike made it difficult for workers to get to the theater.

Two weeks before the theater's originally planned opening, on November 14, the Commissioner of Buildings made a detailed inspection of all Chicago theaters. He found that nearly every one of them violated at least one of the city laws dealing with fire escapes, exits, construction materials, fire equipment, and fire doors. Iroquois Theater management rushed to meet the Commissioner's recommendations. When at last the Iroquois officially opened on November 24, all of the modifications required had in fact not yet been completed. The *Clipper* noted the delay and pointed a finger at the men responsible:

> This is the latest of a series of announcements which have, of necessity, been canceled because of delays in completing the interior furnishings. The executive staff of the new Iroquois Theater has been appointed: Thomas J. Noonan, business manager; Edward J. Dillon, treasurer; William Davis, Jr., assistant treasurer; J. E. G. Ryan, press representative; St. John Lewis, artist; Edward J. Cummings, stage carpenter; G. N. Dusenberry, doorkeeper; Walter Hueston, electrician; and Robert Murray, engineer.[17]

While none of these men were performers, all would soon be front-page headliners.

Chapter 11

I don't believe that from the time it started till the stampede took place and people were smothered in the gallery, could not have exceeded 90 seconds.
from a letter written by Eddie Foy,
January 5, 1904

Racing from New York to Chicago in only twenty hours, the 20th Century Limited streamliner thrilled its passengers. The introduction of a sweet, crunchy confection by the catchy name of *Cracker Jack*, dramatically increased theater receipts. With her skit "Ten Nights in a Bar Room," Carrie Nation had graduated from tent shows to present her saloon-smashing act on the vaudeville stage. Chicago's proud leaders beamed with self-satisfaction when they officially opened what they believed to be the country's most luxurious and beautifully constructed theater, the Iroquois.

The *Chicago Tribune* boasted that the Iroquois Theater was better than any built in the East:

[T]he erection of the new theater has given the Chicago playgoers a virtual temple of beauty — a place where the noblest and highest in dramatic art could find a worthy home. The theater is a place of rare and impressive dignity — a theater about as near ideal in nearly every respect as could be desired.[1]

When the *New York Clipper* correspondent reviewed the Chicago opening of "Mr. Bluebeard," he devoted most of his comments to the theater, marveling at the magnificence of the Iroquois:

The piece has won great favor and its beauties as a spectacular production are widely commented upon. But it is the new theater which is the talk of the town. The house is the most beautiful playhouse in Chicago, and competent judges state that few theaters in America can rival its architectural perfections, the splendor of its decorations, or its facilities for comfort. The lobby is surprisingly beautiful, the auditorium is fitted luxuriantly, and the stage is commodious and perfect in detail.[2]

On November 23, at "Mr. Bluebeard's" opening, the theater was filled with Chicago's social and political elite, along with all those even remotely responsible for its construction. At the end of the second act, the audience called for the appearance of Mr. Davis, the Iroquois' manager, and Mr. Power, its builder. To sustained acclaim, Davis strode out before the curtain with B. H. Marshall, designer and architect of the theater. Amplifying upon the theme of Western initiative and innovation over staid, Eastern self-satisfaction, Davis boldly told the audience that:

> ...the Iroquois was the creation of Western talent, abilities, and enthusiasm, and that Western appreciation and encouragement were all that were desired, and that they were good enough for any man.[3]

The crowded house cheered loudly as the gentlemen retired from the stage. When the orchestra struck up "America," the audience settled into their sumptuous seats to enjoy the remainder of the play.

Reviews of "Mr. Bluebeard" itself were uninspired:

> Appeal to the eye is the all-predominant motive. Music and mirth are subordinated to this one theme, while plot is forgotten.
>
> Of story there is little or none — nobody expected there would be any, and nobody cared because there was none. The music of the piece is hopelessly common. The chorus is admirable for its physical comeliness, and is capable of singing quite well. The ballets are attractive.[4]

In contrast to otherwise perfunctory critiques, Eddie, embraced as Chicago's own, was singled out as the production's "chief and ablest performer":

> Eddie Foy bloomed out in his old-time form and was the lord high jester of the carnival. He was present at every emergency as Sister Anne in garb which became increasingly ridiculous, ever ready with a subdued buffoonery which was like meat and drink to the audience.[5]

Crowds for the two-week run were so large and enthusiastic, management decided to extend "Mr. Bluebeard" through the holiday season, to January 9.

During the production's third week, two incidents occurred that seemed to portend the fragility of life in the theater. On December 16, just down the street from the Iroquois, the Criterion Theater caught fire, gutting its entire facade. Immediately, city inspectors were dispatched to determine what had caused the blaze.

The second incident directly concerned the "Mr. Bluebeard" company. A local gossip column published a rumor that the company would be disbanded at the end of its Chicago engagement. The news upset company members to the point that some balked at doing their jobs until they received a response — yes or no — from Klaw and Erlanger. They received neither confirmation nor denial. Nor was the company told where and when their next engagement had been scheduled.

Eddie was particularly concerned, because his family was traveling with him on tour. When he agreed to sign for the new season, Eddie had asked that the family accompany him. Erlanger not only accommodated him, he even gave the Foy family a separate compartment on the company train.

This was the Foy children's first exposure to their father's stage performance. Often, little Bryan and Charles would be stationed backstage to view the show's preparations and presentation. As the boys commented later, backstage life seemed to them a gigantic playground, filled with colorfully dressed clowns and complicated, mechanical toys. Evidently, the boys were profoundly imbued with the excitement, hyperbole, and "fun" that surrounded them.

The Wednesday, December 30, matinee

Eddie and the five little Foys *(from left to right)* Charles, Bryan, Madeline (on Eddie's lap), Mary, Richard. This picture appeared in the *New York Clipper* shortly before the entire family visited Chicago at the time of the disastrous Iroquois Theater fire.

was a sellout. Eddie had tried to get passes for his entire family, and the box office promised to provide some seats, if possible. Taking Bryan with him to the theater, Eddie left the remainder of the family — Madeline, Catherine, Charles, Richard, Mary, and three-month-old Madeline — to await his call. Upon arrival, however, it was evident the house was jammed. Eddie placed Bryan on a backstage chair, next to the side curtains. A typical holiday crowd, the audience was composed mainly of women and children.

In the middle of Act Two, the entire stage was darkened to introduce the song, "The Pale Moonlight." In jaunty costumes, eight decorative chorus girls and their dashing male escorts entered, dancing and singing. Calcium flood lamps high above flicked on to bathe the performers with a lambent light.

Minuscule sparks from one of these lamps suddenly leapt to an overhead curtain. A thin tongue of flame soon reached the proscenium drape. Electricians stationed in the flies nearby attempted to extinguish the fire manually. Some stagehands joined in the effort.

The flames shot up, igniting another curtain. Again, stage personnel tried to put the fire out by clapping the material between their hands. They were unable to act fast enough. The flames traveled beyond their reach. An electrician shouted to drop the asbestos curtain. Nothing happened.

Herbert Cawthorne, a comedian in the cast, was standing in the wings, ready to enter on cue. He saw a spark ignite a nearby gauze curtain. When he glanced back toward the stage, he realized that none of the performers had yet noticed the fire above them.

A theater fireman rushed in with a cylinder of "Kilfyre." Instead of the stream from the extinguisher striking the flames, it sprayed in the opposite direction, dousing only the fireman.

Long familiar with fire scares backstage, many performers and stagehands quietly attempted to put out the flames. Musicians in the orchestra pit could see something was wrong, but they continued to play. Performers on stage now looked up and saw the flames but, accustomed to a sight they had often seen before, believed the fire would be quickly extinguished. They continued singing and dancing. The musicians' and performers' brief hesitation prompted a subtle, discerning nervousness in the audience; all eyes, however, remained fixed on the stage.

High overhead, flames leapt from curtain to curtain. Efforts by firemen using the "Kilfyre" extinguishers proved ineffective. They called again to have the asbestos curtain lowered. When embers began falling on the performers, they suddenly bolted offstage. Thus alerted, the audience rose from their seats.

In his dressing room, preparing to go on for his elephant pantomime, Eddie heard a noise. Thinking that yet another scuffle had broken out within the anxious company (two had already occurred, attributed to pervasive insecurity concerning the show's closure), Eddie ran out to protect Bryan. Nearing the stage, he saw the entire top of the proscenium in flames. Eddie grabbed Bryan and headed for the stage door. There he encountered Harry Schroeder, a member of the company. Entrusting his son to his colleague, Eddie turned back toward the flaming stage. Though shoved and trampled, Schroeder and Bryan reached the street safely. Schroeder later discovered that he had a number of fractures but was unable to account for how he had received them.

While others ran for their lives, Eddie Foy took the stage. Smoke had already made its way into the auditorium and begun curling around the lower edges of the proscenium arch. Repeatedly, he called out, as serenely as he could, "Ladies and gentlemen, there is no danger. Don't get excited. Just walk out calmly." Between each such command, he turned to the wings, imploring in a hoarse aside, "Drop the fire curtain! Drop the fire curtain!"

Timbers began cracking, like rifles being fired. The lines that held the scenery gave way and the backdrops crashed to the stage with a thunderous roar. The audience was now clearly on the verge of panic.

Again, Eddie tried to calm them. "Get out. Get out slowly."

Focusing on the orchestra pit, he ordered the conductor, "An overture, Herbert. An overture." By that time, only six musicians remained in the pit to follow their conductor's baton. (They played "Sleeping Beauty and the Beast.") Eddie continued to demand that the fire curtain be dropped, but most of the stagehands had already escaped.

Above him, on either side and to the front of the theater, the balcony had now become a furnace. People were jamming the exits but had nowhere to go. At last concerned for his own safety, Eddie jumped down off the stage, into the orchestra pit, and ducked into the basement.

Just then, the asbestos curtain finally fell. It stopped short, however, before the stage opening had been sealed, leaving a fatal space of many feet. Just after the curtain dropped, another door in the rear of the theater was opened to enable backstage personnel to flee. The ensuing draft turned the stage into a blazing inferno, and a mass of flame shot out into the auditorium.

By this time, every available escape route was jammed. People were jostling and struggling with one another, fighting for their lives. Some exits became so densely packed with desperate humanity that no one could pass though. Those behind shoved those in front. Those pushed from behind stumbled and fell over bodies already piled on the floor. Fire exits in the balcony were found to be locked and barred. People tried to force their way through the few open doors. Most of them never made good their escape.

When electric theater lights failed, flames alone illuminated the grisly scene as the lethal draft pushed wildfire in horizontal gusts across the auditorium. Within fifteen minutes, the entire interior of the Iroquois was strewn with ashes, littered with hideous, tangled piles of charred bodies.

When Eddie escaped to the basement, a stagehand led him to a sewer. He followed the sewer to a street entrance, where he emerged into the cold daylight. Crowds of panicked people were dashing in all directions. Someone handed him a coat to cover his costume.

Other cast members — chorus girls and ballet performers — had quickly rushed out backstage doors. Those in dressing rooms on the first tier escaped with little assistance. Those on the second tier confronted an almost impenetrable pall of smoke and had to be guided or carried downstairs. Some of their costumes and hairpieces were aflame.

Outside, company members threw their arms around colleagues exiting the burning building, greeting them with cries of relief. When all the members of the company were counted, they discovered only one of their number missing; but many had been injured or burned. Stagehands working in the upper section of the flies sustained heavy casualties.

By the time that city fire wagons reached the theater, the flames had subsided somewhat. Police were already searching the smoking debris for people who might still be alive. A restaurant across the street — only an hour before filled with high-spirited theatergoers — became a makeshift hospital and morgue, with dead and injured alike carried in and stretched out on its marble-topped tables. Physicians worked feverishly. Constantly arriving ambulances were quickly filled with the injured, transported to an emergency treatment center at Marshall Field's department store. Those who could walk were led to nearby hospitals.

Outside what remained of the Iroquois Theater, the scene was chaotic. Fortunate patrons streaming out of the few available exits were met by shocked passersby, many of whom attempted to console and care for the survivors. Hysterical screams and anguished cries of desperation drowned out fire sirens, police whistles, and vehicular clatter. Policemen shouted to one another, "Look out for the living!" Tight-lipped firemen, their grim faces blackened, their eyes filled with tears, cradled charred bodies and carried them to the street.

In her hotel room a few blocks from the theater, Madeline heard police and fire sirens. Quickly informed that the Iroquois Theater was on fire, she implored, "Where are Eddie and Bryan?" No one was able to answer her.

A few minutes later, however, a runner

(Opposite): **The first picture of the Iroquois Theater aflame. Theater patrons escaping from the fire were met by curious onlookers. Rising from the balconies where hundreds died, flames can already be seen on the roof. The fire department had not yet arrived.**

from the theater informed Madeline that Eddie and Bryan were safe. At that moment, Eddie was being interviewed by reporters to obtain his first-hand account of the tragedy.

When Eddie and Bryan finally returned to the hotel, they were both grimy and bruised. Exhausted and devastated by his ordeal, Eddie collapsed on the bed. More than anything, he mumbled, he was thankful that the family had not received their promised passes to attend the matinee.

The Iroquois had been filled with more than 1,700 people. Nearly 600 were killed, mostly women and children. The exact loss of life and injured was never definitively established.[6]

If a city was ever collectively in shock, so was Chicago the following day. Newspaper headlines graphically told the grim tale:

> Chicago Scene of Greatest Calamity in History of Stage.
> Those in Balcony Found Doors Locked and Escape Cut Off.
> Procession of Dead and Dying From Theater.
> Piles of Dead Bodies in Gallery and Balcony.

Theater manager William Davis had been attending a funeral when he received the news. Upon reaching the theater, he and Power, the builder of the Iroquois, immediately released a statement blaming "Kilfyre," claiming it was ineffective on burning drapes. Thus, when the audience saw the flames, declared Davis and Power, they panicked. In their defense, the men insisted that "the exits and facilities for emptying the theater were ample" and that all efforts had been made to make the house "as fireproof as it could be made." Their statement could not have been more ill-timed.

Mayor Harrison was in Oklahoma when informed of the tragedy. Immediately, he ordered his deputy to close all theaters and move to set up a board of inquiry.

Architect of the Iroquois, B.H. Marshall, was in Pittsburgh on business. When he heard the news, he was reported to have rushed to a long-distance telephone booth and called his mother in Chicago, to determine if any family members had attended the matinee. Then, informed that his own family was safe, he broke down.

January 1, a day usually proclaimed by the sound of bells and steam whistles, was ushered in by somber silence. Mayor Harrison declared a week of civic mourning. He also ordered the arrest of Davis, Power, Building Commissioner Williams, the Iroquois Theater stage manager, electricians, and carpenters. They were to be held over as witnesses in an upcoming trial. In addition, selected members of the "Mr. Bluebeard" company were also detained for the inquiry. Among them was Eddie, whose first-hand testimony was considered crucial.

During the next few days, newspaper stories disclosed additional information about the tragedy. Reports such as these told of victims, harrowing escapes, and heroes. Singled out by the press for his acts of courage, Eddie became a national hero overnight. Reports of the catastrophe almost invariably included photographs of and interviews with Eddie. As much as he attempted to minimize his own involvement, his accounts of the drama were constantly quoted in front-page articles. Whether he wished it or not, regarding the Iroquois tragedy, Eddie had become the survivors' essential spokesperson.

> Eddie Foy Tried to Prevent Panic.
> Eddie Foy Tells Graphic Story of Women in Panic.
> Eddie Foy Tells a Dramatic Story of the Fire.

Accompanying the stories run under such headlines were pictures of himself, Madeline, and the children.

Amy Leslie, the cultivated and celebrated theater critic of the *Chicago Tribune*, wrote a particularly moving piece concerning Eddie's heroism:

Picture Eddie Foy in his ridiculous paint and absurd clothes. A startling, wicked flame licked its hideous tongue out at him and a smothered hurry and strange words near the gaudy draperies told him of more danger than anybody else there dreamed. His merry voice scattered the dancing girls and his muttered commands here and there made him master of the situation, while his heart stood still. "Play, play, for God's sake, play!" begged the actor of the orchestra and they played and Foy played and it did seem for God's sake.[7]

Sequestered in his hotel room, awaiting his turn to testify at the upcoming inquiry, Eddie nervously paced the floor, wondering yet again when and where he might obtain his next engagement. The entire "Mr. Blue-beard" production had been destroyed in the fire, and Klaw and Erlanger would be busy fending off investigations and lawsuits for months, if not years, to come.

Repercussions from the Iroquois Theater tragedy followed rapidly. The closure of all theaters in Chicago put more than 1,000 theater personnel out of work. City fire authorities examined department stores and public schools to determine whether they conformed to fire regulations. Nicholas J. Hayes, who on New Year's Day became the fire commissioner of New York, ordered an investigation of all theaters in that city. Failure to comply with building regulations resulted in the arrest of the managers of seven Washington, D.C., theaters. Every theater in Boston was closed until they could be inspected. Officials in Milwaukee shut four theaters. Similar actions were taking place in cities and towns throughout the country.

Within a week of the fire, more than 5,000 performers were idle. Across the country, theater losses amounted to millions of dollars. The Syndicate reeled from effects of the closures, which would contribute to a gradual decline in their power. Klaw and Erlanger, in particular, were distressed. Since they owned the Iroquois, they were about to be sued by hundreds of families.

Chicago's City Council began a review of all fire regulations to develop new ordinances for theaters. The County Coroner and Fire Commissioner launched an investigation to fix responsibility for the disaster. The official inquiry opened January 7, 1904; hundreds of people jammed the Council Hall to hear testimony. Along with city officials, reporters from newspapers around the world, and theater representatives, were survivors of the holocaust, some still swathed in bandages. Each witness gave a gruesome recital of his or her experience and observations. Many in attendance were so sickened by the stories that they had to leave the room. Some fainted. A nurse in attendance ministered to their needs.

During the late afternoon of the 7th, Eddie was called to testify. By this time, many survivors had already recounted his deeds. When he took the stand, a hush of profound respect and gratitude filled the hall. Marshall Everett, author of "The Great Chicago Theater Disaster," described Eddie's demeanor:

The actor's face was a study. His deep-lined countenance, ordinarily irresistibly funny without effort on his part, took on a truly tragic aspect as he entered upon his story. His indescribable, husky voice that had made hundreds of thousands laugh with merriment, was broken; there was no suggestion of humor in it. Instead it was a wail from the tomb, the utterance of a man broken with the weight of the woe he had beheld in a few brief, fleeting moments.[8]

"Will you kindly tell us, Mr. Foy, or Fitzgerald, in your own way, what transpired?" questioned Coroner Traeger.

Eddie began his narrative by recounting his performance preparations and Bryan's seating in the wings. He went on:

"The second act was on. I was in my dressing room, tying my shoes; and I heard a noise; and I didn't pay much attention to it at first. I says to myself, 'Are they fighting again down there.' There was a fight there about a week or two ago; and I says, 'They're fighting again.'

"I looked out of the door and heard the buzz getting stronger and stronger, with this excitement; and I thought of my boy; and I ran down the steps. I was in the middle dressing room, on the side; and I ran down screaming 'Bryan.'

"I got him at the first entrance, right in front of the switchboard, and looked up and saw a fireman there. He was trying to put the fire out. Then the two lower borders running up the side of this canvas were burning. I grabbed my boy and rushed to the back door, and there was a lot of people trying to get out."

After describing his son's rescue, Eddie recalled his dash to the stage:

"I says: 'Take this boy out,' and ran out on the footlights to the audience. When I did, they were in a sort of panic, as I thought; and what I said exactly I don't remember, but this was the substance. My idea was to get the curtain down and quietly stop the stampede. I yelled, 'Drop the curtain down, and keep up your music.' I didn't want a stampede, because it was the biggest audience I ever played to of women and children. I told them to be quiet and take it easy — 'Don't get excited' — and they started up on this second balcony on my left to run, and I says, 'Sit down; it's all right; don't get excited.' And I says, 'Let down the curtain.' And I looked up, and this curtain was burning...."

Eddie said the curtain wouldn't drop to the floor, that it seemed to be caught. And then, he felt "a sort of a cyclone" behind him.

"What do you mean by a cyclone?" Coroner Traeger asked. "Cyclone of what?"

"It was a whirl of smoke when I looked around. The scenery had broken the slats it was nailed to. It came down behind me, and I didn't know whether to go in front or behind. The stage was covered with smoke, and it was a cold draft; and there was an explosion of some kind, like you light a match and the box goes off."

Under further questioning, Eddie answered that he had seen few fire extinguishers backstage, that the company had engaged in no fire drills, and that only one door in the back appeared to be open.

At the conclusion of his testimony, Eddie recounted his final vision of the auditorium before his escape into the basement: "...my eyes were fastened on the sea of agonized, distracted little ones in the balcony and gallery." Stunned, the Council Hall audience sat in profound silence as he left the witness stand.

After three weeks, only the Auditorium Theater had reopened for business. The City Council attempted to pass new fire ordinances, but so many amendments were introduced that meetings were continued another week. Serious problems were found in nearly all Chicago theaters; special amendments would have to be adopted, or some theaters could not open at all. Representatives of the theater profession attended the meetings, lobbying to return to work as quickly as possible. Finally, at the end of January, the City Council passed new ordinances, and a few theaters reopened. Six more had been inspected and, with minor alterations, could be opened shortly. Municipal and theater officials deemed responsible for the catastrophe were held for trial.

Free now from the inquiry, Eddie diligently contacted theater managers to obtain an engagement. Since he had collected no salary for a month, any kind of employment would do.

The manager of the Empire Theater, in Cleveland, was first to offer him a job, a spot on their vaudeville bill. For a week's run, starting February 1, Eddie played vaudeville for the first time. It had been many years since he had performed on the variety stage. The *Clipper* noted Eddie's new engagement:

> The star feature, and one that appeals to all fun lovers, is Eddie Foy, late of the "Mr. Bluebeard" company, who has gone into vaudeville for a few weeks. Mr. Foy is one of the most popular comedians on the stage, and opens his vaudeville season at the Empire.[9]

When Eddie took the stage in his first appearance at the Empire, the audience rose in unison to applaud and cheer him for ten minutes. At the end of his act, they again stood to acknowledge his heroism. Each of his performances during the week elicited similar reactions.

Eddie received accolades of similar proportions in Detroit, Oklahoma City, Philadelphia, and Brooklyn. A reporter in Philadelphia suggested that Eddie could come on stage just to smile at the audience, and they would applaud appreciatively for ten minutes. In each city he played, there were accompanying newspaper articles about the tragic fire and Eddie's heroic actions.

In early March, when Eddie returned home, he was obviously spent. For all his humorous antics on stage, he admitted that the horror of the scene at the Iroquois continued to smolder deep in his mind.

"My nerves have not yet settled down," he remarked. "But we're pretty thankful and pretty happy. Aren't we, Missus?"

"Yes," Madeline replied. "Now try to get some sleep."

Chapter 12

I've got gold to give away;
They say it's tainted; I say it taint.
The heathen can get my dough any day;
When I die I'll be a saint.
(a song sung by Eddie Foy,
impersonating John D. Rockefeller)

When Eddie appeared on the Brooklyn stage in March 1904, he found himself a legend. It was a most uncomfortable role for him. The audience cheered him lustily for several minutes, urging him to speak. To this suggestion, Eddie walked up to the footlights, nodded recognition, and simply stated, "I thank you from the bottom of my heart."

At the close of his act, the audience again called him insistently. When Eddie attempted to withdraw, someone held the curtain fast so he was unable to escape the limelight. Since there was no other way out of it, he made a second effort at speechmaking.

"I'm not much of a public speaker," he declared, "but I want to thank you again. I was very nervous upon my appearance here, and now I can say that it's the happiest moment of my life."

The audience had come out to see Eddie Foy, the man, to extend him personal honors. Eddie was not only recognized as a comedian, but also as a hero. At this point, his act was of secondary importance. Whatever role he played on stage no longer really mattered. For the past four months, his performances had become an exercise in public adulation, a kind of worship. Most audiences were familiar with his material. But they hadn't come for his comedy. They just wanted to be there, to share an esteemed moment with Eddie.

Just across the East River, in his spare office, Sam Shubert took notice of Eddie's recent rise in popularity. At the moment, he was looking for legends to assist in building his theatrical empire.

In 1900, the three Shubert brothers —

Sam, Lee, and J.J.— had moved to New York when they obtained a lease for the Herald Square Theater, at Broadway and Thirty-fifth Street. The Shuberts already managed five theaters in upstate New York and several touring companies. At the time, the Herald Square represented the uptown migration of theaters in Manhattan. It was located about two miles north of the old theater district around Union Square, only a few blocks south of Times Square.

By virtue of a strategic and financial *coup,* the Shuberts persuaded Richard Mansfield, then at the top of his acting career, to play at their theater. In 1902, they acquired the Casino Theater, a Moorish-decorated, splendid, but aged house, located on Broadway and Thirty-ninth Street. The Casino had been opened in 1882, by impresario Rudolph Aronson, to feature comic opera and showcase his star, Lillian Russell. Over the next two decades, the Casino came under the control of owners and managers, most of whom mounted forgettable shows, except for George Lederer's theatrically innovative musical, "Floradora," in 1900. The Shuberts hoped to capitalize on the Casino's reputation, drawing power, and location.

A slight, extremely energetic man, Sam Shubert, was considered the brains of the Shubert operation. He was a smooth, charming businessman and a highly effective negotiator. Lee served as Sam's strategist and detail man. J.J., an egoistic, volatile personality, had been relegated to handling the brothers' out-of-town business.

In 1903, the Shuberts reluctantly signed an agreement with the Theatrical Syndicate. They didn't care for the organization but believed that, to survive and prosper, they had to belong. The Syndicate offered attractions to play Shubert theaters for the entire season. If the Shuberts did not cooperate with them, they'd be frozen out of the better touring productions. The relationship was tenuous from the very beginning and lasted less than a year.

Syndicate boss Abe Erlanger became suspicious about the Shuberts expansion plans. Erlanger invented a situation that gave him the opportunity to claim the Shuberts had broken their agreement by not playing a specific, Syndicate-sponsored show. Because of this supposed breach of contract, the Shuberts were ousted from the Syndicate. Within a short time, the Shuberts would become the Syndicate's most formidable adversary.

Sam and Lee Shubert were astute observers of Klaw and Erlanger's problems brought about by the Iroquois Theater fire. They immediately contrived to turn the Syndicate's misfortune to their own advantage and enlarge their own domain. One key strategy was to secure top performers, as well as theaters. As with Mansfield previously, the people they now sought to enlist had become legends in what they did best on stage. Eddie Foy was the first such performer they signed. A few months later, they initialed a contract with Lillian Russell. In 1905, by acquiring Lew Fields's Theater, they bought the actor as well, a prize that provided them the imagination and ability to produce their own musical shows.

While Eddie was playing vaudeville dates, Sam Shubert offered Eddie a contract, at $600 a week, to play in a new Shubert-managed musical. Not only was Eddie pleased with the opportunity, it also gave him a chance to affiliate with an organization that was openly hostile to the Syndicate.

"Piff!Paff!!Pouf!!!" opened at the Casino Theater, New York, on April 2. It was tagged a musical cocktail, in two acts. The book was written by Stanislaus Stange, and the show was staged by Gerard Coventry. Song lyrics were written by William Jerome, Eddie's purveyor of personal hits, and the music was by Jean Schwartz, in his initial Broadway show. The duo of Jerome and Schwartz would not only contribute to a number of Eddie's future shows, but also become one of the most popular song writing teams on Broadway. The production's minimal plot was amply fortified by many catchy songs, scenic and costume beauty, an English Pony Ballet, and the

An opulent, Moorish-inspired theater, the Casino featured the best comic opera for two decades. Although its reputation as a venue for stellar productions continued, when the Shuberts bought and renovated the theater in 1902, it had become somewhat shabby.

comic antics of Eddie Foy. At this stage of their planned expansion, the Shuberts spared no expense to produce a high-class show.

August Melon (Joseph Miron), a wealthy widower, is attempting to marry off his four daughters so he can, unencumbered, woo and wed an attractive widow, Mrs. Lillian Montague (Alice Fisher). The deceased Mrs. Melon made provisions in her will that her husband and daughters should divide ten million dollars equally, on condition that the girls marry in succession according to their ages and that her husband remain single until after the youngest is married. Predictably, each of the young women has "peculiar" ideas about men, making it difficult to find them husbands, thus allowing the widow and widower to wed. Nora Melon (Mabel Hollins) can love only a man who has never been kissed; Cora Melon (Grace Cameron) seeks a man who is a paragon of virtue; Encora Melon (Hilda Hollins) is looking for a man who resembles a portrait she has seen; Rose Melon (Amelia Stone) cannot marry until her sisters have been wed. The four men involved in the amorous chase are Peter Pouffle (Eddie Foy), an undistinguished chap resembling a scarecrow; Lord George Piffle (Templar Saxe), an English peer; Marconi Paffle (John Hyams), a caricature of a prominent Italian, and Dick Daily (Maurice Darcy), a newspaper reporter. Resolving these affairs provides the principals with specific performance olios, which include songs, dances, and comic sketches.

Eddie sang two songs. For "The Ghost That Never Walked," a theatrical reference dealing with the actor's weekly paycheck, he was accompanied by the Pony Ballet in a grotesque dance. Eddie performed "I'm So Happy" dressed as a sandman, having just escaped from being buried alive.

In those days, it was common for actors to paraphrase well-known aphorisms and use them in their scripts. Two of his lines selected as the show's best jokes reveal that Foy knew when to borrow an adage. Harking back to Samuel Johnson, he remarked that "when a widow marries it is the triumph of hope over

experience." From William Hazlitt, Foy found inspiration for "a friend in need is a bore indeed."

Eddie's scarecrow-like costume and antics were said to have been suggested by the recent success of the Scarecrow in "The Wizard of Oz." The Pony Ballet was particularly effective in their "Radium Dance." On a darkened stage, sixteen girls in iridescent costumes performed a rope-skipping routine in choreographed ensemble.

Reviewer reactions were mixed. Alan Dale wrote that:

> …people had not quite decided whether they were assisting at its life or death.[1]

The *New York Times* critic called the show "inane" but of the type relished by a "large class of citizens that considers Broadway at midnight just a shade better than Paradise." The *New York Clipper* reported the production a success:

> The audience greeted "Piff!Paff!!Pouf!!!" and gave the production a royal welcome. Its success was proclaimed with the singing of the first number, and was emphasized with every musical that followed.[2]

Whatever the critics concluded about the show itself, all agreed that Eddie "walked away with star honors":

> Mr. Eddie Foy received a riotous welcome when he first appeared. It was the first time we have seen Mr. Foy since his heroic behavior in the Chicago fire, and, naturally, there was a bit of well-deserved sentiment in his ovation.[3]
>
> Eddie Foy was the shining light in the cast.[4]
>
> Prominent in the company is the droll and well remembered Eddie Foy, who was warmly welcomed, and whose familiar methods of extracting fun were as effective as of yore.[5]

Audiences proved undeterred by tepid reviews and crowded the Casino, even as "Piff!Paff!!Pouf!!!" played into the hot summer season. As the production began its fifteenth week, the *Clipper* reported "continued good sized audiences." During the show's unprecedented thirty-third week, when the Shuberts announced the production was about to go on tour, audiences jammed the Casino. The *Clipper* reported continued standing ovations for Eddie when he first appeared on stage.

Everything Eddie said seemed to be quoted in local newspapers. He was reported to be writing a book about his life as a stage clown. He was said to have been consulted on theater safety. A humorous anecdote regarding his perception of New York's new, swanky St. Regis Hotel was printed by the *Clipper*, along with a picture of Eddie, the first time a photo of him had appeared in the prestigious theatrical journal.

"That new St. Regis Hotel must have cost a pile of money to build and furnish," said Eddie, as he and a friend were passing the upscale establishment.

"What would you, an actor, do with a hotel like the St. Regis?" challenged the friend. "You wouldn't know how to run it."

"I know I wouldn't," Eddie responded. "I didn't wish for the hotel. I merely observed I'd like the money."[6]

Of course, money continued a concern for Eddie. When the tour began, he was unable to travel with the company because Madeline had suffered a miscarriage. Any days Eddie missed performing were days he wasn't paid. Eddie caught up with the company in Philadelphia a week later, to everyone's relief.

After Philadelphia, "Piff!Paff!!Pouf!!!" played in Boston, Washington, D.C., Brooklyn — the Shuberts were having scheduling problems — a Philadelphia encore, Newark, and Boston again, arriving for the second time late in February 1905. At all of these engagements, the production played to excellent business. Buoyed by the success of the show, the Shuberts began planning for their next production, again starring Eddie.

Their plans had to be postponed, however, when Eddie unexpectedly demanded salary for rehearsal time. Performers were never paid for rehearsals, one of the primary reasons why rehearsals for new shows were so short, often lasting no more than two weeks. Instead, efforts were made to improve a show during its first weeks in front of an audience. As often as not, this led to a show's premature demise, with losses for all those involved in the production, especially for performers, who then might not get paid even for their performances in front of an audience.

Eddie gambled his recent successes with the Shuberts as leverage to support his demand. The Shuberts refused, and Eddie was "excused" from the show. "Piff!Paff!!Pouf!!!" ran one more week in Boston and abruptly closed.

A week later, Eddie appeared on a vaudeville bill at Keith's Theater in New York. He had signed an eight-week contract with the Keith/Albee Circuit, at $700 a week. He hired three people — Walter Hodges, Eveline Selbies, and Sadie Handy — to assist him in a new routine called "The Man Behind the Gun." It consisted of two specialty sketches.

In the first sketch, Eddie appeared as a soldier calling at the house of his captain. He was put to bed by his superior, in a curtained bedstead, and ordered to snore every time he heard anyone enter the room. The captain wanted his wife to think he was in bed, while he had really gone off to visit a paramour. Eddie pantomimed the entire episode, employing various snoring sounds and sleeping postures.

In the second sketch, Eddie repeated the elephant training scene from "Mr. Bluebeard." The two women he hired played the elephant, just as they had in the original production. For encores — and there were encores at every performance — Eddie appeared in a ridiculous feminine costume and sang "I'm an Unlucky Old Maid."

Eddie played at Keith theaters in Harlem, Boston, Cleveland, Detroit, Buffalo, and Philadelphia, then closed his tour the middle of May back in New York. Albee, noting with approval audience reactions to Eddie, wanted to sign him for another ten weeks. In his final week, at the Keith in New York:

> ...the audience seemed unable to get enough of him, calling him back several times and not letting him go for good, until, after reaching his dressing-room and removing part of his makeup, he came back and made a speech.[7]

In Philadelphia, the *Record* reported:

> Eddie Foy's clowning is as genuinely funny as anything known to the boards; his very personality irradiates merriment. Mr. Foy had to make two speeches of acknowledgment. In the first he burlesqued capitally the Mansfield curtain-call.[8]

Sam Shubert, however, had beaten out Albee. He offered Eddie an excellent contract for a new show. Unfortunately, ten days later, Shubert was killed in a train accident. The growing Shubert dynasty seemed to be on the verge of collapse.

Sam Shubert had been on his way to Pittsburgh to see about leasing the Duquesne Theater. As his train approached Harrisburg, Pennsylvania, it sideswiped a work train on a siding. One of the work train's cars carried explosives. The resulting detonation destroyed both trains, killing twenty-two.

Lee and J.J. were devastated. Within days of the accident, it was reported they would sell out, most likely to Klaw and Erlanger. Instead, surprising the industry, Lee and J.J. announced they not only would remain in the business, but also planned to launch a vigorous program to build theaters in cities where they were unable to lease them. In addition, they made deals with thirteen independent houses around the country, enough venues to present one of their Shubert-owned productions for twenty weeks without duplication. Among the new imports they planned to produce for the fall season was an Ivan Caryll musical called "The Earl and the Girl," the show Sam had had in mind for Eddie. In early August, Lee

Shubert announced he had signed Eddie for the starring role.

Since rehearsals for the new show were not scheduled to start for two weeks, and Madeline was again pregnant (so Eddie needed the money), he performed on vaudeville bills in Manhattan Beach, New York, and at Proctor's Twenty-third Street Theater in the city. His impersonations of Teddy Roosevelt and J.D. Rockefeller were judged "high class and thoroughly enjoyable." Audiences loved Eddie's irreverent impersonation of Rockefeller. Poking fun at New York's economic, social, and political elite was a humorous, cathartic, and immensely popular pastime.

Rehearsals for "The Earl and the Girl" began only three weeks prior to its planned opening. As usual, it was assumed the company could work out any problems during the first few weeks of performance. Hence, the Shuberts scheduled the show to play on the road until it was deemed ready for New York. To their dismay, they discovered a week in Philadelphia was not enough time, because of considerable rewriting and cast changes. Two more weeks in Pittsburgh were needed to get the show in reasonable shape for New York critics and audiences. A review from a Pittsburgh newspaper spoke of the production's progress.

> "The Earl and the Girl" was the attraction, and though the performances during the first week were quite in the rough, a few performances and careful work smoothed this down the second week.[9]

When the company arrived in New York, the show's opening had to be delayed two more days because of further changes in musical numbers. Then, at the last moment, the Shuberts found they would have to keep the production on the road because the Casino Theater itself was not yet ready to reopen.

The previous February, the Casino had sustained considerable damage to its interior because of a fire. Refurbishment was to be completed by September, just in time to open with "The Earl and the Girl." Much to the Shuberts' chagrin, the Casino repairs were not completed on time. They had no choice but to put the show on the road until the Casino was ready. Yet it turned out to be a fortuitous move. "The Earl and the Girl" got such rave reviews while touring that even New York critics were positively influenced, one of the few times that a road show achieved considerable success without Gotham's primatur.

After Pittsburgh, the production played a week-long run in Baltimore, a return engagement in Philadelphia, and two weeks in Chicago. Though Madeline was six months pregnant, she and the children paid Eddie a "flying visit" while the show was in Philadelphia, then accompanied him to Chicago.

It seems that Madeline was concerned about a rumor that suggested Eddie had become involved with a bit player in the cast, Ruth Langdon. One of the show's agents claimed he had seen Langdon and Eddie in bed together. With the entire family on the scene, Eddie's behavior apparently returned to "normal."

Chicago proved the final stop on the road. The Shuberts announced the opening of "The Earl and the Girl" in New York, November 4. At the same time, they declared their plans for the current season. This announcement clearly demonstrated their goals and was an intentional, direct challenge to Syndicate domination.

Star actors signed by the Shuberts included Sarah Bernhardt, Ada Rehan, Lillian Russell, De Wolf Hopper, William Collier, and Eddie Foy. Fourteen Shubert companies would be playing legitimate shows, comic operas, and musical comedies in the fourteen theaters they already controlled, with a promise to double the number of theaters under their management in another year. They also revealed the filing of articles of incorporation, with a capital of $50,000 (the exact amount Sam had left Lee in his will), for the Shubert Booking Agency, to schedule

attractions in their own theaters as well as other theaters whenever the brothers might obtain open time.

When "The Earl and the Girl" opened at the Casino Theater as planned, November 4, the Casino had been dark for more than eight months. Francis Kimball, designer of the original building, was responsible for reconstruction and redecoration of the new one. The entire interior had been gutted, and the stage leveled to the ground floor, with orchestra seats now on street level. A capacious lobby connected the auditorium directly to Broadway. The small, old lobby had been converted to a writing room for ladies, and the café changed to a smoking room for gentlemen. Seating capacity increased from 1,600 to 2,000. The new decorations were Moorish, with a color scheme of gold, green, and scarlet, the draperies and upholstery red. An octagonal ceiling dome and bas-relief panels adorned the space above the proscenium arch. All the interior walls featured decorative murals and elaborate Morroccan stucco work, highlighted by 3,200 electric lights. The Shuberts claimed their stage appliances were the most up-to-date; a steel and water curtain could be deployed to separate the stage and auditorium, and all doors opened with ordinary knobs. They proclaimed the Casino "the handsomest, and one of the safest, theaters in the world."

Billed as "a merry English musical whirl," "The Earl and the Girl" was a play in two acts. The show had been first performed at the Adelphi Theater in London, in December 1903. Seymour Hicks (amusingly referred to as Stealmore Tricks by local critics) wrote the book, Ivan Caryll the music, and Percy Greenbank the lyrics. As usual for a musical comedy, the story was slight.

Dick Wargrove (Victor Morley) and Elphin Haye (Georgia Caine) are engaged, a state of affairs objected to by their uncle, A. Bunder Bliss (J. Bernard Dyllyn), and aunt, Virginia Bliss (Violet Holls). Jim Cheese (Eddie Foy), a dog trainer with a traveling show, is persuaded to impersonate Dick, who has just become the Earl of Stole. In that character, Cheese — leashed to two puppies he declares to be bloodhounds — is presented to the Blisses. (When Wargrove offers Cheese $100 to impersonate him as the earl, Cheese comments haughtily, "I'm an earl, so call me early.") After numerous humorous complications, Elphin's guardians finally accept the real Dick as her fiancé, and Cheese is summarily ousted from society to return to his dogs.

Specialty routines dominated action in the play. In the "Domino Dance," four Pony Ballet members performed a grotesque dance to the accompaniment of a brass band. A song and dance number, "How Would You Like to Spoon with Me," transformed itself into a chorus of eighteen girls on swings. Two groups of nine girls each swung out over the footlights and orchestra seats, while electric bulbs on vine-covered ropes flashed and sparkled. Amelia Summerville, a Marie Dressler-type, played Mrs. Shimmering Black, a socialite and one-time circus strongperson, on the trail of the man who has jilted her daughter. Accusing the Earl (Foy) of this heinous abandonment, she slapped Eddie so hard that he staggered around the stage in a pantomime replete with wobbly-leg movements and facial grimaces so hilarious that they caused audiences to erupt in cheers and applause.

Eddie was on stage nearly the entire show. In an Act One specialty, after becoming the Earl — in lavender tights, medal-studded chest, monocle, red wig, and crown — Eddie impersonated Admiral Togo (Japanese officer in the Russo-Japanese War), the Czar, President Theodore Roosevelt, and J.D. Rockefeller. In Act Two, Eddie sang and danced two songs, "Won't You Change Your Name" and "Famous Men I Have Not Met."

An astute critic noted that one of the hit songs interpolated into the show, "How Would You Like to Spoon with Me," had been written by two talented, young songsmiths, Jerome Kern and Melville Ellis.

"The Earl and the Girl" was well reviewed by critics, some citing its humor, scenery, songs, and pretty girls, others commenting on its "excellent recommendations" from audiences in cities previously performed.

The *New York Times* called the show "…a veritable frolic from start to finish, light, tuneful, full of color, and engaging a company of exceptionally clever people."

Alan Dale, of the *New York American* wrote:

> While there is no startling novelty in "The Earl and the Girl," there is plenty for the money. It is a multi-colored show with many specialties. It is never dull; there is something doing all the time.[10]

The *New York Commercial* reviewer mentioned audiences' enthusiastic reception "for the company that had made so good a name for itself throughout the country." Even the *Evening Mail,* a newspaper not known for its positive reviews of musicals, declared that the company had "received a welcome which should be extended to them for a long time to come."

Eddie was labeled "The Son of the Casino." One critic decried that Eddie was so late in coming on that it seemed he was at home getting the children ready for Sunday School. When Jim Cheese at last came on, it was noted he was "the whole cheese." *New York Herald* headlines called Eddie the star. "The Matinee Girl," feature writer in the *Dramatic Mirror,* was eloquent in her praise of Eddie's acting:

> Eddie Foy is the mildest, least obtrusive comedian on the stage. His is the art that conceals art. When you reflect upon what Eddie Foy's art is not, you realize how deep is the art that is to all appearances so narrow. His methods are as gentle as those of a child under the eye of a watchful mother. If he exaggerates any personal trait it is that air of open-eyed and wondering innocence that sets so well upon him. Eddie's fun-making gets all the comedy there is out of a situation.[11]

A performer knows he has become a star when trains change their schedules for him. One day, during his acclaimed run as "The

Earl," Eddie missed the early train from New Rochelle to New York City. The next train, an express, was not scheduled to stop in New Rochelle. Eddie asked the agent to stop the train, no matter the cost. The agent telegraphed the railroad's general manager to see what he could do. When the express entered New Rochelle station, it slowed down so that Eddie could easily hop on; the conductor assured him he didn't have to pay for the accommodation.

Eddie, Jr., was born on February 4, 1906, which also happened to be the 100th performance of "The Earl and the Girl." Aunt Clara and the children called the theater to tell Eddie the news. The theater manager took the message and, at intermission, announced to the audience that Eddie had just become the father of a baby boy. Audience demands for his appearance finally compelled Eddie to take the stage, where he was given a standing ovation. "How many children do you have now?" came a question from the balcony. "I don't know," Eddie answered, "I haven't been home long enough to count."

The production played at the Casino eighteen weeks, having been previously performed on the road for six. When "The Earl and the Girl" was ready to go on tour again in early March, the Shuberts extended its schedule to May, booking major Eastern cities and small towns in New England. The extended run also meant additional salaries for the company.

When they appeared in Providence, Rhode Island, Eddie was honored with a standing ovation. The *Clipper* reported:

> The demonstration was a personal tribute.[12]

While the company was in Washington D.C., they appeared at the Government Asylum for the Insane. After the performance, company members were escorted through the wards. Eddie did not accompany the cast, admitting that he was afraid. Yet, he seemed unable or reluctant to explain why.

In Boston, a scheduled one-week run turned into a three-week stay, to "excellent returns." New England one-night stands played to SRO houses "and pleased immensely." A performance in Ithaca, New York, closed the season, May 12. "The Earl and the Girl" had been performed 264 times, with highly profitable return for the Shuberts.

Just two days after closing, Eddie was back in vaudeville, playing on a bill at the Colonial Theater in New York. Along with his usual impersonations, he imitated star performer Elsie Janis, while singing "If There Were Not Any Women in the World." The following week, she reciprocated by imitating Eddie, much to the crowd's enjoyment. At each show, he was repeatedly encored. On the bill with Eddie were Blanche Ring, singing some of her famous songs, such as "I've Got Rings on My Fingers," acrobats, a female juggler, trained dogs, a guitarist, and a moving picture, a typical vaudeville bill.

Stage Magazine featured Eddie, a departure for them, since they usually wrote about legitimate stage personalities. They offered him considerable recognition for his comedic talents:

> Mr. Foy has comedy in his eyebrows, eyelids, eloquence in his hands, and a volume of fun in his legs. Mr. Foy has kept pace with the times — kept pace very much, in fact. He has become not only a great favorite in this town of ours, but also has gained a reputation for a unique method, his own, and his only.[13]

From May until July, Eddie played the vaudeville circuit in New York, Chicago, and Atlantic City. With Eddie on the bill were such star actors as Lottie Gilson, Irene Franklin, Peter Dailey, and George Evans. Vaudeville had become so popular an attraction (and one so well-paid for just a few minutes of acting) that many musical comedy personalities now vied for engagements. Presaging the future of popular theater, more vaudeville circuits were being formed, more stars opting for vaudeville contracts, and more theaters converting to vaudeville and moving picture formats. Stars like Eddie found vaudeville booking agencies eager to sign them. Eddie found he was able to earn as much on a vaudeville bill as he earned playing musical comedy, for a fraction of the work.

Still, musical comedy remained Eddie's primary interest. He quickly signed for another season with the Shuberts. At first, they announced he would appear in a play by John D. Gilbert, entitled "The Wild and Wooly Way." It told of a ham-fat actor, turned editor in a Western boom town. But when Gilbert and the Shuberts argued over the author's contract, the show was set aside. Instead, Eddie was announced to play in a second season of "The Earl and the Girl," the Shuberts deciding to gain what they could out of an existing success before having to invest in a new show. They made a profitable decision; the show produced another five months of excellent box-office receipts.

This time, without a battle, Eddie obtained a salary increase from Lee Shubert. He used the money to purchase his first automobile. With a new vehicle came new adventures. Having driven for only two weeks, Eddie ran out of gas and had to walk three miles to get home. It required three days for the auto to be returned.

A few months later, while driving home from the theater one evening, Eddie was stopped by two men who demanded his money. Eddie threw his wallet at them in defiance. The felons became upset when they found only two dollars in Eddie's wallet. In anger, they slashed his two front tires. Again, Eddie had to walk home.

On the other hand, Sundays with the entire family in the auto quickly became legendary in New Rochelle. As the Foys drove along New Rochelle's main street, people stopped to gape at the sight. Dressed in their Sunday finery, Eddie, wearing a bowler, and Madeline, her wide-brimmed, feathered hat blowing in the wind, waved to onlookers.

What amused observers most were the number of children's heads, arms, and legs protruding from the windows. No matter how much Aunt Clara attempted to control them, it always seemed that at least one child was about to fall from the auto. How did they all get into the automobile, wondered neighbors? When they stopped, Eddie exaggerated the impression by jumping out of the auto, helping each passenger to alight, and ostentatiously counting each person assisted to the ground.

When the Shuberts announced their plans for the coming season, observers marveled at the growth of their business in a single year. They now owned or leased forty-six first-class theaters across the country, six of them in New York City. The stars under contract comprised a Who's Who of both the legitimate and popular theaters. They included E.H. Southern, Julia Marlowe, Sarah Bernhardt, Mrs. Leslie Carter, Mrs. Fiske, Margaret Anglin, Ada Rehan, and Virginia Harned among legitimate actors. Among popular theater performers, Blanche Bates, David Warfield, Louis Mann, Clara Lipman, De Wolf Hopper, Jefferson De Angelis, Henry E. Dixey, and Eddie Foy. In addition, the Shuberts now planned to produce ten shows of their own.

"The Earl and the Girl" opened its second season at the Grand Opera House, Columbus, Ohio, on September 3, "to large business." The production remained essentially the same, since most cities on the current tour had not yet seen the show. There were only four changes in the cast. Ruth Langdon remained and, according to rumors, resumed her intimate association with Eddie.

The route took the company to Milwaukee, St. Louis, and a two-week run in Chicago. As had become their habit, Chicago audiences greeted Eddie with admiration and enjoyment. The *Chicago Evening American* seemed to sum up Windy City patrons' appreciation:

> Chicago's own Eddie Foy, with the same tendency to finger a mouth that smiles on the

bias, returned to the Garrick Theater last evening in "The Earl and the Girl," bringing a wealth of joy to a houseful of his admirers.[14]

Following a highly successful Chicago run, the company moved to Kansas City, where another branch of Eddie's admirers filled the theater, demanding encores and speeches. One usher at the Shubert Theater in Kansas City was a young, fair-haired enthusiast of popular theater, Harry Truman. At the same time Eddie played there, a new feature was added to the theater bill — moving pictures.

For the next six weeks, the company made one- and two-night stands in Iowa, Illinois, Wisconsin, and Indiana. That kind of booking usually signaled the end of a road tour, but not for the Shuberts. To avoid long and costly jumps, the Shuberts merely booked the show into smaller towns. This practice maintained a production's profitability. It appeared "The Earl and the Girl" would continue the remainder of the season.

Nevertheless, just after the beginning of the new year (1907), Lee Shubert announced Eddie would be starring in a new musical, "The Orchid," planned to open in March. Reflecting their characteristic scheduling decisions, however, they declared "The Earl and the Girl" would play to February 23. Whether to avoid a confrontation with Eddie or due to their recent financial successes, the Shuberts promised Eddie a salary while in rehearsals for the new show.

After only three weeks of rehearsals, "The Orchid" opened at the New Lyric Theater, Philadelphia, March 18. The opening had to be delayed three days because construction of the theater's interior had not been completed. A fire department inspection finally approved the opening, to everyone's relief. Again, the three-week run in Philadelphia was designed to smooth out the show. At the end of the run, the *Clipper* reported:

> "The Orchid" at the new Lyric is now thoroughly Americanized and is running

smoothly. As a spectacle, it is the finest offering of the season, and Eddie Foy does excellent work.[15]

"The Orchid's" opening in New York took place at Lew Fields' Herald Square Theater, April 8, for an indefinite run. Interestingly, the production had been purchased by Lew Fields in Europe for his own use. When he found the comedy role did not suit his style, he sold the rights to the Shuberts. It was another English play adapted for American audiences. The book had been written by James T. Tanner (English) and Joseph W. Herbert (American). Music was written by Ivan Caryll and Lionel Monckton, lyrics by Adrian Ross and Percy Greenbank, all of them veteran musical comedy authors. The production was in two acts; the second act, with two scenes, staged in a European setting. Americanized shows still maintained the romantic fantasy of a European location, as they had in earlier comic opera.

The plot had a passable story. An American, Aubrey Chesterton (George C. Boniface, Jr.), whose great hobby is orchid growing, sends a professional orchid hunter, Professor Zaccary (William Rock), to Peru in quest of a very rare specimen, with which Chesterton hopes to capture the top prize in the show at Nice, France. Zaccary returns empty-handed, a physical and mental wreck, and recounts his adventures. In reality, however, he has not been in Peru, instead having enjoyed a fling in Paris, spending all the money Chesterton had given him. Sensing his impending doom, Zaccary is distraught, until he comes across Artie Choke (Eddie Foy), the gardener at the local Horticultural College. Artie has grown an exceptionally rare species of orchid but, unaware of its value, is only too glad to sell it to Zaccary for a few dollars and too late discovers that the professor has sold it to Chesterton for $4,000. Chesterton's nephew, Hon. Guy Serymageorn (Alfred Hickman), who is sent to Nice with the orchid, loses it, whereupon it is found by Artie, who sells it back to

Eddie, as Arti Choke, in "The Orchid." It was reported that Eddie had been arrested for stealing his costume hat from a milk-wagon horse. (Museum of the City of New York)

Chesterton for $10,000, just in time for him to win the prize. The matrimonial maneuvers of Caroline Vokins (Trixie Friganza) and her French rival, Zelie Homberg (Laura Guerite), together with the mixed-up marriage licenses of runaway lovers, Lady Violet Anstruther (Amelia Stone) and Dr. Donald Fausset (Melville Ellis) and Josephine Zaccary (Irene Franklin) and Guy Serymageour, add to the amusing complications.

No special effects were featured, but the scenery and costumes were said to be breathtaking, particularly in the ballroom scene, which never failed to elicit applause.

Eddie sang two songs: "College," in the first act; and "He Goes to Church on Sunday," in the second, which became one of the show's hit songs. Some called it risqué because of its lack of piety, but audiences repeatedly demanded encores.

> He goes to church on Sunday,
> He passes round the contribution box;
> But meet him in the office on a Monday,
> He's as crooked and as cunning as a fox,
> On Tuesday, Wednesday, Thursday,
>   Friday, Saturday,
> He's robbing everybody that he can;
> But he goes to church on Sunday,
> So they say that he's an honest man.

Two months into the production, Eddie introduced two new songs, while retaining "Sunday." The first, "Mulberry Street," gave Eddie the opportunity to caricature an Italian from the Bowery, complete with exaggerated costume and rhythmic dialect. The second song, which became an immediate hit, "Why Do They Call Me a Gibson Girl," featured Eddie in a black dress, the train of which extended across and off the stage. As he strolled the stage while singing, he became increasingly tangled in the train, to audiences' delight. Unfortunately, it was a routine almost impossible to encore. Eddie also did impersonations of a college oarsman and Vesta Victoria (a popular English singer who wore outlandish hats), as well as a pantomime of a golfer.

Both the production and Eddie's acting received excellent reviews. The *Clipper,* rarely excited about imported musicals, congratulated the chorus and said the play "had obtained unanimous assent of its success." Of Eddie, the *Dramatic Mirror* noted:

> As Artie Choke, the gardener, he received a royal welcome, and was called upon to make a speech after the first act, which he did, thanking the audience in an almost apologetic way on behalf of the company and himself. He was the same Eddie Foy of yore, very

funny in his own familiar way, as he said, "You can go a long way in this world if you have a weak chin and a sunny disposition."[16]

Alan Dale wrote simply:

> If you wish to pass a pleasant evening, go see Foy's delicious fooling.[17]

A public relations *coup* occurred just prior to the production's 150th performance, one that renewed interest in "The Orchid" at a time when the summer heat was wilting its box-office receipts. A horse pulling a delivery wagon bolted into the front of the Herald Square just as Eddie was entering the theater. The box office was smashed, and one woman was injured before Eddie adroitly seized the horse's reins and stopped its progress. A report of the episode also mentioned that a gilt-framed lithograph of Eddie had been damaged, but customers were assured it would be quickly replaced.

"The Orchid" ran for twenty-one profitable weeks at the Herald Square, to mid-September, before it went on the road. On the way to its first stop, in Pittsburg, a minor train wreck injured a number of the company. Luckily, none of the injured had to leave the cast; the show went on without them until they were ready to return a few days later. The start of the tour also exposed a disagreement between Trixie Friganza and the Shuberts. She complained about being billed second to Eddie, instead of being featured as his co-star. The feud simmered until they reached Chicago, where Friganza abruptly left the cast and announced her intention to enter vaudeville. She claimed that injury in an automobile wreck prevented her from continuing with the show. She also claimed that Eddie was bothering her, whatever that meant. Flavia Acaro took Friganza's place, with no change in the popularity of the show. (A few years later, Acaro became Eddie's premier impersonator in vaudeville.)

While in Chicago, Eddie spent an evening rich with reminiscences when he, Lillian

The Foy family at home in New Rochelle, 1908. There are seven children, but Irving had not yet been born. From left to right, Bryan, Catherine, Charles, Richard, Mary, Madeline, and Eddie, Jr.

Russell, Chauncey Olcott, and Lew Dock-stater had dinner together. It was reported that so many reporters surrounded them, they had little chance to converse, much less eat.

The tour took "The Orchid" company to Milwaukee, St. Louis, Detroit, Baltimore, and three weeks in Philadelphia, with a return to New York for the Christmas holidays. At a Christmas party held by the Shuberts, Eddie met President Theodore Roosevelt. The President greeted Eddie with his characteristic enthusiasm, proclaiming, "Mr. Foy, this is indeed a pleasure, and I have always admired you as a comedian." Eddie shook his hand. Continuing, Roosevelt said, with a sly smile, "And at which theater are you playing?"

After one of the shows, Eddie was approached by a gentleman who identified himself as a music teacher and said, "I have attended several performances of 'The Orchid.'" Eddie nodded. "And I have been somewhat surprised at your lack of ability to sing." Eddie frowned. "I admire you so much personally…" Eddie smiled "…that I would consider it an honor to have you as one of

my pupils. My services will be without charge. I am sure that with a few years of training your voice could be made mellow and sweet." Eddie chuckled, then responded: "Professor, its very kind of you to offer your services, but really I must decline. You see, I have a wife and family and a home in New Rochelle to support. If I could sing, I'd lose my job."

In what became a celebrated move in New Rochelle, Eddie disclosed the family had recently purchased a home consisting of twenty rooms surrounded by nine acres of land. It was reported to be valued at $22,000. Everyone agreed he needed the additional space.

Eddie and the company had time off temporarily when some scenery collapsed on stage and halted performances for almost three weeks. Several members of the chorus were injured. When repairs were made, the company continued its tour late in January 1908, in Washington, D.C., and then visited a number of towns in Pennsylvania, New Jersey, and Connecticut on one-night stands. From February to March, "The Orchid" played to large houses in Providence, Boston, a return engagement in New York for two weeks (at another new theater the Shuberts had just leased), and Pittsburgh, this time at "bargain sale prices." In a move to maintain full houses in cities where the production had played before, the Shuberts reduced ticket prices to half of what they had previously been, and their strategy succeeded in filling theaters. Season's end came in Toronto, early in April. When "The Orchid" cast retired, they believed they had experienced a very successful tour. The Shuberts expressed their satisfaction by asking Eddie to return for another year.

Two weeks later, Eddie appeared at the Orpheum Theater, in Brooklyn, heading a vaudeville bill. Eddie took no vacations; he could not afford the luxury of taking time off, money having become a constant concern. Though he earned an excellent salary, it never seemed to be enough to live comfortably. Nor had he forgotten those periods, not so long ago, when he had been perilously unemployed.

Everyone agreed that Eddie loved to perform; it was his life's blood, according to colleagues. No matter the circumstances, his commitment to the audience was unflagging. But along with this love of performance came a sense of responsibility to his family, a trust he was personally committed to fulfill. At the time, the Foy ménage consisted of Eddie and Madeline, seven children, Aunt Clara, a housekeeper, a large home, and an automobile. Added to these responsibilities were donations to the local church and Madeline's efforts on behalf of homeless children, which often swelled the household by another two or three. And when the entire family accompanied Eddie on tour, those expenses depleted his earnings.

Due to her last pregnancy, Madeline had become ill, and her problems continued after Eddie, Jr.'s, birth. Doctors attributed her illness to too many pregnancies; besides six births, she had had three miscarriages. They instructed her not to get pregnant again if she wished to maintain her health. The doctors' recommendations created a values conflict for Madeline, who rigorously adhered to the tenets of the Catholic church. Still, she had to maintain her health to raise her existing children.

In spite of the doctors' warnings, Madeline again became pregnant. She became so sick during the later stages of this pregnancy, there was serious question whether she and the child would survive. Throughout the summer, Aunt Clara and the housekeeper took over all of Madeline's domestic responsibilities. Whatever the outcome, this would be her last pregnancy.

Both family and friends had noticed minor but significant changes in Eddie's behavior since the Iroquois Theater fire. At the theater, he appeared more serious about performing and less tolerant of the foibles of fellow entertainers. Those whom he believed were less respectful of the stage, he admonished. In one episode, Eddie had a dog trainer taken off the bill because he felt the trainer was abusing his animals. In another episode, he ordered a performer off the stage because of a suggestive remark made to a woman.

At the same time, Eddie's own performances were clearly "at the top of his act." He smoked more and gambled more, particularly on the horses. He increased his efforts on behalf of less fortunate actors, appearing frequently at benefits and charities, and he donated time to the Lambs Club and Friars. When asked about Eddie, William Jerome suggested that his friend had recognized his own mortality. After the Iroquois fire, he indicated, Eddie had become acutely aware that life is finite. So do the best you can, while you can. Eddie did not deny Jerome's astute observation.

Because of Madeline's condition, Eddie played vaudeville dates throughout the summer only in the New York area. "New Foyisms," the critics called his act:

Eddie Foy can always be depended upon to present something decidedly original in the way of fun-making, and his offering at the Alhambra, where he made his reappearance in vaudeville, is of the sort that only he could possibly think of. Grotesque and absurd in the extreme, the act nevertheless appealed to the majority of the spectators, and laughter held full sway while he was on stage.[18]

In these sketches, Eddie played golf with a balloon (a turn likely taken from a sketch he had performed in "The Orchid") and impersonated Governor Hughes as a horse jockey, Gertrude Hoffman (a fellow vaudeville performer whose girth matched her voice) as a Gibson Girl, and Andrew Carnegie, in kilts, giving away libraries.

The annual Friars Festival, an all-star show that attracted top actors and rich patrons, netted more than $15,000 for various actors' charities.

> The people paused along the streets,
> The pikers hurried past;
> The lobby crowd was buying seats,
> The house was filling fast;
> The programs sold for dollars per,
> The day meant joy for all;
> And why? Because the Friars were
> To give their festival.

The New York Theater was filled to SRO to see the best performers in popular theater perform their specialties. Included on the program were Victor Herbert, George M. Cohan, George Beban, Joe Weber, Lew Fields, Mabel Hite, Cecilia Loftus, Louise Dresser, and Eddie Foy.

The performance highlighted the return of Weber and Fields doing their German Senator sketch. This was the first time they had appeared together since their separation in 1904. The crowd gave them a standing ovation; when Fields kissed Weber, everyone shouted their agreement. Eddie appeared in red wig, funny hat, and checkered trousers and "imitated everybody and everything." The *Dramatic Mirror* reported:

> Some have seen fit to circulate stories about Mr. Foy to the effect that he couldn't play Hamlet. In a short speech Mr. Foy put his persecutors to rout by declaring that he had played every hamlet between here and the coast.[19]

In fact, Eddie's playing Hamlet was not idle conjecture. The new Shubert show, starring Eddie, was to be called "Mr. Hamlet on Broadway." An interview by critic Charles Darnton, of the *Evening World,* was headlined: "Eddie Foy Will Go Mad as Hamlet."

"Yes," said Eddie, "it's straight. I'm going to play Hamlet."

When asked about Eddie's new venture, George M. Cohan opined that he "will do a great business."

"I'm changing my name to E. Fitzgerald Foy for the role."

"Are you doing any training?" Darnton asked.

"Well, I'm doing a little in my barn at New Rochelle. You should see the cow and chickens run around when I play Hamlet there. And then I play it to my wife and kids in the house. They dasn't say a word."

"Do you think your playing Hamlet will affect your reputation as a comedian?"

"I've nothing to lose and everything to gain," Foy answered with a grin. "I'm not a Shakespearean actor. I'm not an actor at all. Only a clown who has been buffooning around and making children laugh. If I can get an audience to listen to me I'll be satisfied."

"Will you feel any fear?" Darnton inquired.

"Not a bit. I don't want to seem egotistical, but I don't see why I should be afraid. I got a letter from my insurance company the other day, saying they had increased my premium because they heard I was going to play Hamlet. May Irwin telephoned me to ask: 'Have you got an Ophelia yet?' She would make a great Ophelia, but we'd have an awful job burying her. I'm going to do my best to make Hamlet seem natural."

To prove his point, Eddie performed a sketch at the Music Hall in Brighton, Long Island, in August. He played Hamlet in the graveyard scene. The audience laughed so heartily, Eddie had to repeat his lines so they could hear the dialogue.

Eddie appeared in a dark wig, red tights, and a brown tunic. Tombstones bearing the names of William Jennings Bryan, Governor Hughes, and William Randolph Hearst were seen. "Whose skull is this?" asked Hamlet. "Bingham's," replied the gravedigger. Hamlet answered, "Alas! Poor Bingham. I knew him, Murphy. Oft have I fled from the race track at the mention of his name." Eddie included remarks about people with local reputations, and each such comic dagger was greeted with laughs.

There was no longer any doubts about it. Eddie was going to play Hamlet, starting the new theater season. Seriously.

Chapter 13

To flee or not to flee, that is the question.
Whether it is nobler in the sun to suffer
The slings and arrows of outrageous scorchings
Or to fling his claims against a sea of critics
And, I suppose, offend them;
To fly, to sneak, to "blow" and by that sneak
To say, I end the headshakes and the thousand
Natural wrongs the profesh is heir to.
To fly, to sneak, and when that sneak I make—
What meals may come? For where's the grub?
Oh, who could bear the trips to one-night stands,
The press' wrongs, the crowds' damned contumely,
The trains delay, the prongs of despised hotels,
The insolvency of managers and the spurn of waiting sheriff
When your trunk he takes with a bare suit case;
This makes me rather play the part I have than fly
To authors I know not of.
What! Ho! Some music!

> Soliloquy, Eddie Foy, as Hamlet,
> in *Mr. Hamlet on Broadway*

A. Toxen Worm had recently been hired by Lee Shubert to be his chief publicist. An accomplished and seasoned theatrical promoter, Worm's initial assignment was to make Eddie and "Mr. Hamlet on Broadway"

a winning and profitable enterprise.

Conrad Henrik Aage Toxen Worm was a Danish-born, naturalized American who, for more than a decade, had been recognized as one of the top theatrical public relations experts. Extremely loyal to the Shuberts, he became their chief propagandist and prose-lytizer. A man with a "big, corpulent, Chesterfield frame," Worm conducted his business in flamboyant style. His forte was the "press stunt," many of which have found their way into theatrical legend. His business was to see that mention of Shubert shows appeared constantly before the public. Dictatorial, dogmatic, amusing, spicy, and fiercely competitive, Worm was a perfectionist who demanded the same quality in others. The Shuberts hoped Worm would tolerate Eddie sufficiently to benefit the new production.

Much to everyone's surprise, Worm and Eddie immediately liked one another, a situation that enhanced the success of the new production. Worm respected Eddie's professionalism and his commitment to making audiences laugh. In turn, Eddie quickly recognized Worm's ability to generate interest and enthusiasm for the new show. An interview with Charles Darnton, one of New York's leading theater critics, was Worm's first exercise on behalf of "Hamlet." Other press interviews quickly followed. Numerous articles featuring Eddie's views on playing Shakespeare appeared in newspapers. Eddie readily talked of his early variety experiences and how they motivated him to perform Hamlet.

"Why, I have been yearning to play Hamlet ever since I blacked Edwin Booth's shoes in Chicago, and went to the theater that night, sitting way up in the peanut gallery."

"Of course, I know everybody says, 'Why even if he weren't so identified with burlesque his voice wouldn't permit him to play Hamlet.' But did Sir Henry Irving have a voice? I saw him, and I saw him play Hamlet. When he first came on the stage, you couldn't hear anything but mumble; but he acted Hamlet, and that's what I'm going to try to do."

"Nobody expects to take me seriously. They are all going to come to the theater to give me the laugh. If I catch 'em and hold 'em, than I shall have done something of which I can feel proud. If I only make 'em laugh, what's the odds? They'll come to see it anyhow, and I'll play to big money. So you see, there's a sort of method in my madness, too."

When the Shuberts announced that "Mr. Hamlet" would have its initial opening out of town, the theater public expressed disappointment, exactly the kind of anticipatory behavior the Shuberts wished to create. As they had successfully achieved with previous Foy shows, a few weeks on the road tightened the production and gained enthusiastic reviews prior to any New York opening.

In the view of press and public, the new production would be Eddie's greatest Broadway triumph and the Shuberts most high-profile show to date. Within the confines of the Shubert office, however, expectations were more tentative. Because he was concerned about its conditions, Eddie had not yet signed his contract. The Shuberts offered Eddie $650 a week, plus thirty percent of the royalties after the production had been entirely paid for. In addition, in the event of his death or disablement, his family would receive a two percent royalty on all performances of the play. But how would Eddie know when the production had been entirely paid? And how would the production continue if something happened to him?

The decision became more complicated when Eddie had to ask Lee Shubert for a cash advance, before the new show's opening, primarily to pay Madeline's hospital bills. She had been ill for some months prior to Irving's birth in September. She remained hospitalized afterwards, as well, for how long, no one could estimate. Eddie borrowed $1,800 to be paid back, with interest, at the rate of seventy-five dollars a week for twenty-five weeks. As part of this loan, J.J. Shubert persuaded Eddie to agree to transfer his royalty profits to the Shuberts if he was unable to repay his debt. The Shuberts also took out a $15,000 insurance policy on Eddie's life.

Eddie signed the contract on September 30, just one day before "Mr. Hamlet" opened in Philadelphia. He believed he had no alternative but to agree to the contract terms. To seemingly sweeten the agreement, the Shuberts announced that the "Eddie Foy Company" was presenting "Mr. Hamlet"; the show would be so identified in all future advertising and promotion.

"Mr. Hamlet on Broadway" opened at the Lyric Theater, Philadelphia, October 1:

> Eddie Foy's new show, "Mr. Hamlet on Broadway," opened to a crowded house, which enjoyed every minute of a performance that continued until midnight. The show is lively from start to finish, but there is such a wealth of material that there will have to be considerable pruning to bring it within a three hour show.[1]

Two weeks of performances in Philadelphia did smooth out the production, but the addition of new material and cast changes persuaded the Shuberts to keep it on the road for an extended period of time. A week in Washington, D.C., attracted "packed audiences." Pittsburgh and Cleveland engagements were well patronized, with critics giving the show complimentary reviews. However, in Cincinnati and Toledo, "Mr. Hamlet" ran into problems, both internally and externally created.

As titular manager of the company, Eddie was arrested for presenting children in the show. Ohio labor laws forbade the use of children below fourteen years of age on stage without a permit. Eddie had not been aware of the requirement and was forced to drop the scene. While in Cincinnati, Eddie received a telegram from J.J. Shubert directing him to reduce the size of the orchestra from nineteen to sixteen. J.J. also instructed Eddie to reduce the number of lamps used to light the show. Eddie had no choice but to comply with J.J.'s demands, since they were in the midst of an argument regarding repayment of the loan. Because of personal expenses, Eddie had missed a number of loan

repayments, and Lee had the show's accountant press Eddie for payment, as directed in his note:

> Under no consideration accept any excuses from Mr. Foy, but collect everything he owes us without fail.[2]

Pressure was intense, but Eddie could not comply with Shubert's demands; he needed the money for family expenses, particularly for Madeline. In November, Madeline was reported to be close to death due to complications arising from Irving's birth. Eddie found it difficult to perform, which seemed to be noticed by reviewers in Rochester and Buffalo. Nevertheless, J.J. pushed for repayment of the loan. To the accountant he wrote:

> Will you let me know whether he had paid any of this and the exact balance due by him on this open account. We must collect from him, as he owes too much money. I guess Foy is a pretty hard proposition to collect from.[3]

A week later, the accountant received another note from J.J.:

> Will you kindly tell me how you are getting along collecting money from Foy? Let me know how much you hold in I.O.U. against him, how much you have got from him up to date, and the balance that he owes outside of notes that have been discounted at the bank.[4]

The accountant had not answered J.J. because he had just received a letter from Eddie questioning his own value to the show. Eddie suggested it might be best for the show if he retired from "Mr. Hamlet":

> I have been waiting to hear from you in regards to my leaving the show. I don't want to remain any longer. I have made no arrangements for any other engagement. But this show is no good for me, and if I left it, it may do a better business without me. I will close any time you say. I don't want to walk out on it as that will cause newspaper comment.[5]

The accountant hesitated conveying the message to J.J. Shubert for fear of his strong reaction. Instead, he attempted to humor Eddie by lessening pressure on him to repay the loan. It seemed to be an increasingly strategic, if not mischievous, game being played out by the participants.

In November and December, a series of events apparently took pressure off Eddie, redirecting the Shuberts' attention to maintenance of the production. Female lead Maude Raymond's husband was dying, and she removed herself from the show. Four chorus members were injured in an automobile accident. A number of cast members were stricken with food poisoning and remained out of the show for a week. Lighting malfunctions occurred frequently. And when a critic reported that audiences were concerned about the appearance of gravestones on stage, the Shuberts dispatched Worm to deal with the problems.

In order to prepare for the opening of "Mr. Hamlet" in New York at the end of December, the company had two weeks off to rehearse and integrate new songs and dances into the play. Eddie's letter and loan repayments went unmentioned in Shubert correspondence. He remained with the show, which continued to attract crowded houses and profitable box offices. If not entirely resolved, problems seemed to have been temporarily set aside.

On December 23, at the Casino Theater, New York, "Mr. Hamlet on Broadway" opened to an enthusiastic, SRO audience. The book was written by Edgar Smith, a combination playwright, librettist, and lyricist, who had been responsible for Weber and Fields' Music Hall comedy successes. Music had been composed by Ben M. Jerome and lyrics by Edward Madden. The production was staged by Ned Wayburn. This was the first show starring Eddie that had been an entirely American production, as well as one of the first presented by the Shuberts.

The two acts take place in the Adirondack mountains, the first at a run-down resort hotel, Starvation Inn, the second at the camp of the Utica Reds, Mount Kalish. The boarders at the inn are very much dissatisfied and the landlord is at his wit's end to hold them. A lawn party has been planned by Mrs. Barnaby Bustle (Maybelle Baker), who has engaged a New York actor to play Hamlet, to her Queen. The boarders are eagerly awaiting the event. When word is received that the actor cannot come, the landlord, Jonathan Cheatam (Oscar Ragland), prevails upon Joey Wheeze (Eddie Foy), the clown of a stranded circus, to assume the role. Mrs. Bustle's daughter, Cymbaline (Daphne Pollard), and her admirer, Tom Manleigh (John H. Pratt), are anxious to stay on at Starvation Inn. Mr. Bustle is just as anxious to leave. He and others at the hotel attempt to bribe Wheeze not to appear, but fail.

The beginning of the second act finds Wheeze rehearsing for the role, protected by a local militia company, the Utica Reds. Wheeze's Hamlet is put on to great success. The inn is saved, the patrons having enjoyed the play. Cymbaline and Tom are in love and plan to marry. Wheeze returns to his circus clown persona and leaves as he came.

Eddie wore six different costumes, each of them absurd, except for the character of Hamlet, in which role his appearance closely resembled that of the celebrated tragedian Edwin Booth. He sang three songs: "Everything Depends on Money," in reference to his being bribed not to play Hamlet; "When I Was a Kid Like You," sung to a chorus of children, and "Mr. Hamlet on Broadway" (again with the chorus) at the conclusion of his Shakespearean impersonation.

As the clown of a stranded circus, Eddie entered with his trick bear, Amelie (James F. Cook), and performed an animal training pantomime. Dressed as a soldier, he entertained children to whom he recited nursery rhymes. Later, he drilled recruits in the militia camp. As Hamlet, he declaimed the famed soliloquy, unlike any heard before: "To flee or not to flee, that is the question." At the end of his soliloquy, the King remarked, "Our Ham

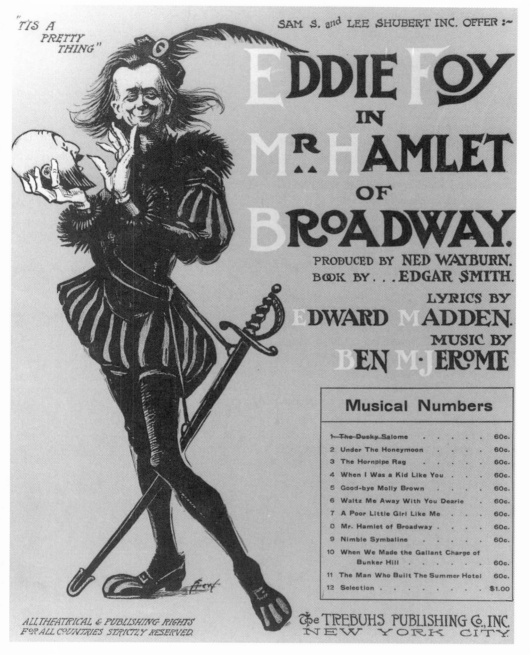

Music sheet cover. "Mr. Hamlet of Broadway" was considered Eddie's most accomplished musical comedy, even though he tried to persuade the Shuberts that he was unsuited for the role.

is cured." Ophelia, with garlands of carrots and turnips in her hair, made it difficult for Hamlet to "plant" her after she died.

Reviews of the production and Eddie's acting were pronouncedly positive. The *New York Globe* declared:

It was to laugh last night at the Casino from the instant Eddie Foy sent his first three-cornered smile beaming over the footlights to the moment of Maude Raymond's final wiggle as Salome.[6]

The *New York Times* noted that "Mr. Hamlet" had the "added value" of Eddie Foy, "an established favorite on the Great White Way":

> The role of Joey Wheeze, a clown in hard luck, is quite in his vein and gives full outlet for an exhibition of those rare whimsical qualities which he projects without effort and which, nevertheless, never fail to bring forth laughter and applause.[7]

By the time "Mr. Hamlet" was in its third week at the Casino (January 1909), much of Eddie's turmoil seemed to have subsided. Madeline's health was improving. A new accountant appointed by the Shuberts worked out an arrangement for Eddie to repay his loan at the rate of $100 a week (which meant he wouldn't be able to pay off the entire loan until the end of April). In addition, the Shuberts increased the size of Eddie's insurance policy.

Excellent reviews for the show and for Eddie continued to generate full houses throughout early February. But because they had booked another show into the Casino in February, the Shuberts had to put "Mr. Hamlet" on the road again, much to Eddie's distress. Not only might the continued success of the show be jeopardized, Eddie was upset that he would be separated from Madeline during her recovery.

Nonetheless, "Mr. Hamlet" continued to be an outstanding success. It was the Shuberts, again, who disturbed the show's fragile equilibrium. Just as Holy Week was approaching, J.J. Shubert announced that he wanted the cast to play at half-salary, because box-office receipts were traditionally lower prior to the Easter holiday. Eddie refused; other cast members threatened actions to dispute J.J.'s demand. After a meeting with Eddie and Maud Raymond, the production's accountant sent a telegram to J.J.:

> Neither Mr. Foy nor Miss Raymond will play for half-salary Holy Week.[8]

J.J. fired back:

> If that is the case we will have to lay off Holy Week. We are not going to pay full salaries and lose money that week.[9]

Coincidentally with this impasse, Eddie suffered a severe case of bronchitis and removed himself from the cast for an entire week. The war of nerves heated up again when J.J. discovered that Eddie had taken an advance of fifty dollars from the box office. J.J. demanded that Eddie pay up his entire debt. Eddie intimated he would leave the show, thus effectively closing it. J.J. relented, but he required Eddie to repay the advance from his next paycheck.

Two weeks of crowded houses in Boston and one-night stands in Massachusetts seemed to satisfy everyone. But when the company reached Providence, Rhode Island, the end of April, the Shuberts abruptly closed the show. "Mr. Hamlet" was reported to be making a profit of $4,000 a week. J.J. claimed that the Shubert's share of the receipts barely covered salaries of $2,700 a week. Eddie, Raymond, and the cast protested; still, "Mr. Hamlet's" season had ended.

But Hamlet and Eddie did not terminate with the closing of the show. Signed for two months of vaudeville, Eddie opened at the Plaza Theater, New York, performing a skit entitled "Hamlet by Freight." Incorporating parts of previous vaudeville routines with the recent "Mr. Hamlet," Eddie presented "his original ideas" on how Shakespeare should be handled on the variety stage. "The offering met with the complete approval of the Plaza audiences," reported the *Clipper*. Included on the vaudeville bill were a male singer, an eccentric musical act, a song and dance team, a dog act, a violinist, a soubrette, a physical culture demonstration, and movies.

Surprising Eddie, the Shuberts announced that he, Lulu Glaser, and Marguerite Clark would be appearing in a new musical, "The Young Guardsman," in the fall. The release, likely Toxen Worm-inspired, wasn't true; it did suggest to Eddie, however, that the Shuberts were still interested in him. Whether because he made profits for them or because he still owed them money, he wasn't sure.

At the end of May, the Lambs Club staged their annual Gambol, a benefit to raise funds for destitute and disabled actors. This year, the Gambol planned to tour for a week of one-night stands to gather more money, the first time they had attempted to expand this charity event. Newspapers called the Gambol the "greatest all-star cast ever gathered together." It included such popular theater luminaries as Victor Herbert and his orchestra, De Wolf Hopper, Charles Evans, Edward Harrigan, Dustin and William Farnum, Raymond Hitchcock, and Eddie Foy. Weber and Fields performed their famous "Poolroom Scene" for the first time since their Music Hall days. Prior to the show, a parade of actors marched from the Lambs Club residence to the Metropolitan Opera House, gathering hundreds of patrons on the way.

Eddie played in a minstrel skit and, in blackface, sang "Down Where the Watermelon Grows." He also played a funny role in a sketch burlesquing an old melodrama rehearsal. The New York show brought in more than $32,000; the entire tour made $130,000. The Gambol tour ultimately took the all-star cast to Chicago, where Eddie played another two weeks at the American Theater, to capacity business.

At home, Madeline was greatly improved, renewing her usual family activities. When Eddie returned home, he had two months to rest and "putter around the farm," as he often said. A number of events evidently highlighted Eddie's summer, but whether they were planted by Toxen Worm or actually happened is unknown.

Worm made sure the press was aware of Eddie's involvement in a benefit the Shuberts put on for old employees. It was reported that twelve-year-old Bryan, upon receiving his first driving lesson from his father, had

taken them both "on a spin" into a rail fence. In another reported episode, while Eddie was taking a trolley to the theater, a thief attempted to rob a woman passenger. The press reported Eddie grabbed the thief and knocked him out. In another episode, the police acknowledged having cited Eddie for "collecting" hats, one of which was a hat he had stolen from a horse pulling a milk wagon on Broadway.

In what was likely the first time the entire Foy family performed in public, a benefit for crippled children, took place at the Polo Grounds on July 29, prior to a baseball game. Led by George M. Cohan, McIntyre and Heath, Fred Stone, Douglas Fairbanks, Marie Dressler, members of the Friar's Club, along with Eddie and the eight little Foys, attired in their Sunday best, a parade started the festivities. Among the sketches presented, the Foy Nine played an inning of baseball, with ten-month-old Irving holding down right field, carefully tended by Madeline. In addition, Eddie met Billy Reeves in a brief boxing match, a serious contest, according to the press. Over 12,000 people attended the event, among them almost every theatrical performer in town.

Prompted by a rapid expansion of their theaters in the South and West, the Shuberts decided to run "Mr. Hamlet on Broadway" another season. Eddie agreed to return, with an increase in salary to $675 a week and a reduction in the remaining amount due on his loan. Rehearsals were to begin in early August, with Eddie getting half-salary. "Mr. Hamlet's" fall opening would begin on the road in September. Although the Shuberts reduced cast size by eliminating some chorus members and stagehands, new songs and material were added to the production.

"Mr. Hamlet on Broadway," second edition, opened August 30, at the Royal Alexandra Theater, Toronto, Canada, to "big business." Eddie sang two songs: the hit "Everything Depends on Money" and "Down Where the Watermelon Grows." When Joey Wheeze complained about not having eaten since his acrobatic job in the circus, Eddie lamented, "I had nothing but hot water for breakfast, so now I'm a tumbler full of hot water."

As Wheeze was rehearsing his Hamlet role, someone asked him if he was familiar with William Shakespeare.

"I knew Bill well, and liked him," Wheeze replied.

"But Shakespeare passed away several years ago."

"And I never knew he was sick," Wheeze answered.

The jokes weren't very good, but Eddie's delivery convulsed the audience.

In some additions to the Hamlet skit, Hamlet's ghost father, Ophelia's ghost, and a band of gravediggers contributed to the comedy. A few weeks into the season, Eddie introduced a third song, "Hamlet's Ghost." Toronto theater critics said of Eddie's acting:

> Mr. Foy, the eminent tragedian, made his first appearance last night. In his hands, the melancholy Dane became quite jolly.

The company played Detroit, Montreal, and Milwaukee successive weeks, to large audiences, with Eddie getting impressive reviews for his Hamlet rendition. In Milwaukee, the audiences filled with his admirers, Eddie received standing ovations.

A week off to make a long jump to Seattle began a six-week tour of major Western cities. The production was running smoothly, the box office profitable, and Eddie comfortable. Shubert Archive notes suggest he had by now repaid his loan.

Returning to the Midwest, stops in Omaha and Kansas City netted "crowded houses." In Kansas City, the opening-night audience had to wait hours because the company was late arriving due to rail delays. Nevertheless, they sat through an orchestra rehearsal, set construction, and the entire presentation, leaving the theater well after midnight, yet fully satisfied with the experience. Because the company had rushed from

the train station to the theater without eating, Eddie ordered out for sardines, oysters, and buns, the cast finishing their meal while performing the first act. The audience loved it. "Eddie Foy, a great favorite in this city, appeared to his usual advantage," reported the Kansas City reviewer.

"Mr. Hamlet" arrived in Chicago for a three-week run over the Christmas holidays. The company was somewhat apprehensive, since the anniversary of the Iroquois Theater fire was being observed. (The astute Shuberts had purposely booked Eddie into Chicago at this time). In a coincidental event, the Peoria theater the company had played in the previous night was reported to have been consumed by an early morning fire.

The entire Foy family joined Eddie in Chicago. It had been some years since they had been together to celebrate the holidays. A dog joke, attributed to Eddie (or Wormplanted), was printed in the *Chicago Tribune*, attesting to the press' interest in everything the comedian said or did while performing in the city.

Turning to the hotel maid, Eddie said, "Take this money. And don't tell the clerk that I've got a dog in my room."

The maid replied, "Indeed, Mr. Foy, I'd lose my job if I took a tip for anything like that." Nevertheless, the maid told the clerk about the dog. Yet when the clerk searched Foy's room, he found no dog. Confused, the clerk confronted Eddie.

"The girl says that you said you had a dog in your room."

Eddie laughed heartily. "Oh no, I didn't. I gave her a quarter and told her not to tell you that I had a dog in my room. I didn't want her to lie, that's all."

On the last night of "Mr. Hamlet's" Chicago run, at the end of the death scene, stagehands were lowering the curtain too quickly. Eddie turned to them and, in a loud aside, cracked, "Take your time there, young fellow. I ain't dead yet." The audience roared their approval and stood up, cheering and applauding his performance. The *Tribune* noted that "Eddie Foy finished his three weeks with a rollicking last night."

"Mr. Hamlet" continued through the Midwest with excellent box offices and reviews. Even when they played return engagements in Kansas City, Cincinnati, and Montreal, theaters filled and reviewers wrote that Eddie "repeated his former successes." When the company returned to Brooklyn in early April, the Shuberts presented Eddie with a new show and a new contract — with a salary increase. He quickly signed. They informed him that "Mr. Hamlet" would be closed in a week, but they neglected to inform the company.

At the end of the week's run at the Majestic Theater, Brooklyn, the Shuberts locked the theater's doors. Although cast members were decidedly angry, they could do nothing about it. In a surprising gesture, J.J. Shubert gave cast members an opportunity to join the new show if they desired. Of course, they would not be paid until the show opened, the usual arrangement. Eddie intervened and persuaded the Shuberts to pay train fare home for those performers who lived outside New York.

At the end of April, A. Toxen Worm, on behalf of the Shubert organization, officially announced that their new production, "Up and Down Broadway," starring "the great comedian," Eddie Foy, would open the summer season at the Casino Theater. Rehearsals were to begin mid-May. While Eddie seemed pleased and eager to perform, he found himself in the middle of an argument between Lew Fields and J.J. Shubert, one that jeopardized the integrity of the new show.

Lew Fields and J.J. Shubert had spent months at odds about the development of productions at the new Winter Garden, a joint Fields/Shubert enterprise. J.J. looked for any opportunity to take over direction of the project and, at the same time, prove to his brother Lee that he could produce more profitable shows than could Fields. Competition for audiences during the summer of 1910 was fierce. Fields' "The Summer Widowers" was

popular, Ziegfeld's "Follies of 1910," featuring Fanny Brice and Bert Williams, was his best production to date, and Fields' "Tillie's Nightmare," with Marie Dressler, had months of good box office. In addition, Fields had half ownership with the Shuberts in "Up and Down Broadway"; in effect, running three shows at one time and competing with himself.

The Shubert/Fields alliance forced Fields and J.J. Shubert into close, daily contact, quickly delineating their distinctly different styles of operation. Fields would make a decision, usually agreed to by Lee Shubert, only to be reversed by J.J., with no discussion. A number of times, Fields discovered these reversals only when he read about them in the newspapers. J.J. borrowed performers from Fields' other shows; Fields balked at having his shows stripped. When J.J. needed additional chorus girls at the last minute, he attempted to abduct them from "The Summer Widowers." Fields loudly protested. The conflict between them escalated further when J.J. forbade a number of prominent theater critics — Channing Pollack, Renold Wolf, Haywood Broun, and Alexander Woolcott — from attending Shubert shows because of their unfavorable reviews. These critics were long-time friends of Fields, and he refused to enforce the Shubert blacklist.

The confrontation went public when both *Variety* and the *New York Clipper* revealed a quarrel between Fields and the Shuberts, reporting that their relationship had "ruptured." The theatrical papers suggested "Up and Down Broadway" was the center of the argument, Fields being angry that the Shuberts would play a show in direct competition to his own.

Fields denied the press accusation, pointing out that he was half-owner of "Up and Down Broadway," so "it is absurd to think that I would be offended in having a show in which I am so deeply interested booked for what looks like a very prosperous engagement at the Casino." He further stated that there was a deep and lasting relationship between him and Lee Shubert. But the Shuberts controlled bookings, and Fields could do little about it. They quickly demonstrated their power by manipulating "Up and Down Broadway's" opening and routing. Unfortunately, this caused considerable financial difficulties for Eddie.

"Up and Down Broadway" planned to open in early June. Yet, because the current production of "The Mikado" at the Casino was doing so well, the Shuberts delayed "Broadway's" opening to early July. Then the Shuberts announced that "Broadway" would open in Boston instead and play there until the Casino was available, effectively delaying the show's New York opening a month. During that time, Eddie's rehearsal salary was insufficient to meet family needs. He had to ask for advances from the Shuberts, which J.J. provided almost gleefully. As before, loan repayments would be deducted from Eddie's weekly salary once the show finally opened.

"Up and Down Broadway," called a musical revue rather than a musical comedy, opened at the Shubert Theater, Boston, June 27. Eddie and veteran Emma Carus were the stars of what the critics called "a typical Parisian revue." The show was an immediate success. So confident was Eddie that they would play an extended run in Boston—as yet, the Shuberts had given no indication when "The Mikado" would vacate the Casino—that he brought the entire family to stay, settling them at the Winthrop Hotel. Reviews supported his certainty:

> The big New York revue, "Up and Down Broadway," in which Eddie Foy and Emma Carus are joint stars, scored an instantaneous hit here. Never has such a wealth of stage settings, not to mention the galaxy of stars, before been seen in a single production in this city.[10]

By its third week, "Broadway" was doing so well, the *Globe* predicted that "a long and pleasant run is anticipated." As if triggered by the statement, the Shuberts immediately announced the production would be moved to the Casino Theater for a July 18 opening. They also informed the press the show would remain at the Casino for only nine weeks before going on tour.

"Up and Down Broadway" was actually a burlesque revue in two acts and eleven scenes, written by Edgar Smith. The music and lyrics were written by Eddie's old friend and personal composer, William Jerome, and his then partner, Jean Schwartz. A cursory plot threaded its way through twenty-two song and dance numbers.

The show opens on Mount Parnassus with a meeting of the "High Brow Club" attended by Momus (Eddie Foy), a janitor found guilty of frivolity. He is condemned to go to Earth, Broadway being the natural place for him to land. Descending in an airship, he is ordered to "highbrowize" Broadway theatrical circles. Other members of the club periodically join him to assist his educational campaign. Instead, Momus become demoralized. Melpomene (Emma Carus), muse of tragedy, comes to rescue Momus just as he is sitting down to a poker game with common mortals. Melpomene vigorously converts the heathen of the Great White Way to divine modes of Grecian dress and manners, but soon she also succumbs to the tawdry pleasures of Broadway life.

Performing in variety-like olios were such principals as George Andrews, Martin Brown, Sylvia Clark, Peggy Merritt, and Mlle. Adelaide, who contributed a compelling exotic dance. Also performing were Irving Berlin and Ted Snyder, as singing and piano-playing entertainers in a Cafe d'Lobster skit. Visits by the "High Brows" to Mrs. Shark's Boarding House (and brothel), Herald Square, Polo Grounds, Chinatown, and the Metropolitan Opera House offered ample opportunity for singing and dancing specialties.

Eddie's two hit songs were "The Ghost of Kelly" and "The Lily," in which he burlesqued Miss Nance O'Neil (from a Belasco play). He also impersonated Forbes Robertson, transformed all the occupants of a

Eddie as Momus in "Up and Down Broadway," a musical review containing twenty-two song and dance numbers. Irving Berlin sang some of his melodies and played the piano in the show. A year later, Berlin would win public recognition with "Alexander's Ragtime Band." (Museum of the City of New York)

boarding house into ancient Greeks, and burlesqued the Stranger in "The Passing of the Third Floor Back," a skit in which the celestial visitor carried his own fireplace into the boarding house and took it with him when he departed.

Considering its reliance on a "more or less incoherent resume of current events — theatrical and otherwise," as described by the *Herald,* "Up and Down Broadway" was reasonably well received:

There is a mighty big show at the Casino and a real jolly one. It is named "Up and

Down Broadway," which means nothing, and has a story so incoherent that it is useless to follow it. But altogether, the Casino has an entertainment that is worthy of the most liberal patronage.

Eddie Foy and Emma Carus appeared under the auspices of the Messrs. Shubert at the Casino Theater last night in a sparkling musical review called "Up and Down Broadway." It was an elaborate production, well staged and excellently costumed. It was set to music above the average and interspersed with several songs that met with cordial approval of an audience that packed the house.[11]

Of Eddie, the *Clipper* reported:

The work of the company was of the gilt-edged variety, Eddie Foy getting his clowning and dancing in to the best possible advantage. He was up to his old little tricks of facial contortions and simulated nonchalance of manner, and the audience liked everything he did.[12]

The *Evening World* headlined: "Eddie Foy's New Warm Weather Show Is Lively and Entertaining," and went on to declare:

Eddie Foy is something more than a grotesque comedian. He is first of all a character, a fact that will probably not be generally realized until he has climbed the golden stairs.[13]

The nine-week New York run of "Up and Down Broadway" did well for the Shuberts, although J.J. seemed to feel that his star comedian had not performed his best, citing various comments from "friends" that Eddie's performances "have not been up to standard." Eddie could not understand what J.J. was referring to, unless it was his delinquent repayment of advances. J.J. was incessantly critical, however, and periodically sent notes to Eddie insisting that he "improve."

The tour took the company to Philadelphia, Baltimore, Washington, D.C., a return to Brooklyn, and again to New York (this time at the West End Theater), then back on the road, heading for a Christmas holiday run in Chicago. Reports from these cities indicated "big business" and "large crowds." But the situation between J.J. and Eddie exploded, prior to "Up and Down Broadway's" opening in Chicago.

A telegram from J.J. to Eddie read:

Dear Mr. Foy:
All along the line people who have seen the show tell me that you are not doing anything to help the attraction.

He went on to remind Eddie that:

We have lost thousands of dollars with this attraction and I feel that the treatment you have accorded us is far from right. You have never looked at the proposition from our point of view.[14]

Eddie was irate. He was unaware of any negative reports regarding his performance. In fact, he believed that "Up and Down Broadway" was one of his best shows. He also knew from perusal of box-office receipts that the show was showing a profit each week. Maybe it was his high salary that so offended J.J.

What J.J. might have been referring to were recent comments made by New York critics that Eddie continued to perform "old stuff," that he might be "getting lazy." One anonymous reviewer suggested Eddie was trading on the good nature of his audience, that it was time he did something new. To some extent, they were correct.

Eddie had been playing similar roles for almost a decade, the last six years with the Shuberts as they built their dynasty. In the meantime, European-style musical comedy was being replaced by more topical American plots, American characters, and the music of American composers on Tin Pan Alley. Vaudeville, too, was fast becoming the dominant popular entertainment, occupying more theaters, stage talent, and press attention than musical comedy could generate.

As it became Americanized, the structure of musical comedy changed from presentation of variety-style olios to more coherently plotted plays in which music was integrated into the performance. This was also an important method by which musical comedy distinguished itself from the familiar vaudeville bill. Plays by George M. Cohan and Lew Fields not only demonstrated that musical comedy could produce good plots, but also that audiences cheerfully embraced and supported such innovations.

Comedy was changing its form, as well. Pantomime was losing its appeal. Audiences were looking for more stage action and snappy dialogue. With the Americanization of productions, comedy became topical, dealing more with real-life situations, real personalities, and current events. Immigrant humor was rapidly fading, as were impersonations. While good impersonations were always funny (and Eddie was the best at using this technique), they often deviated from or broke up the plot line. Audiences were becoming less tolerant of such detours.

Eddie had become so much a unique and eccentric personality that his very success effectively separated him from the show; in fact, the show sometimes hurt because of it. At the same time, his legendary status had influenced audiences to demand familiar material, making him reluctant to stray from previously successful performances.

Blame part of this situation on the Shuberts, who were only interested in repeating box-office successes. Blame Eddie because he had been carried away by his ego and provincial theaters full of admirers who cheered and marveled at his every stage posture. At what point in his career does a legend become so familiar he loses the spark that ignites audiences? New Yorkers were more critical of Eddie's stage persona. When they believed he was not keeping up with the development of popular entertainment, they didn't hesitate to let him know.

Back in 1888, when Eddie had taken his mother to the Chicago Opera House to see him perform in one of David Henderson's extravaganzas, she asked him, "Do they pay y' fifty dollars a week for that?"

"Yes, Mother," he answered.

"Thin fool 'em as long as y' can, Edwin."

Audiences and theater critics had become so sophisticated they were no longer "fooled" by even the best of performers.

Awareness of these shifts in American popular theater could very well have influenced Eddie to assess his career direction. Criticism from New York reviewers surely caught his attention. Events that followed suggest Eddie had carefully evaluated his situation and attempted to address it. His primary concern: could he change his persona — the eccentric comedy, bizarre costumes and makeup, gravelly singing voice, and easygoing manner — and still retain his position as a top comedian? Or had he become so typecast as to face an inevitable, if gradual decline in popularity? Would not too drastic a change create the same negative effect?

Eddie telegramed J.J. Shubert that he wished to retire from the cast of "Broadway." J.J. tried to make him feel guilty about retirement, reminding him of the effect it would have on the company, not to mention Shubert box-office receipts. Eddie responded to J.J.'s admonitions by complaining of the indignities he had suffered during the current season. In turn, J.J. reminded Eddie he still owed the Shuberts money.

Recriminations continued back-and-forth while the company played Midwest engagements through December 1910 and January 1911, ironically, to "packed houses" and excellent reviews. A series of one-night stands in upstate New York, the Shuberts' old stronghold, early in February, ultimately triggered Eddie's action. Unannounced, he departed from "Up and Down Broadway," closing the show.

When questioned by the press, Eddie declared that he was severing all business relations with the Shuberts, that he was disgusted with disagreements involving the Shuberts over the past few years. The Shuberts made no public comment. For almost eight weeks, there was no mention of Eddie in the newspapers.

Early in April, Eddie resurfaced in vaudeville — it seemed to have become his standby job — in a skit entitled "The King and the Jack," with scenery and four women performers in support. He opened in Cleveland, played a week each in Cincinnati and Chicago, and then, pleased with neither the routine nor audience response, disbanded the troupe. On the bill with Eddie in Chicago was a young man whom the local critics called "peculiar, anything but an actor," but his lasso work "is the best we have seen." The kid's name was Will Rogers.

Two weeks later, Eddie was the headliner at Hammerstein's Victoria Theater in New York, playing a solo sketch. Included were some new costumes, new songs, one sung in drag, and his classic Hamlet burlesque. The *Clipper* endeavored to reassure Eddie he was still a New York favorite:

> Foy's faculty of making a travesty of anything and everything carries him straight to the good graces of his hearers, and his star is still "in the ascendant."[15]

Eddie performed the sketch in Chicago and Atlantic City to good effect, returning home in July to decide what he wanted to do in the fall. He was offered a comic role in a musical revue, "The Girl from the Folies Bergère," but rejected it because it resembled "Up and Down Broadway." A.H. Woods, one of a number of emerging New York impresarios, presented Eddie with the leading role, in drag, in a musical farce called "The Pet of the Petticoats." Eddie agreed to try it, although both plot and music seemed uninspired.

"The Pet of the Petticoats" had brief rehearsals and opened at the Savoy Theater, Asbury Park, August 25. After two perfor-

mances, as well as two each in Rochester and Buffalo, Eddie retired from the company. According to Eddie, the show had no "life." But neither was it entirely dead.

In what theatrical observers called a strange move, Charles Dillingham and Flo Ziegfeld bought out the rights to "The Pet of the Petticoats" and persuaded Eddie to return to the cast. But two more weeks of performances in New York convinced everybody the show was a flop. Nevertheless, Dillingham and Ziegfeld retained Eddie's contract and offered him the lead in a remake of "The Man from Mexico," renamed "Over the River." Ziegfeld promised Eddie that a two-week run in Chicago would prepare them for a New York opening.

"Over the River" opened at the Studebaker Theater, Chicago, on September 25. George V. Hobart and H.A. du Souchet wrote the book, and John L. Golden composed the music. Julian Mitchell was stage director. The plot of the musical comedy was adapted from du Souchet's "The Man from Mexico," played by William Collier some years previously.

Madison Parke (Eddie Foy), an elderly man with a fondness for convivial restaurants, visits the Café Cabaret, a New York haunt resembling a Parisian "freedom from propriety" establishment; there, he overindulges. He winds up in a night police court, where an indignant judge prescribes a rest cure of eighty days on Blackwell's Island. Parke persuades the judge to allow him to go home for the night to explain to his family that it is necessary for him to be absent for a period of time. At the suggestion of his friend, Hudson Rivers (Melville Stewart), Parke reveals that he must travel to Mexico with his good friend Timothy Cook (William Sellery).

The second act finds Parke in prison serving his term. His friends have from time

Opposite: A program cover for "Over the River," starring Eddie as Madison Parke. In this show, Eddie introduced the Seven Little Foys. Audience reactions to the children were so enthusiastic that Eddie became convinced the family could become vaudeville headliners.

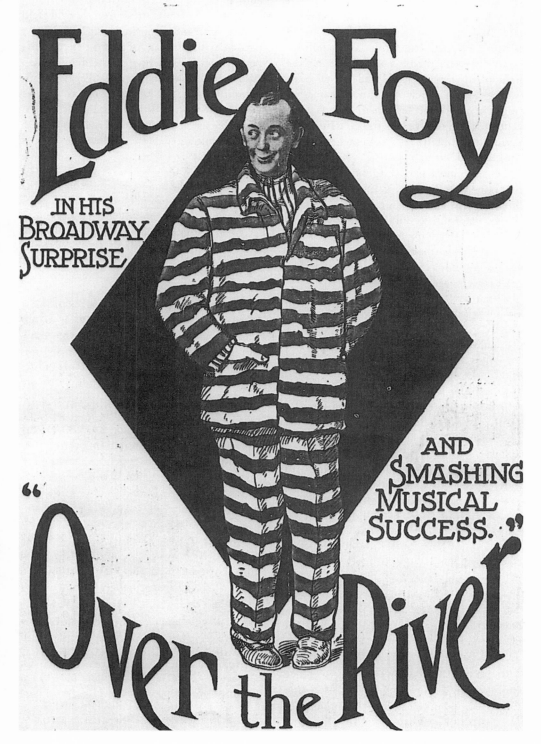

to time conveyed messages to his wife, Mrs. Madison Parke (Maud Lambert), so that upon his return home, he finds a garden party in progress, at which the guests are all in Mexican costume. Explanation failing, Parke discovers that his wife, who on the night of his misadventure had herself been visiting cafés in search of him, was thereupon caught in a raid. He declares that, in fact, he went to prison to save her, thus retaining the reputation of a faithful, if somewhat forgetful, husband.

For the most part, Eddie's comedy was integrated into the plot. Sitting in jail, Parke looks around and observes sadly, "Bars all around me, and yet I'm perishing for want of a drink." Glancing in disgust at the zebra pattern of his garment, Parke laments, "I like this suit all right, except that I get tired of it. I just can't wear it out."

During a scene in the second act, as the warden is making his rounds, he sees Parke laboring. "What are you working at?" inquires Warden Vokes.

"Shoveling coal," answers Parke. "Hard work?" asks the warden. "Nope," Parke replies solemnly. "It's soft coal."

The only time Eddie offered a familiar routine was when his friend Rivers described the elegant lunch he had just eaten at a famous restaurant. As Rivers talked about the meal in detail, Eddie pantomimed facial and body expressions that conveyed acute envy, ravenous hunger, and utter despair, until, at the mention of wine, he could stand it no longer; "with a sigh expressing the anguish of a lost soul," he dragged himself to the corner of his cell.

Eddie sang three songs: "New York Isn't Such a Bad Old Town," at the end of Act One; "Mexico"; and, with the chorus, "When There's No Light at All," at the end of Act Three.

The cabaret scene (a replica of Sherry's Restaurant) featured an extravagant dance exhibition by Maurice and Mlle. Madeline d'Harville, including some dances that were the subject of prudish criticism. Yet such puritanical objections did little to prevent audiences from demanding encores.

Lillian Lorraine, fresh from her Ziegfeld Follies successes, sang five songs, making a particular hit with a song and dance number, "Ring, Ting-a-ling on the Telephone." Also in the cast was an ingénue, Peggy Wood, beginning her rise to stardom, as well as Eddie's girlfriend, Ruth Langdon.

Chicago reviewers called the production familiar but agreeable to audiences:

> The Studebaker was well-filled last night, and the audience seemed to find the warmed over provender of this "new" play's offering a quite comfortable fortification of the first blizzard of 1911–1912. Should auld acquaintance be forgot? Certainly not — and they won't be, so long as Eddie Foy and "Over the River" hold the boards.[16]

Anticipating a quick return to New York, the company was rudely surprised when Ziegfeld announced that the show would go on tour for an indefinite period. What Ziegfeld didn't reveal were his efforts to sell the show to another producer before box-office receipts declined.

The tour stopped at the familiar large cities in the Midwest, then moved East for an extended run in Boston during the Christmas holiday season. Reports indicated good reviews in every city, but box-office receipts were rarely revealed. Finally, after more than four months on the road, the production headed for a Broadway opening.

"Over the River" opened at the Globe Theater, New York, January 8, 1912. New York critics chided the play but complimented Eddie's performance:

> If you haven't seen a real cabaret show you can see a tolerably good imitation in Eddie Foy's new show, "Over the River." Now and then "Over the River" seems like a genuine farce, and now and then like a Broadway musical comedy. However, Eddie Foy is very funny, if you like Eddie Foy's fun, and almost everybody there last night did.[17]

A musical version of "A Man from Mexico" was given by Eddie Foy and his company, and met with approval. Mr. Foy, as usual, was humorously entertaining.

The newspapers also noted that Eddie's entire family attended the opening, jamming "a box which held all eyes, filled with innumerable little Foys, all apparently the same age, who watched all the doings of their father with the greatest glee."

"Over the River" played fifteen profitable weeks, closing the season the third week in April. During the spring, cast changes were numerous. Rose Winters replaced Maud Raymond. Maye Busch took over the lead chorus role. Lillian Lorraine gained press attention by telephoning the theater to say she was voluntarily resigning from the company to get married. When she attempted to return the following night, she was refused entrance.

Deciding she didn't care for dance partner Maurice's antics, Mlle. d'Harville abruptly left. Just arrived from Berlin after two years of study abroad, Florence Walton, a young dancer who had played a small part in Ziegfeld's "Follies of 1910," was immediately auditioned and selected as Maurice's partner. Within a few years, the dance team of Maurice and Walton would be challenging Vernon and Irene Castle as America's premier dance interpreters.

While Eddie spent a quiet summer in New Rochelle, his first real vacation from the stage since having been unemployed during the White Rats' confrontation with the Syndicate, old theatrical legends passed away and harbingers of a new generation of entertainment attracted public attention. When Eddie read the "old reliable" theatrical weekly, the *New York Clipper*, he was sure to have noticed that the Butte, Montana, theater he had played in 1881 had burnt to the ground, along with its historical artifacts. Former flamboyant impresario David Henderson died an obscure death, in poverty. Lottie Gilson, one of the last variety soubrettes, died a worn-out, addicted shell.

In their place, or so it seemed, New Yorkers celebrated the laying of the cornerstone to baseball's newest stadium, Brooklyn's Ebbets Field. The City Council passed an ordinance forbidding women to wear short skirts at beaches. Automobile speeds in Manhattan were limited to fifteen miles per hour, eighteen on wide streets. The church decried such reckless mechanical propulsion as a prime example of the decline of civilization.

Ragtime was at its peak of popularity. Music publishers were distributing a thousand popular songs a year, their sheet music having invaded nearly every home in the country. Moving pictures, with their advanced technology, were capturing the attention and the dollars of nationwide audiences, who increasingly viewed this medium as the new era's entertainment. Its long-appreciated and primary competition, vaudeville, mirrored altered social perceptions and values, as immigrants integrated into the culture and a chauvinistic America flexed its capitalistic muscle. Eddie may not have been able to grasp the profound changes in popular entertainment, but he was clearly aware that such transitions had an effect on his profession. "Over the River" had been a shift from "old familiar routines," but it wasn't yet what Eddie hoped to accomplish.

Eddie's only summer performance was at the Lambs' Gambol, their annual charity benefit. Playing with George M. Cohan, William Collier, Raymond Hitchcock, and Fred Stone in an old-time minstrel skit, Eddie did a cakewalk dance in blackface. There is no record that Eddie ever played in blackface again.

Having demonstrated a successful season with "Over the River," Dillingham and Ziegfeld finally sold the production — or rather Eddie's contract to perform in the production — to Werba and Leuscher, for a reported $25,000. For $1,000 a week, Eddie signed a contract with his new employers. The *Clipper* reported on the agreement, apparently an unprecedented arrangement:

By acquiring Eddie Foy, with the New York production of "Over the River," from Charles B. Dillingham, for the sum of $25,000, Werba and Leuscher have absolutely established a precedent in theatricals. This is the first time in the history of Broadway theatricals that a firm has lifted bodily a star and Broadway success from another manager.[18]

"Over the River" was announced to open its second season in early September. Meanwhile, Eddie was already in closed-door rehearsal for an entirely new and different project.

The Foy family dining room was large enough to contain a long, rectangular, dark oak table, twelve chairs, and a stone fireplace wide enough for children to pedal their bikes inside it. Move the table and chairs, and the dining room easily converted into a small stage, excellent for practicing vaudeville sketches.

A family story has long suggested that Father Manzelli, priest at the New Rochelle Catholic church the Foy family attended, persuaded Eddie and Madeline to perform with their children at a church benefit. Actually, Eddie had already begun preparing the children to appear with him in vaudeville. The church benefit, he calculated, would be good experience for them, their first performance in front of an audience.

Since the time that Eddie and the children first performed at a Polo Grounds benefit in 1908, Eddie had believed a family act could be a successful venture. Yet, as long as he continued to play musical comedies, and as long as the youngest child remained unable to follow stage direction, the timing for such an act was not right. Now, Irving was almost four years old. He could mimic the older children sufficiently to give the impression of a team, yet be sufficiently out-of-step to generate laughter.

Such a family act would be unique in vaudeville. Only a few others currently performed, and they usually consisted of brothers and sisters close in age, performing either songs, dances, or acrobatic feats. No family

act was as large as the Foys, nor presented such a spread in age. In addition, Eddie had an advantage in that the press often referred to his large family, as he himself did whenever he was interviewed; the context was always humorous yet respectful.

Although Eddie was already committed to play "Over the River" for another year, he believed it would be opportune to try out the family act to determine its viability. Thus, on August 19, 1912, at the New Brighton Theater, Long Island, Eddie Foy and the Seven Little Foys made their stage debut. Bryan, the oldest, was almost sixteen; Eddie, Jr., was six years old; Irving would be four in a month. Catherine, Eddie's oldest child (with Lola Sefton), was eighteen and had by now left home to work in the city. She never appeared with her siblings.

Eddie began the performance by appearing in a grotesque costume to sing and dance two songs: "When Shakespeare Was a Boy" and "The Green Grass Grows All Around." He then transformed himself into a suffragette and pantomimed marching in a woman's suffrage parade. (One had just occurred on Fifth Avenue.) Then, with a fanfare, the children, led by Bryan, marched on stage, followed by Eddie carrying a large carpetbag, out of which popped little Irving. The five boys were dressed in dark stockings, white knickers and shirts, and black sailor ties; the two girls wore dark stockings, white blouses and skirts, and black sailor ties. Eddie introduced his children, each of whom in turn stepped forward, danced a few steps, and bowed to the audience, which was already cheering them. Together they sang a song, gave a few impersonations, then joined their father in the chorus of another song. The *New York Clipper* correspondent declared, in the family's first review:

> Eddie Foy is always a treat, and this appearance in vaudeville, with the support of the seven little Foys, is as entertaining an offering as ever appeared on a vaudeville stage. They were a big hit, and would make

good anywhere. The act is a winner, and the seventeen minutes it held the stage is only half long enough.[19]

A week later, they played their first New York engagement, at the Union Square Theater. Audiences enthusiastically received them. Alan Dale reported:

> Eddie Foy, whom everybody knows, and his seven Foylettes, whom everybody does not know, but should, was a riot.[20]

On the Union Square bill with Eddie was a young woman, playing her first New York engagement. Reviewers wrote that she "managed to pull through in fair shape." Her act consisted of singing four songs in a talkative fashion and performing a few dance steps while manipulating minstrel "bones." This less-than-stellar appearance marked the beginning of Mae West's career.

No sooner had the family finished at the Union Square than Eddie was arrested and brought to trial by the Gerry Society for allowing his children to appear on stage without a permit. In his court defense, Eddie stated: "It all hinges on the question as to whether these children of mine sing on the stage. Everybody knows I can't sing, so it follows the children can't either. Besides, I haven't time for the case right now. I'll waive examination and fight it out at Special Sessions."

The judge held Eddie for trial, bail fixed at $100. Harry Fitzgerald, manager of the "Over the River" company, paid the bail so Eddie could begin the tour. This episode proved the first of a long series of arrests and court hearings that Eddie encountered for almost ten years, in cities throughout the U.S., since many states had passed and enforced child-labor laws. Later, the children would joke that they had spent more time in court than on the stage.

"Over the River" opened at the Newark Theater, September 9. "Eddie Foy was a big hit all week," declared the *Clipper*. The production remained much the same, and there were only a few cast changes. But Werba and Leuscher were having problems routing the show and were faced with weeks of one-night stands in small towns interspersed with week-long engagements in larger cities. This placed significant financial pressures on them, making it difficult to properly advertise and promote the show.

Successful weeks in Newark and Brooklyn preceded one-night stands in upstate New York; week-long runs in Cleveland and Detroit were followed by two weeks of one-night stands in Pennsylvania and Ohio. Yet the show continued to attract large houses and good reviews. Eddie was particularly singled out:

> Funny Eddie Foy, the pet of Broadway, never faced an audience without convulsing it with laughter. The instant he appears on stage a smile extends to the last row of the gallery where he is as great a favorite as among the orchestra patrons.[21]

Even in small towns, like Akron, Ohio, Eddie was a hit:

> No play, with Eddie Foy as a top liner in the cast, could possibly fail to attract. This popular comedian is always irresistibly funny; in the prison scene of this piece, when he is seen as a jailbird, he convulses the audience.

Yet, the tour got no easier for the company. They returned to New York for a week and then traveled to Philadelphia where Eddie "was welcomed with showers of applause." Now the company faced two weeks of one-night stands in Connecticut and Massachusetts before arriving in Boston for the Christmas holidays.

Since he would be performing in Boston for three weeks, Eddie brought the entire family there to enjoy Christmas together. Each day, the children attended rehearsals of the show. By the end of the second week, they were performing with members of the company. It was then that Eddie suggested to management that the family be incorporated into the production as an added specialty. For the time being, Werba and Leuscher demurred. Meanwhile, Eddie and Madeline decided the entire family would travel with the company on its tour. A special train car was set aside for them, thirteen people in all—Eddie, Madeline, the seven children, Aunt Clara, a maid, a tutor, and Eddie's manager.

In January 1913, the company and Foy family entourage stopped in Baltimore, Washington, D.C., and, for the first time, traveled South through Virginia, North Carolina, and Georgia. Good business prevailed, although Werba and Leuscher complained about their increased expenses due to the one-night stands. Eddie recognized this all too familiar whining as similar to Shubert protests prior to their cutting costs or reducing cast size.

Two months of one-night stands in the South had exhausted the company, and they begged for a week off to rest. In contrast, the exuberant Foy children were taking in the country, visiting tourist sites in every city, living in hotels, eating at restaurants, and learning what backstage life was like. Management gave the company two weeks to recoup, including Holy Week, a traditionally slow and unprofitable time. It was a wise decision, since it revitalized the cast in preparation for an extensive Western tour.

When Eddie celebrated his birthday in Shreveport, Louisiana, on March 8 (reported to be fifty-two, he was actually fifty-seven), the entire cast gave him a grand party in the theater. A number of cast members donned his own comic costumes and imitated him. When Bryan and Charlie came on stage and mimicked their father, they "brought down the house." No question in Eddie's mind, they were ready for the stage.

In April, the "Over the River" company traveled across Iowa, Nebraska, and Colorado, playing at most two-night stands, even in the large cities, before jumping to Los Angeles for a week's engagement. Since the recent relocation of most moving picture production from the East to Los Angeles, the city was rapidly becoming a Mecca for entertainers. Eddie saw the studios in action, watching movies literally being cranked out daily. When he talked to a number of fellow stage performers who were appearing in movies, he was encouraged by their reports—high salaries, brief periods of work, comfortable living. And think of the national exposure an actor could get by being seen in theaters throughout the country. It surely beat thirty weeks on the road.

It was about this time that Werba and Leuscher told Eddie he could include the family in the production; "but only one skit," they indicated. As the company performed two weeks of one-night stands in California, from San Diego to Sacramento, Eddie and the children rehearsed each day, in preparation for their opening in San Francisco. Area newspapers were already promoting Eddie Foy and the Seven Little Foys in "Over the River"; and advance sales were high. Whether by coincidence or not, songsmith William Jerome was in California; he was seen working with Eddie, presumably preparing the family skit in the show. "Over the River," at the Cort Theater, played to full houses the entire run. The *Chronicle* headlined:

> Eddie Foy in Great Show; Girls, Fun and Dances.
> Seven Little Foys Make as Big a Hit as Father.

In its review of the show, the *Chronicle* went on to report:

> …the seven little Foys, chips and chipettes off the old block, stopped the show like a traffic squad at a busy crossing.[22]

So popular and profitable was "Over the River" in San Francisco, Werba and Leuscher booked engagements in Oregon, Washington, and into Canada, albeit one-night stands, through June. But when the company reached Seattle, they found that weekly salaries had been delayed; there was some question about the bookings in Canada. When they reached Calgary, Alberta, Werba and Leuscher informed the company that the show was closing because of poor business. Not only would remaining salaries be late, but management could not pay train fare to New York. Eddie loaned the money for cast members to return to Broadway. The Foy children had witnessed first-hand an example of a performer's precarious life on the road.

Six weeks later, Eddie filed suit against Werba and Leuscher to recover $7,000. He claimed they owed him four and a half weeks salary, at $1,300 a week, plus $500 he had advanced from his own pocket to bring the company back to New York. Unfortunately, Werba and Leuscher were about to file for bankruptcy. There is no record of Eddie's ever recovering any of the money. The episode, however, convinced him that working for other managers had become high-risk employment. It was time to perform as independently as one could in a complicated business of theater circuits and booking agents.

In July, Eddie completed negotiations with Keith/Albee's United Booking Office for a twenty-week tour at $1,500 a week, starting in September. A brief note in the *New York Clipper* stated:

> Eddie Foy next year will be at the head of his own company, playing with his children, which will play a vaudeville performance in the principle theaters of the country.[23]

Chapter 14

"I'm head salesman in a glove house, and I'm showing my kids."

> Eddie Foy, introducing his children to the audience in their first vaudeville act together.

September 1, 1913. Crowds of patrons jammed the Union Square Theater, New York, to attend a matinee vaudeville show. With the promise of first-class entertainment, they were out in force to inaugurate the new theater season. The theater quickly filled to SRO; there were still hundreds on the street, hoping by some miracle of ticket distribution to witness the first professional performance of Eddie Foy and the Seven Little Foys.

The Foys were the fourth act on the bill, following a soubrette, a "dumb" act, and a farce-comedy skit. The fourth slot in vaudeville preceded intermission and was the star position. As the applause for the farce-comedy skit died down, a quiet fell over the assembled throng, as if the audience held its collective breath, in anticipation of what they believed to be forthcoming.

The lights dimmed. The orchestra began a sprightly overture, and the curtain opened on a simple backdrop. When Eddie, in everyday attire, shuffled on stage, the entire audience rose as one and broke out in loud cheers, whistles, and stomping that lasted five minutes. Beaming across the footlights, Eddie smiled his crooked smile, greeted his admirers, and gave a jaunty wave to friends he could see sitting in the orchestra and box seats.

When the applause subsided, Eddie sang a parody of "The Garden of Roses" in his familiar cracked voice. At its conclusion, the audience demanded an encore. After three encores, Eddie told the crowd he wanted to continue the show "because my kids are getting nervous offstage." Another round of cheers and whistles. Finally, with an orchestral fanfare, Eddie greeted six of his children as they ran on stage. The oldest, Bryan, carried a large cloth bag and handed it to his father. When Eddie opened the bag, out popped the youngest, Irving, who took his place at the end of a line that decreased in size step-wise. The audience erupted in cheers.

The children sang two songs; Bryan and Charlie did some imitations, including one of their father; Mary and Madeline sang a song in harmony, and, in Irving's words, "I was along for the ride." The skit concluded with Eddie singing and dancing a number, with the children in support. After a number of bows, Eddie was forced to make a speech. Then, on cue, Irving ran out, grabbed his father's leg, and attempted to pull him off-stage. "Father," Irving pleaded, "Mother says to come home." It broke up the audience, and they cheered their approval for another five minutes.

At the evening performance (first-class vaudeville now featured two-a-day shows), the Foy family appeared first on the bill, so the young children could be taken home to bed. The audience was aware of the scheduling and cheered all the more.

Two days later, instead of Irving's closing routine, Eddie introduced Madeline, who came on stage for a brief bow with the children, all holding hands. Eddie asked William Jerome, who had written the skit, to supply him with opening and closing lines. For the opening line, as Eddie later recalled, Jerome pondered a moment and then said, "Let's see. You're in front, the kids behind you. The audience gives you an opening hand. You cast a glance back at the youngsters and say with a little smile, 'If I ever move to _____ (whatever town they were playing), it'll be a big city.'"

When the line was used the next night, the crowd howled with delight. Eddie used the opening joke for the entire season. In their reviews, newspapers in each city quoted the line as one of the outstanding jokes in the act.

Reviews of the new act were enthusiastic.

The *New York Telegram* reported:

> They greatly contributed to the satisfaction of the spectators.[1]

The *New York Clipper* declared:

> Eddie Foy and the Seven Little Foys cleaned up. These bright-faced boys and girls, with their talented father, presented a neat offering.[2]

An observer pointed out that Eddie seemed as delighted with the children as was the audience. Performing as a family had been a calculated risk for Eddie, but he believed the kids had a good chance for success. No question it meant a great deal for his own future, as well.

Eddie was fully cognizant that his career had been slowly eroding. The vehicles that had made him a star were in rapid transformation. Musical comedy had matured from variety skits with minimal plots to cohesive stories that integrated song and dance. Burlesque had turned from satire and travesty to girly-shows and "blue" humor. Revues were now modeled after Ziegfeld's Follies. Even vaudeville, the last outpost of variety-style olios, now attracted top performers of the popular stage and screen.

New comedians and comic acts were competing for younger, more sophisticated audiences. Their comedy was more frenetic and slapstick, and their jokes dealt more with exaggerating the realities of daily life, from politics and baseball to automobiles and mothers-in-law. Nor did these new comedians combine their comedy with songs and dances, as did Eddie.

Eddie found that stage legends age, maybe even faster than other performers, because of the ordained status bestowed upon them in the earlier days of their careers. Eddie recognized the evidence. He saw it in the mirror when he had to apply a bit more makeup to cover the lines on his face. He read it when critics identified him as an old performer, although they still mentioned the

Eddie and the Seven Little Foys in 1913, their first full year on the vaudeville circuit. *From left to right:* **Irving, Eddie, Jr., Madeline, Mary, Dick, Charlie and Bryan. They quickly took their place among the most popular two-a-day performers in vaudeville.**

obvious with affection. He felt it after two weeks of two-a-day performances, even though his vaudeville skits were of shorter duration than his roles in earlier musical comedies.

Eddie was only a few years short of sixty, an advanced age for a performer, and he found himself to be one of the oldest active comic actors on the popular stage. Only Lew Dockstater (born the same year as Eddie) and Fred Stone (born in 1873) had been performing as long as Eddie. The new generation of comedians, among them Charlie Chaplin, W.C. Fields, Leon Errol, and Willie Howard, had been born in the 1880s. And another group of young comedians, born in the 1890s, such as Fred Allen, Jack Benny, the Marx Brothers, Eddie Cantor, and Ed Wynn, were only a few short years away from becoming vaudeville headliners themselves.

Eddie's decision to feature himself and the children in vaudeville seemed to offer distinct advantages and opportunities. Vaudeville was approaching the height of its national popularity. Theater managers decried the lack of first-class acts to fill bills. A family act composed of comedy, song, and dance seemed an entertainment particularly suited to the medium. Since there were no other comparable families on stage at the time, the Foy family act was unique. With its obvious size and wide spread of ages, such a family act evoked wholesome nostalgia and, with the promise of clean and wholesome fun, attracted substantial "family" audiences. Each of the Foy children could feature a different routine, and the combination of their talents seemed endless. Moreover, Eddie himself could perform less as each child was featured, with audiences well aware of where the kids' talent and training came from. While Eddie knew his name and reputation helped to make the act a success among theater patrons, he was acutely conscious that the performance itself had to be first-rate. From the beginning, Eddie made sure the act was professionally prepared and presented.

Another advantage of playing the vaudeville circuit was that it allowed the Foys to perform the same routine for an entire season, since they appeared at a given venue but once a year. Within the framework of a particular skit, it was easy to add or subtract material and incorporate new ideas into the act.

Eddie recognized an additional advantage in that he didn't have to rely on managers like the Shuberts, Erlanger, or Lederer, to maintain his employment. A contract with a booking agency like the Keith or Orpheum circuit guaranteed twenty to thirty weeks a year; there were enough circuits competing for talent to ensure good salaries and new venues. With Eddie's history of successes, he could make a strong argument that assured booking agents of banner weeks.

Inevitably, some people accused Eddie of using his children to sustain his career. To some extent, they were probably correct in this assessment. What Eddie might have been able to do in popular theater for the next few years can only be guessed, considering his age and the evolving structure of musical comedy. The fact that he and the family act were highly successful in vaudeville for ten years attests to their ability to capture audiences. Yes, Eddie's career was extended; but we must also admire the enjoyment he and the children gave theater patrons, both the older ones who were familiar with Eddie Foy, the clown, and the younger ones, who discovered a talented family of "born" entertainers.

During their first season, the Foys toured the country from September 1913, to June 1914, visiting thirty-one cities and playing 496 performances. From all reports, everyone loved the experience.

An average day started at 9:00 A.M., when the family arose. Breakfast in the hotel restaurant took place from 9:30 to 10:00 A.M., followed by a half-hour of exercise or a brisk walk. Some days, this time was devoted to learning and rehearsing new material for the act. From 10:00 until noon, the children studied their lessons, given by a tutor who accompanied them on tour. Lunch and rest until 1:00 P.M., when the children had another hour of schooling. At 2:00 P.M., they left for the theater to prepare for a 3:00 P.M. matinee performance. They were back at the hotel by 3:30 P.M. for a rest and additional study, usually homework time. Dinner at a restaurant went from 6:00 to 7:00 P.M., followed by a quick return to the theater for an 8:00 P.M. show. Since they were usually first on the bill at the evening performance, the children would be in bed by 10:00 P.M.

This routine was followed every day except Sunday, when church attendance preceded packing and boarding a train for the next city's engagement. Often, they slept on the train Sunday night.

When rehearsing wasn't necessary and studies had been completed, the working week also included trips to tourist sites, lunches with local dignitaries, park picnics, and tours sponsored by local merchants, who used the occasion of the celebrated family's presence to publicize their products and services. For the family to get around, Eddie rented a car in each city. The Foys stayed at top hotels, with a suite of rooms and assigned clerks available; they ate at the best restaurants. Travel costs were high, but a weekly salary of $1,500 still provided enough money for the summer months at home.

While at home, Eddie was a relaxed father who allowed his children to act their age. On tour, however, he was a stern taskmaster. He demanded full attention to rehearsal time, and performances were sacred. Irving recalled that his father constantly emphasized the need for the children to perform as professionals. Eddie was exacting, Irving said, and his temper was quick. Yet he never hit any of the children. When their father became angry, the children simply stayed away from him; usually his anger disappeared as quickly as it came. Irving remembered, and the grandchildren agreed, that Eddie had been a loving father.

Yet a family such as the Foys performing in vaudeville inevitably had its share of detractors. Nearly every city sustained a puritanical religious faction that railed against the "sins" of vaudeville. A vaudeville act featuring children inspired them to even greater, apocalyptic tirades, picketing, and pulpit-pounding sermons. For the most part, Eddie was unaffected by such complaints. In a number of cities, however, it became more serious when Eddie was arrested for permitting the younger children to appear on stage.

New York City and states like Ohio, Illinois, and Indiana, had child-labor laws in force to "protect children from abuse," a standard strictly interpreted to make sure that underage children would not perform on stage. In New York, the infamous Gerry Society diligently carried out their mission to prevent any child under fourteen from appearing on the popular stage. At the same time, an underage child appearing on the legitimate stage, such as ten-year-old Helen Hayes, was conveniently overlooked. Once an offender was discovered, a court order was issued and delivered. Often, this resulted in both a summons and an arrest.

In other cities, too, Eddie was brought to court, if for no other reason than to obtain a belated permit and pay a small fine. Unfortunately for Eddie, a new permit had to be obtained on each occasion that the family played a given city. This situation continued almost the entire time the Foys performed on stage together, costing Eddie a good deal of time and money, as well as emotional strain.

Just after the Foys closed at the Union Square Theater in New York, Eddie received a warrant for his arrest but was unable to appear in court because the family were already playing in another city. It wasn't until the middle of October, when they returned to New York, that Eddie had a hearing. The case was closed when Eddie paid a $50 fine. When the Foys played Chicago, Eddie

was arrested "for violation of the Child Labor Laws." The *Clipper* reported that:

> This is the first test case of its kind that has ever been brought up in Illinois, and Mr. Foy intends to fight it to the finish.[3]

The Illinois law covered all children under fourteen, without regard to the work they were hired to do. No special provision had been made for show business performers; when the children involved happened to be related to their employer, carrying out the law became a matter of the court's discretion. In many instances, suits against Eddie were dropped when the judge sympathized with his predicament.

When a suit claimed Eddie had allowed his children to sing on stage, he attempted to persuade the judge the children couldn't sing. A brief display of their "limited" talent (they sang off-key or out of harmony), and the judge dismissed the case. Since Madeline accompanied the children, her appearance in court served as an excellent argument for the children's care and supervision. When it was explained the children also had a tutor and maid and went to church every Sunday, few judges pressed charges. By the end of their first year on the road, the Foys had become quite proficient in settling these lawsuits.

The first season had proven successful beyond Eddie's expectations. Crowds filled the theaters at nearly every performance, and audience response to their act had been exhilarating. The tour had taken them to major Eastern cities, the Midwest, the West Coast, and Western Canada. When the Foys returned to New York in early February, they were immediately booked to play the Palace Theater, which had become the epitome of vaudeville theaters, though barely a year old.

The Palace had been opened in March 1913. It was regarded as the finest of the spacious, handsome, and luxurious venues that now exemplified the ascendancy of first-class vaudeville. After struggling the first few months of its existence to attract crowds (bets were being made on Broadway that the theater would close before season's end), successive bills featuring Ethel Barrymore and Sarah Bernhardt attracted large crowds. From that point on, the Palace drew top entertainers and full houses.

On the bill with the Foys were Fanny Brice (making her debut), the Avon Comedy Four, Anna Held, Mae Murray (future silent screen star) and her partner, Clifton Webb, as well as a young dancer, George White (later producer of George White's Scandals). In the *Clipper* review of the entertainment, it was noted:

> Eddie Foy and the seven little Foys were a scream, and responded to several encores.[4]

When management broke with tradition and decided to keep the theater open despite the summer heat, the Foys were signed to reappear at the Palace in July for an extended run. Meanwhile, back on the road went the Foys, to complete their tour of Western states. When they visited Los Angeles, Eddie was approached by the World Film Corporation to appear in motion pictures. It was reported that Eddie rejected the offer, although a refusal was later disputed.

The Foys opened at the Palace in July for a three-week engagement. Thanks to William Jerome, and a few weeks of hard rehearsals in the dining room of their New Rochelle home, most of the act was new. The *Clipper* provided an extensive review of their performance, concluding with the declaration: "The whole act is a winner."

> Eddie Foy and the Seven Little Foys produced the biggest hit of the evening, scoring in a new act which allows Mr. Foy an opportunity for presenting his own famous specialties, and the eight other Foys (there really are eight others, Mrs. Foy appearing) ample latitude for the display of the varied talents of this talented family. Mr. Foy opens in one, singing a rather clever parody of "The Garden of Roses." His high note was immediately recognized and he enjoyed all the endorsement so long accorded this unique comedian.

After the song he "remembers that he had forgotten to remember something that he should not forget." The sight of a policeman's call box on a lamp post reminds him to call up the Foy family in New Rochelle. This he proceeds to do, and the drop rises on a pretty scene of domesticity, Mrs. Foy and the seven youngsters. Papa tells them that he won't be home for supper, and the ensuing dialogue Mr. Foy has with everyone of his offspring in turn contains good comedy. As a finale, the whole family except the Ford car have a singing and dancing number which goes very big and compels them to answer several encores, the last of which is an appearance of the young ones as a band, with the youngest Foy in an impersonation of Sousa.[5]

The summer in New Rochelle was relatively relaxed, except for two week-long performances in New Brighton and Rockaway Beach, where the Foys perfected next season's act. It was announced they would open their second vaudeville season in September, in Brooklyn.

A funny episode between Eddie and Henry Ford was featured in the local press. Apparently, Eddie had cranking problems with the Ford auto that appeared in their act at the Palace. He complained to Mr. Ford about his difficulty in getting the car started. Ford obligingly came by and, with a few flips of the crank, started the car easily. But Eddie still had a grievance: "I've given your car about ten thousand dollars' worth of free advertising, and those mutts of yours won't even give me a nut or a screw when one shakes off on the road."

Ford apologized and replied, "I'll see that you get some service."

A month later, a gigantic box with a Ford Company label on it was delivered to the Foy home. When Eddie opened the box, he found a sample of each nut, bolt, screw, and cotterpin used to put the car together, courtesy of Henry Ford. Eddie admitted it was a fine joke on him. The episode seemed to top off a very enjoyable year.

In contrast, however, the next four years

of Eddie's life were to become an emotional roller coaster, filled with triumphs and disappointments, accolades and embarrassments, domestic pleasures and, ultimately, family tragedy.

The Foys second season opened September 12 at the Bushwick Theater, Brooklyn. The *Clipper* reported:

> Eddie Foy and the seven little Foylettes, in songs, dancing and some good, wholesome comedy, had no reason to complain at their reception. Seldom has an artist received such a welcome as was extended Mr. Foy. As a finale, the little Foys do a fancy military drill that earned the approval of the large audience. Little Mary again excelled, rendering a song assisted by the other members.[6]

A few weeks later, in Pittsburgh, the *Ledger* reviewer declared:

> The same old Foy with the same old grimace, plus a septet of precocious, good looking children. Foy is a real fit, the children are attractive in personality, and at least three of them have more than commonplace talent. The little fellow who imitates his father surely has a bright future. From whatever angle you view the Foy act, it is a substantial success.[7]

Again, Madeline appeared at the conclusion of the act. This time, she was pulled on stage by the children, took a bow, and embraced them lovingly, while Eddie looked on with pride. "Some bread line, that," he remarked. No wonder reviewers in each city extolled the "impression of domesticity" and "family romp," led by a man who had "himself romped and lisped his way into the hearts of hundreds of thousands of theater goers." Not so buried in all of these accolades was a recollection of Eddie's theatrical longevity. The observation became even more obvious when, a few weeks later, Eddie was made a life-member of the Lambs Club, for longtime distinguished service on behalf of the profession's less fortunate actors.

A few days after receiving this honor, however, Eddie was stunned when his sister,

Mrs. Mary Doyle, filed a $15,000 lawsuit against him, to recover the expenses of Catherine's care. Mary claimed she had taken care of Catherine by herself for many years, during which time Eddie had provided little financial assistance. She also hinted that Eddie had not been married at the time of Catherine's birth, the child being a product of a union between Eddie and Lola Conlick (Sefton). In response to the suit, Eddie denied the allegations; he neither admitted nor denied he was the girl's father. The *Times,* like other New York papers, covered the case closely and reported daily on the lawsuit.

As Eddie's work took him away from home, Mrs. Doyle claimed she had accepted, cared for, and educated Catherine, spending more than $10,000 in the process. Under questioning, she further claimed that during the time she had cared for Catherine (until the child was eight years of age), Eddie contributed no more than $500 or $600. The $10,000, Mary said, represented the amount she had actually spent, while the added $5,000 was the value of her services. Mrs. Doyle pointed out to the court that Eddie earned a good salary and was the possessor of property.

The case was ordered delayed because the Foys had to be on the road, but summaries of it continued in the paper for some time.

Eddie's nerves were not soothed when he was brought into court in both Cincinnati and Cleveland for child neglect, a new argument probably concocted just for Foy and presented against his allowing the children to perform. Social reformers in these cities claimed that the stage environment was not conducive to children's morals. Luckily, friendly judges threw out the cases after pleas by the entire family convinced them that the reformers were exaggerating.

In fact, at that very moment, a New York Senate Committee was preparing a bill that would eliminate the code provision making it a misdemeanor to employ children under sixteen to dance, sing, or play musical instruments in a theater. The new bill was specifically designed to prevent authorities from stopping the appearance of the little Foys on the vaudeville stage. Unfortunately, religious forces and the sanctimonious Gerry Society helped table the bill; it was delayed until the legislature's next session. In fact, the bill did not become law until 1923.

While in Cleveland, Eddie had become so weary of the constant arrests and shabby accusations that he wrote Albee he was seriously considering closing the tour. The Foys next stop was Indianapolis, and Eddie knew the city's child-labor laws were even more stringent than in Ohio. Albee quickly solved the problem by booking the Foys into Hammerstein's Olympia in New York City, as well as other more friendly local venues, for the remainder of the season. Nonetheless, when Albee applied for a license for the Foys to play the Palace, New York's mayor refused to allow the younger Foys to perform. In fact, Eddie was arrested and found guilty of permitting the younger children to perform at Hammerstein's. Albee came to his rescue, and the sentence was suspended.

Eddie's entire "morals" situation was made worse when a newspaper revealed that he had been caught in a police raid on a gambling house at Forty-second Street and Broadway. Eddie claimed he had stopped there only to use the phone to call home. Because no evidence was found that he had participated in any gambling, his case was dismissed.

In spite of these distractions, the Foys continued to entertain full houses wherever they played through the remainder of the season. A Lambs' Gambol benefit, staged at the Metropolitan Opera House, featured the family along with headliners like De Wolf Hopper, William Collier, Douglas Fairbanks, Victor Herbert, and Irving Berlin. The show collected more than $15,000 for charity.

A year before, World Film Corporation had offered Eddie an opportunity to appear in a movie. At the time, newspaper accounts indicated that Eddie had refused the offer.

The information was not entirely accurate. In June, World Film Corporation filed an action against the New York Motion Picture Company, representing Mack Sennett's Keystone Studios, over which organization possessed the motion picture acting services of Eddie Foy. The lawsuit suggested Eddie had been negotiating with both companies.

In the action, World Film declared that Eddie was to receive $15,000 for his and his children's appearance. The script was to be prepared by Vincent Bryan, but directors of the company had to approve it before a contract could be signed. Bryan had already collected $250 for his work when Eddie complained that the writer hadn't completed his task. World Film claimed Bryan was ready, willing, and able to finish. Somehow, there appeared to have been miscommunication between World Film and Eddie. Or was it all a dispute over money?

Then the New York Motion Picture Company announced that Eddie and the children were leaving for Los Angeles to begin work on a movie for Mack Sennett. They reported that Eddie had signed a contract for $20,000 and had already received an advance of $2,000.

World Film requested a restraining order to prevent Eddie from appearing for any other studio. Judge Shearn of the New York Supreme Court heard the arguments but delayed decision on the motion. Two weeks later, the judge decided that Eddie could make pictures for the New York Motion Picture Company if he so desired, without hindrance. Since no legal contract had been signed by Eddie with World Film, he was not barred. The family was already packed, waiting for the verdict; Eddie told the press they would leave shortly for the West Coast. Sennett announced that the Foy film had been titled "A Favorite Fool" and stated to the press:

Eddie Foy has signed with the Keystone Film Company for ten weeks, commencing in July at their California studios. Contracts were signed, including the fares for all the Foys.[8]

A week later, before the Foys had left for California, Eddie's name again appeared in New York newspapers. This time, however, he was accused of "misconduct" in a high-profile divorce case. Mrs. Sarah Dean had filed for divorce from her husband, John Wooster Dean, a prominent, and wealthy, local merchant. Dean filed a countersuit, naming Eddie co-respondent, claiming that he had enjoyed a long-term relationship with Dean's wife, whose stage name was Ruth Langdon. The trial lasted four days and generated a thousand pages of testimony, as well as extensive coverage by the press.

According to testimony, Eddie's "misconduct" had occurred from 1905 to 1908 — the liaison had apparently begun when Langdon appeared in the "Mr. Hamlet" company — at the Dean home on West Sixty-fourth Street and from 1908 to 1914 at Pelham Manor. Telling testimony against Eddie came from a theatrical manager and a press agent. They declared that, when the "Mr. Hamlet" company was on tour, Mr. Foy and Mrs. Dean occupied "connecting rooms" and that they had been seen in a bedroom together. The testimony proved sufficient for Mr. Dean to obtain a divorce from his wife, for which she received no alimony. Eddie categorically denied all charges. "It is the rankest perjury I have ever experienced," he declared. "I have known her for five years, but she is only an acquaintance."

Newspaper reporters and theater critics found it hard to condemn Eddie. Yes, they admitted, he may have had a relationship with this woman, but why single out this situation in a business that had tacitly accepted such behavior for years? Among performers, liaisons of this nature, like the other so-called "vices," drinking and gambling, were considered a normal aspect of a profession that required years of constant touring, with long separations from loved ones. Colleagues were aware that Eddie had had women friends. But how would the

general public feel about the issue? The press questioned to what extent this news would affect Eddie's peerless reputation as a "family man." And what about the appeal of the Foy family act? Would audiences continue to accept Eddie as an icon of the popular stage?

How the issue was handled at home was never revealed, but the episode must have produced strains between Madeline and Eddie. She had long been aware of Eddie's previous behavior, dating back to their days appearing together in Henderson's extravaganzas. It is likely that her interest in accompanying Eddie on tour, even with young children in tow, was to some extent a device to protect their relationship. She also had been aware of, as well as a participant in, decisions regarding Catherine, having agreed to let Mary raise Eddie's daughter and, later, accepting her stepdaughter into the family when the Foys moved together to New York.

There is no information available about their efforts to maintain the marriage. They continued to advance the appearance of a cohesive family. No one ever questioned Eddie's love and admiration for Madeline and his children. Yet, a few years later, events involving Eddie and Bryan, who had a deep affection for his mother, may have been precipitated by this affair.

A family tale relates that, when Madeline obtained the details of the Dean divorce, she and the children went to Mrs. Dean's home. The building featured many large windows and a front garden containing decorative stones. Madeline suggested the children use the stones to pepper the windows. Eddie was reported to have expressed great anger, not because of the act itself or its motives, but because it cost him a great deal of money to have the windows repaired.

The trip to California seemed fortuitous, since the Foys could escape the "prying eyes" of the New York press. It might also contribute to a personal renewal of affections. But Eddie quickly discovered that making a motion picture was like nothing he had ever experienced on the stage.

The Foy family were lodged in a cottage in Santa Monica, near ocean beaches. A short automobile drive — Eddie had been given a car to use — transported him and the children to Sennett's studios. Arriving there for the first time, they were greeted by what appeared to be orchestrated chaos. Four movies were being shot at the same time, on sets that seemed to be in constant flux. Stagehands rapidly moved scenery and props, and carpenters appeared to build supports and structures on demand. On another part of the lot, the camera followed a zany car chase, with the director yelling instructions to the drivers through a megaphone. Uniformed acrobats were alternately falling off and climbing onto the racing autos. Eddie became somewhat concerned when he noticed a fully-equipped nurse's station set up nearby.

Indeed, on his first day of shooting, Eddie narrowly escaped being crushed. While preparing for a scene, he emerged from his dressing room. Just as he cleared the door, scaffolding propped against a wall gave way and collapsed upon the spot he had just vacated. It was reported that he laughed off the incident, albeit nervously, and remarked, "Making movies is dangerous."

Eddie and the children were given a small building in which to put on their costumes and makeup, as well as rest between takes. The "shack," as Eddie named it, reminded him of the place he had lived while performing in Leadville. Sennett's plan was to shoot all the scenes involving the children first, so they could return home and enjoy the beach with Madeline, not to mention get off the set as quickly as possible. Eddie and the other actors would be shot on prepared sets. Finally, those scenes involving Eddie in "thrilling" escapades would be completed last.

Within days, if not hours, Eddie found the movie-making experience onerous. He complained about having to get up early, and the long hours repeating scenes challenged his sense of performance fluidity. He was not alone in his feelings; many vaudeville and musical comedy actors experienced similar frustrations. Weber and Fields needed only one Sennett movie to convince them that stage performance was safer and more personally rewarding. Sam Bernard was nearly killed in a staged auto accident. Lillian Russell took one look at the studio's frenetic activity and decided Louis Selznick's barn in New Jersey was more to her liking.

Eddie quickly discerned the differences between stage and screen work, beyond the physical layouts. With a stationary camera, actors were required to work in relatively small spaces. Eddie was used to working on a full stage, which offered him a great deal of latitude for movement in all directions. Without sound, an important part of a comedian's presentation was lost on movie audiences; Eddie, like other stage comedians performing in front of a camera, found it difficult to adjust his acting. Without a live audience, Eddie couldn't tell if his performance was satisfactory or not, and these doubts expressed themselves in his work. Following a specific script was difficult for Eddie. He had boasted that he never repeated the same skit in the same way, an attribute that formed an important part of his stage persona. Yet he was given no such opportunity for flexibility in front of the camera. The situation was made even more arduous because Sennett was a perfectionist and became upset when Eddie deviated from the script.

Eddie and the children had additional problems because they could not all follow the script at the same time. The film's director had never worked with seven young performers, particularly a group that had a propensity for fun-making; he forced them into many repetitive takes. Additional shooting took more time, energy, and money, putting increased pressure on the moviemakers to finish the film. After a long day of repeating only a single scene, Eddie mused, "It makes a burglar's business look as safe as crocheting." Because of delays in completing scenes, his contract had to be extended four weeks.

In 1915, the Seven Little Foys, Eddie, and Polly Moran appeared in Mack Sennett's moving picture, *A Favorite Fool*. Feeling he would be humiliated by Sennett's pie-in-the-face and seltzer-bottle routines, Eddie refused to do them.

It was Sennett's slapstick routines, however, that really exasperated Eddie. Sennett attempted to introduce a number of pie-in-the-face and seltzer-bottle episodes into the picture. Claiming they embarrassed him, Eddie refused to do them. When Sennett pressed him, Eddie threatened to walk off the set. Sennett then persuaded Eddie to use what appeared to be limburger cheese instead;

however, when Sennett wanted to use the actual product for realism, Eddie balked.

Three weeks before the picture was completed (most of Eddie's scenes had already been shot), Sennett fired Eddie. Since Eddie was still due three-week's salary under the contract, at $2,000 a week, Eddie warned Sennett he would sue for salary and damages.

Despite the fact that "A Favorite Fool,"

was considered funny by critics, its exposure in theaters seems to have been restricted and of short duration. The plot has Eddie resting on a farm when "The Widow Wallop's Circus" comes to town. When he falls in love with the widow (played by Polly Moran), she accepts his proposal. He is unaware, however, that she has seven children. When he discovers the family he has assumed, he runs away. Later, he learns that a villainous ringmaster has ousted the widow from her show, taking over its ownership from her. Eddie returns with the papers proving ownership, throws the ringmaster into the lion's cage, and returns possession of the circus to his wife. A tornado releases the villain from the cage, and he cuts the ropes that hold up the tent. The tent collapses on Eddie, his wife, and children. In the closing scene, they poke their heads through the rain-soaked canvas, smiling.

Reviewers called "A Favorite Fool" one of Mack Sennett's most laughable farces. They also declared that Eddie "seems sure to be a great success in motion pictures."

Upon returning to New York, Eddie filed suit against Sennett and Keystone for $7,000—$6,000 for three weeks at $2,000 a week, plus $1,000 for the "humiliation" he had suffered. Walking on limburger cheese and riding a locomotive attired in a nightshirt "with a hose on him," were specified by Eddie as reasons for the charges of humiliation.

In his defense, Sennett replied that the script had been rewritten three times; each time turned down by Eddie for insignificant reasons. Sennett also remarked that this was the first time he had ever discharged an actor for breaking a contract, which everyone knew was untrue. Two months later, the judge found Sennett and Keystone guilty for not honoring the agreed contract. They were required to pay Eddie $6,524 and apologize to him for the inconveniences.

Shortly after the court verdict, Eddie signed a ten-week vaudeville contract with the Orpheum circuit, from mid–November

to the end of January. Apparently to avoid adverse publicity (Eddie's recent court cases still appeared in newspapers), the tour would open on the West Coast and work its way back to the Midwest. No New York engagement was planned. Eddie Foy and the Seven Little Foys opened at the Orpheum Theater in Portland, Oregon, November 13.

The Foys played to full houses at nearly every engagement. Reviews of their act were consistently good, although a few critics mentioned that some songs and gags had been used last season. Actually, the act was exactly the same as the previous season; only the theaters were different.

Just after the Foys returned to New Rochelle, the lawsuit between Eddie and his sister resumed; but, with Eddie's candid testimony, it was quickly resolved. In court, Eddie admitted that Catherine was his daughter and that he had not been married to Lola Conlick (Sefton) when Catherine was born. He also admitted that nine-month-old Catherine had been adopted by Mrs. Doyle, who had cared for her while the child attended elementary school in Chicago. With this admission, the judge ruled in favor of Mrs. Doyle and ordered Eddie to pay her $7,235 for her services. The entire proceedings took only two days and attracted little press coverage.

Except for the annual Lambs' Gambol in July, Eddie received no mention in the press for the entire summer. Friends reported a quiet season at "the Foyer," the name Eddie had given his home.

In mid-September, Charles Dillingham and Flo Ziegfeld announced rehearsals for a new musical revue, "The Century Girl," to open at the Century Theater late in October. Critics applauded the impresarios for engaging a list of performers the envy of theatrical producers nationwide. Victor Herbert and Irving Berlin were to be responsible for the music. The stars of the show included Leon Errol, Elsie Janis, Hazel Dawn, Van and Schenck, Marie Dressler, Sam Bernard, and the Foy family.

Dillingham and Ziegfeld quickly found

that signing a large number of stars was infinitely easier than rehearsing them, let alone satisfying their desire for stage time and funny lines. The usual rehearsal system faltered; at the end of September, Ziegfeld instituted a twenty-four-hour rehearsal plan. Each of three people, Frederick Latham, director of the Century, Irving Berlin, and Victor Herbert, took eight-hour shifts to work with the actors. This novel scheme met with a flurry of complaints.

Latham attempted to satisfy his bosses, Dillingham and Ziegfeld. Berlin and Herbert protested, on behalf of the actors. Then Latham got into arguments with Ziegfeld, to the point that they spoke to each other only when necessary. Ziegfeld wanted Latham fired. Dillingham had hired Latham and considered him one of the best stage producers in the U.S. When Ziegfeld offered Latham's job to other producers, they turned him down because of their respect for Latham.

The Foys were inevitably affected by these disagreements. Initially, their stage time was reduced, which also reduced their salary. Then, when their rehearsal time was changed from day to evening, Eddie refused to make the shift, claiming his children could not rehearse late evenings. It appeared Dillingham and Ziegfeld did little to resolve the situation. A week before the scheduled opening of the show, the Foys retired from the cast.

"The Century Girl" opened November 6, after two delays. A week after opening, Marie Dressler left the company. Two weeks later, Van and Schenck and Elsie Janis all signed on for vaudeville. Shortly thereafter, the production closed. Reviewers had called it a "Gargantuan musical show, full of novelty." Very likely, its immensity was also its undoing.

Within a matter of days, Eddie closed an agreement with the United Booking Office (U.B.O.) and his friend E.F. Albee, for a salary of $2,000 a week. Albee wanted the Foys to open at the Palace Theater, but Eddie hesitated. He felt the recent adverse public

ity might have had an effect on his drawing power. An astute observer of audience behavior, Albee assured Eddie there was no problem; he was correct in his assessment.

The Foys opened at the Palace, October 25, in a skit written by William Jerome and George Hobart, entitled "The Old Woman in the Shoe." Crowds cheered them from the moment they first entered the stage, through the many encores they were obliged to perform. The *Clipper* reported the act to be "the best vehicle the Foys have provided to date" and "one of the big hits of the Palace bill." Somewhat surprised but deeply gratified, Eddie embraced the audiences' enthusiasm.

The act itself had its origins in a Henderson production in which Eddie, in drag, performed parodies of various fairy tales with children, who had emerged from a gigantic shoe. Jerome and Hobart transformed the original skit into a lively singing and dancing vehicle for each Foy child, along with combinations of chorus work with Eddie. While all the children received praise for their specialties, Irving was singled out as a gifted fun-maker, overshadowing the rest of the family. In appropriate costume, Irving imitated Charlie Chaplin and "brought down the house." As a final touch to the act, Madeline came out on stage for a bow, as all the Foys stood before the footlights, hand in hand. Audiences cheered and applauded them vigorously.

One evening, while playing at the Palace, the Foys were visited by President and Mrs. Wilson. Knowing that the President planned to be in attendance that evening, Eddie devised a concluding musical number, humorously interpolating expressions President Wilson had used in his campaign speeches. Audience and President alike responded with laughter and applause. After the show, the Foys were introduced to the President and his wife. Family lore recalls that Mrs. Wilson shook hands and patted each child on the head, specifically noting how cute "little Charlie" was. Charlie was

Eddie Foy and his handsome family in a formal production photograph. This picture was distributed to theater patrons as souvenirs.

seventeen at the time and said to be recovering from a case of the clap. No doubt, the sailor suit he was wearing confused Mrs. Wilson.

Along with various dignitaries the children met while touring the country, they also had the opportunity to meet and observe performances by some of the top vaudeville stars of the day, playing on the same bill as the Foys. These included such luminaries as Harry Houdini, Fay Templeton, Nat Goodwin, the Four Marx Brothers, Sophie Tucker,

Eva Tanguay, and Ruth St. Denis. Irving recalled that it was an exhilarating experience for the children to get to know these people, both on and off the stage. After a while, meeting such stars seemed natural, said Irving; they took one another's popularity in stride. As for the siblings themselves, "We all got along well together," Irving recalled. "We just liked to travel and perform."

The first four months of 1917 were spent playing engagements at first-class theaters in the Midwest, with continued popularity. While in Dayton, Ohio, Eddie was feted at a celebration of his sixtieth birthday, actually his sixty-first. In Cincinnati, a woman wrote an open letter to the local newspaper asking President Wilson to prevent war, with an additional request to remove Eddie's children and put them "in a nice, warm asylum, where they won't have to work on the stage anymore." Dozens of letters were written to the paper, all of them defending the Foys. No letters were received about President Wilson or the war.

The Foys finished their tour with two weeks in New York, one at the Palace Theater, the other at the Riverside. According to the *Clipper*, both weeks were big hits:

> The act has been rearranged since last seen, and is now one of the speediest singing and dancing novelties hereabouts. The children are growing and displaying more talent, and several of the lyrics and jingles called for spontaneous applause. The material in the act, by George Hobart and William Jerome, is of scintillating variety.[9]

In another section of the *Clipper*, buried in a list of new songs that had just been released, William Jerome announced publishing a George M. Cohan song, "Over There," which would soon be introduced by Nora Bayes.

Summers with the Foys revealed additional performances and, inevitably, funny anecdotes. At a National Vaudeville Artists benefit, Eddie and the children appeared on the bill. They were introduced to the audience as "half of New Rochelle." Later in the program, Eddie introduced Stella Mayhew, a remarkably large woman who lived in the same town, as "the other half of New Rochelle."

When Eddie reported for the State Military Census (all men had to register for possible conscription), he was asked about his family. "Anyone dependent on you?" questioned the registrar. "No," Eddie replied. "I am dependent on seven."

Performers from both the Friars' and Lambs' clubs formed a group called "The Lights," scheduled to embark on a summer tour in a revue designed to raise money for the war effort. They planned to travel to each city by boat. The group included George M. Cohan, McIntyre and Heath, Houdini, Jim Corbett, the Foy family, and other vaudeville performers. Their route was shortened considerably when the ship they hired broke down. Transferred to automobile, the tour got as far as theaters on Long Island. Still, attendances were large; "The Lights" tour netted more than $6,000.

Meanwhile, Madeline had to be put to bed due to an undiagnosed illness. She would remain at home during the Foy's entire summer activities. At the same time, Bryan expressed dissatisfaction and intimated that he would like to retire from the act. He cited a recent review that suggested the children were outgrowing their stage roles, and he suggested his father should address the issue:

> Foy will have to change the billing one of these days, for the "little" Foys are growing up, and the two older boys are getting rather big to carry school books and wear kids' costumes.[10]

Even the *New York Clipper* subtly questioned the Foy act. A gossip columnist asked, "What will Eddie Foy do when his Seven Little(?) Foys are little no longer?"

Though Eddie and William Jerome were preparing a new, more grown-up act for the opening of their fall, Orpheum-circuit tour, it was not yet finished, and the Foys had to return to last season's "Old Woman in the

Shoe" skit. Luckily, they opened in Chicago, at the Majestic Theater, August 12, far away from New York critics. Madeline, feeling somewhat better now, journeyed with the family.

Ironically, the Chicago engagement, while attracting full houses, also caught the attention of local police, who arrested Eddie for permitting three of his children to perform without having obtained a permit. Another fine (twenty-five dollars), another reprimand, another court date, and they were on their way to the next engagement. The tour took them to Minneapolis, St. Paul, Duluth, Winnipeg, and Calgary in successive weeks.

Madeline became ill again, and doctors recommended that she return to New Rochelle. Bryan volunteered to accompany her. In Calgary, she collapsed, apparently from a respiratory condition. She was immediately rushed to a sanitarium in Colorado Springs and placed under treatment. Bryan accompanied her, and he informed Eddie he planned to stay with his mother until she was well enough to return to New Rochelle. His decision signaled a dramatic end to the Seven Little Foys. Bryan never again performed professionally with his siblings.

Plans and rehearsals for a new act now had to be curtailed. Instead, the current act had to be revised to reflect Bryan's absence. A Calgary marquee revealed the family's new name, "Eddie Foy and the Younger Foys." The children, now entirely under Eddie's supervision, resumed their West Coast tour.

When the Foys arrived in Los Angeles in mid-November for a two-week engagement, Bryan brought Madeline to spend time with the family. Everyone recognized, though, that Madeline was gravely ill. The *Clipper* received a news dispatch from its Los Angeles correspondent:

> Madeline Foy, wife of Eddie Foy, who is seriously ill, and has been in Colorado Springs for several weeks under the doctors care, has been brought here by her son, Bryan, who

will remain with her. Next week, Bryan will take his mother to Albuquerque, New Mexico, where she will spend the winter.[11]

A profoundly disheartened Foy family left for a Midwestern tour during the winter months. Their tour was made even more problematic by the imposition of war-related restrictions. Citing the need to conserve coal, some railroads had withdrawn completely from the business of transporting vaudeville and musical comedy companies. As their own contribution to the energy crisis, vaudeville theater managers cut intermissions. Managers had to reroute acts to keep their houses open. The first group of performers now joined the armed forces, thus causing a shortage of theater professionals. Not surprisingly, many road shows had to be prematurely closed. As their contribution to the war effort, the New York City Council declared Theaterless Tuesdays and earlier evening curtains.

After playing St. Louis in early January 1918, the Foys had their tour rerouted south, to Texas, Arkansas, and Missouri for six weeks, before returning to Milwaukee in March. There are no published reviews of Foy performances nor audience reactions during this time, but a number of reported episodes suggested family stress.

A newspaper article observed that "the little Foys are beyond control." They wouldn't listen to what their father said and "miss steps by the dozen." The reporter noted that, while Eddie "bawled" his instructions to the children, they "flitted about, apparently not heeding his advice and wisdom."

An episode in Houston was detailed by the *Dramatic Mirror*. Apparently, Eddie got into a scuffle with a waiter at the Rice Hotel over the amount of rationed sugar he was allowed. The management provided each patron three pieces, and Eddie claimed he had not received his full allotment. A fight ensued, and the Foy family had to move to another hotel.

When the Foys arrived in Chicago, Eddie was met with a *Clipper* gossip tidbit that indicated Bryan had enlisted in the Aviation Corps. A call to New Rochelle assured Eddie that Bryan was still at home; however, questioned by his father, Bryan declared that he intended to enlist. Since their Chicago engagement was the tour's last stop, the Foys would be home in a week, and Eddie could address the situation directly.

When the family arrived home, however, they found Madeline failing. Her doctors believed she had only weeks to live. They said she suffered from a congestive respiratory problem that, if it developed into pneumonia, would surely result in her death. The Church had been made aware of the crisis, and Father Manzelli visited Madeline almost every day. With Eddie at Madeline's bedside now, Bryan enlisted in the Navy, temporarily stationed nearby until his mother's condition was resolved. Eddie was angry at Bryan for

leaving home. Yet it was obvious to the family that Bryan, increasingly upset by his mother's illness, had to get away.

As a last attempt to save her life, doctors operated on Madeline to remove a pulmonary abscess. They failed. She died of pneumonia on Friday, June 14, 1918, at home, the entire family at her bedside, Eddie clutching her hand.

Madeline's funeral was held June 17, at 9:30 A.M. In accord with Madeline's wishes, a solemn requiem mass was celebrated by Father Manzelli at the family's parish church in New Rochelle. Her body lay in state at the Foy home the next day, where friends and theatrical people visited her bier to pay their respects. Floral tributes filled the house. Later in the day, Madeline was buried in Holy Sepulcher Cemetery, New Rochelle, the first to occupy the Foy family plot.

Chapter 15

LAWYER: *Your honor, it is unfair to charge this man with being a forger when he can't sign his own name.*
JUDGE: *He wasn't accused of signing his own name.*

Eddie Foy and the Seven Little Foys
"Slumwhere in New York" skit

-Is the ham cured?
-Yes, sir.
-Well, then, it must of had a relapse.

Eddie Foy and the Seven Little Foys
"So This Is a Restaurant" skit

Less than two months after Madeline's funeral, Eddie signed a contract with the Keith circuit for what he anticipated to be a long and profitable tour. Needing the money, he had to return to work. Unfortunately, events prevented the engagement from living up to its promise.

In the late summer of 1918, a highly contagious, lethal strain of influenza broke out in military camps in the East and Southeast. Called the "Spanish Flu," it quickly spread throughout the country, aided unwittingly by the normal dispersal of military personnel. By September, it had become a national epidemic.

Health departments in Eastern cities ordered the closure of all places of public assembly — stores, beaches, athletic events, schools, churches, and theaters. Some cities, like Boston, Philadelphia, and Baltimore, had already been so hard hit by the epidemic that few people could be found in the theaters. In New York, however, the Board of Health claimed they had control of the disease and, instead of closing all theaters, modified operating hours, supposedly to reduce crowding. They declared that the greatest spread of disease occurred in the subways, on elevated trains, and on streetcars. By reducing transportation schedules, the

Board insisted, they would control contagion in the city.

The agreement to stagger hours of operation resulted from a meeting between health department officials and theater managers, among them J.J. Shubert, Alf Hayman, Marcus Loew, and William Fox. A health department announcement communicated the agreement to the public:

> It has been the position of the Department of Health from the first that no individual is in danger if he or she escapes the mouth or nasal secretions of some other person who has it. We believe it is proper to keep the theaters and churches open if we can eliminate the sneezers, coughers, and spitters. We pointed out to the theater managers the importance of making the public who go to their places know that these things are prohibited. Today we ordered these managers to instruct their ushers and attendants to escort from their theaters those who violate the Department rules and to use force if necessary. We will back them up.[1]

Not surprisingly, once managers persuaded the health department to keep their theaters open, actual enforcement of the rules proved minimal. Later, it was revealed that some members of the health department had been "paid off" by theater managers.

Theater closures across the country required an entire rearrangement of routes, along with some company suspensions and abandonment of productions. By early October, nearly all theaters in the country had been closed or were operating on reduced schedules. While large cities had experienced the worst of the epidemic and showed the first signs of recovery, small towns and rural areas were now being hit hard. In Philadelphia, for example, city health officials announced that theaters could reopen in two weeks, while Boston and Baltimore theaters planned to reopen the end of the month.

Pennsylvania health authorities cause a furor among theater managers by announcing that reopenings would be evaluated by

community officials as conditions warranted. Managers telephoned and visited their local health departments arguing vociferously that their town had passed the crisis.

By early November, the influenza epidemic had receded in the large Eastern and Midwestern cities, allowing most theaters to reopen. In New York, theaters continued to operate according to their agreed staggered schedules. A statement by Dr. Copeland, head of the Health Department, complimented the public "for keeping its head, despite the near-hysteria of calamity howlers." He contended that:

> ...the morale of the people in their fight against the contagion must not be weakened by unnecessarily extreme measures.[2]

For example, theater closures.

Now, however, theater managers had to address an even greater challenge — rerouting and rescheduling all of their shows and performers. Already they had experienced sizable financial losses. Now they rushed to get patrons back into theaters and their dollars into box offices. The *Dramatic Mirror* outlined the formidable job ahead:

> Not only will they (managers) be required to disentangle twisted schedules, but in setting the hundreds of companies, now stalled in cities far from their base, into action again, it will not be merely a matter of resuming along original lines. Embargoes will not be lifted simultaneously, therefore detours will have to be made, and substitutions in playing dates will be necessary. Billing will have to be changed, and new printed matter rushed from nearest printing plants of sufficient size and capacity to handle the wholesale orders.[3]

Everyone agreed that restoring the season's momentum would be the most "Herculean job" the industry had ever confronted.

By mid–November, schools and churches reopened. Now only the West Coast suffered the worst of the epidemic, and there all theaters were closed. Across the country, stranded actors were being cared for by fraternal organizations, since churches and relief groups still shunned theater people. All theaters in the East were open, and Chicago theaters were about to reopen. In New York, theaters were back on regular schedules. More than 500,000 people in the U.S. had died of the "Spanish Flu." The virulent disease had killed more than 20 million throughout the world.

The healthy Foys (none had become ill) had opened their season in Washington, D.C., on August 6, about four weeks before the disease reached epidemic proportions. Their new act was entitled, "Slumwhere in New York," written by William Jerome, with a number of songs contributed by Bryan.

Eddie played a sportive old man looking for cheap Italian food in the Bowery. He encountered two groups of children, one Italian, the other Irish, arguing about whose food was better. He separated them, and then talked about playing Hamlet. Under the guise of organizing a Red Cross benefit for soldiers, Eddie sang a song in his familiar style; each of the children indulged in a specialty. The girls sang and danced; Charlie imitated his father; Irving imitated Charlie Chaplin.

The local reviewer declared "the act is one of the best of the series they have presented."

In the first week of September, the Foys played at the Palace Theater, New York. To no one's surprise, the theater was nearly empty. Those few in attendance were treated to a feature not on the program. On furlough, from military service, Bryan stood in the wings, watching his family perform. When Eddie saw him, he brought Bryan out, whereupon what audience there was applauded loudly. It was almost a month, however, before the Foys performed again, in another New York theater.

Reviewers of the new act noted the reduced time Eddie had given himself, as compared to his children. The shift was symptomatic of changes taking place within the family itself. Friends noticed that some family cohesion seemed to have been lost since Madeline's death. Bryan was still in the Navy, and would remain in service even after the war ended. Charlie had been showing signs of impatience and had expressed an interest in going out on his own, intimating that the family act had become stale. Aunt Clara had taken over Madeline's duties in the Foy household, looking after the needs of the younger children.

It seemed Eddie chose to perform less because he was tired, not only because he was sixty-two years old, but also because Madeline's loss and disruptions in the entertainment industry had depressed him. No question Eddie believed his stage career was winding down. These days, he had to depend more on his reputation than his actual performance.

Euphoria returned, however, when the armistice was signed by Germany on November 11, 1918. The U.S. breathed a collective sigh of relief. In a spontaneous outburst of joy, the nation went on a great holiday. Broadway and Fifth Avenue were jammed by milling throngs of people. With office rules and business routines suspended, everyone celebrated the peace in a carnival-like atmosphere. Restaurants were filled with hundreds of people, willing to wait hours for a table. Surface street transportation in New York was halted, causing major tie-ups in the subways and on elevated trains. Theatrical Broadway took part in the celebration, as well.

Actors joined in the festivities and "smiled happily in each other's faces," according to the *Clipper*. Great displays of patriotism, with much flag-waving and outbursts of the national anthem and war-related songs, interrupted shows. All the theaters were "packed to the doors." Ticket speculators reaped a handsome harvest, as patrons were willing to pay any price to get into a theater. Victory matinees were given in all vaudeville houses. One man bought two balcony tickets at the Hippodrome, explaining that one

Eddie and the Seven Little Foys in their skit, "Slumwhere in New York." The backdrop suggests a late-19th-century scene of the Bowery. Irving sold newspapers, as Eddie had actually done on Bowery streets as a child.

was for himself, the other for his bass drum. He was permitted to take the drum into the theater and pound on it vigorously whenever the spirit moved him. Soon there gathered around him an orchestra of horns, rattles, and kitchen utensils, all playing in time with the theater orchestra.

Wherever they happened to be, everyone returned to the streets at night, plunging into the shrieking, swirling, ebullient crowds to celebrate. Crowds were so large at places of business, managers decided that nobody need pay for anything. The celebration on Broadway lasted almost a week.

The combination of peace and abatement of the flu epidemic buoyed the country and inspired the public to flood theaters as fast as they were reopened. At the end of November, the Foys appeared in Pittsburgh and Cleveland, where Eddie took the opportunity to exploit the current patriotic fervor by singing "Rose of No Man's Land" at all performances, always to standing ovations.

The Foys played their Christmas engagement at Chicago's Majestic Theater and enjoyed a fortnight of SRO audiences. The *Tribune* exclaimed:

Eddie Foy and his numerous and talented offspring kept the audience convulsed with their buffoonery.[4]

The *Clipper* noted, somewhat more critically:

Eddie Foy and his gifted family of six lead the field at the Majestic this week. An especial hit was scored by the two young daughters of the famous comedian, who harmonized sweetly and in perfect time. Eddie contented himself for the most part with smiling benevolently on the effects of his youngsters.[5]

While the Foys were playing Midwestern theaters in early 1919, Harry Fitzgerald, Eddie's business manager, announced they would begin rehearsals for a musical show when they returned to New York. Eddie had expressed his belief that an entire production would be better for them than rigorous vaudeville tours.

Their spring tour of the West was punctuated by frequent court appearances by Eddie, to justify the use of his children in the act. More often than not, he won his case. In Seattle, however, he was stymied when the theater manager informed him that no children were allowed on stage.

Nevertheless, playing the Orpheum circuit allowed the children to meet many vaudeville headliners, among them Pat Rooney, Annette Kellerman (from the movies), fellow New Rochellean Stella Mayhew, Trixie Friganza, Blossom Seeley (given to impersonating Eddie), a young Irish dancer, Pat O'Brien (later to appear in movies), and stage veteran Charles Grapewin. If it were possible to increase their natural exuberance, the children seemed energized by sharing the stage with these outstanding performers. In turn, performers seemed to enjoy the "family" feeling back stage.

The appearance of Kellerman and other popular moving picture stars reflected the return of these actors to the vaudeville and musical comedy stage. Movies' drawing power had declined, and studios were cutting back production. Motion picture stars viewed vaudeville work as easier, with comparable salaries, and they were right. Even more important — the essence of what it means to perform — actors preferred to play before live audiences. Given his own experiences in front of the camera, Eddie could readily empathize with those feelings. This return of the prodigals to live theater tended to crowd out lesser performers but gave sizable impetus to filling stage venues.

Upon returning to New York, Eddie found his first federal income tax bill waiting at home. Since it was based solely on property, Eddie had to pay more than $4,000, reflecting his automobile and home ownership. Eddie argued that the property didn't belong to him; he had signed over all personal property to Madeline, and in her will, she had given it to the children. Because he was the family's sole parent and guardian, however, he was deemed responsible. Compared to colleagues like Francis Wilson, who had to pay $50,000, and George M. Cohan, who remitted to the government more than $75,000, Eddie considered himself lucky. On the other

hand, the money that had been put aside for his new show went to pay his taxes. In any case, the show would have had to be delayed, given the extraordinary events of 1919.

The Foys played at a number of theaters in New York, including the Palace, during July, and all the shows were sellouts. As before, the *Clipper* noted Eddie's reduced participation in the act:

> Eddie Foy and the six Foy kiddies, or rather, adults, because they have grown considerably since their last Eastern showing, whooped things up while they were on view. "Slumwhere in New York" gives the Foys a big scope to display their talents. Charlie's imitation of his father is great and the girls harmonize well. The elder Foy has not much to do, but manages to get a few laughs across. Little Irving is rapidly learning the art of comedy, and under Dad's tuition will undoubtedly be a corking performer.[6]

It would be their last engagement for many months.

Just down the street from the Palace, a group of theater owners and actors' union representatives were engaged in an acrimonious debate about actors' rights. A strike seemed imminent.

Back in 1900, the White Rats were formed in reaction to a punitive booking program initiated by the Syndicate. The principal features of this program were that actors' salaries would be reduced; to offset this loss, actors would be guaranteed forty weeks of steady employment. In addition, the program stipulated that agents would be eliminated, and all acts were required to be booked through the Syndicate, at a commission of five percent. The threat of these conditions had pushed the White Rats to strike.

In response, the Syndicate created a blacklist of White Rats members who defied them and blocked their appearance in theaters. (Eddie had been on that list.) The strike was settled when the Syndicate agreed to eliminate the five percent clause. However, the blacklist remained.

Assuming victory over the Syndicate, the White Rats failed to follow up on organizing actors; in a few years, the association gradually declined to fewer than fifty members. Not until 1910, under the direction of Harry Montford, did the White Rats regain influence among actors. An eloquent spokesperson with evangelistic spirit, Montford recruited hundreds of new members, helped erect a clubhouse, and created a sister organization among women playing in vaudeville. Most important, however, he persuaded Samuel Gompers's American Federation of Labor (A.F.L.) to grant the White Rats an official charter of operation. Inspired by this affiliation, White Rats membership grew to many thousands during the next few years. Yet little seemed to be accomplished with this strength. By World War I, membership had again declined, to less than 600.

A resurgence of White Rats activity in early 1917 led to an ill-timed, disastrous strike against theater managers, one that almost completely annihilated the actors' organization. In retaliation against the strike, the managers organized the National Vaudeville Artists, Inc. (N.V.A.), a "company union," the managers called it. Using the familiar blacklist as their weapon of choice, managers forced most actors to join their organization and give up A.F.L. affiliation. Ironically, when the White Rats had to sell their clubhouse, Albee purchased it and placed it at the disposal of the N.V.A.

Further trouble for the White Rats surfaced in early 1918 when a New York court issued a request for their books and records, signaling an investigation of possible fraudulent financial activities. Junie McCree and Walter Waters, White Rats officers, told the court they were unable to recall any of the alleged transactions. Shortly afterward, McCree died, and Waters suffered a nervous breakdown. Then, under questioning by the court, Harry Montford claimed the White Rats books had been stolen. He did admit, however, that the organization had set up a number of dummy corporations and had lost more than $177,000 in the abortive 1917 strike. To further complicate the situation, a former White Rats business manager testified that the association's assets were not real, nor was there any value in their stock.

As the White Rats struggled to survive, a rival actors' group, the Actors Equity Association (A.E.A.), which had been attracting actors to membership for the previous five years, obtained a written pledge from its members to refrain from signing any agreement that provided less than the minimum demands the A.E.A. had established. Surprised that the A.E.A. would challenge them, managers viewed this action as a decided threat to their control. The new President of the A.E.A. was Francis Wilson, Eddie's old friend and a long-time, outspoken critic of the Syndicate.

The impending confrontation between actors and managers had been temporarily delayed due to the influenza epidemic, but hostilities resumed in early 1919. Because of their questionable financial activities, the White Rats were forced to turn over their A.F.L. affiliation to a new actors' labor union dominated by the A.E.A. Immediately, the A.E.A. presented their demands to the managers' organization, calling for a discussion of issues and, if agreement could not be reached, government intervention. Their demands included:

- No more than eight performances a week;
- All salaries to be paid on Saturday only;
- If rehearsals for a play are begun and later abandoned, actors must be paid a week's salary;
- All layoffs, for any reason, must be paid at one-half salary;
- Company layoffs during holidays must be compensated at one-half salary if actors continue to rehearse.

Managers responded by demanding that actors submit to a standard salary arrangement. They scoffed at the actors' group. "Just wait and see!" they declared confidently. "You can't successfully unite an artistic profession with labor unions." This response came after the U.S. Department of Labor had expressed doubt that the federal government had arbitration jurisdiction, asking the question, "Is an actor a laborer?"

The A.E.A. answered the challenge by ordering all members to sign only Equity contracts for the coming season. Managers escalated the confrontation by placing all N.V.A. members under a bond of $10,000 not to sign any Equity contracts or forfeit the money. New York newspapers predicted "war between the two organizations."

At the end of July, the A.E.A. received the mandate they had been seeking for months, official active support from the A.F.L. Hundreds of actors quickly joined the organization, and hundreds more openly voiced their support.

Two weeks later, representatives from opposing sides met secretly to discuss a compromise; it ended badly, with the actors walking out of the meeting. The managers said they refused to do business with Francis Wilson, and demanded that the A.E.A. separate itself from the A.F.L. At the same time, it was announced that George M. Cohan was organizing a rival, non-union, actors' association, made up of members more sympathetic to managers. Managers received further encouragement when the stagehands union declared they wouldn't strike without giving thirty days notice, suggesting they would not support an actors' walkout.

Nevertheless, the A.E.A. voted to strike on August 7, and many New York theaters went dark. Led by the Shuberts and Flo Ziegfeld, managers immediately went to court to restrain the A.E.A. from interfering with production, suing 300 prominent members of Equity for damages of $500,000. They cited as precedent the "Danbury Hatters" case several years before, when judgment had gone against striking union hatmakers for preventing others from working. In a speech to A.E.A. members, Wilson

responded defiantly to the lawsuit: "Sooner or later, we will win. As for yielding to the managers, you can tell them to go to hell."

A managers' spokesperson shot back, "We will never deal with the Actors Equity Association."

To raise money for their cause, the A.E.A. embarked on a series of benefits. Checks poured in from actors and a supportive public. More performers joined the A.E.A., including such headliners as Al Jolson, Ed Wynn, Ann Pennington, Frank Fay, and Gertrude Vanderbilt. A few, like William Collier, Nora Bayes, and E.A. Southern, resigned, saying they were against the closing of theaters.

The conflict escalated further when the managers' association published two full-page ads in the *New York Clipper*, one thanking supporters for their "loyalty and good conscience" (with an accompanying list of managers), the other a warning to all A.E.A. members that they would be held liable to managers for all damages and losses caused by the strike.

An editorial in the *New York Times* urged the adversaries to reach a quick agreement because "both sides have already suffered grave and irreparable losses." The newspaper supported the actors but said they had made a mistake by closing the theaters. The *New York Herald* headlined the conflict "The Battle of Broadway," likening it to the world struggle between labor and capital. They believed the primary issue was one of recognition for the A.E.A. "It is the belief of the public that the time has come for conciliation," the *Herald* declared, because the public "furnishes the money upon which managers and actors alike live."

Even under a persistent rain, hundreds of actors and thousands of cheering spectators participated in an A.E.A.-sponsored parade down Broadway, which elicited extensive press coverage. A benefit at the Lexington Theater collected $6,000. Another at Amsterdam Hall gathered $3,400. Still another, a week later at the Lexington, netted more than $35,000. The Equity ball at the Astor Hotel sold $3,000 worth of tickets. The A.E.A. now boasted a roster of 2,400 actors and actresses. Samuel Untermeyer, one of New York's most prominent attorneys, offered his services, without compensation, to the strikers, even though he was known to have a financial interest in a number of theaters. Untermeyer characterized managers as being "twenty-five years behind the times." Upton Sinclair offered the use of four of his plays at no cost to Equity, to raise money for the strike.

By the end of August, Chicago actors had walked out. All Boston and Philadelphia theaters were closed. Production of new shows had ceased. Losses in gross receipts amounted to more than $245,000 a week. Total losses to theater owners and managers during the four weeks of the strike ran more than $2,000,000: That figure did not include sizable weekly losses among ticket agencies, the printing trades, and trucking companies.

Reversing the statement they had issued a few weeks earlier, the stagehands' union declared support for the A.E.A., voting to walk out of theaters immediately. It was a major blow to managers. When the American Federation of Musicians and the International Alliance of Theatrical Stage Employees and Moving Picture Operators came out in support of the A.E.A., managers knew they were beaten.

But none of these events seemed to deter George M. Cohan, who proceeded to organize his own actors' union, the Actor's Fidelity League. To no one's surprise, he was unanimously elected President of the organization. A number of prominent actors joined Cohan, among them Louis Mann, Otis Skinner, Willard Mack, David Warfield, Holbrook Blinn, and Fay Bainter. Almost immediately, Cohan published an announcement in the *Clipper* claiming his organization was an independent group of actors who "believe that an equitable co-operative spirit" would help "re-establish and maintain friendly relations between actors and managers." He

promised that managers would agree to a satisfactory method of arbitration if given the opportunity. He claimed to have already enrolled 2,500 actors, a questionable boast.

Because they were so angry with Cohan for his allegiance to managers, many actors, including Eddie, refused to talk to him. Although Cohan had been head abbot of the Friars' Club for many years, he was forced to resign because of his actions.

Hastily, managers called for a meeting with actors on August 31 to discuss a settlement, everyone already admitting that the strike should not continue. A day and night of weighty negotiations culminated in a contract, closely resembling A.E.A.'s original demands. Representing Equity were Francis Wilson, Frank Gillmore, Ethel Barrymore, Lillian Russell, Marie Dressler, and Eddie Foy. Representing the managers were David Belasco, William A. Brady, Arthur Hopkins, Sam H. Harris, Henry W. Savage, and A.H. Woods. Within a few days, theaters opened and actors were back at work, ecstatic over the results of the strike and relieved to be earning a salary once more.

Eddie had joined A.E.A. as soon as the organization obtained its charter from the A.F.L. When the strike occurred, Eddie volunteered to participate in fund-raising benefits; the Foys played in four of them. As negotiations with managers were about to begin, Wilson asked Eddie to assist in the process. Members of the A.E.A. negotiating team were all veterans of the stage, and together they could call on myriad experiences dealing with managers. For his part, Eddie was able to bring more than forty years of hard bargaining with managers to the table.

One of the provisions of the new contract stated that neither managers nor producers could blacklist or discriminate against any actor who belonged to Equity or participated in the strike. Easy to state but difficult to monitor. Nor could an actor gather specific evidence to claim he had been blacklisted. Predictably, however, reminiscent of what had occurred after the 1900 White Rats strike, Eddie found himself with no engagements in hand and no manager willing to sign him.

Among the A.E.A.'s negotiating team, only Marie Dressler and Eddie were current stage performers. When Dressler found no work on Broadway, she went to Los Angeles to appear in motion pictures. Eddie chose to continue with the family in vaudeville. For the next six months, the Foys were unemployed.

After the Actors' Equity Strike, the public packed theaters, although the shows of the 1919-20 season were mediocre. The new offerings, however, did showcase the emerging talents of composers like Jerome Kern, George Gershwin, and Oscar Hammerstein II.

Comedy headliners included W.C. Fields, Ed Wynn, Eddie Cantor, and the Four Marx Brothers. Comedy itself was in transition, due to the cultural assimilation and theatrical maturation of urban populations. Vaudeville had become the primary vehicle, assisting the public in accommodating to this change by communicating new cultural meanings of personal success and the American Dream. Vaudeville maintained its popularity because it was live and immediate performance. Moreover, it was personal, allowing audiences easily to identify with its performers. When social messages — ranging from etiquette to education — were conveyed to vaudeville audiences, they were readily accepted and absorbed. Vaudeville also offered its patrons a feeling of good-fellowship, as well as a haven from the anxieties and frustrations of daily life. Above all, it was a place to laugh; when the audience laughed, all those repressed emotions of the moment were washed down the aisles.

Most ethnic comedy had by now all but vanished, although Dutch comics made a brief reappearance after the war. Music was increasingly wedded to comedy; a good comedian must also sing and dance. Blacks on stage became familiar as individual performers, no longer as minstrel-show stereotypes. Some comics became caricatures,

applying this persona to all their roles and routines, which audiences seemed to appreciate. Topical material was prevalent, often based on human (as opposed to ethnic) ridicule and debasement, the more bizarre the funnier. When Ed Wynn played the fool, everyone howled. When the Marx Brothers confused taxi drivers, rich matrons, and hotel clerks with their zany antics, audiences could readily identify with the exaggerated situations. At the same time, the vaudeville milieu served as a splendid source of talent for other media.

It wasn't until April 1920 that the Foys obtained employment, with a small circuit in the Midwest, operated by the Western Vaudeville Managers Association. Chicago was their home base, as the W.V.M.A. had booking agreements with theaters in many smaller cities in Illinois, Wisconsin, Minnesota, and Iowa. The Foys played "Slumwhere in New York" for these audiences, most of whom had never before seen them perform and were unlikely familiar with them. Still, patrons loved their act, and reviews, what there were of them in local newspapers, were uniformly good. Yet no sooner had they returned to Chicago than Eddie was arrested for violating Illinois' Child Labor Act, by permitting his children to perform in vaudeville. He was fined eighty dollars.

For all occasions when they were called upon to deal with authorities, the children had each memorized three distinct ages for themselves: their correct age, the minimum age of the child-labor law in a particular city (where they routinely added three or four years), and their railroad age, since a child paid only half-fare if he or she claimed to be under twelve.

The summer back at New Rochelle was occupied with preparations for a new skit, ably assisted by Bryan and William Jerome. It was a summer of pinching pennies, as well. A sailboat that Eddie had purchased the previous year had to be sold, as did a car that had been bought for Charlie. Since the vehicle was repeatedly in the garage for repairs,

Charlie remarked that his car could find its way back without a driver, it had already been returned so often.

Nor were personal relations between Eddie and Bryan satisfactory. Now out of the Navy, Bryan was living at home and seeking a job, in the entertainment field, he hoped. Eddie had been unable to persuade him to return to the family act. Bryan agreed to write for it, but never again to perform. Bryan seemed nervous and short-tempered, as the rest of the family rehearsed their new act, "So This Is a Restaurant."

Obtaining an engagement remained problematic until the Poli circuit agreed to play the Foys in their Connecticut and Massachusetts theaters. Their weekly salary was $1,250, well below previous rates. The Foys opened in Bridgeport, Connecticut, September 8, to a full house. But Poli's promise of weekly engagements went unfulfilled, and Eddie terminated the agreement. He then appealed to Albee and obtained a booking in Washington, D.C. Albee promised a long-term contract if the D.C. run proved successful.

The Foys' popularity and drawing power remained strong. Consequently, Albee signed them to a ten-week contract, which included an engagement in New York City. After four weeks on the road, the Foys opened at the Palace, to good reviews:

> In their new act, the Foy family has an excellent laugh-getting vehicle which moves easily and gives all of the many children a chance to demonstrate their talent.[7]

"So This Is a Restaurant" opens with the family anticipating a feast. The Foys go to a restaurant, only to find that prices are beyond their reach. The head waiter discovers they are a family of "New Rochelle entertainers"; they are told that, if they will entertain the patrons, they will be fed free of charge. This premise permits a succession of funny dialogue, songs, and dances, with each person doing his or her share.

Eddie sang "The King of Longacre," which was then imitated by Charlie. The six children did a dance in martial time and, all together, the Foys gave an impression of New York police on parade. A new song, written by Bryan, "The Greatest Father of Them All," was sung by the children, closing the act.

The *Clipper* reviewer pronounced the skit "an enjoyable morsel of entertainment" and declared it gave "more opportunity for the Foy youngsters to show their innate gifts for entertaining." While the family was playing at the Palace, Bryan was brought out on stage to take a bow for the songs he had written. A few days later, Bryan entered a sanitarium in West Baden, New York, to be treated for what was described as a nervous breakdown.

Again, reviewers remarked at Eddie's less-than-usual involvement in stage action. One reviewer suggested that "Eddie had better watch out or all of his children will be way ahead of him." Another wrote that the children "give promise of outdoing their talented father." Eddie had apparently chosen to feature his children more since their performing talents had matured, and the uniqueness of their act continued to attract large audiences. Eddie could frame the presentation with his name and reputation; the children could deliver the excitement and appeal.

Two more weeks in New York theaters drew large crowds. The *Herald* reported:

> Eddie Foy and his clan of well-drilled and talented Foys, who represent various stages of development on the road to the Foy millennium, stopped the show as they always do.[8]

However, the *Clipper* correspondent, while acknowledging Eddie's reputation, again reminded readers of his longevity on stage.

> He is the same Eddie Foy who amused us with his drolleries a score of years ago. For

Eddie and the Younger Foys in "So This Is a Restaurant." Bryan had left the troupe to join the William Fox motion-picture organization in its publicity department.

a man his age, he still is light on his feet and, although not as active in the amount of work he does as of former years, is just as interesting.[9]

That the entire act seemed somewhat autobiographical did not go unnoticed by astute critics.

Almost all of the Keith circuit run was performed in the New York area. Not only did Eddie want to avoid taking a long road tour, he wanted the family to stay close to Bryan during his recovery.

Yet another factor may have convinced Eddie to remain in New York. Theaters in other parts of the country were reporting a decline in attendance, one of the first signs of a deepening economic recession. By January 1921, managers reported road shows "flopping" in the South and West. Theater prices were being reduced, and motion pictures were replacing touring companies that had folded.

In spite of dire predictions for New York theaters in 1921, the Foys obtained a contract with the Proctor circuit to play for six weeks in the New York area. Signed with them were old friend Lew Dockstater, Hugh Herbert, Jack Benny, Lillian Roth, and the Four Marx Brothers. The only negative aspect of this extended run in New York theaters was the Proctor penchant for split-weeks — playing the first half of the week in one theater, the second half in another. Some actors felt the system was little better than playing one-night stands. And split-weeks with two-a-day performances were particularly hard on performers. Eddie had to book a hotel room near the theater for everyone to rest a few hours between shows, as well as a place to stay during these engagements. While they were only a few miles from home, they had to play as if they were on the road.

By March, the predicted theater business decline hit New York. Managers were afraid that most of their attractions wouldn't last another month. Vaudeville bills, even those featuring motion pictures, attracted small audiences. The *Clipper* predicted that theater business could be the worst in ten years by summer. For these reasons, booking agents were reluctant to sign acts for long-term tours. Instead, acts were being signed on a week-to-week basis, threatening an actor's already problematic solvency.

Eddie found himself spending a great deal of time searching for engagements, visiting booking agents, and calling theater managers in an attempt to construct a reasonable route that would not make the trip a financial disaster. Thanks to his knowledge of booking methods and familiarity with managers, Eddie secured a two-month route, at a time when theaters nationwide were closing because of low patronage.

The Foys launched their tour in York, Pennsylvania (Keith circuit), the middle of March. From there they played in Scranton (Poli circuit), Harrisburg (Proctor circuit), Youngstown, Ohio, and Louisville, Kentucky, (Keith circuit), Cincinnati and Chicago (Orpheum circuit), and closed in Cleveland (Keith circuit). It was an amazingly adroit bit of scheduling, and the Foys performed successfully at a time when economic conditions had deteriorated so badly that managers felt free to cut actors' salaries, regardless of signed contracts. When actors complained, they were given a choice: work at a reduced salary or don't work at all. The best that Equity could do in response was to threaten managers with a closed shop — no performances unless all those involved (actors, musicians, stagehands, etc.) belonged to a union. In light of current conditions, its impact was insignificant.

By the middle of June, newspapers reported that theater business was in its worst slump in history. All types of entertainment were affected. New York and Chicago were the only cities that attempted to keep theaters open, though they did little business. New York, which normally depended on tourists for summer shows, reported less than half of the usual tourist traffic in town. Poor summer activity also had a dampening effect on the planning of fall productions. Of all types of entertainment, vaudeville theaters were hit hardest, most of them closing for the summer. Around theaters and booking offices, unemployed actors lined the streets.

Eddie spent the summer hard at work, attempting to gain employment for the coming season. Since it appeared that there were going to be few opportunities in vaudeville, Eddie teamed with Willard Mack, a fellow performer and writer, to prepare a comedy in which all the roles would be played by family members. When the *Clipper* reported this novel idea, they kidded Eddie about using the play to dodge Equity closed-shop contracts. The play would be called "Dad" and portray the daily life of a performing family in vaudeville. Unfortunately, the project had to be canceled when Mack filed for bankruptcy a month later.

In late July, Eddie produced the second annual benefit in honor of Madeline for his church in New Rochelle. At the local Lowe's Theater, a full house saw the Foy family perform, along with Blanche Ring, W.C. Fields, and Van and Schenck. More than $2,000 was raised for the church's building fund. Over the years, Madeline had worked hard for the church, from organizing fund-raising benefits to taking in homeless children; Eddie promised to continue her efforts. Attending the benefit and performing with his siblings was Bryan, looking fit. He had just notified his father that he had obtained a position with the William Fox promotion department in New York City.

During this time, the recent death of a friend probably averted severe financial difficulties for the Foys. J. Bernard Dyllyn, a close friend and colleague of Eddie's for many years, had died six months before. When his will was probated, the Foy children discovered they had been left $2,000 by Dyllyn.

While most acts remained idle, the Foys had demonstrated their ability to attract crowds; and the Keith circuit moved to take advantage of the fact. Albee booked the Foys for one of the few touring shows Keith planned to send out. Eddie Foy and the Younger Foys opened at the Palace, New York, August 24, to inaugurate the new season. Although the act was called the "Foy

Fun Revue," it was the same act they had performed the previous season. Nevertheless, they were well received, though Eddie's stage longevity (read: old age) was again highlighted:

> The family made a hit, being recalled for any number of bows, stopping the show, and Foy the elder being compelled to make a speech. Foy said, "What do I do in the act? Nothing. I know it." While it may be true that Foy tells the truth, the audience nevertheless seems to have not forgotten the days when Eddie danced nimbly and amused in *Off the Earth* and other musical comedies.[10]

The Keith run kept the Foys performing through October. Though newspapers reported that more than 5,000 actors were idle and there was little relief in sight, the Foys were signed by the Orpheum circuit for an extended tour of twenty-two weeks, through the middle of April 1922. Not only were they pleased by the booking — and feeling lucky, as well — the Foys weren't required to change their act, because audiences in the Orpheum theaters had never before seen it. The Foys received a salary of $2,100 a week, a princely sum at a time when theater managers claimed losses in the millions. The family opened their tour at the Orpheum Theater, in Portland, Oregon, December 21.

The theater situation at the beginning of 1922 reflected an economy that was beginning to stabilize. Most theaters were open, although business was below average, even for the holiday season. Unemployment remained high, especially so for actors. Few new shows opened in New York, as managers were afraid to risk presenting attractions to half-filled theaters. Vaudeville circuits initiated lower prices for balcony and gallery seats and saw some positive response to the bargains. Orchestras were trimmed in size. The Shuberts suffered a major financial blow when their vaudeville circuit had to close because of low attendance.

Now, however, the Orpheum management saw an opportunity to dominate markets by offering vaudeville headliners at moderate prices. With fewer road companies playing and many vaudeville houses closed, Orpheum heavily promoted their bills, thereby attracting most of the available theater patrons. The Foys were one of a group of top acts, which included Chic Sale, Trixie Friganza, Julian Eltinge, Billy Van, and Jim Corbett, as well as the Four Marx Brothers, who benefited from the Orpheum strategy.

When Eddie played in San Francisco, he noticed a decided difference in audience theater etiquette. Bay Area audiences had always been loud, outspoken, and responsive to stage action, often voicing their likes and dislikes demonstrably. Suddenly, so it seemed, the audience had become more subdued, more polite, applauding at more appropriate times. It was a little disconcerting to Eddie because it was harder to judge audience reactions to stage business, not knowing how well it was received until the end of the act. This newly refined behavior was not unique to San Francisco.

The war had already discouraged boisterous encores. Theaters were required to conserve coal; encores lengthened programs. By eliminating encores, a program could be shortened by up to an hour. Unfortunately, the elimination of such encores also erased spontaneous recognition for performers, as well as audience participation.

In addition, many theaters now prohibited smoking in the auditorium. The increased presence of women and children influenced patrons to temper their behavior. Foot stomping, whistling, and yelling from the gallery were now banned, as were spontaneous insults or encouraging comments made by the audience. Although they continued to join in when performers sang, audience involvement with actors had markedly declined. Theater managers hung signs in strategic places reminding patrons to behave in a proper manner.

Professionals in the industry offered many reasons for this change in theater etiquette. Some attributed the change to the increased sophistication of audiences. Others suggested the Emily Post–like articles in magazines and newspapers often pointed with disapproval at "rowdy" and "ungentle-man-like" behavior in public places, particularly theaters. (Baseball games were excluded because they were primarily patronized by men.) Entertainment people suggested that perceptions of the acting profession were changing, that somehow actors were gaining respect.

The most important impact on live entertainment, however, was likely that of motion pictures. They had created a different set of norms for theater behavior, which was now governed by darkness, enforced quiet, anonymity, and focused attention. As more theaters presented combination bills of vaudeville and motion pictures, movie deportment gradually became the norm for the entire theater experience.

The Foys' tour took them to West Coast cities, back East to Salt Lake City and Denver, and into the Midwest. While in Los Angeles, the family celebrated Bryan's new job with William Fox. He had been transferred to Los Angeles to join Fox's motion picture scenario staff. They also shared in Bryan's happiness about the sale of a song he had written for the comedy team of Gallagher and Shean, for which he was paid the grand sum of fifty dollars. Called "Mr. Gallagher and Mr. Shean," it quickly became the team's theme song and was published by Jack Mills, Inc., a national music publisher. When Bryan later filed a lawsuit to obtain a portion of the profits made by the comedy team and Mills, the suit was thrown out of court because Bryan had signed his rights away when he was paid for the song. According to family members, Bryan was upset about the outcome for a long time.

In early April, Orpheum announced they were closing all theaters at the end of the month. That meant the Foys would conclude their tour in Chicago, where they were favorites. Audiences jammed the theater, and the *Tribune* reported "a great time was had by all":

Eddie Foy and family caused a near riot with their combination of comedy, songs and dances. The elder Foy was forced to make a speech or two and several extra bows before he could stop the cheering. No show was ever stopped more completely.[11]

While playing in Chicago, Eddie was a sad witness to the demolition of the Mc-Vicker's Theater, where he had learned a good deal of stagecraft in his early career. The McVicker's had been originally opened in 1857, rebuilt in 1871, six weeks before the Great Fire, and rebuilt again in 1872. Eddie had appeared there in the late 1870s, on the same stage as Edwin Booth and Joseph Jefferson. The McVicker's was the last of the great Chicago theaters to be razed.

The success of the Orpheum tour seemed to rejuvenate Eddie, and he began planning again for a comedy that featured the entire family. Williard Mack and William Jerome were recruited to write the play, with songs by Jerome. But their work was interrupted by the unexpected death of Lillian Russell.

The entire theater community went into mourning, and a number of memorial services were held on Russell's behalf. At one, sponsored by the Keith organization, Eddie gave a short speech, recalling Russell's generosity to other actors and her role in the success of the Equity strike. At another, held in the Hippodrome, Eddie, representing the Lambs' Club, sang a song in remembrance of Russell. When an "old timers" act was proposed to honor her, Eddie was asked to participate, still another reminder of how long he had been performing.

Returning to the new family project, Eddie was surprised when Charlie announced he no longer wished to play with the family. He stated a firm desire to perform on his own, and he had been exploring the possibility of doing a solo act in vaudeville. As with Bryan, Eddie could not convince him to remain. New material now had to be modified to reflect Charlie's defection, though this seemed to make no difference to Albee and the Keith circuit, as the Foys were signed for a twelve-week run in New York and Eastern cities, at $2,000 a week.

For the first time since the Foys had begun their act in 1913, Eddie did not have to worry about breaking child-labor laws, nor deal with arrests and court appearances. Lobbied by Samuel Gompers and the A.F.L. in Washington, D.C., a Senate subcommittee agreed to an amendment to existing child-labor law, one that allowed children under eighteen to perform on stage. Gompers expressed his desire to promote the career of stage children, citing, as an example, Eddie's continuous court battles to allow his children to perform. Gompers pointed out the difference between factory labor for children and their employment on stage, "which is more like play than work and does not involve any hardship." While Eddie was not able to benefit from the new law, his encounters with authorities and zealots for close to a decade likely were the impetus for its passage.

The Foys' new act, "The 1922 Revue," opened at Keith's Theater, Washington, D.C., August 23. Audiences crowded the theater. In fact, audiences were now crowding theaters all across the country, as the recession waned. Managers predicted a good season, maybe even the best in years.

For "Revue," Eddie played the role of a poor cabby, a single parent responsible for his children. As he arrives home in his dilapidated rig, the children tell him they want to celebrate his birthday and plan to get money for his party by going on stage. Pop informs them they are too young. The remainder of the act is composed of specialties intended to demonstrate the kids' talents. Mary and Richard perform a song and dance double. Mary and Madeline sing in harmony, backed by ensemble dancing. Madeline and Eddie, Jr., perform a fast double waltz. Irving imitates some well-known actors. For the finish, all change to striped sweaters and caps for "Walking," an ensemble song and dance in which Eddie ad libs and jokes out in front of the line. Eddie is handed a telegram, offering

him $5,000 a week to act in pictures, as the only surviving cab driver with a horse. Eddie notes that he doesn't recognize the handwriting; then, with his trademark sigh, remarks, "It must have come from Mack Sennett." William Jerome and Bryan were the authors of the sketch, possibly autobiographical.

Reviewers considered the act even better than the Foys had done before:

> Eddie Foy shows up to great advantage in his new act. His voice is better and he shows his old time dance stuff. The Younger Foys sing and dance and show up well as "chips off the old block."[12]

In Boston, Eddie was interviewed by a *Globe* reporter, who asked him how he had been able to take care of the children and tour at the same time. Eddie jokingly remarked that the reason he had put together the act in the first place was to be able to raise the children. In addition, Eddie declared he was writing a book, "The Care and Rearing of Children," which would include all of his child-raising pointers. Recently, he added, he had to carry a club to keep would-be suitors away from his two daughters. "None of the prospective applicants," he concluded, "appeared as though they would make good actors." The reporter closed the interview, wondering whether Eddie was serious or not.

For the remainder of 1922, the Foys played in Keith-Circuit theaters in Brooklyn, Philadelphia, and Baltimore, then back to the Palace in New York for a two-week engagement. They appeared on the second half of the bill, following Fanny Brice. In what seemed a temporary arrangement, Charlie reappeared with the family. The *Clipper* reported:

> Their stuff went strong, as all of Foys' stuff always does.[13]

The *Herald* was equally complimentary, comparing Eddie's performance with his earlier days:

Foy is more like himself in his present offering, and after seeing Foy's work here this week it takes you back to the days when Eddie Foy started out as the very same sort of comedian and with the same spirit that is shown in his present characterization.[14]

For the first time in a long while, the Foys spent the Christmas holidays at home. Eddie announced that, following the brief respite, the family would be appearing in a comedy drama, "That Casey Girl," rehearsals to begin in January.

Eddie's evident cheerfulness, however, went beyond his recent stage successes. Unknown to the children, Eddie had been keeping company with a young woman. Described as "a dashing brunette from Dallas," Marie Combs (née Reilly) was a widow, her husband having died the year before. She claimed to be twenty-nine (or thirty), an heiress to an oil fortune (no evidence to prove it), part Cherokee (her mother was one-fourth Cherokee), and to have appeared in the movies (naturally).

She and Eddie had actually met four years previously in San Francisco, introduced by some friends at a dinner party. Although married at the time, she had been living apart from her husband. Whenever Eddie visited San Francisco, the two spent time together. Shortly after her husband's death, Marie moved to New York, taking an apartment on West Fifty-first Street.

One night, prior to putting on their vaudeville act, when the Foys were playing New York in early January, Eddie revealed to his children his intention to wed. "I'm thinking of getting married," he said rather uneasily. Once the children realized their father was not joking, they could only respond with inarticulate gasps. "I'm growing old," he continued. "I'm beginning to feel lonely. You're all growing up, and you'll soon marry and leave the old home."

Somewhat surprised, Eddie found the children's response was less than enthusiastic. They asked many questions, not only to discover more about the mysterious Marie,

but also the better to understand their father's reasons. After consulting among themselves, they declared, "Pop, you can marry if you like, of course. But we won't have any other woman in mother's home." After the show, the children drove back to New Rochelle. Eddie retired to Marie's apartment.

The next day, Eddie brought Marie to the theater, hoping her presence would make the children more sanguine about the marriage. Yet, after dutifully shaking her hand and saying hello, they departed.

On January 8, 5:30 P.M., at the Holy Cross Catholic Church, on Forty-second Street, between Eighth and Ninth Avenues, Reverend Francis P. Duffy officiated at the marriage of Edwin Fitzgerald and Marie Combs. Eddie said he was sixty-four (he was actually two months short of sixty-seven). Only a few close friends attended the ceremony, among them, J.W. Whelan, Eddie's best man, and Dolly McGrath, the bride's attendant. The children were conspicuous by their absence.

With typical humor, William Jerome sent Eddie a congratulatory telegram:

> This is the best-staged of all your marriages. Always knew you were a great showman. You made only one mistake; should have had the marriage public and sold the motion picture rights.

When Eddie and Marie arrived at the theater after the ceremony, he called the children together and announced, "I married Mrs. Combs this afternoon." The children wished them happiness and quietly departed, to prepare for their act. On stage that evening, the Foys played as they always had.

Rehearsals for "That Casey Girl" were scheduled to begin, but family tensions delayed them. Instead, the Foys obtained a four-week booking with the Orpheum circuit, starting in Chicago, January 21. Since Eddie's plan was to open "That Casey Girl" in Chicago, this was a fortuitous trip.

However, midway through the Chicago

On January 8, 1923, Eddie and Marie Combs were married. Eddie was 66; Marie 29 or 30. A few months later, Eddie retired from the stage. The couple moved to the original Foy house in New Rochelle.

engagement, Charlie was stricken with appendicitis, which would take him off the boards for at least a month. The new show had to be delayed again. The Foys returned to New York to discuss future plans. Eddie to his apartment with Marie; the children to "The Foyer," now under Aunt Clara's supervision.

Newspaper reporters attempted to uncover and exploit the apparent rift between Eddie and the children. They interviewed Charlie, the designated spokesperson for his siblings. He confirmed the children's possession of the family home, noting that all property had indeed been put in his mother's name and willed to the children when she died. "She was great at taking care of money," Charlie said. "Father liked to play billiards. Or, when it wasn't billiards, it was the horses." To support their brother's statement, the girls reported that Eddie slept in a feather bed with three pillows. On one of them, he kept his racing form, glasses, and a pencil.

"She was a perfect mother," continued Charlie. "We can't let anybody take her place. We haven't a thing against Pop's new wife, but we couldn't stand seeing anybody else sit at Mother's place at the table or in her rocking chair on the porch."

Nor did Eddie seem to be angry. In fact, he seemed resigned to the situation. "If I had all the money I've spent making my children happy, I'd be a millionaire today. But I wouldn't want a dollar of it back. Not a dime. Not a cent."

"I don't blame the children for their feeling," he added. "Every one of them is wonderful."

As if to reinforce the relationship between Eddie and his children, the Foys jointly announced they were returning to vaudeville after an absence of several months. Signed by the Loew circuit, at $1,650 a week, the Foys were promised an extended tour if their initial work proved profitable. After they had worked in Cleveland and Buffalo, however, the tour abruptly ended; the family returned to New York, again to begin rehearsals for their new comedy drama.

"That Casey Girl" opened October 3, at the Playhouse Theater, Wilmington, Delaware, for an indefinite run. Willard Mack and George Hobart had written the book, with lyrics and music by William Jerome and Jean Schwartz. Jack Mason was in charge of musical and dance numbers, with "a dancing chorus of Broadway beauties." The show was now called a "musical comedy."

As Martin Casey, Eddie played the role of a hen-pecked husband who loves his children but, more often than not, misunderstands them. The play presented incidents and vignettes of family life in the Casey home, in something of an uproar over Mary's impending marriage. While the local reviewer recognized Eddie as "the funniest man in the world," and the children "a talented family," the best he could say about the play was to applaud its wholesomeness and note that there was "not so much as one risqué statement throughout the whole piece." Three songs appeared destined for popularity, "That Casey Girl," "Casey Is a Wonderful Name," and "Every Day Is Mother's Day." The play was heralded as "glorifying the American family."

"That Casey Girl" played in Wilmington, Philadelphia, and Paterson, New Jersey, closing less than a month after opening. With tears in his eyes and cap in his hand, Eddie announced his retirement from the stage.

Chapter 16

Memories are the only beautiful things in life that no one can take away from us.
Eddie Foy in *The Fallen Star*

It was the second year Marie and Eddie had spent in their home — the family's original cottage in New Rochelle — since Eddie's retirement. What Eddie especially liked about the home was the place they were now sitting, a back porch that looked out upon the old barn where his young children had first played and where they had begun practicing vaudeville sketches.

"Aren't you going to visit the Lambs' today?" Marie asked. It had become an almost daily routine for Eddie to spend some time at the Lambs' Club, reminiscing about the old days with his cronies. Each morning, Eddie took the train to New York. Taxi drivers at the station knew Eddie, clad in his familiar brown overcoat, and vied with each other to drive him to the club. Knowing, as they did, when he usually returned to the train station, there was always at least one taxi waiting to take him there.

Eddie had been staring at the barn,

seemingly deep in thought, perhaps grappling with fond, fleeting memories. Finally, he stood. "Time to go. I've got a meeting with a manager this morning to discuss a sketch I wrote." He said something like this every morning now, Marie noted. Retirement seemed improper for Eddie, she thought.

After the closure of "That Casey Girl," Eddie had returned to Marie at their Fifty-first Street apartment. Not much press had been given to Eddie's claim about retirement. Too many stars had made similar claims, only to return for "final tours." So Eddie's withdrawal seemed to pass quietly, with no fanfare, no nostalgic newspaper articles, no benefits honoring his career. It was pretty much the way he wanted.

When Marie and Eddie moved into their New Rochelle house, however, newspaper articles suggested the couple was living in poverty, with little food on the table. Yet when reporters interviewed Eddie, he did not appear destitute. Actually, he seemed well fed and content. With his old, characteristic grin, Eddie told the reporters, "The clown still laughs."

"Save your tears," he counseled them. "I've had life tickle my ribs. And I've had it hit below the belt. Someday I'll write it as I lived it, pages from the life of a clown." And with that, he'd dance a few steps, make a funny face, and smile that trademark smile.

Reporters noticed that the walls of the Foy home were covered with photos, playbills, and reviews, reminders of Eddie's glory years. As he lovingly referred to them, they could see that these mementos helped to sustain Eddie's belief that he might still return to the stage. "I'm not through," he insisted. "I still have my face. And I can still make people laugh."

Actually, the original Foy home in New Rochelle was a roomy cottage (it had to be, to have housed all the children), and Marie and Eddie lived comfortably. Charlie acknowledged that his father received one hundred dollars weekly, as rental for the big house, in which the children lived.

Beyond that, however, there was little closeness between the new couple and the children. When they did get together, Eddie would go alone to visit his family. While the children did not dislike Marie (she was a pleasant woman who obviously cared for their father), they remained uncomfortable about her replacing their mother as Eddie's wife.

Even his daily trips to the Lambs' Club were grim reminders of Eddie's past triumphs. They served to keep him informed of Broadway activities, as well as giving him the opportunity to share souvenirs of the past. Yet, as Eddie turned toward home at the end of the day, observers noted an elderly man with head drooping and shoulders slumped.

When Eddie visited his doctor to report heart palpitations, he was diagnosed as suffering from angina. The doctor recommended he avoid situations that produced stress, but Eddie refused to give up his daily excursions to the Lambs' Club.

In fact, Eddie had become so despondent about his chances to perform again, that he even wrote George M. Cohan, albeit reluctantly, to explore job opportunities. Cohan responded in a friendly manner but gave Eddie no encouragement. Nor was Eddie pleased about Cohan's references to "open shops" and broken friendships:

> If conditions during the next couple of months become so I can operate my business along open-shop lines for the coming season, I should be glad to sit down and talk with you.
>
> It was a great pleasure to talk with you the other day and renew the old friendship which should never have been broken, as I have always been one of your most ardent admirers and always a rooter for your success.

Cohan concluded the letter with an ambiguous brush-off:

> Some time when you are around this way, drop in and say hello.[1]

When Eddie walked the streets of Broadway, as he often did, he observed the dramatic changes taking place in popular entertainment. He did not feel he had been rejected, just forgotten by a public that increasingly sought new theatrical experiences.

Show business was fast becoming big business. The country's burgeoning prosperity permeated Broadway, with flush Wall Street investors and entrepreneurial "angels" underwriting shows. As producers vied for their talents, star salaries had jumped to unprecedented figures.

Vaudeville had reached its peak of popularity but couldn't buck movies, with hundreds of stories and casts of thousands. Unable to change its format, vaudeville began a gradual decline. On the other hand, movie studios had become giants of entertainment, building elegant theaters, controlling distribution, and promoting technological advances that suggested movie-going itself was an exciting fantasy.

Jazz brought new zest to popular music. It brought the rhythmic movements of the Charleston and Black Bottom to a larger public and invigorated the phonograph record business. It helped to popularize the more intimate, noisy atmosphere of cabarets and Prohibition-inspired speakeasies. Once assimilated by Caucasian musicians, jazz became America's unique contribution to musical invention.

In the course of a single year, radio grew from a curious fad broadcasting music and baseball scores through headsets — many called it a "passing novelty" — to an industry manufacturing and selling home appliances that covered concerts, sporting events, and Presidential campaigns. By late 1922, there were over 200 radio stations and 3,000,000 radio sets. Within a few years, nearly every home in the U.S. had access to radio, widely promoted as a something-for-nothing entertainment. On Broadway and throughout the country, box-offices dreaded its competition and worried it would kill live theater.

The combination of passage of the Nineteenth Amendment (women's vote), the publication of F. Scott Fitzgerald's "This Side of Paradise," and the popularization of Sigmund Freud's psychoanalytic theories, brought sex out of the closet. The pervasive "Gibson Girl" image of an elegantly dressed, corseted, stately woman, devoted to home and children, had given way to a new ideal: a gregarious, iconoclastic "flapper" with bobbed hair, short skirts (ten inches above the ground), flat breasts, and straight hips, defying convention by smoking, drinking, and kissing in public.

Popular music had reached a level of sophistication well beyond the dreams of Tin Pan Alley song pluggers. In fact, some of the graduates of the Alley, like Irving Berlin, Jerome Kern, and George Gershwin, expanded musical horizons with singable, danceable tunes that quickly identified the singers, authors, and shows in which they were featured. The composers themselves became popular icons. From 1924 on, American musical theater entered its golden age, with such names as Gershwin, Kern, Berlin, Rodgers and Hart, Youmans, Friml, and Romberg, contributing infectious rhythms and memorable lyrics to such landmark hits as "Lady Be Good," "Rose Marie," and "No, No Nanette." They were now only two years away from the precedent-setting "Showboat."

Old-fashioned burlesque, featuring travesty and satire, had changed to a decidedly modern presentation of unabashed sexual display. Ziegfeld had helped to legitimize this mutation by featuring statuesque, revealingly costumed women. Each year, his Follies displayed ever more abbreviated costumes. By 1925, girls were appearing in splendid tableaux nude or nearly so from the waist up. Ziegfeld was able to cloak his shows' sexuality in terms of art and glamour to gain the approbation of his more prudish patrons.

Just down the street from Ziegfeld's theater, burlesque for the working class (men) packed theaters presenting the new sensation called striptease. Instead of closing theaters for "corrupting the morals of youth," the NYPD raid on Minsky's in 1925 so sensationalized and popularized burlesque that it became one of New York's most profitable entertainments for a decade.

Comedy was now in the capable hands of Al Jolson, Ed Wynn, Eddie Cantor, W.C. Fields, Fanny Brice, and the Four Marx Brothers, all vaudeville graduates who were earning generous salaries appearing in musicals, movies, and on the radio. Not to be outdone, movie studios promoted their own comedians — Chaplin, Keaton, Lloyd, Turpin, Langdon, Laurel and Hardy. Slapstick, pantomime, and exaggeration weren't exactly dead: but, now such comedy had become heavily scripted.

No wonder Eddie was bewildered by what he observed, not to mention visibly

Six of the grown-up Foys. *From left to right:* **Irving, Dick, Mary, Madeline, Eddie, Jr., and Charlie. Irving, Mary, Madeline, and Eddie, Jr. were appearing in vaudeville as "The Foy Family: Real Chips Off the Old Block." Dick had recently joined Bryan in Hollywood. Charlie was performing a solo vaudeville act.**

reminded of the yawning gap between his own stage triumphs and those of the comedians who had replaced him.

The Foy children, however, continued their careers in entertainment. Bryan was in Hollywood, learning the trade, on his way to becoming a movie producer. Performing solo in vaudeville, Charlie was earning $300 a week for his efforts, which included an imitation of his father. Dick had joined Bryan and was attempting to break into the movie business. The remaining four — Mary, Madeline, Eddie, Jr., and Irving — continued the Foy tradition by playing the vaudeville circuits. A critic noted that, while each of them possessed unique talent, a touch of the "old man" could always be seen in their work. Reliable Aunt Clara kept the house in shape

for those infrequent periods when the younger Foys came home to rest.

A few years before, Eddie had boasted he would someday write about his career in show business. His chance came when Alvin Harlow and *Colliers* magazine approached Eddie to serialize his life for their readers. (Other magazines were currently publishing the lives of various old-time stars.)

Offered $400 for his cooperation, Eddie readily accepted. The first episode appeared in the December 18, 1926, issue of *Colliers* and covered Eddie's youthful years. In all, nine episodes were published; popular response to his story was so pronounced, it was decided to publish it in book form.

Eddie wove an entertaining story, most of which was true, though sketchy, with the usual amount of revisionist history that an autobiography concedes. His later years, which included adventures with the Seven Little Foys, were only briefly noted. As in life, in print, Eddie tended to minimize his triumphs and contributions to popular theater. Except for a few funny anecdotes, Eddie, the comedian, rarely appeared.

Nonetheless, the *Colliers'* story persuaded the team of Frank Fay, a comedian and vaudeville producer, and Tom Barry, a writer, to prepare a skit for Eddie, convinced he would be interested in performing it. To their surprise, Eddie hesitated to accept. Could he still perform? Did audiences remember him? Fay, Barry, and Lambs' Club colleagues assured Eddie he could meet the challenge. In January 1927, Fay announced that Eddie Foy would be featured in a new vaudeville skit opening sometime during the summer.

No sooner had Eddie signed a contract for $700 a week, than he was stricken with a slight heart attack. Doctors ordered him to bed, to rest for an indeterminate period. To many, it appeared that Eddie's return to the stage had been arrested. But while Eddie remained at home, he learned the script and blocked out his stage moves. When Fay visited him, Eddie clearly demonstrated his mastery of the role. In fact, he could have gone on stage the next day. Thanks to old friend E.F. Albee, Fay booked Eddie to open at the Palace Theater, New York, early in August. It could not have been a more auspicious return to the popular stage.

Entitled "The Fallen Star," the skit was eerily close to autobiography. Eddie portrayed a stage doorman, the charity of the theater being to give an old actor and forgotten Broadway star a job.

In the title role, Eddie is advising a young vaudeville dance team whose partnership has become a love relationship, one that, unfortunately, threatens their career. At the theater, late one night, the old actor wanders onto the stage, triggering memories of the days when he too was a star. Recalling in monologue the entertainment of his time emboldens him to repeat a few of the old dances and songs. He recollects a scene in a cafe on Broadway, dining with imaginary friends of yore, such as Al Smith, John L. Sullivan, Lillian Russell, and O. Henry. By contrast, he philosophizes on contemporary show business. With fists clenched, he decries the fact that youth has lost the spirit of the Great White Way, that the "religion" of Broadway is not viscerally felt by the newer generation. "For some strange reason," he laments, "they don't think of it in terms of relating to themselves. They think of it only in terms of a street."

"We called the street Broadway. We gave it religion. We gave it spirit. To youth, it all seems funny." From the wings, a stagehand witnesses the old man's reveries, eyes him pityingly, and suggests that he "come in out of the rain."

Shuffling offstage in his final exit, the fallen star exclaims, "Memories! Memories! The only beautiful thing in life that no one can take away from us."

On August 8, 1927, Eddie returned to the Palace Theater stage in "The Fallen Star." Despite a heavy rain on opening night, the house was full, awaiting Eddie's appearance. The stage setting was simple; a fragment of wall with a stage entrance on it the only scenic suggestion, the remainder of the stage covered by drapes. When Eddie made his entrance, he received a standing ovation, the audience rising as one to greet him. When he broke into a song and dance, it immediately elicited a shout of recognition. And when he finished the skit, he received tremendous acclamation. In show-biz jargon, the audience tore down the house.

Later, in his dressing room, stage manager Max Gorden found Eddie crying. "Max," he declared, "they didn't talk to me at the Astor yesterday. They hardly knew me. But they'll talk to me now."

Reviews of Eddie's performance were outstanding. The *New York Times* reported:

> Eddie Foy announces his farewell tour in conjunction with this sketch. It is a fitting

Eddie in "The Fallen Star," a nostalgic, semi-autobiographical vaudeville skit that elicited both cheers and tears from his host of admirers. As William Jerome wrote: "He passed on as he wished to pass on — with his theatrical boots on." (Harry Ransom Humanities Research Center–University of Texas)

and touching vehicle.... Eddie Foy in this sketch is among the surest things in big-time vaudeville.[2]

The *Herald* declared that audience response "was both a tribute to his acting and a recognition of his fifty-odd years on the stage. As always," they continued, "Eddie took the reception admirably, retiring with just a few words of thanks."

In response to the reviews, Albee immediately signed Eddie to a full season's contract. After playing the Palace through Christmas (an unprecedented five-month booking at the theater), Eddie went on tour.

To celebrate the new year — and his new triumph — Eddie held a family party on the Palace roof. Everyone attended, except Bryan. Wishing them a joyous 1928, he chided them, perhaps only half in jest, "Be good. Attend strictly to business. Go home after the performance."

"The same advice he's always given us," said Eddie, Jr. "It's good advice."

As they parted, Eddie patted his chest, just over the diaphragm. "Something the matter here," he remarked, with a rueful grin. "A touch of indigestion," Charlie suggested. It would be the last time the children saw their father alive.

Colleagues, particularly E.F. Albee, showed concern for Eddie's health. He had suffered a number of minor heart problems during the preceding months, but nothing to take him off the stage. Worried about his friend, Albee wrote Eddie at the Palace Theater in Chicago. The letter was dated January 12, 1928.

My dear Eddie:
I understand that you are going along, making good everywhere. Neither you nor myself should forget that we are getting along in years. We should take it easy and rest as much as possible when we are not actually employed.
Don't eat too much. Restrict all of your habits, such as smoking, drinking, or anything else in excess; and there is no reason

why you shouldn't go along for a great many years yet. But one must know how to take care of oneself and realize he cannot do what he did in his younger days.[3]

To what extent Eddie heeded Albee's advice — or the advice of his doctors — no one knows.

After performing his sketch at the Orpheum Theater in Kansas City, the evening of February 15, Eddie complained of having eaten something that did not agree with him. Forgoing his usual after-performance meal, he retired to his hotel room, to be cared for by Marie, who had been accompanying him on the tour.

Eddie was awakened early the next morning by severe heart pains. The house physician and a priest were called. Within an hour, however, without a word, Eddie died. Marie and the doctor were at his side. The priest arrived just before he died and administered the last rites.

The Foy children, temporarily united for a vaudeville tour through the Midwest, were about to open an engagement in Madison, Wisconsin. They were notified and made plans to join the funeral party in Chicago, on its way back to New Rochelle.

It was reported that Eddie had been subject to mild heart attacks for several months, but his condition had not been regarded as serious. Ironically, just before Eddie's turn Tuesday night, a friend had found him seated on a trunk backstage. He had felt almost too weak to go before the footlights. He confided to the friend that he did not believe he would be able to finish out the season. Yet, when talking to newspaper reporters after the show, he expressed no intention to retire.

"Quit the stage? Me!" he declared. "Say, I'll fall over into the orchestra pit first." In a more serious voice, he observed, "On the whole, life has been a pretty jolly affair. I have no complaints to make. A few regrets."

Newspapers across the country spoke of Eddie in warm, familiar, sympathetic terms. They all agreed that Eddie had died as he wanted to, on the stage, doing the work he so wholeheartedly loved. Tributes came from multitudes of colleagues, critics, and theater managers. Whether new to the business or veterans, they all knew Eddie and tendered him great respect, admiration, and affection.

The *Herald Tribune* summarized his career in a few simple sentences, befitting the man:

> He used to stroll out from the wings dressed like a ballet dancer in pink tights, a skirt that flared out in all directions and a great wig of yellow hair. He walked with a strut, like a bantam rooster looking for a fight, and his voice had that odd lisp that made every syllable drip with molasses.... He was funny when he sang. He was funny when he walked. He was funny when he just stood there and blinked across the footlights. The spirit of nonsense and foolishness — that was Eddie Foy. He was one of the world's great clowns. There was no other quite like him, and we shall not look upon his like again.... Eddie Foy belonged to a generation that is gone. His sense of pantomime and humor was tuned to the theater of twenty-five years ago, when wisecracking was not such a virtue as it is today.[4]

Old friend and colleague William Jerome prepared a eulogy for Eddie, to be read at his funeral. It was published in newspapers, as well:

> Very few people knew the real Eddie — the man Eddie Foy, not the clown. His courageous heart was a storehouse of tragedies.... In success, he never high-hatted anybody. He never passed you in a hurry; always had time to stop and say something nice to you.... It was the boy in Eddie Foy that kept him a boy to the end. He passed on as he wished to pass on — with his theatrical boots on.... Others will still clown and win renown. But there will never be another Eddie Foy.[5]

Before being returned to the East, Eddie's body lay in state at Sheehan's funeral home in Kansas City. For a full day, friends and admirers came to pay their respects. A special service was held, led by clergy of the Catholic Church and civic representatives. That evening, the casket was put on a train bound for Chicago, its final stop New Rochelle.

On the morning of February 21, at the Church of the Blessed Sacrament, old family friend and confidant, the Reverend Manzelli, celebrated a requiem mass. More than 600 actors and neighbors filled the church to SRO. Standing beside the casket were Marie, still suffering from shock, and Eddie's eight children. Bouquets of flowers had arrived from Albee, the Lambs Club, the Friars, and the Actors Guild, along with more than 700 telegrams from colleagues and fans across the country. When the service ended, the pall-bearers, all members of the Lambs, bore the casket to the hearse, which was followed to the cemetery by a long procession of automobiles. Eddie was buried in Holy Sepulcher Cemetery, next to Madeline.

At the cemetery, the snow was deep; a chilly wind swept the crowd. Actors stood bareheaded to pay their last respects. After a brief, final blessing, the casket was lowered into the frozen ground. The children said simply, "Good bye, Pop," as the first spade of earth struck the casket.

Probably the greatest compliment that could be paid Eddie Foy was his own deep, sincere love for and respect of the theater and its patrons. Many times during his career, he was questioned about what the theater meant to him. Without hesitation, he always recited his personal credo, the sacred tenets by which he entertained. They were simple, yet demanding:

You have to want to entertain people. It is hard work. Make sure the man who pays fifteen cents to sit in the last row, at the very top of the theater, hears every word you say. Please the audience. Make people laugh. Make sure no one gets hurt in the process. Give 200 per cent to your acting. Always leave your audience wanting you again. Respect the theater.

Eddie Foy was never simply a funny clown; he was also a serious student of the theatrical process. Even after his evening performances, he read late into the night. He could discuss knowledgeably all the great actors of the American stage, their lives, their performing characteristics. He could lecture on Greek drama and the methods employed by the players of past centuries. He could analyze the psychology of acting more profoundly than most of his colleagues.

Spectators who laughed heartily at Foy's comedy did not think his work was anything more than mere clowning. Yet Foy took a serious view: you have to know your audience. Based on that knowledge, you have to deliver.

"The first thing I do when I make my entrance is to endeavor to size up the audience. If I can strike the right chord, my work goes well; for I have a feeling of confidence. The subtle something comes back to me, and the circuit is completed. I have established communication. That was the trick of the great actors of the past. They kept the closest tabs and found out quickly as possible the temperament of the people before them and swayed them accordingly."

Theater critic Alan Dale, in his appraisal of Eddie Foy, noted that he had seen it all. Indeed, Foy played in all forms of popular theater from the 1870s to the 1920s. He performed in an exceptionally wide variety of venues, from urban beer halls and frontier saloons to the prestigious Palace Theater. Through all of this, he endured frigid, rat-infested dressing rooms, dirty theaters, infrequent meals, exhausting travel, frequent boredom, frenzied rehearsals, and bitter salary disputes. Success fulfilled his yearning for family, his desire for a fine home, and the comforts of "traveling in style."

Foy observed and experimented with many different acting roles, gradually perfecting his characteristic clownish persona. He was intimate witness to changes in audience behavior and possessed in abundance the ability to give them what they wanted. That took strength and perseverance. And Foy was the ultimate survivor.

Never afraid to change and update his

material, Foy participated in and contributed to the development of American comedy. He helped define the role of the comedian in musical comedy. He personified the antics of the popular theater clown. Ed Wynn and Eddie Cantor carried the legacy from the '20s to the '40s. Milton Berle, Sid Caesar, Jackie Gleason, Jerry Lewis, and Red Skelton developed and extended it from the '50s to the '80s. None have yet fully emerged to continue the tradition.

Foy perfected the family act. No group before or since can claim that accomplishment. It was not simply his family's size, nor even their respective talents. Rather, they were imbued with their father's joy of performing, of pleasing the audience: these ineffable vibrations projected across the footlights.

Comedy is the most fragile and ephemeral of art forms. Brilliance comes from making it look easy. Longevity is the result of keeping it funny. Comedy, as Foy saw it, is uncomplicated. Make your own rules. Develop your own style, material, delivery, and personality. Learn timing and body control. Believe you can make people laugh.

Comedy is a kind of communication. It has a distinct language. It has rules. Don't hesitate to push it beyond its apparent limits. Comedy is hard labor; it takes all of your intellectual and emotional effort. Above all, keep it simple.

For more than fifty years, Eddie Foy was a gifted comedian whose clever creations made him one of the most endearing and entertaining artists in American theater. He imparted the sincerity of his deep-rooted convictions in his versatile interpretations, sparkling originality, keen conceptual abilities, and mastery of the comedic spirit.

Upon taking the stage, America's clown prince was able to relieve stress and dispel gloom, all with a magical, apparently effortless wave of his comedic baton.

Performance Chronology

1873–74
Edwards and Foy, various beer halls, honky tonks, and wine rooms; Chicago, Illinois and nearby towns

1875–76
Collins and Foy, various beer halls in Chicago area

Collins and Foy, circus company; two months; Chicago, touring through northern Illinois and southern Wisconsin; minstrel company; one month; northern Illinois

1877
Collins and Foy, superluminaries at McVicker's Theater, Chicago; one year; various plays including legitimate productions featuring Edwin Booth and Joseph Jefferson; Collins and Foy played at local concert halls and variety theaters in Chicago when not working at the McVicker's

Fry and Foy, variety theaters, Chicago, Illinois

Collins and Foy, variety theaters, Chicago, Illinois, and Iowa; three months

Collins and Foy, Coliseum Theater, Chicago, Illinois; variety; three months

Collins and Foy, Academy of Music, Chicago, Illinois; variety; two months

1878
Edwin Foy, Academy of Music, Chicago, Illinois; variety; three months

Edwin Foy, Atlantic Garden Theater, Ft. Wayne, Indiana; variety; one month

Thompson and Foy, theaters in Ft. Wayne, Chicago, St. Louis, and Kansas City; variety; three months

Foy and Thompson, Springer's Concert Hall, Dodge City, Kansas; variety; three months

Foy and Thompson, Theater Comique, Leadville, Colorado; variety, minstrel, and stock; four months

1879
Foy and Thompson, Theater Comique, Leadville, Colorado; variety, minstrel, and stock; five months

Foy and Thompson, Theater Comique, Dodge City, Kansas; variety and minstrel; three months

Foy and Thompson, Theater Comique, Coliseum, Athenaeum Theater, Leadville,

Colorado; variety, minstrel, and melodrama; four months

1880

Foy and Thompson, Grand Central Theater, Leadville, Colorado; variety, minstrel, and melodrama; five months

Foy and Thompson, Palace Theater, Denver, Colorado; variety and minstrel; six months

1881

Foy and Thompson, Palace Theater, Denver, Colorado; variety and minstrel; six months

Foy and Thompson, Adelphi Theater, San Francisco, California; variety, minstrel, and melodrama; six months

1882

Foy and Thompson, Adelphi Theater, San Francisco, California; variety, minstrel, and melodrama; three months

Foy and Thompson, Emerson's California Minstrels, Standard Theater, San Francisco, California; minstrel; three months

Foy and Thompson, Gus Bruno's Company, Virginia City, Nevada; variety; one week

Foy and Thompson, Theater Comique, Butte, Montana; variety and minstrel; four months

1883

Foy and Thompson, Carncross' Minstrels, Philadelphia, Pennsylvania; January 22 to May 26; minstrelsy

Edwin Foy, Carncross' Minstrels, Philadelphia, Pennsylvania; August 30 to December 31; minstrelsy

1884

Edwin Foy, Carncross' Minstrels, Philadelphia, Pennsylvania; January 1 to April 30; minstrelsy

Edwin Foy, Haverly's Minstrel Company, London, England; May 31 to August 20; minstrelsy

Edwin Foy, Carncross' Minstrels, Phila-

delphia, Pennsylvania; August 24 to December 31; minstrelsy and farce comedy

1885

Edwin Foy, Carncross' Minstrels, Philadelphia, Pennsylvania; January 1 to May 10; minstrelsy and farce comedy

Edwin Foy, Barry & Fay, "Irish Aristocracy," "All Crazy," "Dynamite"; farce comedy; 10 cities, 10 weeks

Edwin Foy, Kelly & Mason, "The Tigers"; farce comedy; 21 cities, 14 weeks

1886

Edwin Foy, Carrie Swain's Company, "Jack-in-the-Box"; farce comedy; 12 cities, 24 weeks; Foy's first performance in New York, February 8

Edwin Foy, Alcazar Theater, San Francisco, California; stock; 10 weeks

Edwin Foy, Mr. and Mrs. George Knight's Company, "Over the Garden Wall"; farce comedy, 20 cities, 18 weeks

1887

Edwin Foy, Mr. and Mrs. George Knight's Company, "Over the Garden Wall," "Baron Rudolph"; farce comedy; 18 cities, 18 weeks

Edwin Foy, Alcazar Theater, San Francisco, California; farce comedy; appeared with Gus Williams in "Oh, What a Night," "One of the Finest," "Captain Mishler," and "Kepler's Fortune"; 5 weeks

Edwin Foy, Kate Castleton's Company, "Crazy Patch"; farce comedy; 31 cities in 13 weeks

1888

Edwin Foy, Kate Castleton's Company, "Crazy Patch"; farce comedy; 27 cities, 15 weeks

The Crystal Slipper, opened June 19, Chicago Opera House, Chicago, Illinois; Foy as Yosemite; comedian; 12 weeks; on tour September 8 to December 31, 8 cities

1889

The Crystal Slipper, on tour January 1 to May 9, 15 cities

Bluebeard, Jr., opened June 11, Chicago Opera House, Chicago, Illinois; Foy as O'Mahdi Benzini; comedian; 12 weeks; on tour September 3 to December 31; 11 cities

1890

Bluebeard, Jr., on tour January 1 to May 15; 15 cities

The Crystal Slipper (revised), opened June 19, Chicago Opera House, Chicago, Illinois; Foy as Yosemite; comedian; 12 weeks; on tour September 8 to December 31; 13 cities

1891

The Crystal Slipper (revised), on tour January 1 to May 9; 25 cities

Sinbad, opened June 11, Chicago Opera House, Chicago, Illinois; Foy as Fresco; comedian; 14 weeks; on tour September 14 to December 31, 8 cities

1892

Sinbad, on tour January 1 to May 9; 19 cities

Ali Baba, opened June 2, Chicago Opera House, Chicago, Illinois; Foy as Cassim; 24 weeks; on tour November 6 to December 31; 5 cities

1893

Ali Baba, on tour January 1 to April 28; 15 cities

Ali Baba, Chicago Opera House; May 28 to October 10 (in conjuction with the Chicago World's Fair)

Sinbad (revised), opened October 12, Chicago Opera House, Chicago, Illinois; Foy as Fresco; comedian; 4 weeks; on tour November 12 to December 31; 4 cities

1894

Sinbad (revised), on tour January 1 to May 7; 15 cities (Foy leaves company April 23)

Off the Earth, opened September 10, Davidson Theater, Milwaukee, Wisconsin; Foy as Cluster; comedian and head of company; 1 week; on tour September 17 to December 31; 12 cities

1895

Off the Earth, on tour January 1 to May 2; 23 cities

Little Robinson Crusoe, opened June 15, Schiller Theater, Chicago, Illinois; Foy as Dare Devil Willie; comedian; 13 weeks; on tour August 25 to January 5, 1896; 22 cities

1896

The Strange Adventures of Miss Brown, opened March 11, Hooley's Theater, Chicago, Illinois; Foy as Miss Brown; comedian; 2 weeks; on tour March 25 to June 2; 26 cities

Off the Earth (revival), opened September 28, Davidson's Theater, Milwaukee, Wisconsin; Foy as Cluster; comedian; 1 week; on tour October 5 to December 31; 13 cities

1897

Off the Earth (revival), on tour January 1 to March 26; 45 cities

In Gay New York, opened August 28, Metropolis Theater, New York; Foy as Edgardo Macbeth Boothand Barrett Todd; comedian; 1 week; on tour September 5 to December 31; 29 cities

1898

In Gay New York, on tour January 1 to March 6; 18 cities

Hotel Topsy Turvy, opened September 19, Lafayette Theater, Washington, D.C.; Foy as Lebeau; comedian; on tour September 19 to December 31; 5 cities (11 weeks in New York, at Herald Square Theater, opening October 3)

1899

Hotel Topsy Turvy, on tour January 1 to April 1; 11 cities

An Arabian Girl and Forty Thieves, opened April 27, Herald Square Theater, New

York; Foy as Cassim D'Artagnan; comedian; 4 weeks

Hotel Topsy Turvy, opened August 19, McVicker's Theater, Chicago, Illinois; Foy as Lebeau; comedian; on tour August 19 to December 31; 33 cities

1900

Hotel Topsy Turvy, on tour January 1 to March 31; 33 cities

A Night in Town, opened September 2, Olympic Theater, St. Louis, Missouri; Foy as ?; comedian; on tour September 2 to October 31; 10 cities

1901

The Strollers, opened June 24, Knickerbocker Theater, New York; Foy as Kamfer; comedian; 12 weeks; on tour September 9 to December 31; 13 cities

1902

The Strollers, on tour January 1 to April 1; 18 cities

The Wild Rose, opened April 22, Garrick Theater, Philadelphia, Pennsylvania; Foy as Paracelsus Noodle; comedian; on tour April 22 to December 31; 27 cities (17 weeks in New York at Knickerbocker Theater, opening May 5)

1903

The Wild Rose, on tour January 1 to January 15; 5 cities

Mr. Bluebeard, opened January 21, Knickerbocker Theater, New York; Foy as Sister Anne; comedian; 18 weeks; on tour September 28 to December 30 (Iroquois Theater fire); 17 cities

1904

Eddie Foy, vaudeville, opened February 1, Empire Theater, Cleveland, Ohio; 5 cities

Piff!Paff!!Pouf!!!, opened April 2, Casino Theater, New York; Foy as Peter Pouffle; comedian; 33 weeks; on tour November 23 to December 31; 5 cities

1905

Piff!Paff!!Pouf!!!, on tour January 1 to March 4; 9 cities

Eddie Foy, vaudeville, opened March 4, Keith's Theater, New York; 12 weeks, 12 cities

The Earl and the Girl, opened September 4, Lyric Theater, Philadelphia, Pennsylvania; Foy as Jim Cheese; comedian; on tour September 4 to November 2; 6 cities; opened November 4, Casino Theater, New York; 8 weeks

1906

The Earl and the Girl, Casino Theater, New York; 19 weeks; on tour March 12 to May 12; 9 cities

Eddie Foy, vaudeville, opened May 14, Colonial Theater, New York; 9 weeks, 7 cities

The Earl and the Girl, opened October 1, Shubert Theater, Kansas City, Missouri; on tour October 1 to December 31; 13 cities

1907

The Earl and the Girl, on tour January 1 to January 17; 3 cities

The Orchid, opened March 18, Lyric Theater, Philadelphia, Pennsylvania; Foy as Artie Choke; comedian; on tour March 18 to April 6; 3 cities; opened April 8, Herald Square Theater, New York; 22 weeks; on tour September 16 to December 31; 15 cities

1908

The Orchid, on tour January 1 to April 1; 13 cities

Eddie Foy, vaudeville, opened April 27, Orpheum Theater, Brooklyn, New York; 6 weeks; 4 cities

Mr. Hamlet on Broadway, opened September 29, Lyric Theater, Philadelphia, Pennsylvania; Foy as Joey Wheeze; comedian; on tour September 29 to December 12; 10 cities; opened December 23, Casino Theater, New York; 1 week

1909

Mr. Hamlet on Broadway, Casino

Theater, New York; 6 weeks; on tour February 8 to April 23; 10 cities

Eddie Foy, vaudeville, opened May 8, Plaza Theater, New York; 6 weeks, 5 cities

Mr. Hamlet on Broadway, on tour August 30 to December 31; 18 cities

1910

Mr. Hamlet on Broadway, on tour January 1 to April 9; 14 cities

Up and Down Broadway, opened June 27, Shubert Theater, Boston, Massachusetts; Foy as Momus; comedian; on tour June 27 to July 16; 1 city; opened July 18, Casino Theater, New York; 9 weeks; on tour September 19 to December 31; 15 cities

1911

Up and Down Broadway, on tour January 1 to February 11; 6 cities

Eddie Foy, vaudeville, opened April 9, Keith's Columbia Theater, Cincinnati, Ohio; 7 weeks, 7 cities

The Pet of the Petticoats, opened August 25, Savoy Theater, Asbury Park, New Jersey; Foy as ?; comedian; on tour August 25 to September 2; 1 week; 1 city

Eddie Foy, vaudeville, opened September 4, Keith's Theater, New York; 2 weeks, 1 city

Over the River, opened September 25, Studebaker Theater, Chicago, Illinois; Foy as Madison Parke; comedian; on tour September 25 to December 31; 14 cities

1912

Over the River, on tour January 1 to January 7; 1 week; 1 city; opened January 8, Globe Theater, New York; 15 weeks

Eddie Foy and the Seven Little Foys, vaudeville, opened August 19, New Brighton Theater, Long Island, New York; one week; opened August 26, Union Square Theater, New York; two weeks

Over the River, opened September 9, Newark Theater, Newark, New Jersey; on tour September 9 to December 31; 16 cities

1913

Over the River, on tour January 1 to June 19; 24 cities

Eddie Foy and the Seven Little Foys, vaudeville, opened September 1, Union Square Theater, New York; on tour September 1 to December 31; 17 weeks, 13 cities

1914

Eddie Foy and the Seven Little Foys, on tour January 1 to June 27; 26 weeks, 21 cities

Eddie Foy and the Seven Little Foys, Palace Theater, New York; 3 weeks

Eddie Foy and the Seven Little Foys, New Brighton Theater, Long Island, New York; 2 weeks

Eddie Foy and the Seven Little Foys, vaudeville, opened September 12, Bushwick Theater, Brooklyn, New York; on tour September 12 to December 31; 19 weeks, 9 cities

1915

Eddie Foy and the Seven Little Foys, on tour January 1 to April 28; 17 weeks, 14 cities

A Favorite Fool, moving picture; Eddie Foy and the Seven Little Foys, Polly Moran, Charles Arling, and Mae Busch; Triangle-Keystone; shooting July through September; release–September 22, 1915

The Great Vacuum Robbery, moving picture, Eddie Foy supplies scenario; Triangle-Keystone; release–November 5, 1915

Eddie Foy and the Seven Little Foys, vaudeville, opened November 13, Orpheum Theater, Portland, Oregon; on tour November 13 to December 31; 6 weeks, 5 cities

1916

Eddie Foy and the Seven Little Foys, on tour January 1 to March 11; 10 weeks, 9 cities; on tour April 10 to April 29; 3 weeks, 3 cities

Eddie Foy and the Seven Little Foys, vaudeville, opened November 1, Alhambra Theater, New York; on tour November 1 to December 31; 5 weeks, 5 cities

1917

Eddie Foy and the Seven Little Foys, on tour January 1 to April 4; 13 weeks, 13 cities

Eddie Foy and the Seven Little Foys, Palace, Royal, and Henderson's Theaters, New York; 3 weeks

Eddie Foy and the Seven Little Foys, vaudeville, opened August 12, Majestic Theater, Chicago, Illinois; on tour August 12 to December 31; 20 weeks, 18 cities

1918

Eddie Foy and the Seven Little Foys, on tour January 1 to April 10; irregular schedule — 7 weeks, 4 cities

His Wife's Friend, moving picture; Paramount Pictures Corp.; under supervision of Mack Sennett; Charles Murray, Gonda Durand, Harry McCoy, Wayland Trask, Phyllis Haver, Myrtle Lind, Laura LaVarnie, Eddie Foy, Al McKinnon, Larry Lyndon; in final cut, Foy is removed from the film; release — September 8, 1918

Eddie Foy and the Younger Foys, vaudeville, opened August 17, Keith's Theater, Washington, D.C.; on tour August 17 to December 31; 9 weeks, 9 cities

1919

Eddie Foy and the Younger Foys, on tour January 1 to June 11; 22 weeks, 19 cities

Yankee Doodle in Berlin, moving picture; Mack Sennett Comedies Corp.; Bothwell Browne, Ford Sterling, Mal St. Clair, Bert Roach, Eva Thatcher, Marie Prevost, Charles Murray, Ben Turpin, Wayland Trask, Fanny Kelly, Heinie Conklin, Eddie Foy, Sennett Bathing Girls; use of previous film takes: a Foy routine from *His Wife's Friend*

Eddie Foy and the Younger Foys, Palace, Riverside, Orpheum, and Royal Theaters, New York; 4 weeks

Eddie Foy and the Younger Foys, vaudeville, opened September 15, Keith's Theater, Washington, D.C.; 1 week

1920

Eddie Foy and the Younger Foys, vaudeville, opened May 19, Chateau Theater, Chicago, Illinois; 1 week

Eddie Foy and the Younger Foys, vaudeville, opened September 8, Poli's Theater, Bridgeport, Connecticut; 2 weeks, 2 cities

Eddie Foy and the Younger Foys, vaudeville, opened September 29, Keith's Theater, Washington, D.C.; on tour September 29 to December 31; 12 weeks, 7 cities

1921

Eddie Foy and the Younger Foys, on tour January 1 to May 18; irregular schedule-15 weeks, 10 cities

Eddie Foy and the Younger Foys, vaudeville, opened August 24, Palace Theater, New York; on tour August 24 to December 31; 12 weeks, 13 cities

1922

Eddie Foy and the Younger Foys, on tour January 1 to April 26; 16 weeks, 14 cities

Eddie Foy and the Younger Foys, vaudeville, opened August 23, Keith's Theater, Washington, D.C.; on tour August 23 to December 31; 13 weeks, 6 cities

1923

Eddie Foy and the Younger Foys, on tour January 1 to January 13; 2 weeks, 1 city; on tour January 24 to February 6; 2 weeks, 1 city; on tour May 21 to June 4; 2 weeks, 2 cities

That Casey Girl, opened October 3, Playhouse Theater, Wilmington, Delaware; with the Younger Foys; Foy as Martin Casey; comedian; on tour October 3 to October 31; 4 weeks, 3 cities

1924–1926

Retired from stage.

1927

Eddie Foy, vaudeville, "The Fallen Star," with Monica Skelly and Hall Munnis; opened

August 8, Palace Theater, New York; August 8 to December 31 at Palace Theater

1928

Eddie Foy, vaudeville, "The Fallen Star"; on tour January 1 to February 16; 6 weeks, 5 cities; died while playing at the Orpheum Theater, Kansas City, Missouri

The Foy Family, moving pictures; *Vitaphone Varieties*: #2579: "Foys for Joys," a satire on talking motion pictures; directed by Bryan Foy; songs: "Sal," "My Blue Heaven"; #2580: "Chips of the Old Block," songs and dances, with a comedy monologue by Eddie Foy, Jr.; songs: "I Just Roll Along," "Bye-Bye Pretty Baby," "Smile"

Notes

CHAPTER 1

1. Mormon Library, Salt Lake City, Utah.
2. New York City Vital Statistics, Death Records.
3. New York City Vital Statistics, Death Records.
4. See: K. Sawislak, *Smoldering City,* Chicago, University of Chicago Press, 1995, anti–Irish prejudice, Chapter 3.
5. Dr. W.A. Evans, *Mrs. Abraham Lincoln,* New York, A.A. Knopf, 1932.
6. See: William H.A. Williams, *'Twas Only an Irishman's Dream,* Urbana, University of Illinois Press, 1996, Chapter 6 — The Irish and Vaudeville.
7. See: John Culhane, *The American Circus,* New York, Henry Holt & Co., 1990, Chapter 6 — The Wild Frontier.

CHAPTER 2

1. *New York Clipper,* July 28, 1877.
2. *Clipper,* April 6, 1878.
3. Eddie Foy and Alvin Harlow, *Clowning Through Life,* New York, E.P. Dutton & Company, 1928, p. 93.
4. See: Stanley Vestal, *Queen of Cowtowns-Dodge City,* New York, Harper & Bros., 1952.

5. *Ford County Globe,* July 9, 1878.
6. Lily-B Rozar, *Kanhistique,* December, 1981, p. 7.
7. *Ford County Globe,* August 6, 1878.
8. Robert DeArment, *Bat Masterson,* Norman, University of Oklahoma Press, 1979, p. 112.

CHAPTER 3

1. See: William S. Greener, *The Bonanza West,* Norman, University of Oklahoma Press, 1963, Chapters 7 and 8, and Don and Jean Griswold, *History of Leadville and Lake County, Colorado,* Colorado Historical Society, 1995.
2. *New York Dramatic News,* April 19, 1879.
3. *Dramatic News,* May 17, 1879.
4. *Leadville Chronicle,* March 3, 1879.
5. *Ford County Globe,* June 13, 1879.
6. *Dramatic News,* September 17, 1879.
7. Foy and Harlow, p. 138.
8. *New York Clipper,* June 19, 1880.
9. Greener, pp. 158–174.
10. *Denver Daily News,* July 22, 1881.
11. See: Edmond M. Gagey, *The San Francisco Stage,* New York, Columbia University Press, 1950, Chapters 5 and 6.
12. *San Francisco Chronicle,* November 6, 1881.

13. *Chronicle,* February 11, 1882.
14. *Chronicle,* April 29, 1882.
15. *Dramatic News,* May 13, 1882.
16. Greener, pp. 238–39.
17. *Montana Standard,* October 14, 1882.

CHAPTER 4

1. *New York Clipper,* July 9, 1883.
2. *Philadelphia Ledger,* August 31, 1883.
3. *Clipper,* October 6, 1883.
4. Foy and Harlow, p. 202.
5. See: Roger Baker, *Drag,* New York, New York University Press, 1994, Part III, pp. 161–174.
6. *Philadelphia Ledger,* November 26, 1883.
7. *Ledger,* December 11, 1883.
8. *Ledger,* January 15, 1884.
9. *Ledger,* January 15, 1884.
10. *Clipper,* June 7, 1884.
11. *Ledger,* August 25, 1884.
12. *Clipper,* August 30, 1884.
13. *Clipper,* April 25, 1885.

CHAPTER 5

1. See: Jeffrey D. Mason, *Melodrama and the Myth of America,* Bloomington, Indiana University Press, 1993, Chapters 1 and 7.
2. *San Francisco Chronicle,* June 20, 1885.
3. *New York Clipper,* September 26, 1885.
4. *Boston Globe,* December 26, 1885.
5. *Chronicle,* July 10, 1886.
6. *Chronicle,* June 20, 1887.
7. *Philadelphia Ledger,* November 5, 1887.
8. *Clipper,* November 12, 1887.
9. *Clipper,* February 11, 1888.

CHAPTER 6

1. *New York Clipper,* June 23, 1888.
2. *Clipper,* September 15, 1888.
3. *Clipper,* December 8, 1888.
4. *Clipper,* December 8, 1888.
5. Foy and Harlow, pp. 235–36.
6. *Clipper,* January 19, 1889.
7. *Chicago Tribune,* June 22, 1889.
8. *Clipper,* June 29, 1889.
9. *Clipper,* September 28, 1889.
10. *New York Herald,* November 23, 1889.

11. *Boston Globe,* December 21, 1889.
12. *Clipper,* January 18, 1890.
13. *New York Dramatic Mirror,* February 1, 1890.
14. *Clipper,* June 28, 1890.
15. *Clipper,* July 26, 1890.
16. *Clipper,* August 9, 1890.
17. *Chicago Tribune,* December 20, 1890.
18. *Clipper,* December 21, 1890.

CHAPTER 7

1. *New York Clipper,* June 13, 1891.
2. *Clipper,* June 20, 1891.
3. *Clipper,* June 20, 1891.
4. *Chicago Tribune,* July 4, 1891.
5. *Clipper,* Juny 25, 1891.
6. *Clipper,* August 1, 1891.
7. *Clipper,* August 22, 1891,
8. *Clipper,* September 19, 1891.
9. *Boston Globe,* January 23, 1892.
10. *Clipper,* February 6, 1892.
11. *Clipper,* June 11, 1892.
12. *New York Dramatic News,* June 11, 1892.
13. *San Francisco Chronicle,* December 17, 1892.
14. *Chronicle,* December 24, 1892.
15. *Clipper,* March 4, 1893.
16. *Clipper,* June 3, 1893.
17. *Clipper,* July 8, 1893.
18. *Clipper,* December 30, 1893.
19. *Clipper,* February 10, 1894.
20. *Philadelphia Ledger,* March 17, 1894.
21. *Clipper,* May 12, 1894.
22. *Clipper,* May 12, 1894.

CHAPTER 8

1. *Milwaukee Sentinal,* September 15, 1894.
2. *Sentinal,* September 17, 1894.
3. *Chicago Tribune,* September 18, 1894.
4. *New York Clipper,* September 22, 1894.
5. *Boston Globe,* November 3, 1894.
6. Foy and Harlow, p. 252.
7. *Clipper,* April 13, 1895.
8. *Clipper,* June 22, 1895.
9. *Clipper,* June 22, 1895.
10. *Clipper,* June 29, 1895.
11. *Clipper,* July 6, 1895.
12. *Clipper,* August 3, 1895.

13. *Clipper,* November 30, 1895.
14. *Clipper,* January 4, 1896.
15. *Chicago Tribune,* January 11, 1896.
16. *Chicago Tribune,* March 7, 1896.
17. *Clipper,* March 21, 1896.
18. *Clipper,* May 9, 1896.

CHAPTER 9

1. *Chicago Tribune,* November 21, 1896.
2. *New York Clipper,* September 4, 1897.
3. *Clipper,* February 5, 1898.
4. See: Norman Hapgood, *The Stage in America: 1897–1900,* New York, The Macmillan Co., 1901, p. 18.
5. *Ibid,* p. 18.
6. *Ibid,* p. 21.
7. *Washington Times,* September 19, 1898.
8. *Clipper,* October 8, 1898.
9. *Clipper,* November 5, 1898.
10. *New York Times,* October 9, 1898.
11. *New York Telegraph,* October 24, 1898.
12. *Philadelphia Ledger,* January 28, 1899.
13. *Cleveland Plain Dealer,* March 18, 1899.
14. *New York Times,* April 30, 1899.
15. *Clipper,* August 26, 1899.
16. *Clipper,* January 20, 1900.

CHAPTER 10

1. See: George Fuller Golden, *My Lady Vaudeville and Her White Rats,* New York, Broadway Publishing Co., 1909.
2. *New York Clipper,* September 15, 1900.
3. *New York Mirror News,* June 25, 1901.
4. *New York Times,* June 25, 1901.
5. *Times,* June 25, 1901.
6. *New York World,* June 25, 1901.
7. *Green Book,* July 1, 1901, p. 263.
8. *Clipper,* December 28, 1901.
9. *Clipper,* April 22, 1902.
10. *New York Herald,* May 6, 1902.
11. *Philadelphia Ledger,* September 20, 1902.
12. *Chicago Tribune,* November 11, 1902.
13. *New York Morning Telegraph,* January 31, 1903.
14. *New York Telegram,* January 22, 1903.
15. *Pittsburgh Dispatch,* September 29, 1903.
16. *Cleveland Plain Dealer,* October 13, 1903.
17. *Clipper,* November 21, 1903.

CHAPTER 11

1. *Chicago Tribune,* December 5, 1903.
2. *New York Clipper,* November 24, 1903.
3. *Chicago Chronicle,* December 31, 1903.
4. *Clipper,* December 3, 1903.
5. *Chicago Tribune,* November 24, 1903.
6. A thorough report of the fire and later investigation can be found in Marshall Everett, *The Great Chicago Theater Disaster,* Chicago, Publishers Union of America, 1904.
7. *Chicago Tribune,* January 3, 1904.
8. Everett, pp. 220–229.
9. *Clipper,* February 6, 1904.

CHAPTER 12

1. *New York American,* April 3, 1904.
2. *New York Clipper,* April 9, 1904.
3. *American,* April 3, 1904.
4. *Life Magazine,* April, 1904.
5. *New York Sun,* April 3, 1904.
6. *Clipper,* November 12, 1904.
7. *New York Dramatic Mirror,* March 11, 1905.
8. *Philadelphia Record,* May 20, 1905.
9. *Pittsburgh Leader,* September 19, 1905.
10. *American,* November 6, 1905.
11. *Dramatic Mirror,* November 13, 1905.
12. *Clipper,* April 7, 1906.
13. *Stage Magazine,* April, 1906.
14. *Chicago Evening American,* September 24, 1906.
15. *Clipper,* March 30, 1907.
16. *Dramatic Mirror,* April 20, 1907.
17. *American,* April 9, 1907.
18. *Dramatic Mirror,* May 16, 1908.
19. *Dramatic Mirror,* September 26, 1908.

CHAPTER 13

1. *New York Clipper,* October 10, 1908.
2. Letter, Lee Shubert to J.A. Reed, November 2, 1908, Shubert Archive.
3. Letter, J.J. Shubert to J.A. Reed, December 21, 1908, Shubert Archive.
4. Letter, J.J. Shubert to J.A. Reed, December 1, 1908.
5. Letter, Eddie Foy to J.J. Shubert, December 6, 1908.
6. *New York Globe,* December 24, 1908.
7. *New York Times,* December 24, 1908.

8. Telegram, W.W. Freeman to J.J. Shubert, March 17, 1909, Shubert Archive.

9. Telegram, J.J. Shubert to W.W. Freeman, March 17, 1909, Shubert Archive.

10. *Clipper,* July 9, 1910.

11. *New York Herald,* July 9, 1910.

12. *Clipper,* July 23, 1910.

13. *New York Evening World,* July 23, 1910.

14. Letter, J.J. Shubert to Eddie Foy, December 8, 1910, Shubert Archive.

15. *Clipper,* June 3, 1911.

16. *Chicago Tribune,* September 26, 1911.

17. *New York Times,* January 9, 1912.

18. *Clipper,* July 27, 1912.

19. *Clipper,* August 24, 1912.

20. *New York American,* August 31, 1912.

21. *Boston Globe,* December 21, 1912.

22. *San Francisco Chronicle,* May 24, 1913.

23. *Clipper,* July 26, 1913.

CHAPTER 14

1. *New York Telegram,* October 11, 1913.

2. *New York Clipper,* November 29, 1913.

3. *Clipper,* February 7, 1914.

4. *Clipper,* February 28, 1914.

5. *Clipper,* July 18, 1914.

6. *Clipper,* September 19, 1914.

7. *Pittsburgh Leader,* October 12, 1914.

8. *Clipper,* June 26, 1915.

9. *Clipper,* May 9, 1917.

10. *Clipper,* June 20, 1917.

11. *Clipper,* November 14, 1917.

CHAPTER 15

1. *New York Dramatic Mirror,* September 26, 1918.

2. *Dramatic Mirror,* November 2, 1918.

3. *Dramatic Mirror,* November 2, 1918.

4. *Chicago Tribune,* December 21, 1918.

5. *New York Clipper,* December 21, 1918.

6. *Clipper,* July 16, 1919.

7. *Clipper,* November 10, 1920.

8. *New York Herald,* December 8, 1920.

9. *Clipper,* December 15, 1920.

10. *Clipper,* August 24, 1921.

11. *Chicago Tribune,* April 19, 1922.

12. *Clipper,* September 20, 1922.

13. *Clipper,* December 1, 1922.

14. *New York Herald,* November 30, 1922.

CHAPTER 16

1. Letter, George M. Cohan to Eddie Foy, January 22, 1924.

2. *New York Times,* August 10, 1927

3. Letter, E.F. Albee to Eddie Foy, January 12, 1928.

4. *New York Herald Tribune,* February 16, 1928.

5. *New York American,* February 21, 1928.

Selected Bibliography and
Source Material

ARCHIVES, COLLECTIONS, LIBRARIES

Academy of Motion Picture Arts and Sciences
California Historical Society, San Francisco
Chicago Historical Library
Colorado Historical Society
Denver Public Library, Western History Department
Dodge City Historical Society
The Free Library of Philadelphia, Theater Collection
Harvard University, Performing Arts Library
Institute of the American Musical
Leadville Library
Library of Congress
Mormon Library, Salt Lake City
Museum of the City of New York
National Portrait Gallery, Smithsonian Institution
New Rochelle Public Library
New York Public Library at Lincoln Center, Billy Rose Theater Collection
Princeton University Libraries, Department of Rare Books and Special Collections
Shubert Archive

University of California, Los Angeles, Microfilm Library
University of Southern California, Special Collections Library
University of Texas, Harry Ransom Humanities Research Center
University of Wisconsin, Wisconsin Center for Film and Theater Research
University of Wyoming, American Heritage Center

PERIODICALS, NEWSPAPERS

New York Clipper, January 1874 to July 1923
New York Dramatic Mirror, January 1880 to December 1922
Variety, December 1905 to December 1928
Selected issues of *Colliers, Green Book,* and *Theater* magazines
Selected newspaper articles from 1876 to 1955: *Boston Globe, Chicago Tribune, , New York Herald, New York Times, Philadelphia Ledger, San Francisco Chronicle*

BOOKS: HISTORICAL AND SOCIAL BACKGROUND

Brown, Harry C. *In the Golden Nineties*. Hastings-on-Hudson: Valentine's Manual, Inc., 1928.

Everett, Marshall. *The Great Chicago Theater Disaster*. Chicago: Publishers Union of America, 1904.

Grau, Robert. *The Business Man in the Amusement World*. New York: Broadway Publishing Co., 1910.

Morris, Lloyd R. *Incredible New York*. New York: Random House, 1951.

BOOKS: MINSTRELSY, VARIETY, VAUDEVILLE, MUSICAL COMEDY

Atkinson, Brooks. *Broadway*. New York: Macmillan Publishing Co., 1970.

Baker, Roger. *Drag*. New York: New York University Press, 1994.

Beadle's Dime Burlesque Speaker. New York: M.J. Ivers & Co., Publishers, 1880.

Bordman, Gerald. *American Musical Theater*. New York: Oxford University Press, 1978.

Broadbent, R.J. *A History of Pantomime*. London: Simpkin, Marshall, Hamilton, Kent & Co., 1901.

Cahn, William. *The Laugh Makers*. New York: G.P. Putnam's Sons, 1957.

Courtright, W. *The Complete Minstrel Guide*. Chicago: The Dramatic Publishing Co., 1901.

Csida, Joseph, and J.B. Csida. *American Entertainment: A Unique History of Popular Show Business*. New York: Billboard Publications, 1978.

Dick's Variety Sketches and Stump Speeches. New York: Dick & Fitzgerald Publishers, 1879.

Fields, Armond, and L. Marc Fields. *From the Bowery to Broadway: Lew Fields and the Roots of American Popular Theater*. New York: Oxford University Press, 1993.

Franklin, Joe. *Encyclopedia of Comedians*. New York: Bell Publishing Co., 1979.

Gilbert, Douglas. *American Vaudeville*. New York: McGraw-Hill, 1940.

Golden, G.F. *My Lady Vaudeville and Her White Rats*. New York: The Board of Directors of the White Rats of America, Broadway Publishing Co., 1909.

Green, Abel, and Joe Laurie, Jr. *Show Biz*. New York: Henry Holt & Co., 1951.

Hapgood, N. *The Stage in America, 1897–1900*. New York: Macmillan, 1901.

Johnson, Charles. *Why the World Laughs*. New York: Harper & Bros., Publishers, 1912.

Kleiser, Grenville. *Humorous Hits and How to Hold An Audience*. New York: Funk & Wagnalls Co., 1908.

Loesser, Arthur. *Humor in American Song*. New York: Howell, Soskin Publishers, 1942.

Logan, O. *Before the Footlights and Behind the Scenes*. Philadelphia: Parmelee & Co., 1870.

Marks, Edward B. *They All Sang*. New York: The Viking Press, 1935.

Modern Jokes and Monologues. Baltimore: I. & M. Ottenheimer, 1915.

Paskman, Dailey and Sigmund Spaeth. *Gentlemen Be Seated*. New York: Doubleday, Doran & Co., 1928.

Rice, E.L.R. *Monarchs of Minstrelsy*. New York: Kenny Publishing Co., 1911.

Samuels, Charles, and Louise Samuels. *Once Upon a Stage*. New York: Dodd, Mead & Co., 1974.

Slide, Anthony. *The Vaudevillians*. Westport, Conn.: Arlington House, 1981.

Sobel, Bernard. *A Pictorial History of Vaudeville*. New York: The Citadel Press, 1961.

Spitzer, M. *The Palace*. New York: Atheneum, 1969.

Stearns, Marshall Winslow, and Jean Stearns. *Jazz Dance*. New York: Da Capo Press, 1994. (Reprinted from 1968 edition.)

Toll, Robert C. *The Entertainment Machine*. New York: Oxford University Press, 1982.

BIOGRAPHIES, AUTOBIOGRAPHIES

Fields, Armond. *Lillian Russell: A Biography of America's Beauty*. Jefferson, N.C.: McFarland, 1998.

Foy, Eddie, and Alvin F. Harlow. *Clowning Through Life*. New York: E.P. Dutton & Co., 1928. (Serialized version appeared in *Colliers*, December 18, 1926 to February 19, 1927.)

Hopper, DeWolf. *Once a Clown, Always a*

Clown. Garden City, N.Y.: Garden City Publishing Co., 1927.

Lake, Stuart N. *Wyatt Earp: Frontier Marshall*. New York: Houghton Mifflin Co., 1931.

Leavitt, M.B. *Fifty Years in Theatrical Management*. New York: Broadway Publishing Co., 1912.

Leslie, Amy. *Some Players*. New York: Herbert S. Stone & Co., 1890.

Moody, Richard. *Ned Harrigan*. Chicago: Nelson-Hall, 1980.

Sennett, Mack. *King of Comedy*. San Francisco: Mercury House, Inc., 1954.

Stone, F. *Rolling Stone*. New York: Whittlesey House, 1945.

Interviews with: Irving Foy, Eddie Foy III, Madeline Foy O'Donnell, Frank and Suzanne Foy.

Index